W9-AQV-450

THE CLOTHING OF THE RENAISSANCE WORLD

EUROPE · ASIA · AFRICA · THE AMERICAS

IA

Cesare Vecellio's *Habiti Antichi et Moderni*

THE CLOTHING OF THE RENAISSANCE WORLD

EUROPE · ASIA · AFRICA · THE AMERICAS

MARGARET F. ROSENTHAL AND ANN ROSALIND JONES

with 540 illustrations, 77 in colour

Thames & Hudson

We dedicate this book to our husbands, Peter Stallybrass and Robin Shakeshaft, with love and many thanks for every kind of help

pp. 2–3 Jost Amman, "Procession of the Doge in Venice," 1560
p. 4 Giovanni Battista Moroni, *Portrait of a Man* (*The Tailor*) (detail), c. 1570

First published in the United Kingdom in 2008 by Thames & Hudson Ltd, 181A High Holborn, London WC1V 7QX

www.thamesandhudson.com

British Library Cataloguing-in-Publication Data
A catalogue record for this book is available from the British Library

ISBN 978-0-500-51426-9

Printed and bound in China by C&C Offset Printing Co. Ltd.

CONTENTS

The folios given above refer to the pagination of this book: Vecellio's original pagination is given at the top of the page in the translation (pages 50–574). Since the titles of sections in Vecellio's work do not name all the places whose costume he discusses, the list of contents above indicates in brackets the other countries covered.

INTRODUCTION
VECELLIO AND HIS WORLD

Cesare Vecellio's two books on the clothing worn throughout the world have fascinated artists, costume designers, and historians since they came out in Venice at the end of the sixteenth century. The first sections of both *Degli habiti antichi et moderni di diverse parti del mondo* (*The Clothing, Ancient and Modern, of Various Parts of the World,* 1590) and *Habiti antichi et moderni di tutto il mondo* (*The Clothing, Ancient and Modern, of the Whole World,* 1598) deal in breadth and rich detail with Italian clothing, beginning with ancient Rome and then focusing on the history and range of clothing worn in medieval and Renaissance Venice. More than this, however, both books are ambitious anthologies of dress all over the globe: in 1590, Europe, Asia and Africa, and in 1598, the Americas as well. The title pages of both books were designed to advertise this global coverage: they present a quartet of differently dressed allegorical female figures, each representing one of the four known continents—Europe and Asia at the top, America and Africa below.

As a writer, too, Vecellio calls attention to the breadth and variety of the styles of dress he shows in his woodcuts. In his titles and his preface he emphasizes the immense efforts he has put into gathering clothing from "the various nations of the world," including places so far away that it has been difficult to acquire trustworthy information about them. Presenting 428 woodcuts in his first edition and 503 in the second, Vecellio offers more information about nearby and faraway costume and custom than any of the dozen costume books published before his. He promises that the labor and art he has devoted to collecting the images will delight readers curious about the diversity of dress and culture, from Italy to the farthest reaches of the known world.

OPPOSITE Map of Venice, engraved by Bernardo Salvioni and printed by Donato Rasciotti, 1597

BELOW Venetian possessions in the Adriatic and Aegean regions, c. 1580

TRAMONTANA
VENE TIA
MVRAN
TORCELO
MAZORBO
BVRAN
LA GIVDECA
CANAL DELLA GIVDECA
PONENTE
LEVANTE
CHIOZA
MALAMOCHO
OSTRO
GOLFO DE VENETIA
Piazza di S. Marco
Ponte de Rialto
Processione del Corpus Domini con la compagnia de Pelegrini che vanno in Gierusalemme
Donzele
Principessa
Matrone
Gentildonne

The four-hundredth anniversary of Vecellio's death in 1601 was the occasion in Belluno, the central town of the region where he was born, for a series of conferences, research publications and exhibits of his work. This celebration coincided, by the wonderful magnanimity of Fortune (as he might say), with our first year of translating his 1590 costume book. We present his lengthy 1590 commentary in English for the first time here, in a translation much enriched by the decade of research that culminated in Belluno in 2001.

VECELLIO'S VENICE

Venice in the 1590s had lost some of its vast imperial power in the Mediterranean, but it was still a highly international city, receiving immigrants from its neighboring possessions and merchants by ship from its former territories and from all over the world. Trading high-quality luxury goods such as textiles and glass with the rest of Europe and the Levant, receiving visitors including popes, kings and ambassadors, and inhabited not only by Italians but also by Germans, Spaniards, Greeks, Albanians, Slavs, Mamluks, Persians and Africans, the city also had great appeal for tourists attracted by the myth of its prosperity, its constitution and political stability, and the beauty of its women, both aristocrats and (more accessibly) courtesans.[1] At its spring fair, the Sensa, thousands of customers came to admire and buy from the displays of finely crafted goods produced by artisans from the city and all over the world. Vecellio enthusiastically describes this two-week festival, when a spectacular outdoor market was held in Piazza San Marco:

BELOW, LEFT Giacomo Franco, engraving, "Gentildonna con mercante" from *Habiti delle donne Venetiane intagliate in rame*, Venice, 1610

BELOW, CENTER Giacomo Franco, engraving, "Noblewoman with a small fan" from *Habiti delle donne Venetiane intagliate in rame*, Venice, 1610

BELOW, RIGHT Titian, *Young Woman with a Fan*, c. 1555 (possibly Titian's daughter Lavinia in her wedding dress)

RIGHT Venetian bookbinding in leather for the commission certificate of Girolamo da Mula as Procurator, Venice, 1572

FAR RIGHT Drinking glass, Venice, c. 1590

an extremely rich display of the work of goldsmiths, jewelers and everything else crafted in metal, with shops on both sides of a wide street covered with awnings. Here for fifteen continuous days more Venetian nobles and foreign lords assemble than at any other time. (folio 152 in the original book)

Venice was also a center of publishing and bookbinding: 453 printers, publishers, booksellers and book-binders worked in the city over the course of the sixteenth century.[2] Visitors could take away a range of goods, including a book like Vecellio's that pictured and named the fabrics, lace, gloves, colored and patterned glass, fans and other luxuries made in this cosmopolitan city. By the middle of the sixteenth century, the entrepreneurial networks of the city linked together artists, craftsmen, merchants—and writers who could publicize their wares.[3]

VECELLIO'S WORLD

Vecellio shared the civic pride of Venetians during the Cinquecento. In the final phrase of his paean to Venice, he expands conventional praise of the city as a moral and political ideal by emphasizing its status as an international depot of sumptuous goods: "a mirror of beauty, a model of good customs, a fount of virtue, the home of good men, a shelter for the industrious, *and a warehouse for the whole world of merchandise of all kinds*" (38, emphasis ours). He arranges his prints of Venice in an order that corresponds to the city's social hierarchy, showing the uniforms of every state official from the doge to the Senators down through professional men, merchants and shopkeepers to galley slaves and porters; and, for women, from the *dogaressa* (the wife of the doge) through noblewomen and artisans' wives down to prostitutes and state-supported orphans. His admiration for the luxurious and elegant dress of high officials and members of the aristocracy appears in many of his comments, but he also praises the practical dress and dependable work of porters and housemaids in the city and in the farming communities near it.

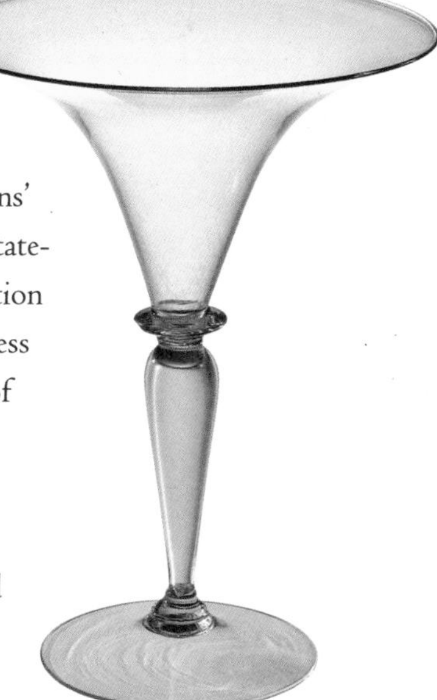

In his prints and text, he pays particular attention to the merchants of the city, whose expertise he specifies in several cases: for example, Paolo dello Struzzo, a skilled apothecary, and Bernardo Pilotto, the owner of a shop famous for luxurious cosmetics. What Vecellio adds here is striking: both men are also collectors of "paintings and many valuable objects" (116v)—not only businessmen but also connoisseurs, intellectuals, and potential subsidizers or buyers of his book. So, too, are the noblemen of the Veneto, the region around the city. Vecellio names and thanks several of them for help in his research. His pleasure in markets, whether in Venice or far away, even overcomes the rivalry with the Levant in his remark about demand from the Turkish sultan's court for the brocades of the Venetian cloth-maker Bartolomeo Bontempele. Even greater enthusiasm colors his description of the textile market in Aleppo (now Halab, in northwest Syria), a city where, as in Venice, many exchange routes met.[4] In his description, he revels in the crowds of buyers and sellers and in the quantity and variety of merchandise there, which, like the rich fabrics and trims made in Venice, embellish the local noblewomen with grandeur appropriate to their station:

> *The city of Aleppo, because it is very rich in merchandise, is also very rich because of the great numbers of people...who meet there from all over the world.... Many fabrics are brought here...very fine linen...the whitest* lisaro *[fine cottons].* (459v)

The most Venetian aspect of Vecellio's costume book may be his praise of *homo economicus*—the international businessman. In a passage on Venetian merchants given special licenses to trade in Constantinople, he claims that the commercial instinct is innate and universal: "Because man is by nature inclined toward profit and commerce...he leaves his paternal dwelling behind...and...moves to faraway lands" (412v). Such international mercantile adventures had been as central to the prosperity of the medieval Venetian patriciate as they were to Vecellio, a late sixteenth-century artist traveling between Italy and Germany. The entrepreneurial spirit he naturalizes in this passage sums up the composer of *Degli habiti antichi et moderni* and the ideology of the book itself. Both typify the practices and values of "La Serenissima" most vividly when they focus on costume, custom, buyers and regions beyond the confines of Venice.

VECELLIO'S CAREER

Though he would come to embody the entrepreneurial activity of the city, Vecellio was not himself a native of Venice.[5] He was born around 1521 in Cadore, a self-governing protectorate of Venice near the larger town of Belluno, then called the Cividal di Belluno; he would later show the dress of noblewomen of Belluno in his costume book. His family, well known in the region, had included political and military

ABOVE, LEFT Cesare Vecellio, *Degnamerita, Countess of Porcia*, 1575

ABOVE, CENTER Cesare Vecellio, *Giorgio Piloni*, 1575

ABOVE, RIGHT Cesare Vecellio, *Odorico Piloni*, after 1594

OPPOSITE, ABOVE Cesare Vecellio, *Madonna and Child in Glory*, 1585

OPPOSITE, LEFT Cesare Vecellio, *Odorico Piloni*, c. 1570

OPPOSITE, RIGHT Cesare Vecellio, *Laura, Countess of Terlago and Lodrone*, c. 1570

men and several artists. He was a cousin once removed of Titian—Tiziano Vecellio—the most celebrated painter of the Vecellio clan. An earlier member of the family, Marco, was also a painter, as was Vecellio's brother Fabrizio.[6]

Cesare probably started painting as an apprentice to the older Francesco Vecellio, the brother of Titian, in Cadore, and then worked with Titian himself.[7] It is certain that in 1548 and later he went with Titian on trips to Augsburg, accompanied by Orazio, Titian's favorite son, and by the Dutch painter Lambert Sustris. He probably worked in Titian's workshop, though no works signed by him during that time survive, and he is known to have lived in Titian's house in the Biri Grande, in the parish of San Canciano in Venice.

The first paintings known to be by Vecellio are portraits of the twin sons of his principal patron Odorico Piloni: Paolo (painted in 1550) and Cesare (1552).[8] He painted several portraits of Odorico throughout his life, including a pair of him and his wife Laura, Countess of Terlago and Lodrone, and two of the patron as an old man. He also painted another of Odorico's sons, Giorgio, and his wife Degnamerita, Countess of Porcia. For the Piloni library, he painted the fore-edges of valuable books, which during this period were stored facing outward on their shelves. In the 1560s he restored paintings for churches in the Veneto, but he began to sign his work only after Titian's death in 1576. This work included paintings for churches in towns near Belluno—Cadore, Pieve, Capo di Ponte and Feltre—including altarpieces, ceilings, and a fresco representing the Four Evangelists. He also painted frescoes for private houses in the region, including a cycle of the four seasons for the Piloni household. His early work for Belluno included an

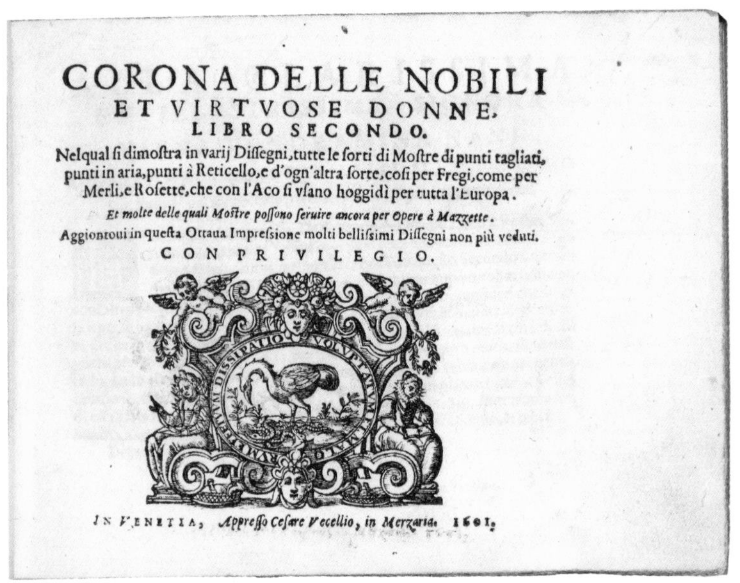

CORONA DELLE NOBILI
ET VIRTVOSE DONNE.
LIBRO SECONDO.
Nelqual si dimostra in varij Dissegni, tutte le sorti di Mostre di punti tagliati, punti in aria, punti à Reticello, e d'ogn'altra sorte, così per Fregi, come per Merli, e Rosette, che con l'Aco si vsano hoggidì per tutta l'Europa.
Et molte delle quali Mostre possono seruire ancora per Opere à Mazzette.
Aggiontoui in questa Ottaua Impressione molti bellissimi Dissegni non più veduti.
CON PRIVILEGIO.

IN VENETIA, *Appresso Cesare Vecellio, in Merzaria.* 1601.

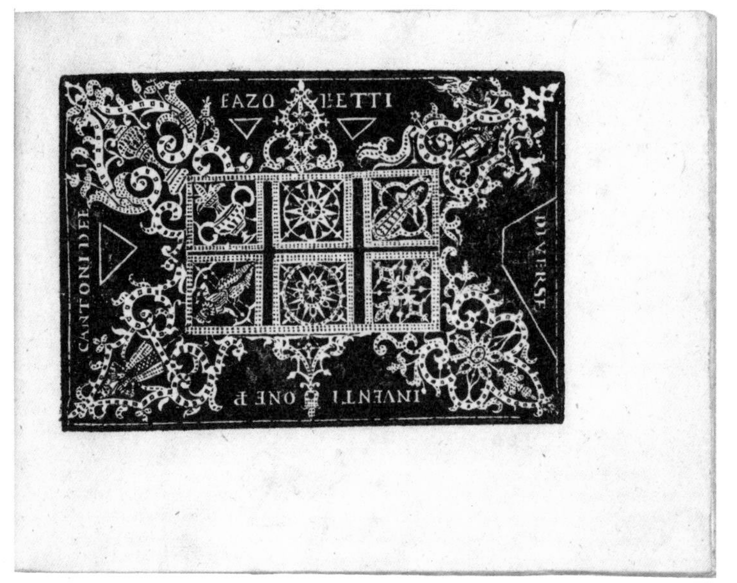

altar painting of Saint Sebastian for a chapel in the cathedral when it was rebuilt in 1557.[9]

His first recorded print, granted a ducal privilege in 1575, represented Christ's circumcision and adoration by angels and monarchs. A second print, a woodcut entitled *Il Collegio di Venezia*, recorded a visit by ambassadors to the Ducal Palace in Venice. A four-page pamphlet in Latin, predicting events to come in 1578, was issued from his printing house in the Frezzaria, a major commercial thoroughfare connecting Piazza San Marco to the Rialto, where he established contacts with merchants of textiles, luxury goods and prints, and worked until his death.[10] In Germany throughout the 1590s, Vecellio carried out church-commissioned work begun by Titian's son and his own brother Fabrizio. It may have been during these trips over the Alps that he met the Nuremberg woodcut artist Christoph Chrieger, whom he identifies in *Degli habiti antichi et moderni* as the maker of the prints based on his own drawings.[11]

In 1591, Vecellio published a four-book collection of lace patterns with the title *Corona delle nobili et virtuose donne*, two books of which were dedicated to the Venetian noblewoman Viena Vendramin Nani. Lace was made by women in Venice but worn by both men and women, in beautiful patterns and at high cost, which helps to explain why this book was republished in 1596, expanded by a fifth section, and again in 1601 by Vecellio's Frezzaria printing house, under a copyright that he renewed every year.[12] The book continued to be reprinted after his death in 1601. Another reason for the success of this lace book, which belonged to a genre that had been popular in Venice since the 1530s,[13] may have been its completeness: it combined 450 intricate illustrations with practical advice about lace-making, suggesting that Vecellio had accurately foreseen his audience: people interested in luxury textiles from many places. Captions in the book name patterns as coming from all over Europe, and from Turkey and Algeria. Vecellio offers patterns for specific purposes—making trim for handkerchiefs, for example—and he emphasizes the elegance of his patterns with names such as "Imperiali Cantoni di punto in aria, Mostra Bellisima et superba, per ogni lavoro" ("corners of needlework lace

ABOVE, LEFT Cesare Vecellio, woodcut, title page of *Corona delle nobili et virtuose donne*, Venice, 1592/1601

ABOVE, RIGHT Cesare Vecellio, woodcut, diagram of a design for handkerchief corners from *Corona delle nobili et virtuose donne*, Book 2

BELOW Paintings by Cesare Vecellio on the fore-edges of four books.

worthy of emperors, of a most beautiful and noble appearance suitable for any technique").[14] This informative interplay of word and image would reappear later as the basis for his costume books.

REPRESENTATIONS OF CLOTHING IN THE SIXTEENTH CENTURY

The popularity of Vecellio's lace book was related to the larger project of his books on clothing: he knew there was a demand for detailed representations of local and international costume. A clear parallel between the *Corona* and *Degli habiti* is that in both, visual detail is combined with detailed commentary. As a source of practical patterns, the *Corona* belonged to a range of texts offering models for clothing. Another kind was the tailor's sample book, in which detailed robes and gowns were drawn or painted in watercolor. One such book, assembled by two tailors and entitled *Il libro del sarto* by later scholars, included court dress and costumes for masques from the 1540s to the 1570s.[15] One of the tailors, Gian Giacomo, was employed at the court of Prince Renato Borromeo of Milan in the 1570s, and annotated many watercolors with the names, colors and quantities of fabrics he had used for these garments. Such books recorded ceremonial and festive costume and presented courtly attire in sufficient detail to allow followers of court fashion to order similar garments to be made for themselves.

The 1550s, however, saw the birth of a very different kind of costume book. These, like Vecellio's, focused on far-away places, on clothing intriguing for its strangeness rather than for the possibility of imitating it. Early modern maps, aimed at a similar audience, often included borders filled with figures dressed in clothing associated with the regions being shown.[16] David Woodward's summary of the appeal and significance of the world maps collected with increasing

BELOW, LEFT TO RIGHT

François Deserps [Desprez], woodcut, title page of *Recueil de la diversité des habits*, Richard Breton, 1562

Jost Amman, woodcut, title page of *Gyneceum, sive Theatrum Mulierum*, Frankfurt, 1586

Hans Weigel and Jost Amman, woodcut, title page of *Habitus praecipuorum populorum tam virorum*, Ulm, 1639

Giacomo Franco, engraving, title page of *Habiti delle donne Venetiane*, Venice, 1610

frequency by Venetians from the 1550s onward applies equally to the costume book as a genre:

> *As maps became more and more a part of everyday life, they played a subtle but important role in the shaping of ideas about the world. Beyond conveying knowledge factual or otherwise about strange places and events, they symbolized through a complex iconography some overarching themes: the magic of capturing the world as a [set of] ordered image[s], the replacement of the content of classical geography with a "modern" geography that incorporated "the new discoveries," and the secularization of the world image from the representation of spiritual to geometric space.*[17]

Like maps, costume books appealed to curiosity about countries and continents far from France, Germany, northern Italy and Belgium, the places where these books were being published.[18]

Why should ethnographic curiosity have been channeled into books on clothing? In early modern Europe, clothing wasn't mainly an expression of personal style or an imitation of fast-changing fashion; rather, as in the Middle Ages, it marked the gender, age, marital status and rank of its wearers, and reflected their city or regional identity. Individuals weren't free to dress as they pleased. Sumptuary law, in Venice and in other cities, controlled the fabrics, colors, and cut of clothing in an attempt to limit inequality among citizens (although in Venice such laws were suspended on great state occasions in order to demonstrate the splendor of the Republic).[19] Every public official dressed in a robe and hat that indicated his position, and a woman wore rich silk and satin or good wool or cheap linen in particular colors according to her family's wealth and social status. To dress was to be *invested* with a public identity according to a system of fixed codes. In a largely pre-literate society, people learned to read the value of textiles and the meaning of their cut as signs of profession, wealth, social status and geographical provenance. The newly rich man dressed as well as he could, but doing so meant dressing as wealthy men in his city already dressed, not inventing some extravagant style of his own. Women's headgear clearly announced their marital and economic status: single girls went bareheaded indoors, brides usually wore their hair loose at their weddings, wives always covered their hair whether with simple linen caps or elaborate headdresses, and widows wore veils of cotton, linen or silk. Therefore, a traveler who recorded clothing was recording richly meaningful signs of shared cultural identity rather than the whims of personal taste.

At the same time, however, clothing was fascinating because of its variation from place to place. In an era when many people died where they had been born, styles of dress remained distinct; tradition governed the costume of city dwellers and peasants alike. Costume summed up local custom. Bronwen Wilson offers a useful definition of *habiti* (or *abiti*), the Italian word associated with traditional costume as custom:

> *Derived from the Latin* habitus, *or aspect, the word* [h]abiti *signified the ways in which apparel invested bodies with meaning through the quality of the fabric and the tradition and conventions attached to dress. The word is also defined as* contegno, *meaning attitude and behavior and thereby conveying those attitudes to which people are inclined habitually or innately.* Abiti, *then, identified those aspects of clothing that were aligned with place, and these were the ideals inscribed in costume prints: the social roles and characteristics that distinguished regional diversity across time.*[20]

Greater physical mobility was required of merchants, soldiers, and courtly ambassadors, but they still wore a style of clothing that announced their regional origin and their professions. As Vecellio recognizes, political changes affecting the elite—for example, the takeover of the court of Naples by the Spanish—did lead to the adoption of new styles.

OPPOSITE Jean-Jacques Boissard, engraving, *Habitus variarum orbis gentium*, Cologne, 1581, plate 39

Virgo Macedonica

Nobilis fœmina Alexandrina

Fœmina Macedonica

Fille de Macedoine
Junckfraw aus Macedonia

Dame Alexandrine
Edele Fraw zu Alexandria

39

Femme de Macedoine
Fraw auss Macedonia

But for most classes the difficulty and expense of traveling gave regional costumes, as presented in printed costume books, a startling novelty. The anthropologist Daniel Defert points out two ways in which costume books appealed to readers: first, they provided pleasant armchair travel (cheaper and less arduous than actual voyages); and second, in printed form, they appealed to the same interests as the elaborate "cabinets of curiosities" assembled by prosperous collectors. Both the title pages and the prints in costume books, presented singly or in groups, promised wide coverage and exotic details.[21]

Such curiosity was also the motive for an earlier, more portable, collection focused on clothing: the illustrated manuscript book or *album amicorum*, assembled by students from Germany or other northern countries as they traveled farther south during their studies.[22] In cities such as Padua and Venice they selected particular drawings and watercolors of local costume from the ranges available in printers' and stationers' shops, as well as directly from artists, and had them bound into books as souvenirs of their youthful travels. Each city and its people were summed up by brightly colored, conventionalized images of the clothing worn by their

RIGHT Watercolor and gouache, "Sposa Venetiana in Gondola," 1575–7, from an *album amicorum*, Egerton ms. 1191, fol. 63

OPPOSITE, LEFT Watercolor and gouache, "Il Rettore in Padova," 1575–7, from an *album amicorum*, Egerton ms. 1191, fol. 72

OPPOSITE, RIGHT Watercolor and gouache, "Una Gentildonna Veneziana," 1575, from ms. 451 "Mores Italiae," fol. 49

officials and citizens. The watercolorists who produced the paintings are rarely named in the albums, but the watercolors can be dated since the students who collected them had their friends add their signatures on them, often with a date.[23] Such books were easy to carry, and they were organized, like costume books, into a hierarchical grid beginning with monarchs and nobles and descending to workmen and paupers. Sometimes the images collected in the albums also included individual prints from previously published costume books. Unlike costume books, however, these collections were personalized, assembled according to the preferences of the individual collector, and they became part of the private holdings of the elite families to which the students returned in the north.

Printed costume books claimed a more systematic and broader coverage. They consisted of woodcuts or engravings of single or grouped figures, with short captions, usually in several languages. The costume books that preceded and followed Vecellio's provided visual information and identifying captions, but they normally included no commentary and they usually focused on present-day clothing, as some representative titles show:[24]

Recueil de la diversité des habits qui sont de present en usage dans les pays d'Europe, Asie, Affrique et Isles sauvages (Collection of the Variety of Costume Presently Worn in the Countries of Europe, Asia, Africa, and the Wild Islands), Paris, 1562

Omnium fere gentium nostrae aetatis habitus (The Clothing of almost All the Peoples of Our Age), Venice, 1563

Omnium fere gentium nostrae aetatis nationum habitus et effigies (The Clothing and Images of Almost All the Peoples and Nations of Our Time), Antwerp, 1572

DEGLI HABITI ANTICHI ET MODERNI

In contrast to previous costume-book makers, who had focused on present-day dress, Vecellio wrote a history of costume. He begins with the Old Testament, moves on to ancient, medieval and modern Rome, and then records shifts in Venetian fashion from the Middle Ages to the present, especially from the 1550s to 1590. He follows each woodcut in his book with a page or more of commentary, in which he typically explains the geography, agriculture, diet and customs (especially marriage ceremonies) of the countries he covers; he always describes in detail the clothing represented in each woodcut. Jean de Glen's costume book, printed in Liège in 1601, is largely an abridged, reordered imitation of Vecellio's book. Its title spells out the historical depth, cultural comprehensiveness, and geographical breadth that Vecellio aimed at: *Des Habits, moeurs, cérémonies, façons de faire anciennes & modernes du monde* (*The Clothing, Customs, Ceremonies and Forms of Behavior, Ancient and Modern, of the World*). These claims are fully lived up to in Vecellio's work, by far the largest, most diverse, and richest in commentary of all the costume books printed up to 1590.

Vecellio's history of costume starts with Genesis. In his twelve-page "Discorso sopra gli habiti antichi et moderni, origine, mutatione et varietà di quelli" (Discourse on Ancient and Modern Clothing: Their Origin, Transformation, and Variety), he works out a synthesis of Old Testament, Christian and classical narratives, starting with Adam and Eve in Paradise and continuing through the ancient Babylonians, Phrygians and Persians until he arrives in the West, whose center he considers to be ancient and modern Rome. Book I, *Degli habiti, costumi et usanze di tutta l'Europa*, begins with ten figures from ancient Rome, including a patrician, a consul, six soldiers and a noblewoman. Vecellio then moves forward in time by including two prints of women from medieval Rome and ten figures of women from modern Rome and its countryside.

The next section is a "Breve descrittione della Città di Venetia," opening with a "Prima Perspettiva della Piazza di San Marco" (the first of four perspective views of Venice) and leading to 119 prints of men's and women's costume from medieval, early sixteenth-century and modern Venice. The prints and commentaries are ordered from the highest social status to the lowest—the doge, his officials, and the noblemen down through porters, galley slaves and beggars; and, in the case of women, from the doge's wife through noblewomen to housemaids and produce sellers in the city's markets. In all, the clothing of Venice and the Veneto takes up the first third of Book I.

The ambitious scope of the rest of the book is evident in its divisions and subdivisions. Seventy-one prints cover the rest of Italy, from west to east and north to south, organized by region, city and era: medieval and later Lombardy (Parma, Ferrara, Mantua), Piedmont (Bologna, Ancona, Turin, Genoa), and the Venetian territories (Verona, Brescia, Vicenza, Padua and the smaller towns of the Veneto). The last thirty-six woodcuts of Italian costume present clothing worn in Tuscany (Florence, Siena and Perugia), Naples, Romagna, and the islands of the south, ending with Sicily.

Book I then moves to France, opening with a discussion of its terrain, products and history and presenting fourteen prints. Spain is given eleven prints, Germany twenty-nine. Forty-four prints of northern dress conclude the first section of Book I, including Livonia (north of present-day Lithuania and south of Estonia), Silesia, Sweden, Bohemia, Switzerland, Prussia, the Low Countries, Hungary and Croatia, Schiavonia (Dalmatia), Slovenia, Poland, Muscovy, Brabant, England and Gothland. The final section of Book I moves east toward Asia. It contains thirty-three prints of clothing worn in Turkey, eleven of the dress worn by Greeks throughout Europe and Asia Minor, and six of costume from Macedonia, Thessaly and the islands of Crete, Mytilene, and Rhodes.

The title of Book II, *Degli habiti, costumi et usanze dell'Asia, et dell'Africa* (*The Clothing, Customs and Ways of Life of Asia and Africa*), promises a more explicit ethnographic focus: social conventions and rituals will be described. Vecellio admits in his opening "Discorso" that this book is more conjectural than Book I, based on second-hand reports rather than the evidence of his own eyes or dependable testimony. Book II is considerably shorter than Book I, consisting of fifty-nine prints in all, but its geographical range is vast. The countries typified by costume include eastern and southern regions of Asia Minor (Caramania, Armenia, Georgia, Persia, Syria), then India, East Asia (China and Japan) and the region of Ethiopia considered to lie in Asia. Finally, Vecellio turns to Africa, from the old Mamluk Empire in Cairo to North Africa (Barbary, Tunisia, Morocco) and then to sub-Saharan Africa and the island regions of Zanzibar and the Canaries.

In 1598, the second edition—*Habiti...di tutto il mondo* (*Clothing...of the Whole World*)—included twenty prints of the clothing of the New World, which we have added at the end of the 1590 images. In addition to correcting some mislabeled prints from the first edition, Vecellio divided the book into twelve shorter books, each defined by a national identity; he added eight prints of rulers, beginning with the pope and ending with the King of Persia. He also included additional prints of merchants in Italy and other European countries, added figures from each of the European countries he described in the 1590 volume (particularly from the north) and put in fifteen new figures from Persia, the Far East and Arabia. The twelfth of these books contains New World costume, as he promised in 1590: its title is "The Clothing of America." Another major difference in the 1598 book is that the Italian commentary from 1590 is cut to fit on only half a page, so that a Latin translation could be printed on the lower half of each page. Though the dedication and letter to the reader remain the same, this edition also omits Vecellio's opening "Discorso" on the history of clothing.

So for readers interested in Vecellio's commentary, the 1590 book is more useful. The section on the New World in the 1598 edition, however, ties Vecellio to the enormous interest in exploration and colonization shared by early modern Europeans in every region.

In contrast to the brief captions typical of costume books preceding Vecellio's, he adds comments full of precise terminology relating to textiles and trim.[25] His vocabulary materializes the global history of cloth condensed into the fabrics worn by Cinquecento Venetians. A light silk, *ormesino,* was named after Hormuz, an island in the Persian Gulf where the fabric had been made for centuries before its production was taken up by the Venetian *ormesini*—for whom a Fondamenta in Canaregio is still named. *Tabino* or *tabì,* a rich, heavy silk often given a watered or moiré finish, was originally made in al-Attabiya, a district of Baghdad. The *sbernia,* a loose cape, probably took its name from the *burnous,* an Arab mantle. And *damasco,* damask, a figured silk, echoes the name of the city where it was first made, Damascus in southwest Syria. Venice had been importing the splendid textiles of the East for a long time before Venetian cloth makers began exporting their own *damaschino,* a textile patterned in arabesques of golden or silk flowers, sent especially to Constantinople.[26]

Textile terms also came from closer by, from the cities and nations of Europe. *Rascia,* a twill of silk or wool, originally came from Raskia, a city in Serbia. *Cambrai* or *cambrada,* a kind of very fine white linen, came from the Flemish city of Cambrai; another fine linen, *renso,* echoed the name of its city of origin, Reims. *Scotto,* a rough wool tweed, took its name from Scotland, the country from which the best kinds came. And *ferrandina,* the term for a light fabric of mixed silk and wool, records the region in which it was first made: *Fiandra,* that is, Flanders. The textile economies of northern and eastern Europe made their way both into the shops where Venetians bought cloth and into the language they spoke.

Venice also put new words into circulation, especially the names of the rich silk velvets that textile masters produced in the city using new technologies. *Velluto soprariccio,* or pile on pile velvet, was woven around circular and elliptical rings that gave it a pile of different heights, hence a dense, three-dimensional surface with a chiaroscuro effect; *velluto allucciolato* sparkled with the tiny gold or silver loops woven into it; *velluto ad opera* had designs of contrasting color or gold worked across its surface. Another Venetian specialty was *brocadello,* a silk and linen textile in which the silk threads stood out in lustrous relief above the stiffer linen warp. Most of all, Vecellio sings the praises of the multicolored brocades designed by Bartolomeo Bontempele and sold at his shop, La Calice (The Chalice), which, as mentioned earlier, received orders from as far away as Constantinople. Venice gained distinction from the rich array of foreign fabrics its citizens wore, but Vecellio also insists that these citizens themselves produced dazzling new textiles, able to compete with cloth produced all over the world.[27]

What was new in Vecellio's book? In his dedicatory compliment to Count Montalbano he nimbly ties the Count's family's virtues to the qualities he wants to associate with his own volume: antiquity, variety and wealth. Each of these qualities does in fact set Vecellio's book apart from earlier costume books. While his predecessors in the genre presented figures mainly from the present, he presents costume from the ancient and medieval West as well as the two centuries preceding his. This long timeframe provides

BELOW Damask kaftan, Turkey, c. 1530

RIGHT Gown of *velluto sopraricco.* Detail from Vincenzo Catena, *Doge Andrea Gritti*, after 1523

him with a wide range of styles, a variety far greater than that found in costume books recording only what was worn in the present. He proudly presents "ancient" styles recoverable only by the first-hand observation he describes himself carrying out. And he explains each of his figures in rich detail from head to foot, including information about social customs as well as the cut, fabric, and trim of their clothing and minute description of coiffures, headdresses, and accessories.

VECELLIO'S SOURCES: THE VISUAL ARTS

Vecellio speaks only briefly of his own travel beyond Venice to the Veneto and to Germany. Instead, he emphasizes the geographical and cultural centrality of Venice as a city to which visitors come from all over the world; most of his sources have been actual living people. In addition to direct observation, he presents himself as an investigator of visual remains of various kinds, an archaeologist of dress. He is careful to explain his research into local historical costume, citing Latin and Italian historians but emphasizing his own success in discovering direct physical evidence.

Vecellio was in his seventies by the time the 1590 book reached print. This and his comments on his sources suggest that the images took years to assemble. He drew upon a wide range of visual materials. He tells his reader that he studied wall paintings in Padua for early costume (82) and he thanks certain gentlemen of the Veneto for showing him old frescoes and portraits in their private houses (77). As sources for early Venetian dress, he names painters including Luigi Vivarino (76), Vittore Scarpa (Carpaccio) (84v), and Giovanni Bellini (91). He also made use of architectural decorations and sculpture: for example, the capitals on columns at the Ducal Palace and funeral monuments from churches in Venice and on islands in its lagoon. And he drew upon mosaic figures from San Marco, inside and outside the cathedral.

Vecellio also makes a point of his collaboration with contemporary artists. As contributions to the book, he mentions a drawing by the miniaturist Giovan Maria Bodovino (26); he credits Erasmo Falte, a bookseller of Parma, for sending him a drawing by a local painter that he used for the print of a duchess of Parma (186v); he thanks Christoforo de Maganza, a Piedmontese artist, for an image he used for the print of a married woman of Turin (203v). He says that Antonio Zappello, a Genoese artist, sent him the drawing on which he based his print of the dress of a modern Genoese noblewoman (207v); and Francesco Curia, a Neapolitan artist, sent him sketches on which he modeled his present-day women of Naples (253).[28] He invokes a network of intellectuals and artists spanning all of Italy, not only to guarantee the accuracy of the book but also to demonstrate the wealth of his professional connections.

Another visual source for Vecellio was earlier costume books. He used many of his predecessors, including François Desprez, Pietro Bertelli, Jost Amman and Bartolomeo Grassi. He also used engravings published by the Frankfurt printer Theodor de Bry in the early 1590s, based on watercolors and sketches by artists who had accompanied explorers to the New World.

SOURCES FOR VECELLIO'S COMMENTARY

Among the various sources for his descriptions of costume and custom Vecellio mentions conversations with travelers from Venice and other places.[29] From the young Angelico Fortunio, for example, he got a report on Poznań, the Polish city in which Fortunio had just spent three years (352). He also recalls hearing about a dazzling cargo of Chinese goods, including paintings and bedsteads, brought back to Lisbon by the Portuguese captain Ribora Alguazil (475v). It may well be that scrolls in Alguazil's shipment provided Vecellio with his figure of the Chinese noblewoman, which he says he took from "paintings from that land" (473v). Eyewitness accounts obviously meant a lot to Vecellio, judging from his apology at the beginning of Book II for the second-hand information he has had to use when writing about Asia and Africa.

He demonstrates his training as a humanist by explaining that he has based his history of costume on a range of Roman historians, including Plutarch, Suetonius, and Aulus Gellius; he refers, in addition, to medieval and early

LEFT Detail of a manuscript map of Africa by Guillaume Le Testu, showing Tunisia and Algeria, *Cosmographie universelle selon les navigateurs, tant anciens que modernes*, Paris, 1556

Renaissance writers such as Macrobius and Flavio Biondo. (The Piloni library contained most of these books.) He also says he has used official reports, such as the account of the Bellunese Zaccaria Pagan, who accompanied the Venetian ambassador Domenico Trevisan on his trip to the Mamluk court at Cairo in 1512 (478v). He cites the Venetian Francesco Sansovino several times in his section on Venice, particularly Sansovino's history of the costume of the doges in his *Venetia città nobilissima* of 1581, and he echoes Sansovino in his interpretation of early Venetian costume as a sign of its citizens' sober republican character.

Once past his large section on Venice, however, Vecellio rarely names written sources, and once outside Europe he hardly ever does. One exception is Ludovico Varthema (Barthema), the Bolognese author of an account of his travels to India, whom the Venetian Senate paid to report to them in 1508.[30] Vecellio repeats Varthema's story about being asked to sleep with an East Indian bride before her husband did, according to local custom, and he names Varthema for the first time when he retells his story of the East Indian sultan who ate poison every day so as to be able to kill his enemies by spitting at them (465v). He uses old sources such as Ptolomy's *Geographica* for his map of Africa but also, in a highly selective way, the *Description of Africa* written by Leo Africanus (Hasan ben Mohammed al-Wazzan al-Zaiyati) and published in Giovanni Battista Ramusio's first volume of accounts of voyages in 1550. Possibly because he had seen images of clothing worn by the inhabitants of Barbary, Tunis and Marrakesh, he focuses on Leo's description of these cities.[31] But he omits most of Leo's historical and genealogical details, concentrating rather on the customs of the present. He quotes Leo respectfully on Barbary noblemen's erudition and interest in the humanities and the Tunisians' respect for learned and religious men (487), but he is also interested in bizarre or shocking details: the display of the bloodied sheet after the marriage night in Marrakesh (486), or the use of hashish in Tunis (487). This selectivity suggests that his way of working was to begin with an image—in the case of Africa, probably a figure taken from previous costume books—and then to assemble a text to explain it, rather than the other way around.

THE PRODUCTION PROCESS

Vecellio's own printing house seems to have been big enough to produce his book on lace. However, the many woodcuts and long commentaries of the 1590 and 1598 books would have made them very expensive to print, which probably explains why Vecellio handed them over to two large-scale publishers. Damian Zenaro produced the 1590 volume, setting his device, a crowned salamander, on its title page. The Sessa family (Giovanni Battista and Giovanni Bernardo at the time) printed the 1598 book; their device, a cat with a mouse in its

BELOW, LEFT Detail of Damian Zenaro's emblem, from the title page of *Degli habiti antichi et moderni*, 1590

BELOW, CENTER Detail of the Sessa brothers' emblem, from the title page of *Habiti antichi et moderni di tutto il mondo*, 1598

BELOW, RIGHT Detail of the Sessa brothers' cat with a kitten, from the last page of *Habiti antichi et moderni di tutto il mondo*, 1598

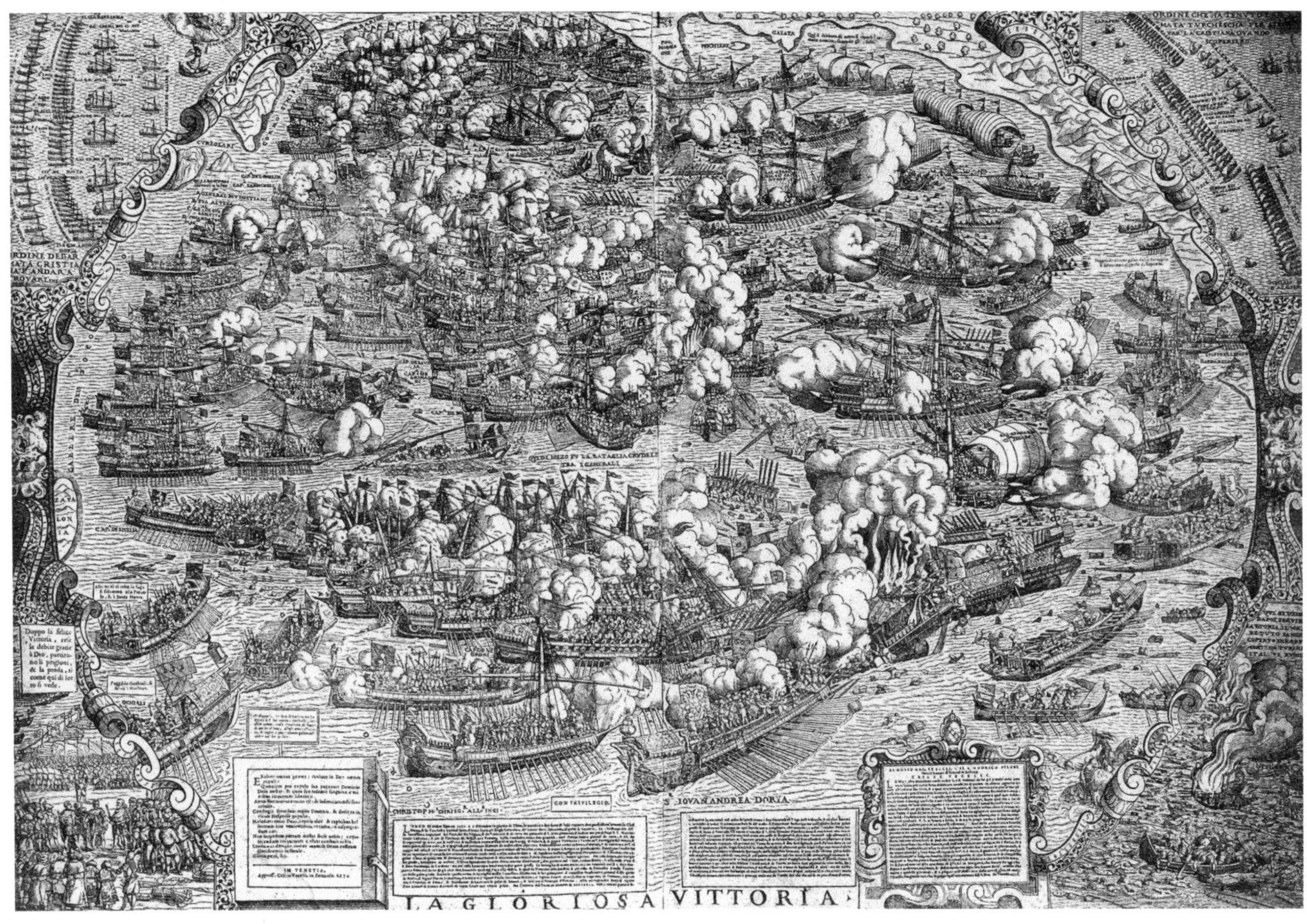

LEFT Cesare Vecellio and Christoforo Guerra [Christoph Chrieger], woodcut, *Battaglia di Lepanto e delle Curzolari*, 1572

mouth, appears on the title page, and a cat with a kitten appears on the final page. These men were powerful members of the booksellers' guild, as the minutes from the *arte*'s meetings from the 1570s through the 1590s show.[32] And the Sessas' publication of the book in Roman typeface and Latin, still an international language, suggests their confidence that it would be bought by readers all over Europe. They gave the 1598 book a larger print run than the 1590 volume, judging from the higher number of copies in rare book libraries today, but this seems to have caused them to work in haste. The 1598 book mixes type sizes in order to fill out pages; the woodcut borders of the prints are often imprecisely registered, leaving gaps at the corners; and the same print is used for merchants of Rome, Florence and Naples and, in the section on Venice, relabeled as "Mercanti d'Italia moderni."

Degli habiti arose from a kind of collaboration between Italian and German artists that had a long history. Albrecht Dürer's travels to Italy in the 1510s began a tradition of artistic exchanges between the two countries. German patrons such as the Fuggers employed Italian artists, and many German engravers and woodcut printers settled in Venice.[33] Titian traveled to Augsburg twice, to join the court of the Emperor Charles V, in 1548 and 1550—through this connection he obtained many later portrait commissions.[34] Vecellio's scornful description of the disorderly, violent German Coachman ("Carattiero Thedesco", 338), though the image is based on earlier costume books, suggests that his own travels in Germany were less than blissful. In the 1590 book Vecellio writes about his collaboration with the printmaker Christoph Chrieger (translating the German *Krieg*, meaning war, into the Italian *Guerra*). Together they produced a print of the Battle of Lepanto, drawn in 1572, a year after the battle, and published in 1591. Chrieger (the usual spelling) may also have provided woodcut portraits for the second edition of Vasari's *The Lives of the Artists* (1568).[35]

Vecellio spells out the work routine he shared with Chrieger in his comment on the print of a noblewoman of Bologna: "I saw this attire in Venice, and then it was drawn and incised by Christoforo Guerra, a German from Nuremberg and a most excellent maker of woodcuts" (200). In the north, Chrieger, as the cutter of a durable woodblock, would have been paid more by the publisher than Vecellio, who provided an ephemeral and more quickly made drawing.[36] But Zenaro must have paid Vecellio a good deal, too, for his role as researcher and writer of *Degli habiti*. The Vecellio/Chrieger collaboration was evidently long-lasting and amicable. Vecellio included a written and illustrated memorial to Chrieger in *Degli habiti*: in his "Third View of the Piazza of San Marco" he explains that the image is incomplete because Chrieger, "my friend, and an excellent printmaker of our time" (155), died before they could add the recently completed stretch of new apartments for the Procurators to the image. Fittingly, this print of the Piazza represents a funeral procession—though that of a doge rather than of an artist.

More hands than Vecellio's and Chrieger's contributed to the book. The seven woodcut borders repeated throughout both books probably belonged to the Zenaro printing house; their intricate strap-work and witty grotesques, typical of the Sansovino frame, also recall Fontainebleau designs.[37] Chrieger most likely made the woodcut for the title page of the 1590 edition, with its four female allegories of the continents, but his death around 1590 raises the possibility that another printmaker cut the block for the title page of the 1598 book, with its differently clothed and positioned figures. Some of the new figures late in the European section of the 1598 volume, more clumsily outlined and with longer bodily proportions, also suggest the work of another printmaker.

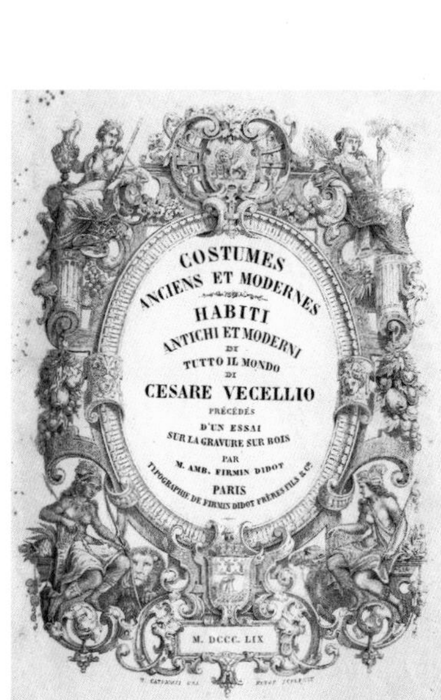

ABOVE Ambroise Firmin Didot, wood engraving, title page of *Costumes anciens et modernes. Habiti antichi et moderni... di Cesare Vecellio*, Paris, 1859–60

VECELLIO'S READERS

Vecellio's letter "To the Reader" reveals a good deal about his intentions for the book. One of the audiences he intends to "entertain and please" is that of people interested in his profession—the visual arts. This remark is a good guide to the prints themselves. They are not models for tailors but images meant to be useful to painters.[38] This is why he explains so specifically the textures and quantities of fabrics and the colors worn by different ranks and genders, gives detailed descriptions of accessories and hair styles, shows figures in a variety of postures (front views, but also profile and back views), represents various gestures appropriate to his figures, and even describes items not shown in the prints: undergarments, breeches covered by a cape, doublets covered by long robes, and colored shoes hidden by floor-length hems.

Later, revised editions of Vecellio's 1590 book provide further evidence for its relevance to artists. The shortening of the commentary in 1598 emphasizes the images over the text. The third edition, published by Giovanni Giacomo Hertz in Venice in 1664, makes a fictional claim that Titian contributed to the book and that Vecellio was his brother; its long title elaborates on the book's usefulness to artists of various kinds: *Habiti antichi overo raccolta di figure delineate dal gran Titiano e da Cesare Vecellio suo fratello, diligentemente intagliate, conforme alle Nationi del Mondo. Libro utilissimo a pittori, dissegnatori, scultori, architetti et ad ogni curioso, e peregrino ingegno* (*Clothing of the Past, or a collection of images outlined by the great Titian and by Cesare Vecellio, his brother, carefully incised, according to the nations of the world. A book extremely useful to painters, designers, sculptors, architects and to every curious and wide-ranging mind*). When the 1598 book was remade in Paris in 1859–60, under the title *Costumes anciens et modernes. Habiti antichi et moderni di Cesare Vecellio,* its French publisher, Ambroise Firmin Didot, wrote an essay focusing on the technical superiority of the newly made prints—wood engravings—in comparison to woodcuts. The modern edition published by Dover Press (New York, 1977) omits the commentary. It offers only the images from the 1598 book, on the assumption that costume designers and other visually oriented users will need only the pictures, not the words.

The books were indeed owned and used by artists. Inigo Jones, collaborating with Ben Jonson on masques for the English court in the early 1600s, probably used Vecellio's print of the "Gentildonna di Caramania" (Noblewoman of Modern Caramania, 436) for the character played by Lady Anne Clifford in *Berenice,* and Vecellio's "Hebrea in Soria" (Jewish Woman in Syria, 464) for a female captive in *Albion's Triumph.*[39] Vecellio's figure of a Mexican soldier appears in costume drawings for Italian pageants; it seems that Leonardo da Vinci used early sources similar to Vecellio's for his sketch of a Mexican in a feathered headdress.[40] And one extant copy of the 1590 book was owned by the English Pre-Raphaelite painter John Martineau (1789–1854).

Portraits from the period soon after Vecellio's books show that the international distribution planned by his publishers did indeed materialize. In 1605 the Spanish court painter Juan Pantoja de la Cruz painted Margaret of Austria, wife of Philip III of Spain, standing with her right hand on an open book. The frame and single-figure format of the page at which this book is opened resemble those in Vecellio's

ABOVE Detail showing a costume book, from Werner Jacobszn, *Members of the Company of Captain Albert Coenraetsz and Lieutenant Pieter Evertsz*, 1625

ABOVE, RIGHT Werner Jacobszn, *Members of the Company of Captain Albert Coenraetsz and Lieutenant Pieter Evertsz*, 1625

OPPOSITE Juan Pantoja de la Cruz, *Margaret of Austria*, 1605

costume books exactly. And in Holland in 1625, the Dutch painter Werner Jacobszn, in a group portrait of the members of the military defense team of Albert Coenraetsz, included a gentleman holding a book in which he points to a print of a single male figure dressed in a *berretta à tozzo* and wide breeches, and holding a staff—as the members of the order did to have their portraits painted. The format of the print is like the one Vecellio uses, although no print of his resembles this one exactly; the image may come from a collection of military figures, a genre related to the costume book. But in both cases, the artist uses this type of book to mark the identity of his sitter.

VECELLIO AS A VENETIAN AUTHOR

Vecellio's treatment of Venetian and global costume and custom suggests that he was also writing for his own city's merchants and their wives, informing them about modern clothing throughout the world. But he also invokes ancient Venetian values to remind them of proper gendered behavior. This backward focus was ideologically motivated. Vecellio produced his retrospective catalogue of Venetian costume not to encourage his readers to recognize the otherness of the past but to recommend traditional dress as a continuing model for behavior in the present for the men and especially the women of his city. Looking at the capital of a column at the Ducal Palace, he interprets a pair of medieval lovers as an exemplary couple: "Habito Antico di Giovane Nobile Ornato per Fare l'Amore" (Early Clothing of a Young Nobleman Dressed to Go Courting, 55) and the matching maiden, "Donzella Innamorata" (Maiden of Early Times, in Love, 56). Assigning the man an active gesture with expressive hands, to which he contrasts the sculpted maiden's modest gesture of surprise or self-defense, Vecellio uses pose and costume alike to materialize the model behavior of this couple.

Such interpretation takes the costume print far beyond reportage. Vecellio presents costume as an indicator of character, in which an old style of dress reveals a virtuous way of being. In his commentary, he interprets a man's gown with the long, full *dogalina* sleeve as a sign of dignity and political wisdom: "This dress is very sober and Senatorial" (54). In modern times too, he writes, clothing makes material civic virtue: the young noblemen of present-day Venice wear bright colors and delicate silks, but in the street they hide them under their cloaks: "They wear all these colors in as concealed a way as possible, according to the modesty appropriate to this Republic" (108v). He also takes the simplicity of early noblemen's clothing, resembling boys' clothing in modern Venice, as evidence that they were sexually innocent. He claims that they maintained their chastity until the age of thirty, for "the clothing they wore permits no other conclusion" (65 v)—surely a conclusion more hopeful than plausible. Vecellio's interpretations of *habiti antichi* are prescriptive, those of a moralist as much as a historian of dress.

Vecellio also represents early women as exemplifying values he wants to promote in contemporary Venice, setting up a model of modest wealth and energetic domesticity. A striking example is his image and commentary on a fifteenth-century noblewoman: "Donne Antiche per Casa" (Noblewoman of Early Venice at Home, 58). A modern viewer of this print is likely to notice the elaborate headdress and the rich brocade

ABOVE, LEFT AND RIGHT Filippo Calendario, sculpted marble capitals, a young man and a young woman courting, Ducal Palace, Venice, c. 1340

of the puffed upper sleeves and the underskirt. But Vecellio's description translates this rich costume into evidence of feminine virtue. He explains that women of this era rejected the *dogalina* and wore narrow sleeves instead, with a light veil thrown back over their shoulders, a combination that facilitated good wifely behavior in the style of ancient Rome:

> *And so, fit and quick to attend to their household duties with the greatest diligence and to care for their children and husbands, they strove to avoid idleness, following the example of the Roman Lucretia, a true model of chastity, whose fame is eternal because of...the love she bore for her husband Collatinus, equal to any woman of antiquity in the purity of her soul.* (58)

Here Vecellio fits women out according to ancient texts—the Roman historian Livy's account of Lucretia's rape and subsequent suicide.[41]

Similarly, in his section on contemporary Venetian dress he defines an umarried woman as exemplary because of her enveloping costume and her restrained pose: "Donzelle, et Fanciulle di Venetia" (Maidens and Girls of Venice, 124). The darkly inked, heavily incised vertical lines representing the black veil obscure the girl's face entirely, and Vecellio assures us that such a veil prevents a girl from being seen. This is precisely his point: an unmarried noblewoman isn't supposed to be seen. In contrast, the later copy of this image, the wood engraving published by Firmin Didot in Paris in 1859–60, transformed Vecellio's original by representing the girl in a white veil. Her face can be clearly seen (and to our eyes she looks distinctly coquettish).[42] This modernization contradicts Vecellio's insistence that the virtue of such a girl corresponds to the invisibility provided by her costume:

The greatest…modesty characterizes the…tradition of bringing up noble girls in Venice, for they are so well guarded…in their fathers' houses that very often not even their closest relatives see them until they marry…. [When] they are fully grown, they dress entirely in black, with a fazzuolo *called a* cappa *of very delicate silk, very full and ample, thick and* stoccato *[crimped]…which covers their face, so they are unseen but can see others. But girls of the nobility and high ranks go out rarely, only on principal festivals and holy days.* (124v)

RIGHT AND FAR RIGHT
Cesare Vecellio, "Donzella Antica" and "Giovane Antico"

The *donzella*'s gloved hands, firmly held handkerchief, and gesture of touching her necklace with her hand all correspond to Vecellio's model of contained, modest femininity—though her schematically drawn cleavage and fashionable pinked gloves complicate the image.

Vecellio's image of the Venetian widow is free of any such ambiguity ("Delle Vedove," 134). He informs his readers that widows who wish to remarry can acceptably signal their intent by wearing simple jewelry and letting some of their hair show. But the woodcut erases this possibility: it represents a woman whose body is turned away from us, with her hair entirely covered by a dark veil and a prayer book in her dark-gloved hand. According to Vecellio, this sober costume signals chaste custom:

> *With the death of their husbands widows in Venice embrace the death of all vanity and bodily ornament. For in addition to wearing black they cover their hair, fasten a very thick veil over their breast...and go through the streets sadly and with lowered heads.* (133v)

Interestingly, though, Vecellio names this woman as a member of the Contarini clan, identifying her in a way that contradicts his implication that the modest dress and deportment of Venetian widows preserve their anonymity.

Vecellio also uses the past to warn women against contemporary fashion. In his print of "Habiti Venetiani antichi di cento anni" (Venetian Clothing of Former Times, 93), the upward-swooping headdress and repeated horizontal trim on the skirt and sleeves suggest a lively extravagance. But the high-waisted cut of the gown is what Vecellio admires:

> *This style...is still more comfortable than our present-day long bodices, which, while they may give a slimmer silhouette, cause discomfort. And I recall...that these new bodices reached such an extreme that the* Magistrato sopra le Pompe[43] *had to intervene, for such bodices were being worn long and broad beyond all measure, and with iron stays set into them to hold in the waist more tightly. Warnings were issued that this was the cause of many injuries to pregnant women, and so it was prohibited by law....* (93)

We might ask how Vecellio knew that this bodice was so uncomfortable. But comfort is not the central issue for him; rather, he wants to argue that the natural maternal role of women calls for a more "natural" cut of costume. The long, flat bodice threatens not only sartorial moderation but also the safety of Venice's future progeny.

Yet Vecellio's civic loyalty also leads him to contradict this elevation of plain women's dress as a model of modesty. Typifying the tension in Venice between praise for traditional sobriety in dress and the entrepreneurial invention of new products and fashions, he emphasizes that the glory of the city depends on the public magnificence of its citizens' clothing.[44] The long bodice that he denounces in contrast to the gowns of a century earlier is clearly visible in a print he uses to illustrate how lavishly Venetian noblewomen dress on state occasions, when they are not only allowed but encouraged to dazzle visitors with the splendor of their costume and jewels: "Nobile ornata" (Noblewomen at Public Festivals, 131). In his commentary on this image, Vecellio tells us about the visit of Prince Henri of Valois to Venice in 1574, when the women of the city were paraded before him as exemplars of sumptuous wealth and the newest fashion.[45] In the meeting room of the Great Council a hundred pairs of *gentildonne,* dressed in white satin and covered in pearls, gold and jewels, passed by the prince. On an occasion like this, Vecellio explains, the Republic suspended all sumptuary laws in order to impress foreign visitors. He reports an estimate that each woman in this procession was wearing a gown and jewelry worth 50,000

ABOVE Cesare Vecellio, woodcut, "Donzelle, et Fanciulle di Venetia," 1590

BELOW Ambroise Firmin Didot, wood engraving, *Costumes anciens et modernes*, 1859–60, plate 101

scudi (131v). Patrician women, however often they were praised for remaining indoors and invisible, were also expected to perform in public on state occasions, as metonyms of their prosperous Republic. Like Shakespeare's company in London, the King's Men, who were given livery of red cloth to march in during public occasions, Venetian gentlewomen were summoned to participate in a living frieze assembled to glorify Venice.

Henri's visit was an exceptional event. But Vecellio suggests that women were allowed—expected, even—to display the Republic's splendor annually at the Sensa festival. He describes the Venetian bride during this festival as the pinnacle of the wealth, sartorial elegance, and allure of the city: "Spose in Sensa" (Brides at Ascension Time, 128). The woodcut of the bride hardly does justice to the prose poem describing her:

> *If ever there is a time that the brides of Venice make an effort to look beautiful and to appear richly dressed, it is during the fifteen days of the Sensa holiday.... Then [they] set about inventing...the greatest luxury and elegance they can, because they will be seen not only by their fellow citizens but also by the many foreigners of all ages and sexes who come...to see that splendid display of merchandise. During these days the brides show off the richness of their largest pearls...with which they ornament their ears, hair, necks and breasts. Shining with gold and gems...they stroll through the Sensa [wearing] overgarments of white satin.... The rest of their overgarment...is made of lightweight black silk...with a train.... And from their hair hangs a black veil of very beautiful transparent silk.* (129)

This veil, in contrast to the kind worn by girls of the nobility, allows its wearer to be seen and admired. Vecellio's print and comment reveal again the tension between Venetian pride in contemporary fashion and respect for plain, traditional virtue.

A pair of prints from the end of Vecellio's section on Venice further illustrates these conflicting ideologies. As an example of virtuous traditionalism, Vecellio presents the female market gardeners of Chioggia, who come to sell fruit and vegetables in the city: "Hortolane" (Market Gardeners, 151). Their clothes, like their goods, seem to arise naturally from the town's unchanging, fertile terrain. Vecellio praises the land itself, suggested by the flowers at the gardener's feet: "Surrounding the ancient city of Chioggia...are several villages or towns rich in beautiful orchards and vineyards... expertly cultivated, so that in every season they provide everything needed for food" (151). He describes the young gardener admiringly: she wears her hair in "modest little curls" and covers her breast completely with a veil; she wears inexpensive colors suited to her rank—"negro, o turchino" (black or turquoise)—and flat shoes. In their habit and their habits, Vecellio suggests, such women display an instinctive generosity related to the land from which they come: "dressed in this way, with some lovely gift of fruit, they appear before their friends and masters." The straw basket in the print is more than a decorative accessory: it signifies regular seasonal work by people who know their station, and the availability to Venice of all good things. Such images point to an unchanging country–city economy that exists outside history.

But at the same time, Vecellio celebrates Venetian merchants' newly designed textiles and their appeal in international markets. Describing his sumptuously dressed "Donne per Casa" (Women at Home, 139), he praises the silk brocades designed by the Venetian merchant Bartolomeo Bontempele and adds that the noblewomen of Venice wear these brocades because they are attracted by Bontempele's new pink, blue and green dyes. But in an attempt to resolve a potential contradiction, Vecellio also claims that the wearing of these luxurious fabrics by high-ranking women is a sign of wifely virtue: they dress as richly as they do to keep their husbands' "conjugal love" (139v). That is, he defines patrician women not as consumers of Venetian merchandise to attract the publc gaze of visitors but as embodiments of a virtuous at-home style meant to keep the eyes of husbands from straying.

VECELLIO AND WOMEN BEYOND THE LAGOON

Vecellio constructs a different notion of the virtuous woman when he transfers his attention from Venice to cities of the north. In a reversal of the enclosure "*per casa*" through which he models good Venetian women, he praises the public engagement and business acumen of northern women merchants in a series of prints and comments in which his business ethic overrules his loyalty to the habit of sequestering noblewomen at home. The geographical distance of such merchants presents no threat to Venetian order, and their skills resemble those of Vecellio himself, a publisher and artist working for urban rather than courtly patrons. He focuses approvingly on how skillfully foreign women sell their goods and train their daughters to be equally sharp buyers and sellers. A woman merchant from contemporary Genoa is shown with a narrow bag for utensils hanging from her waist: "Habito moderno di Nobile Genovese" (Modern Clothing of a Genoese Noblewoman, 208). This noblewoman is also a businesswoman who combines the charm of the ideal court lady with a sisterly chasteness of speech:

> *These are the most affable and pleasant-spoken women of all Italy.... They go about buying and selling without any loss of reputation because women who buy and sell at the greatest profit are very highly esteemed; so they are shrewd and sharp-witted.... They...almost always wear a purse hanging from their belt, and a* thing [emphasis ours] *embroidered all over with gold...that is used to hold sewing needles or other objects.* (207)

In this final reference to sewing needles, Vecellio seems to be trying to assimilate these Genoese merchant women with Venetian women doing needlework in their houses—the kind illustrated in his *Corona delle nobili et virtuose donne.* In fact, Genoese women probably used these reticules to carry account books and small weights and measures, not sewing implements, which they would have kept and used at home.

Vecellio is similarly impressed by the merchant women of Silesia (then a part of present-day eastern Germany and Austria). His print of the "Donna di Mediocre Conditione in Slesia" (A Woman of Middle Rank, 324) includes three details signifying her mercantile skill: her purse, her keys, and a wide belt from which she hangs them. He comments: "The women of middling rank in Silesia are very expert in business, so they go throughout the city buying and selling what they need" (324). For this northern region, he accepts a method of raising girls strikingly different from Venetian custom: "They usually take their daughters with them, dressed as they are, whom they teach from an early age to buy and sell, so that they become skillful and experienced in business".

Jeannine Guérin Dalle Mese sees a wishful vision here of what high-ranking Venetian women ought to be allowed to do: maneuver in public without being criticized for risking their chastity.[46] It is equally likely that Vecellio, writing as a merchant himself, sees these women vendors as more useful to their local economies than the patrician women of his own city. Indeed, he admires businesswomen whenever he comments on them, whether of Antwerp or Bohemia (361, 334). He also writes approvingly about the women of England, who work harder at the market and in their shops than do their husbands (370). While respectfully recording the Venetian nobility's strict internment of its daughters, as an entrepreneur Vecellio also admires the public activity of the wives and daughters of the international merchant class.

Vt Matronæ Dasamonquepeuc liberos gestant. X

IN oppido DALEMVNQVEPEVC, quatuor aut quinque miliaribus a ROANOAC distante, matronæ eadem ratione qua ROANOACENSES amiciuntur & pungũtur; corollas tamen capiti non imponunt, nec crura punctiunculis picta habent. Miram habent liberos gestandi rationem, & a nostra plane diuersam: nam nostræ brachiis ante pectus liberos sustinent, illæ vero prehensa pueri dextra manu, in tergo gerunt, crus illius sinistrum sinistro brachio amplectentes, ratione satis mira & peregrina, vt ex pictura videre licet.

B 2

RIGHT Theodor de Bry, *Les Grands voyages*, Frankfurt, 1590, vol. I. An engraving of a Virginian woman carrying her child, based on a watercolor by John White in Thomas Harriot's *A briefe and true report of the new found land of Virginia*, London, 1588, plate 10

FAR RIGHT Cesare Vecellio, woodcut, "Habito delle Donne dell'Isola Virginia," 1598

In 1598, Vecellio's presentation of New World women suggests a different assumption. For his prints of women of the Americas, he used contemporary texts illustrating New World expeditions. One source was De Bry's Latin commentary and engravings (*Les Grands voyages,* Frankfurt, 1590), based on Thomas Harriot's English account of Virginia (*A briefe and true report of the new found land of Virginia,* London, 1588), which included John White's watercolours from 1585. De Bry added rich details of flora and fauna to his version, setting his figures in a frame of human use of natural surroundings.

In contrast, Vecellio removes his New World women from any inhabited landscape, isolating them from the natural and social world shown in his sources, and setting his description of cultures into the text—which in the 1598 edition is very brief. This format puts New World women and their dress into an ahistorical realm that contrasts with the detailed chronology of costume he constructs for both sexes in Europe and, to a lesser extent, for New World men.[48]
In general, Vecellio admires the cultures of the New World. But as a genre, his costume book, by centering a single figure in a small print, diminishes the social contexts verbally and

visually supplied by earlier explorers and artists. He acknowledges the history of Spanish occupation by calling attention to the mixed clothing of New World men—the Spanish mirror held by a young man of Mexico (472), the Cuzco nobleman's Spanish shirt (488v). But European gender attitudes and visual conventions combine to cut his American women off from their social relationships and the locally varying kinds of work they do.

Vecellio's print of a woman of Virginia carrying her child on her back typically reworks De Bry's engraving and text. De Bry, expanding on White's watercolor, gives the viewer a back and front view of this mother and surrounds her with a landscape.[49] This presentation turns the Virginian mother into an ethnographic exemplum, but the Frankfurt printer also makes her engage the observer directly, gazing toward us on the left and looking back at her child on the right. Vecellio, in contrast, gives us a single image—"Habito delle Donne dell'Isola Virginia" (Clothing of the Women of Virginia Island, 503v)—in which the mother gazes off to the left in profile, not at the viewer or at her child. He also puts less emphasis on this novel way of carrying a child in his commentary than does Harriot. Harriot stresses the action by describing it as "quite contrarie to ours," and De Bry's title also emphasizes the mother's behavior with her child. Vecellio

Regis & Reginæ prodeambulatio recreandi animi gratia. XXXIX.

39

PRODIT interdum Rex sub vesperam deambulatum in proximam sylvam solus cum primaria conjuge, tectus cervina pelle tam eleganter parata, & varijs coloribus picta, ut nihil elegantius depictum conspici queat. Bini adolescentes latera ejus claudentes, flabella ad ventulum faciendum gestant, tertius globulis aureis & argenteis è cingulo propendentibus ornatus, pone sequitur, pellem ne terram verrat, sustinens. Regina & ejus pedissequæ ornatæ sunt ex humeris propendente vel eas cingente musci quodam genere in nonnullis arboribus nascente, tenuibus staminibus invicem cohærentibus catenularum modo prædito, viridis in cæruleum tendentis coloris, adeo venusti, ut sericea stamina videantur. Iucundum præbent spectaculum hoc musco oneratæ arbores: nam è summis nonnumquam ramis etiam prealtæ arboris ad terram usque demittitur. In venationem aliquando profectus cum aliquot commilitonibus in sylvas habitationi Regis Saturioua vicinas ipsum cum Regina ita comptos reperi.

Porrò monendus lector, omnes istos Regulos, eorumque uxores, corporis cutem puncturis quibusdam varias picturas imitantibus ornare (ut ex sequentibus iconibus videre licet) sic ut interdum in ægritudinem septem vel octo dierum incidant: puncta tamen loca, herba quadam fricant, quæ tincturam addit indelebilem. Ornatus etiam & magnificentiæ gratia, digitorum in manibus & pedibus ungues crescere sinunt, quorum latera scabentes concha aliqua, acutissimos reddunt: oris etiam circumferentiam cæruleo colore pingere soliti.

FAR LEFT Theodor de Bry, *Indorum Floridam provinciam inhabitantium eicones*, Frankfurt, 1591, engraving of a king and queen of Florida, based on a 1565 drawing by Jacques le Moyne de Morgues

LEFT Cesare Vecellio, woodcut, "Habito della Regina," 1598

describes the gesture more briefly—though positively—as "fine": "un bel modo di portar i loro fanciulli" (a fine way of carrying their children).

Dalle Mese takes this adjective as proof of Vecellio's admiring rather than exploitative view of the people of the New World.[50] But we would add that De Bry's engraving frames the mother's role as a significant particularity of her culture (rather than a natural fact) in a way that Vecellio's woodcut cannot do. De Bry, in addition to representing two aspects of this child-carrying technique, places both figures in a landscape, including a river on which men row long boats, situating the Virginian mother in a larger Roanoke culture. Like De Bry, Sulstazio Gratiliano, the Sienese humanist who translated Vecellio's text into Latin, clearly appreciated the ingenuity of this method of carrying a child; he describes it with the adverb "aptissimè"—that is, very capably, neatly, efficiently. By contrast, in his brief comment Vecellio focuses on the woman's clothing rather than her behavior, and his remark that she wears "only an animal skin" deculturates her further. The comment and image attribute a wild roughness to her loincloth, in contrast to the neat fringe that White depicts in his watercolor and De Bry repeats in his engraving. We are a long way from Vecellio's admiring account of the culture of the Silesian mother who educates her daughter to barter and keep accounts.

The format of the 1598 book similarly isolates Vecellio's "Queen of Florida" from her culture: the marriage ritual and process of tattooing narrated by the French traveler Jacques Le Moyne de Morgues, who accompanied the Huguenot captain René de Laudonnière to Florida in 1565 and then sold his paintings to De Bry in 1587.[51] Le Moyne tells his readers that after he watched the elaborate ceremonies uniting the chief Saturiba and his new wife, he saw them walking with their attendants in a forest—the site of the bush whose leaves they used to tattoo their bodies with an indelible blue (113). In De Bry's crowded engraving, we see the queen offering a small branch of this plant (indigo?) to her husband, while her attendants gather it in a basket.[52] In Vecellio's print "Habito della Regina" (Clothing of the Queen, 498), however, the queen stands alone, a semi-nude with downcast eyes, offering not indigo to her husband but a round fruit to the viewer. Like De Bry's queen, Vecellio's is fashioned in *contrapposto*, but now, removed from her context, she seems only to be looking at the fruit in her hand. Is this Eve's apple? Perhaps so. In his comment, Vecellio mistranslates Le Moyne's commentary (in Latin in the De Bry volume). Interpreting De Bry's text through the lens of Genesis and probably also through European views of the New World as a paradise on earth, Vecellio interprets the dye leaves as fig leaves, with which, he says, the Floridians conceal their genitals (as Adam and Eve did after the Fall). He writes that the Virginians, too, cover their shoulders and genitals with the leaves of trees: "Coprono le spalle e le vergogne con foglie di arbori."

Vecellio's print of a Virginia woman carrying a gourd similarly effaces her cultural situation. In his commentary, Harriot, motivated by the desire to convince Elizabeth I of the economic value of Virginia and the docility of its people, enumerated a range of cultural practices in addition to the physical bounty that he represented as there for the taking. He identifies this woman as the wife of a Pomeiooc chieftain, and he links her, through her smile and pointing finger, to her daughter at play. Focusing again on cultural practices, Harriot writes that such gourds are usually "full of some pleasant drink" and that these women use their necklaces of copper or bone beads "to give support to one of their arms." He also comments on the daughter's toys: she holds a doll supplied by the English explorers, with which, he says, the Florida children were "highly delighted". But Vecellio omits the ethnographic details of White's painting and of Harriot's prose, which locate both figures in a history not only of indigenous culture but also of new international exchange. Vecellio, rather, shows a timeless single woman, looking downward with an averted gaze: "Habito delle matrone, donzelle" (Clothing of Married Women and Girls, 501). Rather than commenting on this married woman's gesture of resting her arm on her necklace, he describes a gesture unrelated to the print, quoting a comment from Harriot about how Pomeiooc unmarried *girls* "place their hands on their chest to hide their breasts." Vecellio's modest Pomeiooc Eve (or Venus) registers European discomfort with adult female nudity—or, rather, the convention of translating it visually into classical poses and implicit references to the Christian myth of innocence and fall.

Vecellio's book, then, embodies the mentality of a forward-looking Venetian artist and businessman at the end of the sixteenth century. In many ways, Venetian cultural assumptions and the loyalties and aspirations of Vecellio's entrepreneurial artist-publisher class shape his images and judgments of his own city and of other people. His long section on Venice affirms the traditional values shared by its citizens and, simultaneously, celebrates the new goods they make, consume, and export. His pride in Venetian textiles coexists with wholehearted admiration for the sumptuous cottons and silks worn in Turkey, sold in Middle Eastern market cities and made in the New World. As a result, the book is a rich historical record of dress in Venice, Europe, the rest of the Old World, and the Americas—and of the mentality of Cesare Vecellio himself.

VECELLIO'S LANGUAGE

Vecellio usually writes in standard Italian, but he also uses Venetian dialect, especially in his history of the clothing of Venice. One example is the *dogalina* sleeve, derived from *ducale* (in Venetian dialect *dogale*), meaning suitable for a doge—that is, rich and splendid. Vecellio explains that such long, full sleeves gave their name to an overgarment of various styles, and he cites his source for this early version as a painting in the monastery of San Domenico (62). He adds that medieval women began to imitate this style and later he offers an image of a bride of former times dressed in an overgown with similar wide sleeves, also worn turned back onto the shoulders (94v).

Vecellio uses Venetian dialect again to name another early style of sleeve, worn with a short overgown: *maniche a comeo* in the print (*à cometo* in the text, 64). These are long sleeves that hang down deeply below the elbow: *il gomito,* Tuscan for elbow, had become *comio* or *comeo* in Venice by the fifteenth century. Vecellio is most explicit about the fact that he's using a Venetian word when he describes the hats worn by merchants and shopkeepers in Venice: "Et questi portano le berrette alte, che essi chiamano à tozzo" (They wear a cap they call a *beretta à tozzo,* 116). A *tozzo* was a light, small boat; near Padua, the word also meant a small, plump man.[53] The hat, arched at its high top, as young men wore it, was given a full, rounded shape by its pleats or gathers. Its flat crown (*à tagliere*), in the form in which older men usually wore it, gave it the shape of a platter (in Florentine Italian of the time, *una taglia*). Vecellio reports that the young women of Venice, too, have particular words for their garments and accessories. The long sashes of silk net that they tie around their waists they call *poste* (126). Young girls wear a sheer white veil they call a *fazzuolo,* but young noblewomen wear a stiff, crimped veil of black silk, which they call a *cappa.* This is the style of veil that the print illustrates, completely concealing the girl's face. He celebrates his city by retelling its history and describing its architecture, and also in the texture of his prose by using words unique to Venetian sartorial vocabulary. He never employs dialect for comic or satiric purposes, but to affirm the longstanding particularity of his culture.

Vecellio sometimes domesticates foreign fashions by comparing them to styles familiar in Venice or in Italy at large. For example, he explains the fur cloak of "La

Nobilis Matrona Pomeioocenſis. VIII

CIRCITER viginti ab ea inſula miliaribus, proxime lacum PAGVIPPE, aliud eſt oppidum POMEIOOC nuncupatum, mari vicinum. Eius oppidi nobiliorum matronarum amictus paululũ ab illarum quæ in ROANOAC viuunt veſtitu differt: nam capillos in nodum implexos gerunt vt virgines iam dictæ, eodemque modo ſunt punctæ, torque tamen craſsiorum vnionum aut æ rearum ſphærularum, oſsiculorumve perpolitorum quinquies aut ſexies collum cingunt, in eo alterum brachium imponentes, altera manu cucurbitam ſuaui quodam liquore plenam gerentes. Altius reliquis & ſub pectore pelles duplicatas cingũt, quæ anteriore parte ad genua vſque fere propendent, poſteriore parte propemodum nudæ. Pone ſequuntur plerumque illarum filiolæ ſeptennes aut octennes, coriaceo cingulo cinctæ, quod a tergo propendens ſub natibus inter crura reducitur, & ſupra vmbilicum adſtringitur, interpoſito ad pudenda tegenda arborum muſco. exacto autem decennio, pellibus cinguntur vt reliquæ. Pupis & tintinnabulis ex Anglia delatis, maxime delectantur.

ABOVE, LEFT Detail of a girl's doll from Theodor de Bry, "A cheiff Ladye of Pomeiooc"

ABOVE, CENTER Theodor de Bry, *Les Grands voyages*, I, "A cheiff Ladye of Pomeiooc"

ABOVE, RIGHT Cesare Vecellio, woodcut, "Habito delle matrone e donzelle," 1598

matrona di Svetia" (Married Woman of Sweden, 330)—whose costume is, in fact, quite unlike any worn in southern Italy—via a familiarizing comparison: "These married women wear an overgarment of squirrel fur, in the same style as a Roman woman does, according to Italian custom." His English widow (370), likewise, is a very strange, bleak figure, but he makes her seem less strange by comparing her twisted hood with its hanging stole to the "cappuccio" of Jesuit friars. Yet Vecellio does not always see through a European lens, and is capable of appreciating the international variety of dress in an objective way. One instance is the admiring simile he uses to describe wealthy traders from Caramania, in Asia Minor, whose brightly colored clothes contrast with those worn by the black-clad gentlemen of his own city. He writes, "those who come to Venice dress for the most part in very fine wool or in scarlet, which makes one think that when they wear them in their own piazzas, they must seem like meadows full of various beautiful and lovely flowers" (438).

Such open-mindedness is especially evident in his treatment of the Ottoman court at Constantinople, in which he carefully uses the words the Turks themselves apply

ABOVE A feather headdress from Peru, 15th or 16th century

to their clothing. Of the Sultan himself, he writes, "It is impossible to say or imagine how very rich and more than beautiful the clothing of this Great Lord is. As far as color is concerned, he appears now in one, now in another...he wears...a *dulimano*" (376v)—that is, a dolmen, a loose-cut formal overgown whose sleeves are cut of the same piece of fabric as the robe. Similarly, when he describes the Aga, whose title he gives in Turkish before translating it as "the General of the Janissaries," he labels his turban a *dulipante*, using an Italianized form of *tulipant*, the Turkish word for the

Persian turban (*dolband*). Describing the Peceqs—footmen to the sultan, who were mostly Persians—Vecellio is respectfully precise: he cites the titles they give themselves in their own language, *Peich* and *Pieudur* (385v). He also cites their words for the garments they wear: the *Siuf* (a high, silver and gold hat) and the *Chochiach*, a striped silk scarf tied around their waists, to which they attach a *Bechiach*—a dagger. By recording Persian and Turkish words in his representation of these officials, Vecellio textualizes his respect for their rich costume and for the languages spoken in their culture.

His attitude toward a New World figure, the Nobleman of Cuzco, is similarly respectful. For one thing, he acknowledges that the name Europeans give this man's land is their invention, not his: "this country that *we* call America" (489, emphasis ours). He downplays the strangeness of the nobleman's costume at first by comparing his cotton or woolen cloak to a *lenzuolo*, that is, a large piece of cloth that Italians used as a mantle. But then he gives the Indian word for this mantle, *hacola*, recording the linguistic specificity of the Cuzco people. Further, he calls attention to a strange hybrid detail: the ruffled shirt collar showing above the nobleman's mantle. Such men, he says, delight in wearing shirts given to them by the Spanish. Rather than presenting this man as a noble savage, fixing him in an unchanging past and present, Vecellio shows that he occupies a changing culture, one being transformed by contact with Europeans. In a later print of a Mexican page carrying a mirror, another import from Europe, and in his comment that many Mexicans have converted to Christianity (493), Vecellio seems to judge these Indians of "New Spain" from an unquestioningly ethnocentric perspective. Yet in the last line of his description of the Cuzcan nobleman, he focuses on the social hierarchy not of Spain but of Peru: this costume is reserved for the elite of the tribe, signifying their exclusive right to wear two feathers attached to the front of a "beautifully colored headband."

And in Vecellio's opening "Discourse" on the evolution of costume, at the end of his list of the materials from which clothing has been made, he places the glorious feather clothing of the New World:

> *extremely beautiful, well-woven garments, divided into sections of feathers of different birds, skillfully and artfully made, in such a variety of well-matched colors that for this reason and for their rarity, they can be considered the most delicate and sumptuous clothing to be found anywhere. And these are worn by the Indians of America and in other places very far from our country.* (4v)

This is the conclusion not of an ethnocentric European but of an enthusiastic man of the world.

VECELLIO AND THE COSTUME BOOK: CONCLUSION

In *Renaissance Clothing and the Materials of Memory*, Ann Jones and Peter Stallybrass argue that early modern clothing not only signaled social identity but also produced it. Through processes of formal investiture, daily dressing, and textile memory systems, people became what they wore. Costume books, as both of Vecellio's suggest, contributed to this process on a global level, using costume to affirm custom.

However, by the 1590s the regional and temporal continuity assumed by costume books as a genre corresponded less and less to the facts of international European economies, transnational commerce, and New World exploration. As Vecellio admits in his "Letter to the Reader":

> *...clothing as a subject allows no absolute certainty, for styles of dress are constantly changing, according to the whim and caprice of their wearers. Add to this, if you will, that many regions of the*

world now are too far away for us to have news of them, although they are nonetheless being discovered. We hardly know the names of many places discovered within our and our fathers' memories, let alone their costumes and customs; and dress shares the changeability to which all worldly things are, and always have been, subject.

Vecellio registers all of these changes. At the same time that he glorifies Venetian traditions of dress, he acknowledges the loss of identity among Neapolitans, who now dress like their Spanish conquerors; he laments the loss of sartorial distinctiveness by Swiss girls, who now dress like German ones. Yet he admires the beauty of American feather cloaks recently imported to Europe. Similarly, after the pages in which he presents medieval dress as a model for the present, he advertises a Venetian textile firm and links its owner to new textile processes and to new fashions. He puts on view the newest of the new, in Venice and in the wider world.

In fact, the costume book as a genre aimed for a geographical range and pictorial diversity that were bound to challenge narrowly local assumptions. Vecellio, investigating European cultures beyond Venice and its territories, confronts a broader range of social possibilities for men and women of his class than those he knows as typically Venetian. But the very notion of the "typically Venetian" is problematic in a book that records sweeping historical and mercantile change and, in Europe and the New World, the rapid process of cultural hybridization. Vecellio's book was shaped and transformed by the border-crossing exchanges that remade both costume and custom in early modern Europe.

NOTES TO THE INTRODUCTION

1 Three useful general studies of Venice include: F. C. Lane, *Venice: A Maritime Republic* (Baltimore, 1973); E. Muir, *Civic Ritual in Renaissance Venice* (Princeton, 1981); and A. Zorzi, *Una città, una repubblica, un impero: Venezia 697–1797* (Milan, 6th ed., 1999). See also *Venice Reconsidered: The History and Civilization of an Italian City-State, 1297–1797*, ed. J. Martin and Dennis Romano (Baltimore, 2000).

2 E. Pastorello, *Bibliografia storico-analitica dell'arte della stampa in Venezia* (1933), cited in Bronwen Wilson, *The World in Venice: Print, the City, and Early Modern History* (Toronto, 2005), p. 3. For a higher estimate of 500 printers and up to 18 million copies of books produced throughout the Cinquecento, see P. Burke, "Early Modern Venice as a Center of Information and Communication," in *Venice Reconsidered*, p. 398.

3 For a study of artists who used such new circuits of direct sale and in-city publicity, see P. Wills, "Tintoretto's Marketing," in *Venedig und Oberdeutschland in der Renaissance*, ed. B. Roeck, K. Bergdolt and A. J. Martin (Sigmaringen, 1993), pp. 107–120.

4 On commercial and cultural exchange between Venice and the Levant, see D. Howard, *Venice and the East: The Impact of the Islamic World on Venetian Architecture 1100–1500* (New Haven, 2000) and R. Mack, *Bazaar to Piazza: Islamic Trade and Italian Art, 1300–1600* (Berkeley, 2002).

5 On Vecellio's life, see T. Conte, "Note biografiche," in *Cesare Vecellio 1521c.–1601*, ed. T. Conte (Belluno, 2001), pp. 13–34.

6 Both Marco and Fabrizio Vecellio received commissions to paint portraits of Venetian officials and scenes of political events. See, for example, Marco's portrait of the Procurator Turno Querini (c. 1546, Pincoteca Querini Stampalia) and his scene of the meeting between Pope Clement VII and the Holy Roman Emperor Charles V (c. 1560, Palazzo Ducale).

7 On Vecellio's apprenticeship to Francesco Vecellio, Conte cites Francesco Valcanover's study in the exhibition catalogue *Mostra dei Vecellio* (Belluno, 1951). See also F. Heinemann, "La Bottega di Tiziano/ Titian's Workshop," in *Tiziano e Venezia: Convegno internazionale di studi, Venezia 1976* (Vicenza, 1980).

8 On the Piloni family, see M. Perale, "Stemmi tra storia e costume: il caso dei Piloni," in *Il vestito e la sua immagine: Atti del convegno in omaggio a Cesare Vecellio nel quarto centenario della morte, Belluno 20–22 settembre 2001*, ed. J. G. Dalle Mese (Belluno, 2002), pp. 207–22.

9 For Vecellio's fresco cycle for the Piloni palazzo, see E. Zadra, "La committenza privata," in *Cesare Vecellio 1521c.–1601*, pp. 192–97. On Vecellio's altar painting for Belluno Cathedral, see T. Conte and E. Zadra, "La committenza ecclesiastica nelle diocesi di Belluno, Feltre e Ceneda," in *Cesare Vecellio 1521c.–1601*, p. 215.

10 On early prints by Vecellio, see T. Conte, "Note biografiche," in *Cesare Vecellio 1521c.–1601*, p. 17.

11 On Christoph Chrieger, see E. Bénézit, *Dictionnaire critique et documentaire des peintres, sculpteurs, dessinateurs et graveurs* (Paris, 1911, rpt. 1999). The skills of Nuremberg printers working in Venice are discussed by D. Landau and P. Parshall in *The Renaissance Print, 1470–1550* (New York and London, 1994), Chap. 3, "How Prints Became Works of Art: The First Generation", esp. pp. 43–4.

12 On *La Corona*, see C. Paggi Colussi, "Alcune osservazioni sui modellari di ricami e merletti del XVI e XVII secolo," in *Il vestito*, pp. 159–76. See also S. M. Levey and P. C. Payne, *'Le Pompe,' 1559: Patterns for Venetian bobbin lace* (Bedford, England, 1983) and D. Davanzo Poli, *Il Merletto Veneziano* (Novara, 1998).

13 For a short illustrated history of lace-making manuals in Venice prior to Vecellio's, see P. Fortini Brown, *Private Lives in Renaissance Venice* (New Haven, 2004), pp. 115–18.

14 A modern facsimile of the prints and an English translation of *La Corona* is entitled *Pattern Book of Renaissance Lace: A Reprint of the 1617 Edition of the "Corona delle Nobili et Virtuose Donne"* (New York, 1988).

15 For a facsimile and study of this book, see *Il libro del sarto della Fondazione Quirini Stampalia di Venezia/saggi di Fritz Saxl* [et al.] (Modena, 1987).

16 For the observation that clothed figures on maps emphasize how identities in this period were defined through cities more than nations, see B. Wilson, *The World in Venice*, 72 ff. On the gender-normative use of clothed figures on maps, see V. Traub, "Mapping the Global Body," in *Early Modern Visual Culture: Representation, Race,and Empire in Renaissance England*, ed. P. Erickson and C. Hulse (Philadelphia, 2000), pp. 44–92.

17 D. Woodward, "The Camocio Atlas," James Ford Bell Lecture, University of Minnesota, 1996, available on line at http://bell.lib.umn.edu/wood. html © University of Minnesota.

18 On costume books, see J. A. Olian, "Sixteenth-Century Costume Books," *Dress* 3 (1977): 20–48; D. Defert, "Un genre ethnographique profane au XVIe: Les livres d'habits (Essai d'ethno-iconographie)," in *Histoires de l'Anthropologie (XVIe–XIXe siècles)*, ed. Britta Rupp-Eisenreich (Paris, 1984), pp. 25–41; and O. Blanc, "Images du monde et portraits d'habits: les recueils de costumes à la Renaissance," *Bulletin du bibliophile* No. 2 (1995): 221–61. For a more recent analysis, see U. Ilg, "The Cultural Significance of Costume Books in Sixteenth-Century Europe," in *Clothing Culture, 1350–1650*, ed. C. Richardson (Aldershot, England, 2004). On costume books with particular attention to Venice, see B. Wilson, *The World in Venice*, chap. 2, "Costume and the Boundaries of Bodies."

19 For a discussion of the fixed meanings of Venetian dress in the period preceding Vecellio's books, see S. M. Newton, *The Dress of the Venetians, 1495–1525* (Aldershot, England, 1987), Introduction and Chap. 1. On Venetian sumptuary law, see Brian Pullan's description of the government agency that enforced limits on spending and display, the *Magistrato alle Pompe*, in *Rich and Poor in Renaissance Venice* (Cambridge, Mass., 1971), pp. 126 and 568. See also, in D. Chambers and B. Pullan, *Venice: A Documentary History, 1450–1630* (Oxford, 1992), the edicts assembled in the section entitled "Conspicuous Consumption and Styles of Living," pp. 177-80. More generally, see Pierogiovanni Mometto, "'Vizi privati, pubbliche virtù': Aspetti e problemi della questione di lusso nella repubblica di Venezia (secolo XVI)," in *Crimine, giustizia e societa veneta in età moderna*, ed. L. Berlinguer and F. Colao (Milan, 1989).

20 B. Wilson, *The World in Venice*, p. 102.

21 D. Defert, "Un Genre ethnographique," p. 26. On the cabinet of curiosities in general, see P. Findlen, *Possessing Nature: Museums, Collecting and Scientific Culture in Early Modern Italy* (Berkeley, 1994).

22 On the illustrated *alba*, see J. L. Nevinson, "Illustrations of Costume in the *Alba Amicorum*," *Archaeologia* 106 (1979): 167–80.

23 On autographs in *alba*, see P. Amelung, "Die Stammbucher des 16/17. Jahrhunderts als Quelle der Kultur- und Kunstgeshichte," in *Zeichnung in Deutschland: Deutsche Zeichner 1540–1640*, ed. H. Geissler (Stuttgart, 1980), pp. 211–22.

24 The following list expands the one provided by J. A. Olian in "Sixteenth-Century Costume Books":

Enea Vico, *Libri della diversità degli habiti de diverse nationi del mondo* [*Books on the Variety of Clothing of Various Peoples of the World*]. Venice, 1558.

Anonymous (François Desprez), *Recueil de la diversité des habits qui sont de present en usage dans les pays d'Europe, Asie, Affrique et Isles sauvages* [*Collection of the Variety of Costume Presently Worn in the Countries of Europe, Asia, Africa and the Wild Islands*]. Paris, 1562.

Ferdinando Bertelli, *Omnium fere gentium nostrae aetatis habitus [The Clothing of almost All the Peoples of Our Age]*. Venice, 1563.

Nicolas Nicolay d'Arfeuille, *Les Quatre premiers livres des navigations et peregrinations orientales* [*Four Books of Sea Voyages and Travels to the East*]. Lyons, 1567.

Joannes Sluperius, *Omnium fere gentium nostrae aetatis nationum habitus et effigies* [*The Clothing and Images of almost All the Peoples and Nations of Our Time*]. Antwerp, 1572.

Hans Weigel and Jost Amman, *Habitus praecipuorum populorum, tam virorum quam foeminarum singulari arte depicti* [*The Clothing of the Principal Peoples, Men as Well as Women, Depicted with Rare Artistry*]. Nuremberg, 1577.

Abraham de Bruyn, *Omnium poene gentium imagines, ubi oris totiusque corporis et vestium Habitus in ordinis cuiuscunque ac loci hominibus diligentissimé exprimuntur* [*Images of almost All the Peoples, in which Their Features, Bodies and All their Habits of Dress Are Carefully Shown, in Order of Rank and Place*]. Cologne, 1577.

Abraham de Bruyn, *Omnium pene Europae, Asiae, Aphricae atque Americae gentium habitus* [*The Dress of almost All the Peoples of Europe, Asia, Africa and America*]. Antwerp, 1581.

Jean-Jacques Boissard, *Habitus variarum orbis gentium/Habitz de nations estranges/Trachten Volcker des Erdskreys* [*The Dress of the Peoples of the World*]. Malines (Mechelen, Belgium), 1581.

Bartolomeo Grassi. *Dei Veri ritratti degl'habiti di tutte le parti del mondo intagliati in rame, Libro primo* [*Accurate Portraits of the Clothing of Every Part of the World, Book I*]. Rome, 1585.

Jost Amman, *Gynaeceum, sive theatrum mulierum* [*The Women's Quarters, or The Theater of Women*]. Frankfurt, 1586.

Pietro Bertelli, *Diversarum nationum habitus* [*The Clothing of Various Nations*]. 3 vols. Padua, Alciato Alciati, 1589, 1594, 1596.

Alessandro Fabri, *Diversarum nationum ornatus* [*The Apparel of Various Nations*]. 3 vols. Padua, 1593.
Jean de Glen, *Des Habits, moeurs, cérémonies, façons de faire anciennes & modernes du monde* [*The Dress, Customs, Ceremonies, and Forms of Behavior, Ancient and Modern, of the World*]. Liège, 1601.
Zacharias Heyns, *Dracht-Thoneel* [*The Theater of Dress*]. Amsterdam, 1601.
Giacomo Franco, *Habiti d'huomeni et donne Veneziane* [*The Dress of Venetian Men and Women*]. Venice, 1610.
Giacomo Franco, *Habiti delle donne Venetiane intagliate in rame* [*The Dress of Venetian Women, in Engravings on Copper*]. Venice, 1610.
See also the longer concluding list in O. Blanc, "Images du monde et portraits d'habits."

25 For a thoughtful study of Vecellio, including his interest in contemporary textiles, see J. G. Dalle Mese, "Abiti di Cesare Vecellio: Venezia e 'il Veneto,'" in *Cesare Vecellio 1521c.1601*, pp. 125–154.
26 For interesting illustrations of textile designs that went both ways between Venice and Constantinople, see R. Mack, *Bazaar to Plaza*, Chap. 2, "Patterned Silks." and Chap. 10, "From Bazaar to Piazza and Back," esp. pp. 175–9.
27 Mack remarks that such competition might better be described as "reciprocal copying" of a peaceful kind, since "it benefited both parties" (*Bazaar to Plaza*, p. 179).
28 On Francesco Curia, including citations from letters between him and Vecellio, see I. Di Majo, *Francesco Curia: l'opera completa* (Napoli, 2002).
29 This kind of eager questioning of a recently returned traveler repeats a pattern of behavior typical of official Venetian treatment of voyagers. An early example is the Maggior Consiglio's listening to the Vicentine Antonio Piggafeta's story of his travels with Magellan, recorded by Marin Sanudo (P. Burke, "Information and Communication," in *Venice Reconsidered*, p. 392 and n. 15, 415). Venetian travelers were similarly questioned in other Italian cities: the merchant Nicolò Conti, for example, was asked to describe his journey to Asia to the secretary of Pope Eugene IV, Poggio Bracciolini. For this episode and a general argument that secular travelers and urban humanists combined their perspectives to produce Renaissance accounts of foreign lands, see J.-P. Rubiés, *Travel and Ethnology in the Renaissance, South India through European Eyes* (Cambridge), Chap. 4.
30 On Varthema, see J.-P. Rubiés, *Travel and Ethnology in the Renaissance*, p. 125 ff.
31 *La Descrizione dell'Africa di Giovan Lioni Africano*, in G. B. Ramusio, *Navigazioni e viaggi*, ed. M. Milanesi (Turin, 1978), I: 19-460.
32 The *Atti dell'arte* from the 1550s to 1600 record men of the Zen and Sessa families in major positions in the guild, including that of Chancellor. Brian Richards, in *Print Culture in Renaissance Italy: The Editor and the Vernacular Text, 1470–1600* (Cambridge, 1994), gives a good sense of how long-lived a publishing family the Sessa were ("Index of Editions," pp. 248–9), and he remarks in *Printing, Writers and Readers in Renaissance Italy* (Cambridge, 1999) that Melchior Sessa the younger during the 1560s and 70s had booksellers working on commission for him as far away as Genoa, Calabria, Sicily and Spain (p. 35). See also S. Curi Nicolardi, *Una società tipografico-editoriale a Venezia nel secolo XVI: Melchiorre Sessa e Pietro di Ravani, 1516–1525* (Florence, 1984).
33 On German/Venetian exchange, including the work of Christoph and Giovanni Chrieger in Venice, see G. J. van der Sman, "Prints and Printmakers in Late Sixteenth-Century Venice," in *Renaissance Venice and the North: Crosscurrents in the Time of Bellini, Dürer, and Titian*, ed. B. Aikema and B. L. Brown (New York, 2000), pp. 154–5.
34 B. W. Meijer, "Titian and the North," in *Renaissance Venice and the North*, p. 500.
35 Van der Sman, "Prints and Printmakers," p. 155.
36 For the distinction in pay between draftsmen and the makers of woodblocks or plates, see L. Voet, *The Golden Compasses: A History and Evaluation of the Printing and Publishing of the Officina Plantaniana at Antwerp* (Amsterdam and London, 1972), II: 223–5.
37 On the Sansovino frame, see N. Penny, *National Gallery Catalogues: The Sixteenth-Century Paintings*, vol. I (London, 2004), pp. 170–80.
38 J. G. Dalle Mese points out Vecellio's interest in earlier artists and his wide network of fellow artists in "Abiti di Cesare Vecellio," pp. 130–32.
39 For juxtapositions of the Vecellio prints and Jones's sketches, see R. Strong and S. Orgel, *Inigo Jones: The Theatre of the Stuart Court* (Berkeley, 1973), vol. II: 145–8.
40 On the Mexican drawings, see J. Pellerano Ludmer, "Echoes of Columbus' Discoveries: Early Visual Images of the New World with Speculations on Notes and Drawings by Leonardo da Vinci," in *1492, Dos mundos: paralelismos y convergencias: XII coloquio internacional de historia del arte* (Mexico City, 1991), pp. 133–45.
41 Livy (Titus Livius) tells the story of Lucretia in his history of Rome, *Ab Urbe Condita*, Book 1, LVII–LX.
42 A. Firmin Didot, *Costumes anciens et modernes/Habiti antichi et moderni di Cesare Vecellio* (Paris, 1859–60), wood engraving 101.
43 Vecellio's term is *il Magistrato sopra le Pompe*, the official who prosecuted Venetians for illegally extravagant dress and banquets. Brian Pullan briefly describes this government agency, the *Magistrato alle Pompe* in *Rich and Poor in Renaissance Venice*, pp. 126 and 568. See also, in D. Chambers and B. Pullan, *Venice: A Documentary History*, the edicts assembled in the section entitled "Conspicuous Consumption and Styles of Living," pp. 177–80.
44 P. Fortini Brown analyzes this long-standing conflict between legislative control and ostentatious display in *Private Lives in Renaissance Venice*, especially pp. 150–57, 182–87, 278, fn 70.
45 On the fact that women in this royal entry were displayed as luxury commodities themselves, see P. Fortini Brown, *Private Lives in Renaissance Venice*, p. 157. For a discussion of contradictory attitudes specifically toward women's costume in Venice and throughout Europe, see J. Haraguchi, "Debating Women's Fashion in Renaissance Venice," in *A Well-Fashioned Image: Clothing and Costume in European Art 1500–1850*, ed. E. Rodini and E. B. Weaver (Chicago, 2002), 22–34. Bronwen Wilson provides an interesting argument about debates over women's fashion as the context for changes in certain maps of Venice, in *The World in Venice*, pp. 180-85.
46 J. G. Dalle Mese, *L'Occhio di Cesare Vecellio*, p. 112. Dalle Mese argues throughout her book that Vecellio's visual treatment of women outside Europe, especially Turkey, is less culturally and erotically exploitative than the perspectives implicit in other Italian, French and German costume books, partly because Venetian relations with the Ottomans were long-standing, practically informed and commercially central to the Republic. Her comparisons of prints are convincing.
47 T. Harriot, *A briefe and true report of the new found land of Virginia* (London, 1588), reprinted with engravings by Theodor de Bry in *Les Grands Voyages* (Frankfurt, 1590). We cite from this 1590 edition. A facsimile and English translation, including White's watercolors and De Bry's engravings, can be found in S. Lorant, *The New World: The First Pictures of America* (New York, 1946), pp. 226–77. See also the recent facsimile of a hand-colored version of De Bry's prints of Virginia, *A briefe and true report of the new found land of Virginia, Thomas Hariot/The 1590 Theodor de Bry Latin Edition*, trans. J. C. Robertson *et al.* (Charlottesville and London, 2007). Commentary on Harriot and other explorers involved in colonial projects of the 1570s–90s is now very rich; see, for example, S. Greenblatt, *Marvelous Possessions: The Wonder of the New World* (Chicago, 1991) and M. Campbell, *The Witness and the Other World: Exotic European Travel Writing, 400–1600* (Ithaca, 1988). A more recent study is J. P. Sell, *Rhetoric and Wonder in English Travel Writing, 1560–1613* (Aldershot, 2006). On Italians in the New World after Vespuccci (Columbus belongs to the Spanish context), see L. Hodorowich, "Armchair Travelers and the Venetian Discovery of the New World," *Sixteenth Century Studies*, 36: 4 (Winter 2005): 1039–62, and J.-P. Rubiés' study of Ludovico de Varthema in *Travel and Ethnology in the Renaissance*, Chap. 4.
48 For examples of this association of New World peoples with nature rather than culture in frontispieces and costumed natives on maps, see V. Traub, "Mapping the Global Body," in *Early Modern Visual Culture: Representation, Race, and Empire in Renaissance England*, ed. P. Erickson and C. Hulse (Philadelphia, 2000), pp. 44–92. On European observers' assumption that natives had no history, see B. Fuchs' analysis of Spanish-authored texts in *Mimesis and Empire* (Cambridge, 2001).
49 The De Bry engraving is Plate 10 of the first book of his *Grands Voyages*. For a lightly modernized version of Harriot's commentary on this image and on the Woman of Pomeiooc (Plate VIII), see *A briefe and true report* (Charloteville and London, 2007), pp. 63–4.
50 Dalle Mese, *L'Occhio di Cesare Vecellio*, p. 215.
51 J. Le Moyne de Morgue's narrative was published, along with engravings based on his drawings of Florida, by Theodor de Bry in Frankfurt in 1591 as *Indorum Floridam provinciam inhabitantium eicones* in Book I of *Les Grands Voyages*. For the text and engravings, we have used Lorant's *The New World*.
52 *Indorum Floridam*, print 39, Lorant, *The New World*, p. 113.
53 G. Boerio, *Dizionario del dialetto veneziano* (Venice, 1856; rpt. Florence, 1993).

BIBLIOGRAPHY

Primary Sources

Printed Costume Books (in date order)

Enea Vico, *Libri della diversità degli habiti de diverse nationi del mondo.* Venice, 1558.

Anonymous (François Desprez), *Recueil de la diversité des habits qui sont de present en usage dans les pays d'Europe, Asie, Affrique et Isles sauvages.* Paris, 1562.

Ferdinando Bertelli, *Omnium fere gentium nostrae aetatis habitus.* Venice, 1563.

Nicolas Nicolay d'Arfeuille, *Les Quatre premiers livres des navigations et peregrinations orientales.* Lyons, 1567.

Joannes Sluperius, *Omnium fere gentium nostraq aetatis nationum habitus et effigies.* Antwerp, 1572.

Hans Weigel and Jost Amman, *Habitus praecipuorum populorum, tam virorum quam foeminarum singulari arte depicti.* Nuremberg, 1577.

Abraham de Bruyn, *Omnium poene gentium imagines, ubi oris totiusque corporis et vestium habitus, in ordinis cuinscunque ac loci hominibus diligentissimé exprimuntur.* Cologne, 1577.

——. *Omnium pene Europae, Asiae, Aphricae atque Americae gentium habitus.* Antwerp, 1581.

Jean-Jacques Boissard, *Habitus variarum orbis gentium/Habitz de nations estranges/Trachten mancherley Völcker des Erdskreys.* Malines (Mechlin), 1581.

Bartolomeo Grassi, *Dei Veri ritratti degl'habiti di tutte le parti del mondo intagliati in rame, Libro primo.* Rome, 1585.

Jost Amman. *Gynaeceum, sive theatrum mulierum,* Frankfurt, 1586.

Pietro Bertelli and Alciato Alciati. *Diversarum nationum habitus.* 3 vols. Padua, 1589–1596.

Alessandro Fabri, *Diversarum nationum ornatus.* 3 vols. Padua, 1593.

Jean de Glen. *Des Habits, moeurs, ceremonies, façons de faire anciennes & modernes du Monde.* Liège, 1601.

Zacharias Heyns, *Dracht-Thoneel.* Amsterdam, 1601.

Giacomo Franco, *Habiti delle donne Venetiane intagliate in rame.* Venice, 1610.

——. *Habiti d' huomeni et donne Venetiane.* Venice, 1610.

Selected Illustrated *Alba Amicorum*

Ms. Egerton 1191, 1573–8. British Library.

Ms. 451 "Mores Italiae," 1575. Beinecke Rare Book and Manuscript Library, Yale University.

Ms. PML 5675, c. 1600. Pierpont Morgan Library

Ms. 91.71, 1595. Los Angeles County Museum of Art.

Ms. 16000, c. 1595. National Library of Scotland.

Ms. Douce d. 11. c. 1585. Bodleian Library, Oxford University.

Early Modern Guidebooks to Venice

Casola, P. *Canon Pietro Casola's Pilgrimage to Jerusalem In the Year 1494.* Trans. M. Margaret Newett. Manchester, 1907.

Coryat, T. *Coryate's crudities...five months' travels in France, Savoy, Italy...* London, 1611; rpt. Glasgow, 1905.

Doglioni, N. *Le cose notabili et meravigliose della città di Venezia,* Venice, 1624.

Garzoni, T. *La Piazza Universale di Tutte le Professioni del Mondo.* Venice, 1599.

Goldioni, L. *Le Cose Notabili, et Maravigliose della Città di Venetia. Riformate, accommodate, et grandemente ampliate.* Venice, 1649.

Sansovino, F., and G. Stringa. *Venetia Città Nobilissma, et Singolare.* Venice, 1581.

Secondary Sources

Cesare Vecellio: Biography and Criticism

Bellecin, F. "La decorazione pittorica della Biblioteca Piloni," in *Cesare Vecellio 1521c.–1601,* ed. T. Conte. Belluno, 2001. pp. 95–123.

Conte, T. "Note biografiche," in *Cesare Vecellio 1521c.–1601.* pp. 13–34.

—— and E. Zadra, "La committenza ecclesiastica nelle diocesi di Belluno, Feltre e Ceneda," in *Cesare Vecellio 1521c.–1601.* pp. 203–227.

Dalle Mese, J. G. *L'Occhio di Cesare Vecellio: Abiti e costumi esotici nel '500.* Turin, 1998.

——. "Abiti di Cesare Vecellio: Venezia e 'il Veneto,'" in *Cesare Vecellio 1521c.–1601.* pp. 125–54.

Grazioli, G. "I libri dipinti della raccolta Piloni: conferenza di Giovanni Grazioli, Belluno, 4 giugno 1999." In *Archivio storico di Belluno, Feltre e Cadore* 70 (1999), no. 3: 213–14.

Hodorowich, L. "Armchair Travelers and the Venetian Discovery of the New World." *Sixteenth Century Studies,* 36: 4 (Winter 2005): 1039–62.

Paulicelli, E. "Geografia del vestire fra vecchio e nuovo mondo nel libro di costumi di Cesare Vecellio," in *Moda e moderno: Dal medioevo al Rinascimento,* ed. E. Paulicelli. Rome, 2006, pp. 129–53.

Perale, M. "Stemmi tra storia e costume: il caso dei Piloni," in *Il vestito e la sua immagine: Atti del convegno in omaggio a Cesare Vecellio nel quarto centenario della morte,* Belluno, September 20–22, 2001, ed. J. G. Dalle Mese. Belluno, 2001, pp. 207–22.

Ticozzi, S. *Vite dei pittori Vecelli di Cadore.* Bologna, 1977.

Valcanover, F. *Mostra dei Vecellio.* Belluno, 1951.

Vecellio Online

http://vecellio.net

http://alpagocansiglio.it/cesarevecelli.asp

http://realmofvenus.renaissanceitaly.net

Histories of Clothing and Costume Books

Allerston, P. "L'abito come articolo di scambio nella società dell'età moderna: Alcune implicazioni," in *Le trame della moda,* ed. A. Giulia Cavagna and G. Butazzi. Rome, 1995. pp. 109–124.

——. "Wedding finery in sixteenth-century Venice," in *Marriage in Italy 1300–1650,* ed. T. Dean and K. J. P. Lowe. Cambridge, 1998. pp. 25–40.

——."Clothing and early modern Venetian society," *Continuity and Change* 15:3, 2000: 376–77.

Arti e Mestieri Tradizionali, ed. M. Cortelazzo. Milan, 1989.

Belfanti, M. and F. Giusberti. "Global Dress: Clothing as a Means of Integration (17th–20th Centuries)."

Blanc, O. "Images du monde et portraits d'habits: les recueils de costumes à la Renaissance." *Bulletin du bibliophile* No. 2 (1995): 221–61.

Bridgeman, J. "Dates, Dress, and Dosso: Some Problems of Chronology," in *Dosso's Fate: Painting and Court Culture in Renaissance Italy,* ed. L. Ciammitti, S. Ostrow, and S. Settis. Los Angeles, 1998.

——. "'Condecenti et netti...': beauty, dress and gender in Italian Renaissance art." In *Concepts of Beauty in Renaissance Art,* ed. F. Ames-Lewis and M. Rogers. London, 1998.

——. "Dress in Moroni's Portraits," in *Giovanni Battista Moroni, Renaissance Portraitist,* ed. P. Humfrey. Kimball Art Museum, Fort Worth, 2000.

——. "'Troppo belli e troppo eccellenti.' Observations on Dress in the Work of Piero della Francesca," in *The Cambridge Companion to Piero della Francesca,* ed. J. M. Wood. Cambridge, 2002.

Burnham, D. K. *Warp and Weft: A Dictionary of Textile Terms.* New York, 1980.

Cocks, A. S. and C. Truman. *Renaissance Jewels, Gold Boxes and Objets de Vertu.* New York and London, 1984.

Colas, R. *Bibliographie générale du costume et de la mode.* New York, 1969.

Colussi Paggi, C. "Alcune osservazioni sui modellari di ricami e merletti del XVI e XVII secolo," in *Il Vestito e la sua immagine.* pp. 159–76.

Il costume al tempo di Pico e Lorenzo il Magnifico, ed. A. Fiorentini Capitani, V. Erlindo and S. Ricci. Milan, 1994.

Curatola, G. "Tessuti e artigianato turco nel mercato veneziano." In *Venezia e i turchi: scontri e confronti di due civiltà.* Milan, 1985.

Currie, E. "Textiles and Clothing [in Florence]," in *At Home in Renaissance Italy,* ed. M. Ajmar-Wollheim and F. Dennis. London, 2006, pp. 342–351.

Davanzo Poli, D. "Abbigliamento Veneto: Attraverso un'iconografia datata: 1517–1571." In *Paris Bordone e il suo tempo: Atti del Convegno Internazionale di studi,* Treviso, 1985. pp. 243–53.

——. *Abiti antichi e moderni dei Veneziani.* Venice, 2002.

——. "Le cortigiane e la moda," in *Il Gioco dell'Amore: Le cortigiane di Venezia dal Trecento al Settecento: Catalogo della Mostra. Venice. Casino Municipale Ca' Vendramin.Calergi, 2 Febbraio–16 Aprile 1990.* Milan, 1990.

——. *I mestieri della moda a Venezia, dal XIII al XVIII secolo: The Crafts of the Venetian Fashion Industry from the Thirteenth to the Eighteenth Century.* Venice, 1995.

——. *Il merletto veneziano.* Novara, 1998.

—— and S. Moronato. *Le stoffe dei Veneziani.* Venice, 1994.

Davenport, M. *The Book of Costume.* New York, 1948, 8th rpt. 1968. 2 vols.

Defert, D. "Un genre ethnographique profane au XVIe siècle: Les livres d'habits (Essai d'ethno-iconographie)." In *Histoires de l'Anthropologie (XVIe-XIXe siècles),* ed. B. Rupp-Eisenreich. Paris, 1984. pp. 25–41.

Emery, I. *The Primary Structures of Fabrics: An Illustrated Classification.* Washington, D.C., 1980.

Fauro, G. "L'enigma di due vesti bizantine tra Oriente e Occidente." In *L'arte di Bisanzio e l'Italia al tempo dei Paleologi, 1261–1453,* ed. A. Iacobini and M. Della Valle. Rome, 1999.

Fornasari, F. *Splendors of the Renaissance: Princely Attire in Italy. Reconstructions of Historic Costumes from King Studio.* Catalogue by J. Cox-Rearick. New York: Art Gallery of the Graduate Center, The City University of New York, March 10–April 24, 2004.

Foulkes, C. *The Armourer and his Craft: From the XIth to the XVIth Century*. New York, 1988.
Frick, C. "Cappelli et copricapi nella Firenze del Rinascimento: l'emergere dell'identità sociale attraverso l'abbigliamento," in *Moda et Moderno: Dal Medioevo al Rinascimento*. Rome, 2006, pp. 102–128.
——. *Dressing Renaissance Florence: Families, Fortunes, and Fine Clothing*. Baltimore, 2002.
Grimes, K. I. "Dressing the World: Costume Books and Ornamental Cartography in the Age of Exploration," in *A Well-Fashioned Image: Clothing and Costume in European Art 1500–1850*, ed. E. Rodini and E. B. Weaver. Chicago, 2002. pp. 13–21.
Hackenbroch, Y. *Renaissance Jewellery*. London and Munich, 1979.
Haraguchi, J. "Debating Women's Fashion in Renaissance Venice." In *A Well-Fashioned Image: Clothing and Costume in European Art 1500–1850*, ed. E. Rodini and E. B. Weaver. Chicago, 2002. pp. 13–21.
Herald, J. *Renaissance Dress in Italy 1400–1500*. London, 1981.
Hollander, A. *Seeing through Clothes*. New York, 1975.
Hunt, A. *Governance of the Consuming Passions: A History of Sumptuary Law*. New York. 1996.
Ilg, U. "The Cultural Significance of Costume Books in Sixteenth-Century Europe," in *Clothing Culture, 1350–1650*, ed. C. Richardson. Aldershot, 2004. pp. 29–47.
Küp, K. and M. Baldwin. *Costume, Gothic and Renaissance: Some Early Costume Books, 1400–1600*. New York, 1937.
Kybalova, L., et al. *Das grosse Bilderlexikon der Mode vom Altertum zur Gegenwart*. Gütersloh, 1966.
Levey, S. M. *Lace: A History*. London, 1982.
Levi, G. "Comportements, resources, procès: avant la 'revolution' de la consommation." In *Jeux d'echelles: la micro-analyse et l'experience*, ed. J. Revel. Paris, 1996. pp. 187–207.
Levi, R. P. *Il costume e la moda nella società italiana*. 5 vols. Turin: Einaudi, 1964–1971. Vol. 1.
Mayer, A. Hyatt. "Two Renaissance Costume Books." *Bulletin of the Metropolitan Museum of Art* 37 (June, 1942): 158–9.
Molà, Luca. *The Silk Industry in Renaissance Venice*. Baltimore, 2000.
Mortier, B. M. du "'Hier sietmen Vrouwen van alderley Natien:' kostuumboeken bron voor deschilderkunst." *Bulletin van het Rijksmuseum* 39 (1991), no. 4: 401–413.
Muzzarelli, M. G. *Gli inganni delle apparenze: Disciplina di vesti e ornamenti alla fine del medioevo*. Turin, 1996.
Nevinson, J. L. "Origin and Early History of the Fashion Plate," *United States National Museum Bulletin* 250 (1967): 65–92.
——. The dress of the citizen of London 1540–1640. London, 1978.
Newton, S. M. "The Dress of the Venetians, 1495–1525." In *Collectanea Londinensia. Studies presented to Ralph Merrifield*. Aldershot, 1988.
Olian, J. A. "Sixteenth-Century Costume Books," *Dress* 3 (1977): 20–48.
Paulicelli, P., ed. *Moda e moderno: Dal Medioevo al Rinascimento*. Rome, 2006.
Payne, B., et al. *The History of Costume: From Ancient Mesopotamia Through the Twentieth Century*. New York, 1992.
Picken, M. B. *A Dictionary of Costume and Fashion*. New York, 1957.
Richardson, C., ed. *Clothing Culture, 1350–1650 (The History of Retailing and Consumption)*. Aldershot, 2004.
Roche, D. *The Culture of Clothing*, trans. J. Birrell. Cambridge, 1996.
Scott, P. *The Book of Silk*. New York, 1993.
Strocchia, S. T. *Death and Ritual in Renaissance Florence*. Baltimore, 1992.
Studies in European Arms and Armor: The C. Otto Kienbusch Collection in the Philadelphia Museum of Art. ed. C. Blair et al. Philadelphia, 1992.
Tessuti italiani del Rinascimento: Collezioni Franchetti Carrand, Museo Nazionale del Bargello (1981 exhibition catalogue). Florence, 1981.
Thiel, E. *Geschichte des Kostüm: die europaische Mode von den Anfängen bis zur Gegenwart*. Wilhelmshaven, 1982.
Tilke, M. *Costume Patterns and Designs*. New York, 1990.
——. http://vecellio.net
Le trame della moda, ed. A. G. Cavagna and G. Butazzi. Rome, 1995.
Vecellio's Renaissance Costume Book: All 500 Woodcut Illustrations from the Famous Sixteenth-Century Compendium of World Costume. New York, 1977.
Velvet. ed. F. de' Marinis, trans. A. Shugaar. New York, 1994.
Il vestito e la sua immagine: Atti del convegno in omaggio a Cesare Vecellio nel quarto centenario della morte, Belluno 20–22 settembre 2001, ed. J. G. Dalle Mese. Belluno, 2002.
Weiditz, C. *Authentic and Everyday Dress of the Renaissance: All 154 Plates from the "Trachtenbuch."* New York, 1994.
Welch, E. "From Retail to Resale: The Second-Hand Market in Renaissance Italy." In *The Art Market in Italy, 1400–1600*, ed. S. Matthews Grieco and L. Matthews. Florence, 2002.
Wilson, B. "*Foggie diverse di vestire de' Turchi:* Turkish Costume Illustration and Cultural Translation," *Journal of Medieval and Early Modern Studies* 37, 1 (Winter 2007), special issue, "Mapping the Mediterranean," ed. V. Finucci: 97–139.

Glossaries of Textile Terminology

Cortelazzo, M. A., A. Da Rin, and P. Frattaroli, "Glossario," in *Tessuti nel Veneto, Venezia e la Terraferma*, ed. G. Ericani and P. Frattaroli. Verona, 1993.
Dal Borgo, M. "Fonti e documenti dell'Archivio di Stato di Venezia per la storia della produzione serica nei territori della Serenissima" in *Tessuti nel Veneto: Venezia e la Terraferma*, ed. G. Ericani and P. Frattarola. Verona, 1993.
Davanzo Poli, D. "Glossario." In *I mestieri della moda a Venezia*. pp. 149–56.
Ferrari, D. "Glossario Stivini." In *L'Inventario dei beni del 1540–1542*. Milan, 2003. pp. 1–23.
Frick, C. "Glossary." In *Dressing Renaissance Florence*. pp. 301–320.
Vitali, A. *La moda a Venezia attraverso i secoli. Lessico ragionato*. Venice, 1992.
Zanetti, A. A. *Dizionario tecnico della tessitura*. Udine, 1987.

Alba Amicorum

Amelung, P. "Die Stammbucher des 16/17. Jahrhunderts als Quelle der Kultur- und Kunstgeshichte," in *Zeichnung in Deutschland: Deutsche Zeichner 1540–1640*, ed. H. Geissler. Stuttgart, 1980. pp. 211–22.
Fechner, J.-U. "Some sixteenth-century albums in the British Library," in *Stammbücher als kulturhistorische Quellen*. Munich, 1981.
Nevinson, J. L. "Illustrations of Costume in the *Alba Amicorum*." *Archaeologia* 106 (1979): 167–80.
Klose, W. *Corpus Album Amicorum: CAAC, Beschreibendes Verzichnis der Stammbucher des 16. Jahrhunderts*. Stuttgart, 1988.
O'Dell, I. "Jost Amman and the Album Amicorum: Drawing After Prints in Autograph Albums," *Print Quarterly* 9 (1992): 31–36.
Rosenheim, M. "The Album Amicorum," in *Archaeologia* 62 (1910): 251–308. *Zu gutem Gedenken: Kulturhistorische Miniaturen aus Stammbüchern des 1570–1770*, ed. L. Kurras. Munich, 1987.
Nickson, M. A. E. "Early Autograph Albums in the British Museum." London, 1970.

Art History

Art and Cartography: Six Historical Essays, ed. D. Woodward. Chicago, 1987.
Circa 1492: Art in the Age of Exploration, ed. J. A. Levenson. New Haven, 1992.
Dackerman, S. *Painted Prints: The Revelation of Color in Northern Renaissance and Baroque Engravings, Etchings & Woodcuts*. Pennsylvania State University Press and the Baltimore Museum of Art, 2002.
Di Majo, I. *Francesco Curia: L'Opera completa*. Naples, 2002.
Findlen, P. *Possessing Nature: Museums, Collecting and Scientific Culture in Early Modern Italy*. Berkeley, 1994.
Grieco, S. M. and L. Matthews, eds. *The Art Market in Italy, 1400–1600*. Florence, 2002.
Hale, J. R. *Artists and Warfare in the Renaissance*. New Haven, 1990.
Harbison, C. *The Art of the Northern Renaissance*. London, 1995.
Heinemann, F. "La bottega di Tiziano/Titian's workshop." In *Tiziano e Venezia: Convegno internazionale di studi, Venezia, 1976*. Vicenza, 1980. pp. 433–40.
Mack, R. E. *Bazaar to Piazza: Islamic Trade and Italian Art, 1300–1600*. Berkeley, 2002.
Orgel, S., and R. Strong. *Inigo Jones: The Theatre of the Stuart Court*. 2 vols. Berkeley, 1973.
Pastoureau, M. *Blue: The History of a Color*. Princeton, 2001.
Penny, N. *National Gallery Catalogues: The Sixteenth-Century Paintings*, vol. I. London, 2004.
Pope-Hennessy, J. *The Portrait in the Renaissance*. Princeton, 1979.
Revaluing Renaissance Art, eds. G. Neher and R. Shepherd. Aldershot, 2000.
Sarti, R. *Europe at Home: Family and Material Culture 1500–800*. Trans. A. Cameron. New Haven, 2002.
Simons, P. "Portraiture, Portrayal, and Idealization: Ambiguous Individualism in Representations of Renaissance Women," in *Language and Images of Renaissance Italy*, ed. A. Brown. Oxford, 1995. pp. 263–311.
Snook, B. *Florentine Embroidery*. New York, 1967.
Traub, V. "Mapping the Global Body." In *Early Modern Visual Culture: Representation, Race, and Empire in Renaissance England*, ed. P. Erickson and C. Hulse. Philadelphia, 2000. pp. 44–92.
Venturelli, P. "La moda come 'status symbol': Legislazione suntuaria e 'segnali' di Identificazione sociale." In *Storia della Moda*, ed. R. Varese and G. Butazzi. Bologna, 1995.

Social and Art History: Venice

Aikema, B. and B. L. Brown, eds. *Renaissance Venice and the North: Crosscurrents in the Time of Bellini, Dürer and Titian.* New York, 1999.

Ambrosini, F. "Ceremonie, feste, lusso." In *Storia di Venezia dalle origini alla caduta della Serenissima, IV: Il Rinascimento: politica e cultura*, ed. A. Tenenti and U. Tucci. Rome, 1996.

——. *Paesi e mari ignoti: America e colonialismo europeo nella cultura veneziana (secoli 16–17).* Venice, 1982.

Art Markets in Europe, 1400–1800, ed. M. North and D. Ormond. Aldershot, 1998.

"Behind the Walls: The Material Culture of Venetian Elites." In *Venice Reconsidered: The History and Civilization of an Italian City-State, 1297–1797*, ed. J. Martin and D. Romano. Baltimore, 2000. pp. 219–29.

Bistort, G. *Il Magistrato alle Pompe nella Republica di Venezia.* Bologna, 1912.

Brown, P. F. 'The Venetian *casa*,' in *At Home in Renaissance Italy*, ed. M. Ajmar-Wollheim and F. Dennis. London, 2006, pp. 50–65.

——. "Measured Friendship, Calculated Pomp: The Ceremonial Welcomes of the Venetian Renaissance Republic," in *Art and Pageantry in the Renaissance and Baroque*, ed. B. Wisch and S. Scott Mushower. University Park, 1990. pp. 136–86.

——. *Art and Life in Renaissance Venice.* New York, 1997.

——. *The Renaissance in Venice: A World Apart.* London, 1997.

——. Private *Lives in Renaissance Venice: Art, Architecture and the Family.* New Haven, 2004.

Burke, P. "Early Modern Venice as a Center of Information and Communication," in *Venice Reconsidered: The History and Civilization of an Italian City-State, 1297–1797*, ed. J. Martin and D. Romano. Baltimore, 2000. pp. 387-419.

Chambers, D. and B. Pullan. *Venice: A Documentary History, 1450–1630.* Oxford, 1992.

Chojnacka, M. *Working Women of Early Modern Venice.* Baltimore, 2001.

Chojnacki, S. *Women and Men in Renaissance Venice: Twelve Essays on Patrician Society.* Baltimore, 2000.

Cità Excelentissima: Selections from the Renaissance Diaries of Marin Sanudo, trans. L. Carroll, ed. P. H. Labalme and L. Sanguineti White. Baltimore, 2008.

Crouzet-Pavan, E. *Venice Triumphant: The Horizons of a Myth.* Baltimore, 1999.

Davis, R. C. *The War of the Fists: Popular Culture and Public Violence in Late Renaissance Venice.* Oxford, 1994.

Goffen, R. *Piety and Patronage in Renaissance Venice: Bellini, Titian, and the Franciscans.* New Haven, 1986.

Hinton, J. "By Sale, By Gift." *Journal of Design History* 15, no. 4: 245–62.

Howard, D. *Jacopo Sansovino: Architecture and Patronage in Renaissance Venice.* New Haven, 1975.

——. *Venice and the East: The Impact of the Islamic World on Venetian Architecture 1100–1500.* New Haven, 2000.

Hughes, D. O. "Sumptuary Laws and Social Relations in Renaissance Italy." In *Disputes and Settlements: Law and Human Relations in the West*, ed. J. Bossy. Cambridge, 1983. pp. 64–99.

Labalme, P. H. and L. Sanguineti White, "How to (and How Not to) Get Married In Sixteenth-Century Venice," *Renaissance Quarterly* 52 (1990): 43–72.

Lane, F. C. *Venice: A Martime Republic.* Baltimore, 1973.

Mack, R. *Bazaar to Piazza: Islamic Trade and Italian Art*, 1300–1600, Berkeley, 2002.

Mackenney, R. *Tradesmen and Traders: The World of the Guilds in Venice and Europe, c. 1250–c. 1650.* London, 1987.

Mallett, M. *The Military Organization of a Renaissance State: Venice, c. 1400–1617.* Cambridge, 1984.

Manno, A. *I mestieri di Venezia, storia, arte e devozione delle corporazioni dal XIII al XVIII secolo.* Cittadella, 1995.

Martineau, J. and C. Hope, ed. *The Genius of Venice, 1500–1600.* London, 1983.

Mazzarotto, B. T. *Le Feste Veneziane.* Florence, 1961.

McCray, W. P. *Glassmaking in Renaissance Venice: The Fragile Craft.* Aldershot, 1999.

Molmenti, P. *La Storia di Venezia nella vita privata dalle origini alla caduta della Repubblica.* Bergamo: 1927–9, 3 vols.; rpt. Trieste, 1973.

Mometto, P. "'Vizi privati, pubbliche virtù'": Aspetti e problemi della questione di lusso nella Repubblica di Venezia (secolo XVI)," in *Crimine, giustizia e società veneta in età moderna*, ed. L. Berlinguer and F. Colao. Milan, 1989.

Muir, E. *Civic Ritual in Renaissance Venice.* Princeton, 1981.

Newett, M. M. "The Sumptuary Laws of Venice in the Fourteenth and Fifteenth Centuries," in *Historical Essays First Published in 1902 in Commemoration of the Jubilee of the Owens College, Manchester.* Manchester, 1907.

Padoan Urban, L. "La festa della Sensa nelle arti e nell'icongrafia," in *Studi Veneziani* 10 (1968): 291–353.

Pauletti, A. G. "Tessili da abbigliamento e arredamento nella pittura Cinquecentesca del Basso Veneto," in *Il vestito.* pp. 191–206.

Perry, M. "Saint Mark's Trophies: Legend, superstition and archaeology in Renaissance Venice," *Journal of the Warburg and Courtauld Institutes* 40 (1977): 27–49.

Pullan, B. *Rich and Poor in Renaissance Venice: The Social Institutions of a Catholic State, to 1620.* Cambridge, 1971.

Queller, D. *The Venetian Patriciate: Myth versus Reality.* Champaign Urbana, 1986.

Romano, D. *Patricians and Popolani: The Social Foundations of the Venetian Renaissance State.* Baltimore, 1987.

——. *Housecraft and Statecraft: Domestic Service in Renaissance Venice, 1400–1600.* Baltimore, 1996.

Rosand, D. *Painting in Cinquecento Venice: Titian, Veronese, Tintoretto.* New Haven, 1982.

——. *Myths of Venice: The Figuration of a State.* Chapel Hill, 2001.

Rosenthal, M. *The Honest Courtesan: Veronica Franco, Citizen and Writer in Sixteenth-Century Venice.* Chicago, 1992.

Ruggiero, G. *The Boundaries of Eros: Sex Crime and Sexuality in Renaissance Venice.* New York, 1985.

Schmitter, M. A. "The Display of Distinction: Art Collecting and Social Status in Early Sixteenth-Century Venice." Ph.D. dissertation, University of Michigan, 1997.

Schulz, J. *The New Palaces of Medieval Venice.* University Park, Penn., 2004.

Sperling, J. *Convents and the Body Politic in Late Renaissance Venice.* Chicago, 1999.

Thubron, C. *The Venetians*, in *The Seafarers* (a Time-Life Series). Alexandria, Va., 1980.

Timmons, T. E. "*Habiti Antichi et Moderni di Tutto il Mondo* and the 'Myth of Venice.'" *Athanor* 15 (1997): 28–33.

Valensi, L. *The Birth of the Despot: Venice and the Sublime Porte*, trans. A. Denner. Ithaca, 1993.

van der Sman, G. J. "Prints and Printmakers in Late Sixteenth-Century Venice," in *Renaissance Venice and the North: Crosscurrents in the Time of Bellini, Dürer, and Titian*, ed. B. Aikema and B. L. Brown. New York, 2000. pp. 154–5.

Venice Reconsidered: The History and Civilization of an Italian City-state, ed. J. Martin and D. Romano. Baltimore, 2000.

Wills, P. "Tintoretto's Marketing," in *Venedig und Oberdeutschland in der Renaissance*, ed. B. Roeck, K. Bergdolt and A. J. Martin. Sigmaringen, 1993. pp. 107–120.

Wilson, B. *The World in Venice: Print, the City, and Early Modern History.* Toronto, 2005.

Woolfson, J. *Padua and the Tudors: English Students in Italy, 1485–1603.* Toronto, 1998.

Zorzi, A. *Una Città, una Repubblica, un Impero: Venezia 697–1797.* Milan, 6th ed., 1999.

——. *La vita quotidiana nel secolo di Tiziano.* Milan, 1990.

History of the Book and of Prints

Bartsch, A. *Le Peintre graveur.* Wurzburg, 1920.

Bénézit, E. *Dictionnaire critique et documentaire des peintres, sculpteurs, dessinateurs et graveurs* (Paris, 1948 ,rpt.) 1976).

Chartier, R. *Culture écrite et société: l'ordre des livres, XIVe–XVIIIe siècle.* Paris, 1996.

——. *Forms and meanings: texts, performances, and audiences from codex to computer.* Philadelphia, 1995.

The Culture of Print: Power and the Uses of Print in Early Modern Europe, trans. L. G. Cochrane, ed. R. Chartier. Princeton, 1989.

Eisenstein, E. L. *The Printing Revolution in Early Modern Europe.* Cambridge, 1983.

Febvre, L. P. V. *The Coming of the Book: The Impact of Printing 1450–1800*, trans. D. Gerard, ed. G. Nowell-Smith and D. Wootton. London, 1976.

Hind, A. M. *An Introduction to a History of Woodcut*, Vol. 1. New York, 1963.

——. *A History of Engraving and Etching from the 15th Century to the Year 1914.* New York, 1963.

Hollstein, F. W. H. *German Engravings, Etchings and Woodcuts ca. 1400–1600.* Amsterdam, 1949.

Landau, D. and P. Parshall. *The Renaissance Print: 1470–1550.* New Haven, 1994.

Lauri, M. *The World of Aldus Manutius: Business and Scholarship in Venice.* Oxford, 1979.

Lehmann-Haupt, H. *An Introduction to the Woodcut of the Seventeenth Century.* New York, 1977.

Pastorello, E. *Tipografi, editori, e librai a Venezia nel secolo XVI.* Florence, 1924.

Rhodes, D. E. *Silent Printers.* London, 1995.

Richardson, B. *Print Culture in Renaissance Italy: The Editor and the Vernacular Text, 1470–1600.* Cambridge, 1994.

——. *Printing, Writers and Readers in Renaissance Italy*. Cambridge, 1999.
Voet, L. *The Golden Compasses: A History and Evaluation of the Printing and Publishing of the Officina Plantaniana at Antwerp*. 2 vols. Amsterdam and London, 1972.
Woodward, D. *Maps as Prints in the Italian Renaissance: Makers, Distributors and Consumers*. The 1995 Panizzi Lectures, London, 1996.

Atlases, Maps, Travel Books, European/New World Contacts, Global Economies

Ambrosini, F. "'Descrittioni del Mondo' nelle case venete dei secoli XVI e XVII." *Archivio Veneto* 5 (1981): 67–79.
Arbel, B. *Trading Nations: Jews and Venetians in the Early Modern Eastern Mediterranean*. Leiden, 1995.
Atlas of World History. London, 1981; rev. ed., 1995.
Bentley, J. *Old World Encounters: Cross-Culture Contacts and Exchanges in Pre-Modern Times*. Oxford, 1993.
Black, J. *Maps and History: Constructing Images of the Past*. New Haven, 1997.
Blackburn, R. *The Making of New World Slavery, 1482–1800*. London, 1998.
Braudel, F. *Capitalism and Material Life, 1400–1800*, trans. M. Kochan. New York, 1973.
——. *The Wheels of Commerce*. New York, 1982.
Campbell, M. B. *The Witness and the Other World: Exotic European Travel Writing, 400–1600*. Ithaca, 1988.
Coded Encounters: Writing, Gender and Ethnicity in Colonial Latin America, ed. F. Javier Cevallos-Candau et al. Amherst, 1994.
Defert, D. "The Collection of the World: Accounts of Voyages from the Sixteenth to the Eighteenth Centuries," trans. M. Diamond, *Dialectical Anthropology*, 7:1 (September 1982): 11–20.
Dirks, N. *Colonialism and Culture*. Ann Arbor, 1992.
Dorling Kindersley World Reference Atlas, ed. A. Dougell et al. New York, 1994.
Europe and Its Others: Proceedings of the Essex Sociology of Literature Conference, 1984, eds. F. Barker, et al. University of Essex, 1985.
Fabian, J. *Time and the Other: How Anthropology Makes its Object*. New York, 1983.
Fuchs, B. *Mimesis and Empire*. London, 2001.
Gillies, J. *Shakespeare and the Geography of Difference*. Cambridge, 1994.
Greenblatt, S. *Marvelous Possessions: The Wonder of the New World*. Chicago, 1991.
——, ed. *New World Encounters*. Berkeley, 1993.
Greene, R. *Unrequited Conquests: Love and Empire in the Colonial Americas*. Chicago, 1999.
Harriot, T. *A briefe and true report of the new found land of Virginia* [facsimile], Charlottesville, 2007.
—— *A briefe and true report of the new found land of Virginia*, London, 1588, Reprinted with engravings by Theodor de Bry (Frankfurt: Johann Wechels, 1590. Facsimile in S. Lorant, *The New World: The First Pictures of America*. New York, 1946. pp. 226–77.
Harris, J. *Textiles: 5,000 Years*. New York, 1993.
Harris, N. *Mapping the World: Maps and Their History*. San Diego, 2002.
Histoire naturelle des Indes: The Drake Manuscript in the Pierpont Morgan Library, trans. R. Kramer. New York, 1996.
Hodgen, M. *Early Anthropology in the Sixteenth and Seventeenth Centuries*. Philadelphia, 1964.
Hulme, P. *Colonial Encounters: Europe and the Native Caribbean, 1492–1797*. New York, 1986.
Impey, O. and A. MacGregor, eds. *The Origins of the Museum: The Cabinet of Curiosities in Sixteenth- and Seventeenth-Century Europe*. Oxford, 1985.
Jardine, L. *Worldly Goods: A History of the Renaissance*. London, 1996.
Jennings, F. *The Invasion of America: Indians, Colonialism and the Cant of Conquest*. New York, 1976.
Karrow, R. W. Jr. *Mapmakers of the Sixteenth Century and Their Maps*. Chicago, 1993.
Leo Africanus (Hasan ben Mohammed al-Wazzan al-Zaiyati). *La Descrizione dell'Africa di Giovan Lioni Africano*. In G. B. Ramusio, *Navigazioni e viaggi*, ed. M. Milanesi. Turin, 1978, I: 9–460.
Lestringnant, F. "The Philosopher's Breviary: Jean de Léry in the Enlightenment." In *New World Encounters*, 127–38.
——. *Mapping the Renaissance World*. Berkeley, 1994.
Levenson, J. A. *Circa 1492: Art in the Age of Exploration*. National Gallery/Yale, 1991.
Macdonald, J. G., ed. *Race, Ethnicity and Power in the Renaissance*. Cranbury, N. J., 1998.
Magocsi, P. R. *Historical Atlas of East Central Europe*. Seattle, 1993.
Portinaro, P. and F. Knirsch. *The Cartography of North America, 1500–1800*. New York, 1987.
Pratt, M. L. *Imperial Eyes: Travel Writing and Transculturation*. New York, 1992.
Relaño, F. *The Shaping of Africa: Cosmographic Discourse and Cartographic Science in Late Medieval and Early Modern Europe*. Burlington, Vermont, 2002. Part I.
Rubiés, J.-P. *Travel and Ethnology in the Renaissance: South India through European Eyes*. Cambridge, 2000.
Silverberg, R. *The Realm of Prester John*. Athens, Ohio, 1977; rpt. 1996.
The Times Atlas of European History. New York, 1994.
Todorov, T. *The Conquest of America*, trans. R. Howard. New York, 1985.
Traub, V. *The Renaissance of Lesbianism in Early Modern England*. Cambridge, 2002.
Travel Knowledge: European Discoveries in the New World, ed. I. Kamps and J. Singh. New York, 2001.
Wallerstein, I. M. *The Modern World-System: Capitalist Agriculture and the Origins of the European World-Economy in the Sixteenth Century*. New York, 1976.
Woodward, D. "The Camocio Atlas," James Ford Bell Lecture, University of Minnesota, 1996, available on line at http://bell.lib.umn.edu/ wood.html. © University of Minnesota.
Writing Culture: The Poetics and Politics of Ethnography, eds. J. Clifford and G. Marcus. Berkeley, 1986.
Zamora, M. *Reading Columbus*. Berkeley, 1993.

TRANSLATORS' NOTE

Our translation includes all of the text from the 1590 *Degli habiti antichi et moderni di diverse parti del mondo*. We also include the twenty prints of New World dress and the commentary about them from the 1598 *Habiti antichi et moderni di tutto il mondo*. It has been set page for page as in the original editions, with the costume illustrations in the same positions. The ornaments and almost all the decorative initials are taken from Vecellio's books.

We have followed Vecellio's phrasing closely, but at times we have divided very long sentences into shorter ones and long passages into shorter paragraphs. We have replaced Vecellio's many "ands" with semi-colons and omitted some, and we have translated his often-repeated "bello" with a variety of synonyms.

The first time a technical costume term appears in the text, we set it in bold type and follow it with a short definition in brackets. A full definition of these terms can be found in the Glossary. After their first use, we repeat them in Italian, in roman type. We translate some very frequently used words silently into English. When Vecellio uses a costume term in the plural, we reproduce his spelling rather than add an "s" (e.g., *sottane*).

A comment on a crucial term in both of Vecellio's books: the Italian *habito*. This word has no exact equivalent in English. Its general meaning is "clothing," but it can imply traditional costume and modern fashion alike, as well as "custom." *Habito* rarely refers to a single garment; usually it means an ensemble or collection of garments, including accessories, among which hats and headdresses are highly significant. One thing *habito* does not mean is an idiosyncratic, one-of-a-kind outfit. Rather, it refers to a commonly recognizable assemblage of garments in a style that defines the region, rank, age, profession, and marital status of its wearer. We have translated it as "clothing," "dress," and, less often, "costume," in the sense not of theatrical costume but of customary apparel.

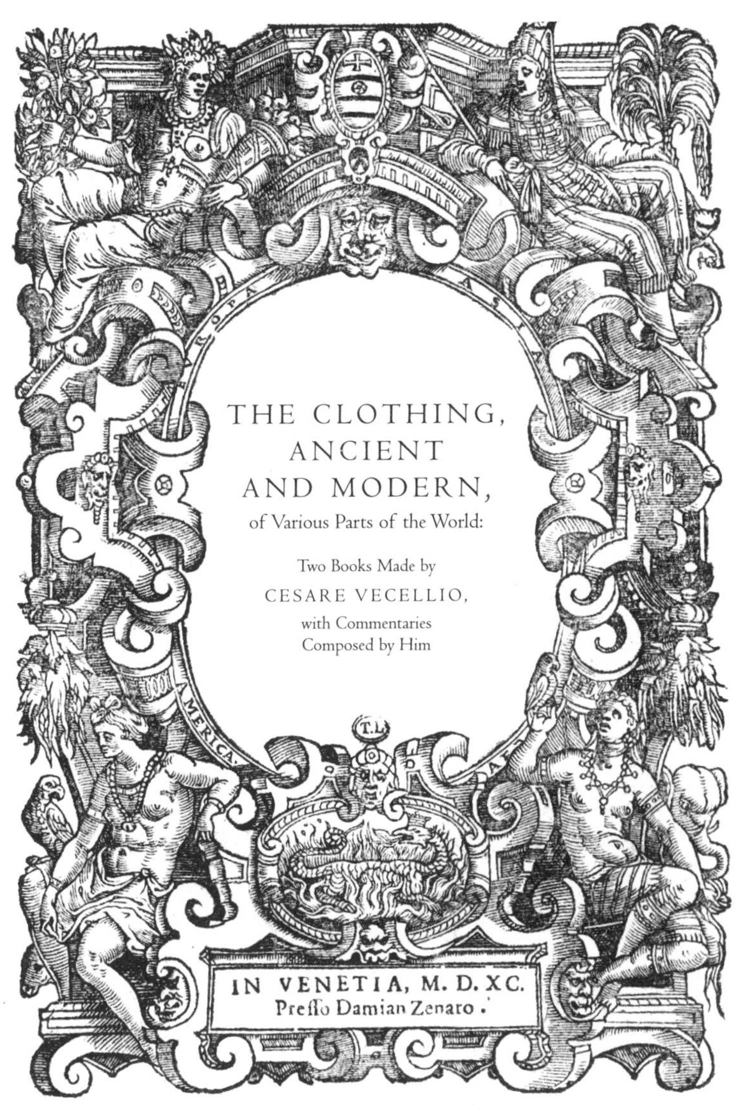

THE CLOTHING, ANCIENT AND MODERN,
of Various Parts of the World:
Two Books Made by
CESARE VECELLIO,
with Commentaries Composed by Him
AMERICA
IN VENETIA, M. D. XC.
Presso Damian Zenaro.

TO THE MOST

ILLUSTRIOUS LORD PIETRO MONTALBANO,

COUNT, KNIGHT, ETC.,
MY MOST HONORED LORD:[1]

DEDICATION

s I was considering what qualities would bring praise and appeal to this work of mine about the clothing of diverse nations, ancient as well as modern, which I have assembled and explained with such great effort, I selected three criteria as the most important: antiquity, variety, and richness. Any one of these by itself can arouse curiosity in the hearts of men, but even more when they are joined together. Eager to increase the splendor and beauty of these qualities as much as I could through the person to whom I chose to dedicate my book, I thought that this concept of mine would be greatly embellished by finding a dedicatee who demonstrates that he, in fact, unites all three of them in himself. For in addition to bringing fame to the work through the use of his name, by this balance of qualities he would bring a certain harmony to the minds of those who would open the book and see his name inscribed at its beginning.

Considering this, I immediately thought of your most illustrious Lordship. For when I contemplate the qualities that your distinguished family has shown to the world, and those belonging to you yourself, and the greatness of your spirit, which fame reports to me, I can think of no one better suited for my purpose than you. For if I want a high degree of ancient lineage, it is obvious that the noble Fratta family, of German origin, from which your Lordship descends, is of very great antiquity, as witnessed by written records and marble monuments attesting to the line's many years of existence and its origin in the distant past. This can be seen in Conegliano, where the family began, while further witnesses to its size and grandeur, in addition to its antiquity, are the noble monuments visible in Bologna, Ferrara and Venice.

Your family is no less admirable for its diversity. For in addition to the range of places already mentioned where the memory of your highly esteemed bloodline lives on in happy perpetuity, its great nobility can be discerned in the variety of names in which it has been preserved, always abundant and always among the most distinguished wherever the family has taken up residence, and through which, always splendidly famous for its magnanimity and grandeur, it has kept its ancient dignity. Thus, along with the surname Fratta, which the family originally used when it came from Germany, the line has continuously produced men worthy of note and full of wisdom and valor, modest in prosperity, constant in adversity, and in good and bad fortune faithful preservers of the patrimony bestowed on them by their ancestors.

Among these was Enrico dalla Fratta, Bishop of Bologna, who perhaps brought the most honor to the family because of the way he was chosen as bishop rather than for the title itself. For he was elected in 1130, as records attest, by popular acclaim, a true sign of his goodness and of the universally shared religious faith that he generated in the city, the excellent guidance to be counted on from his learning, and the sanctity of his life. This man, in addition to the magnificence he showed in many fine buildings, also showed his Christian zeal and piety by erecting and consecrating many churches; and he was so greatly favored by God that he was graced with the rediscovery of the head of Saint Petronius, held in such veneration in that city. I shall say nothing of two other men, Henrico and Vittorio, who, after him, were equally worthy of admiration, for I should be too long-winded, which would be out of place here. Yet to honor the glorious variety of famous men that this family name of Fratta has engendered, like a fertile plant, I will say that under its other name Montalbani (a name derived from the high, steep mountains that the family owned and ruled), it was by no means sterile. We know that under this name, too, as if under a new banner displaying their power and elegance as it waves in the air, the family produced other men who flourished in various professions and, because of their greatness, married into the noblest families of Venice, who, for the sake of brevity, shall go unnamed.

I will speak briefly first of the wealth that has always been owned by the great Fratta Montalbana family, who have always succeeded in making their sons famous as honored and impressive knights. And, without mentioning others, I will speak of the riches left to you by the most illustrious Lord Marco, your father, of blessed and enduring memory for the fame of his writing, riches that your Lordship spends and saves with such splendor and reputation; for they are so great that you need envy no one of your rank. Among other things, these riches include the palace of Conegliano, at different times the welcoming shelter for a King of France and an Empress. From that king, Henri III, you received the well-deserved title of knight; and she, Madame Maria of Austria, passing through Conegliano on her way to Portugal, remembered, now remembers, and will always remember, your most illustrious Lordship as her magnanimous and courteous host.[2]

To your Lordship, finally, so richly deserving that the Emperor Maximilian of glorious memory made you a count, together with the illustrious Lord Marco, your son, honored with many titles and powers, I too have wanted to make an offering and to adorn my book with your name and with the admirable balance of qualities I mentioned earlier. Accept, your Lordship, both tokens of my affection in the truly generous spirit in which you have always favored and embraced all skillful works, and deign to accept me among the number of your servants. I offer myself as one of these, praying to our Lord to grant you every blessing.

From Venice, October 9, 1589,
your Lordship's most affectionate servant,
Cesare Vecellio

CESARE VECELLIO

TO THE READER

Several years ago, with the intention of both entertaining and pleasing anyone interested in my profession through my art and industry, I set out to draw the styles of dress of the various nations of the world. To these drawings, I have added descriptions and commentary for the greater clarity of the work and the satisfaction of the viewer. No one would believe the effort I have devoted to this work, especially to collecting these styles of dress. For it is difficult to acquire dependable information about them because they come from such distant places and from unknown lands, some of them without the direct contact that would provide us with accounts worthy of belief. I have assembled all these drawings, though I know I have not included all that I should, or at least could. So it might seem that I have given birth prematurely. But let anyone who makes this judgment remember that someone who waits for the end of a thing that has no end would be thought foolish indeed! And it is very true, as I said at the beginning of this work, that clothing as a subject allows no absolute certainty, for styles of dress are constantly changing, according to the whim and caprice of their wearers.

Add to this, if you will, that many regions of the world now are too far away for us to have news of them, although they are nonetheless being discovered; we hardly know the names of many places discovered within our and our fathers' memories, let alone their costumes and customs; and dress shares the changeability to which all worldly things are and always have been subject. For these good reasons, may the reader excuse me and appreciate the effort recorded here. If I find that it is well received, I am ready to add to this work other styles of dress that I have already collected but not yet organized according to style, which I can show the reader—as well as others that I am now acquiring, of the New World and other less-known places. Accept these from me now, of which there are 415, and hope for others still more exotic and novel if you show, as I think you will, that you have enjoyed this work of mine. This alone will strengthen me and lighten all my labors.

Live in happiness!

Candida cursum.[1]

DISCOURSE
BY CESARE VECELLIO

ANCIENT AND MODERN CLOTHING: THEIR ORIGIN, TRANSFORMATION, AND VARIETY

CHAPTER 1
The Changes and Variety of Regions and Cities That Have Led to Changes and Diversity in Clothing

aving promised to speak of the diversity of clothing, both ancient and modern, to clarify the present work, I will begin by using everything that can shed light on their description. Human undertakings flow onward like a river and have no permanence or stability: mighty cities have existed in the world, full of people, whose walls or ruins we do not see today, and whose sites we do not even know; and even if we know of and can see some of the most famous, it still seems almost impossible to believe that in past times so many people should have gathered together and lived in them, resplendent with such great nobility. Proof of this is Troy in Asia, Tyre in Palestine, Corinth in the Peloponnese, Babylon in Senahar,[2] Athens in Attica, and many other regions and other noble and famous cities, which are now only plowed fields, flattened to the ground and deserted, even when formerly, not satisfied with sculptures made of the finest stone, they increased their grandeur with proud memorials to guarantee eternal memory of their names.

We also read in histories that in past times some regions and cities extended the boundaries of their empires so far that they filled the world with wonder; and yet they have fallen in our day into such ruin and weakness that they have succumbed to the rule of cities that were previously of no account whatsoever. And some, completely devastated, have left nothing behind but their names. We also see some kingdoms so violently attacked that they have become mere provinces; and, similarly, one city turn into a powerful state and dominate many nations, while another falls from its previous height down into servitude, as well as peoples moving or being taken from one region to another through brute force or by being organized into a colony. It can be said that the cause of all this is the fury of heaven and the cruel onslaught of our enemy, time. It can also be explained by fires, floods, destruction brought about by earthquakes and other misfortunes. Sicily can serve as an example, for it was split off from the mainland by an earthquake, as people believe also happened to Cyprus and some other places.

Similarly, we can find many plains once fertile in every necessity now turned into the bottom of the sea. Likewise, some regions are now rich in every resource that they used to lack, and others lack today what they earlier had in abundance. This is demonstrated to us by balsam, which in the past could be found only in Jericho;[3] but after the fall of Jerusalem, according to Josephus, it ceased to occur there.[4] In the same way, some lands now abound in wine that previously had no knowledge of it, although this change can be explained as the result of human effort. Does it not also often happen that an infertile country, once full of inhabitants, becomes depopulated because its inhabitants are forced by necessity to seek a more fertile land? This is what the Goths did, the Cimbrians, the Longobards, and the Swiss, who originally inhabited the region where the Danube has its source and who now live in the Alps and other mountains. For this reason, cosmographers call the earlier place "the desert of the Swiss." It is equally clear that the Saxons were forced by war to move into Transylvania. From this brief discussion, then, we can understand the origin of the great variations and diversity of dress that has come into being and still exists, highly susceptible to change. Of this fact we have reliable information from literature, history, paintings, carvings in the finest marbles and other hard stone, and sculptures cast in ringing bronze.

CHAPTER 2
The Regions of the Earth

Wishing to speak about the diversity of clothing worn by the peoples of various nations, which reflect the regions they come from as well as those who wear them, I think it is relevant to provide a general scheme of the whole world and the provinces found in it, so that I can then speak in the best possible order about the dress normally worn in one place or another. The world, then, was divided into three principal parts by ancient cosmographers, though they did not divide these parts equally: one of these is called Europe, the second Africa, and the third Asia. We read that Europe and Asia took their names from two women so named. Europa, it is claimed, was the daughter of Agenor, and

Jove fell in love with her, turned himself into a bull, and took her from Phoenicia to Crete.[5] *Asia was the queen of that region and the daughter of Teude and Loceano, and the region of Asia took its name from her, although many others claim that this name is derived from Asius, the son of Matrea and Lidus.*

As for Africa, it is said that it was named for Afrus, the son of Abraham, who captured Lydia by force of arms and established the seat of his government there, after having defeated his enemies and Cetura.[6] *Others equally claim that this name Africa is derived from the Greek language, because "a" means lack and "frie" means cold. But this is little to our purpose, since one part of it derives from fable and the other has passed from memory as an uncertain thing.*

Because I intend to include many styles of dress from Europe in the present work, I will mention something in honor of this third part of the world. Even though Europe is smaller than the other two in area, breadth and length, it is still far superior in dignity to those others because of its wealth in everything needed to feed and clothe human beings, owing to the kindly disposition of heaven, so beneficent that it makes the earth suitable for growing every sort of crop in its most perfect form. In Europe there is hardly any uninhabited or uncultivated place, and it is rich in every region and full of cities, farmlands, castles and villas, whose inhabitants are both of livelier intellect and greater strength than the peoples of Asia and Africa. And this lovely part of the world is bordered on the west by the Atlantic Sea, on the north by the sea of England; on the east it has as a border the River Don and the Meotide Marsh,[7] *and on the south the Mediterranean Sea. What is more, Europe is habitable everywhere except for a small area untenable because of its extreme cold, that is, the region that faces the Don and the Meotide Marsh, where the inhabitants dwell on raised platforms, even though the mountainous areas of all its regions are afflicted by the cold. In this part of the world, Europe, there are no deserts or sands so sterile or so extremely hot as to scorch the things that grow there, as is the case in Africa.*

This part of the world begins at the tip of Spain and stretches all the way across to Constantinople. Its northern territories are very wide, but in length it almost exceeds the two other parts of the world. Ample proof of the grandeur and magnificence of Europe is the fierce war waged by the Carthaginians against the Romans in Italy, and for Sicily and Sardinia, which the Africans wanted to occupy, driven by greed for the riches they hoped to take from these islands once they became their rulers. It can also be said that the Europe of our days includes all parts of the world where the Christian faith is practiced, and part of the territories of Turkey. The specific regions of Europe are many: Albion, now called England; Ireland; Spain; France; Germany, called the land of the Tedeschi; Italy; Sarmatia, also called Poland; Lithuania; Hungary; Valacchia;[8] *Greece; and many islands as well, which for the sake of brevity I will not name.*

CHAPTER 3
The Regional Dress That Will Be Discussed in this Work

Of the illustrations of clothing in this work, many, indeed most, are from Europe, such as those of Italy, Greece, and other nations or regions. As far as Italy is concerned, it should be remembered that after the great Flood mentioned in the Scriptures, the government of the world was given to the great father Noah, whom the ancients later called Janus and who many believe was Saturn. Then he, leaving Ramea (which was later called Armenia), came to Italy and built Janua there, named after him and now called Genoa. From this name the region as a whole was called Janicola. This Noah, also called Janus, had a wife named Vesta at the beginning of the time that the ancients called the Golden Age, because after the Flood the world was as if reborn and new, or rather entirely cleansed and pure. The world continued in this state of purity for two hundred and fifty years, as had been foretold to Noah and as he told his descendants. He was then called Janus, according to a Hebrew word that in our language means wine. He was also depicted by the ancients with two faces, so that with one he could see the past and with the other he could look ahead.

The region of Italy was then known as Hesperia, and the same name was given to Spain, because Hesperus, driven out of Spain by his brother Atlantis, came to this country and made himself its lord. Macrobius,[9] however, says that Italy was named after the star Hesperus, because this star had a great influence over the area. It was then called Camasena after Camese, Saturnia after Saturn, Taurina after the Egyptian god Osiris (later called Jove). The ancients also frequently called the area Enotria, either because of the abundance of wine it produced, since this word in Greek means wine, or because the name was derived from a certain Enotrius, king of the Sabines. But all we need to know is that it was finally called Italy, as it is still called, after a certain Italus, king of Sicily, who taught farming to the Italians and also gave them the custom of living under just laws. This beautiful country of Italy is surrounded by two seas, the Tyrrhenian and the Adriatic. The Adriatic took its name from the city of Adria, or Atria, situated not far from the Po river. The Tyrrhenian took its name from a certain Greek, Tyrrhenios, who, disagreeing with his brother Lidos, who wanted to rule alone, was driven by destiny to leave him and to abandon the country not large enough for the two of them. So, leaving it behind, he came to Italy, calling the region where he took up residence Tyrrhenius, after his name. This happened, according to the consensus of writers, not long after the fall of Troy.

CHAPTER 4
The Variety of Fabrics and Materials Used to Make Clothing in Ancient Times

After the sin of our first parents, when they recognized that they were naked, God gave them tunics made of animal skins, although we don't know specifically what kind of animals they came from. And it is certain that this mode of dressing and the materials used for it lasted a very long time. Indeed, on this subject we read that up to the present, some nations, such as the Scythians, today called the Tartars, still dress in this way. Then, as the second material for clothing, men started to use wool, dyed different colors, a custom that has come down to us today. The third material, then, and the most delicate of all, was silk, woven

in different ways with various designs worked into it, and into which ingenious people gradually began to mix silver and gold to make it richer and more splendid. The fourth material for clothing, in the region of Thebes, as a result of the wild forests found there, was made of goat and badger skins and of palm leaves, woven in the way we see baskets and straw mats woven from reeds today. The fifth material was cotton, and along with this we can mention linen, and also broom and hemp and other similar materials, which I will not list, to avoid going on at great length—and there are also extremely beautiful, well-woven garments, divided into sections of feathers of different birds, skillfully and artfully made, in such a variety of well-matched colors that for this reason and for their rarity, they can be considered the most delicate and sumptuous clothing to be found anywhere. And these are worn by the Indians of America and in other places very far from our country.

CHAPTER 5
The Various Colors That Have Been Used Over Time to Dye Fabrics for Clothing

Diverse writers, ancient and modern, have said that the finest and most illustrious colors were porpora [bright red to purple] and giacinto [purplish blue],[10] and these colors were used for the garments of the most eminent persons, although white, too, was customary in many nations, especially ancient Rome, during the election of magistrates, who as a result were called candidates.[11] These three colors continue in wide use today, but red and blue are those most widely used in republics, especially Rome and Venice. Grana [a red dye; cf. cremesino], however, according to Pliny[12] was used to dye the mantles, that is, the military garments, of emperors; Julius Caesar was the first to appear dressed this way in public, sitting on a golden chair. This red, because of its nobility, was liked and valued so much by princes that a specific law was written to prevent its use by private citizens.

The origin of this porpora as the most beautiful and highly valued color must not be omitted. Know, then, that Hercules had a dog that always followed him around because of its faithfulness. Once, as this Hercules was passing by some rocks washed by the sea, there appeared to the eyes of his dog a shellfish, or oyster, fixed to a rock, which, as soon as he saw it, seizing it in his mouth, he ate. As a result, the dog's lips were deeply dyed with this color. When Hercules returned home with his dog, his beloved saw the dog's lips, so, entranced by the beauty of the color, she told Hercules that he should never come to see her again unless he brought her a garment dyed that color. So Hercules, with his mind fixed on the beauty of the color, left the house with his dog and, setting out for the place he had been before, reaching the same rock, he sought again what had befallen the dog, and he finally found the color, resembling blood, and gathered it up and made a present of it to his lady. So the Tyrians claim that Hercules was the first discoverer of this dye.

CHAPTER 6
The Number of Cities in Italy

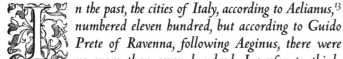

In the past, the cities of Italy, according to Aelianus,[13] numbered eleven hundred, but according to Guido Prete of Ravenna, following Aeginus, there were no more than seven hundred. I prefer to think, however, that these writers used the word "city" to describe any fortified town or large village, in contrast to the Church of Rome, which called no place a city, however large, unless it had a bishop. But if we accept the opinion of Biondo,[14] we must believe that in his tim, the cities of Italy numbered no more than 260. However, because several popes between then and now have set up bishoprics in many fortified towns, the number of cities is now much greater, though not as great as the number mentioned above. I decided to discuss this question briefly in order to show how often this beautiful country of Italy has been subject to ruin and how many diverse inhabitants and foreign invaders and barbarians have trod underfoot and plundered this most fertile region, feasting on and helping themselves to all her most desirable goods. But Italy derived no benefit from them except its wide and changing array of languages, clothing and customs.

CHAPTER 7
Of the Various Peoples Who Have Lived in Italy and the Number of Major Cities, Their Provinces, and Their Ancient and Modern Names

The provinces of Italy are many, and they have different names now from those they originally had. For example, the coastal region around Genoa was called Liguria; Tuscany was called Etruria; the duchy of Spoleto, Umbria; the Roman countryside, Latium; the Terra di Lavoro, Fertile Campagna; the region around Basilicata, Lucania; lower Calabria, the Brutii; upper Calabria, Magna Graecia; the land around Otranto, Salentini; the land around Bari, Puglia Peucetia; the plain of Puglia, Apulia Daunia; Abruzzo, Sanniti; the Marches of Ancona, Ager Picenus; Romagna, Flaminia; Lombardy on this side of the Po, Emilia; Lombardy beyond the Po, Transalpine Gaul; the Marches around Treviso, Venetie; and Istria and Friuli, Julius' Forum. Then among the islands of Italy in the sea of Genoa, Corsica was called Cimus; Sardinia, Sandoliatin; Elba, Ilva. Among the islands of the Tuscan sea, Procida was called Prochita and Ischia, Aenaria. Among the islands of the Sicilian Sea, Sicily was called Trinacria; Lipari, Eolie; Malta, Melita. Among the islands of the Adriatic, Santa Maria di Tremiti was called the Diomedean Islands.

Now that I have named many provinces of this beautiful region of Italy, it seems to the point to mention in addition some of their principal cities. The fertility and beauty of Italy, after the Flood, drew many and various peoples to live there, who, attracted by the bounty of its fertile and pleasant lands, began to build towns, villages, fortified manors, farmlands, and cities, and to name these places as it suited them. As a result, Istria and Friuli have the ruined city of Aquileia (a patriarchal city[15]), Trieste, and Udine. The Romagna has Bologna, Ferrara, and Ravenna, though some think Ravenna belongs to Emilia. Lombardy includes Milan; the Trevisan Marches, Venice; Liguria has Genoa; Tuscany has Florence, Siena, Pisa and Lucca. Umbria has Perugia and Spoleto; Latium has Rome, whose people were called Latins; Campagna has Capua and Naples; Puglia has Brindisi, Tarento, and Siponto; Calabria has Reggio and Otranto; the Marches of Ancona have Ancona, Ascoli, Fermo, and Macerata. From all this, we can conclude that this Italy of ours has often fallen prey to foreigners and been the crossroads of Fortune. For this reason, it is no wonder that we can see a greater diversity of dress here than in any other major nation or region.

And now I recall an amusing anecdote about the topic of this diversity, once told to me by Signor Baldo Antonio Penna, a man of great learning and a renowned professor of humanities in Venice. He said that there was once a man who, as we have just been doing, depicted in his book the clothing of all the provinces, and when he came to the man of Italy, he represented him naked but carrying a piece of cloth on his shoulder. When he was asked why he had not shown him clothed, as he had all the others, he answered that he saw the Italians as so changeable, mutable and capricious in their dress that this one had decided to carry cloth on his shoulders so that he could have the tailor cut his garments according to his whim.

CHAPTER 8
Rome, the Ruler of the World

Because we should begin with the noblest subjects, I will not proceed in this description according to geographical borders—that is, by starting at one end of Italy and continuing on to the furthest point—but by speaking first of the glorious city of Rome, the reigning city of this land because of its majesty and its position as seat of the pope, who, as the true vicar of Jesus Christ our Lord, is the religious leader of the whole world, and also because it formerly ruled the universe and maintained its empire over all living people, as the trumpets of its glory and fame announce on every side.

First I will say something about its origins, on which all authors agree. It was founded by Romulus and took its name from him, even though others claim that it was called Roma because of a certain Romola, the wife of a king who lived, reigned and died in Italy. Even so, we must concede that Romulus built the encircling walls and fortified the city with towers and every other kind of fortification then in use. This city, then, gradually expanded and grew to the extent that the valor and strength of its inhabitants rose to such glory and grandeur that we can justifiably say that there has never been, before or after, any city to equal it. The towers that surrounded it like a crown and reinforced it amounted to 634, and because the wall extended so far, it could contain thirty-seven gates. It is also said that in front of the wall was a cleared plain two thousand feet across, the equal of five German miles, which made it look more like a territory than a city.

Our age, however, sees it in a very different state, because now it has only twenty usable gates still standing and not all of *these are open; and in the wall surrounding the city, only 360 towers remain. It is not at all surprising that in the era of its great good fortune and glory, when it was so powerful and had such a vast empire, it reached such a height of happiness that at times it refused to assume power over kingdoms that sent it their keys and surrendered to it voluntarily. It seems fitting to say here that in the city of Rome one could see many extravagant and varied styles of dress, compared to the long, unchanging run of dress among the Greeks and barbarous nations elsewhere. This is the origin of the great variety of styles that we see today, a good part of which we can still gather from famous and triumphal arches, statues, columns, and the ancient writings of reliable men. For at different times, Rome was subject to changing princes and leaders, so it is no wonder that both men and women kept transforming their clothing and adopting new styles of dress.*

I have decided, in the proper place, to speak first of the clothing I have found in written descriptions and then of the dress, still more beautiful, worn in this city today. In my discussion of these styles of dress, I will try to be brief, mentioning the materials used to weave these ancient garments and their colors, and assuming that everyone can imagine the rest, given the wealth of this city and the splendor and lavishness of its clothing.

CHAPTER 9
The Magnificence and Extraordinary Cost of the Luxurious Ornaments Worn by Ancient Roman Senators and Noblewomen

he magnificence and sumptuousness of the clothing of the Romans were so great that they seem almost incredible to anyone who reads about them in ancient writing, such as that of Pliny, who claims that Roman women of the past adorned and dressed their hair with great numbers of pearls or other jewels, and that such splendor and expense corresponded to their high rank. In addition, around their necks they wore necklaces and on their arms bracelets so rich and of such beauty that wherever they went, the sight of their amazing splendor made everyone marvel. From the same author we read that Lollia Paulina, the wife of Caligula, not just when she went out to public ceremonies but when she dressed up to be seen at a dinner or wedding, was so coiffed and bejeweled, with her head weighed down by superb emeralds and huge pearls, with earrings in her ears and necklaces around her neck, that she astonished everyone. He estimates that these ornaments were worth four thousand sestertii.[16]

Pliny writes the same thing about Cleopatra, who, at the height of her prosperity, was often invited by Mark Antony to dine at his sumptuously laid table. He once asked her whether it was possible to put together a more splendid meal, and she answered that she, on one dinner alone, would spend a hundred thousand sestertii. This answer inspired Mark Antony to wager that such a thing was impossible, and he laid down a bet that it was impossible to spend so much money on a single dinner. To which Cleopatra responded that she had not only seen this done but she herself would swallow in one mouthful the sum of a hundred thousand sestertii. When the night of the dinner came and everybody was seated at the table, Mark Antony looked over everything laid out upon it to see what dish or food could have cost so much, and of what single food she could take a mouthful worth a hundred thousand sestertii. Finally, there appeared on the table rich goblets full of precious liqueurs, including one full of very strong vinegar; the cup was made of a highly precious kind of stone. Into it Cleopatra dropped an enormous pearl that she had taken from her ear; this was of great value and expertly worked. As she dropped it into the vinegar, it immediately dissolved, and she swallowed it down. She prepared to do the same with the second pearl, but those judging the bet stopped her, acknowledging that she had won. Antony was astonished at such bravura and pride. The second pearl, taken from Egypt, was saved and brought to Rome, where it adorned the statue of Venus Genetrix placed in the Pantheon.

CHAPTER 10
Government and Dress of the Roman Empire

After Tarquin, for the indecent and wicked violence he did to Lucretia, was deprived of rule and banished from Rome,[17] *the Romans began to create consuls instead of kings, though they were given the same regalia and privileges as kings, except for the right to wear a crown and toga. In those days many citizens, as a result of this past corruption, were led to make an oath that they would never allow any single man to rule or have power over them in the future. The number of Roman senators was then three hundred, but Valerius, the third consul, formulated and set up certain laws that allowed the consulship to be given to the common people, adding afterward a law that if anyone should try to become a tyrant, he should be killed and his killer, rather than being punished, should be given unending praise. He also ordered that the Temple of Saturn should become the treasury building, where public monies could be kept and saved. He also allowed the people to choose two tribunes. Soon after this a magistrate's position was created that they called the dictatorship, without naming anyone particular to it, to which no one was appointed or promoted except on the occasion of some great suspicion or fear that a manifest and serious danger could befall the city of Rome. This dictator was allowed to appoint the Master of the Horsemen, whose rank was directly below his and who accompanied the dictator, as the tribune previously accompanied the king.*

Then it was granted to the plebeians that they should have their own magistrate, so tribunes began to be appointed, but they became so arrogant that they disregarded and annulled the orders and laws of the senators and consuls whenever they didn't suit them. Two censors were also created, whose authority grew so much over the course of time that they regulated and reformed all customs and civic discipline, inspected all public and private places, taxed the people, took the census, removed senators from the senate, exposing them for evil doing; and the term of this magistrate lasted five years. Then another magistrate was created, who judged law cases; he was called the praetor, and to him was given the authority to judge public and private cases. And it was also up to him to review cases already judged and to distinguish what was lawful from what was unjust. At first there was only one praetor, called the urban, that is, of the city, but realizing this man alone could not suffice for such an important responsibility, another was created, who passed judgment on foreigners. This, then, was the system of government of the Roman republic, which lasted until the era of Julius Caesar, who turned the state back into a monarchy again. I wanted to say this by way of explanation, thinking it very important to our subject, because these magistrates will often be named in our discussion of the clothing of the Romans and of what particular people were permitted to wear.

CHAPTER 11
The Organization of the Roman Militia

aving briefly described the government of the Romans, I think it is proper to say something about their military organization. For we can see clearly that art, virtually the imitator of nature, maintains the same order in artificial things that nature maintains in natural ones; and the more such art reflects the good, the more it maintains good order. For disorder can create nothing but confusion and loss. So the ranks and order of command were established as follows: the private soldier obeyed the centurion, who commanded one hundred soldiers, and the centurion obeyed the tribune or captain. The tribune reported to the legate, the legate to the consul, the consul to the master of the horsemen, and this last to the dictator. Young men who joined the army had an obligation to serve from the age of seventeen to forty. In peacetime they wore the toga, a long, loose garment, but in war Roman noblemen wore the color porpora, and the noble horsemen wore gold rings. Before I go on, I will mention that in mourning the ancient Romans wore black clothing, but women wore white mourning clothes, without ornament.

CHAPTER 12
The Names of Garments, Especially Those of the Romans

o avoid any confusion that might arise from my comments on our clothing, and so as not to repeat any single garment, which would bore the reader, it occurred to me to present the following brief discussion of ancient clothing, especially of the Romans. Let it be known, then, that the praetexta was a very ancient garment worn by the censors, who dressed this way (according to Athaneus[18]) and, wearing crowns, killed sacrificial animals with a hatchet or axe. We read that this ancient garment was used by Romulus, according to Plutarch,[19] who says he wore a porpora-colored mantle and the praetexta. This praetexta was also given as a special honor to Roman women, because when Romulus had unfurled his banners against the Sabine men, who had already seized the Capitol, these women brought about the end of the fighting, for they interposed themselves between the two armies and spoke so effectively that peace followed between the two sides. For this reason, not only did they have the honor of wearing the porpora praetexta, but also no unchaste words could be said in their presence.

The trabea, next, was an embroidered garment worn by captains in triumphs, which they kept on even after the triumph. It was perhaps for this reason that Ammianus[20] called it the consular trabea, and later, Martial[21] the palmata, probably in reference to such victories. Suetonius[22] mentions three kinds of trabea: one, consecrated to the gods, was made entirely of porpora-colored cloth; the second, in porpora, belonged to kings and was bordered in white; and the third was worn by augurs and was woven in porpora and scarlet.

The paludamentum *[a long, one-piece mantle] was a military cloak worn by emperors, though some claim that it was also used and worn by members of the army. According to Atheneus, it was also worn by the horsemen and noblemen of Greece. This garment, in my opinion, is none other than the one that army men wear in our time, which they call the* casacca *[an ample cloak]. It was first worn by the Macedonians and then by the Romans.*

The chlamys, *in my opinion, was similar to a very wide shoulder cape, cut in a round shape almost like a veil covering the shoulders, and it was worn by highly placed people with such pomp and splendor that we read that Demetrius gave one to Polycrete to embroider, and it was exceptionally lovely. On this (Pliny writes) were embroidered the whole world and all the principal signs of the heavens—that is, the pole stars and the twelve signs of the zodiac. This* chlamys, *then, was worn on the shoulders and because it was so comfortable and light, the Greeks wore it in warfare.*

The toga *was a senatorial garment, and from what we can gather from sculptures, it was a floor-length robe, with a cloak worn in various ways, tied over the shoulders, called the* paludamento. *Many people wore the toga belted, and it was worn by notable married women, as can be seen in many medallions and statues. Soldiers going to war wore a shorter and looser toga, while women always wore it much longer and always in the same style. But women of high rank wore it with a stole over it, hanging down in back, like those worn by priests in our day.*

The tunic, according to Aulus Gellius,[23] *was not worn by ancient Romans; and yet we read that Cato, after eating, used to go into the Forum without shoes or a tunic, wearing only a toga, and once there, he would walk about and talk to his friends—which we assume did not detract from his dignity as praetor, for we can be sure that the elders he knew never wore tunics, either. Ennius*[24] *later called the youth of Carthage the tunic-wearers, because in winter they wore a kind of tunic that scarcely covered their shoulders, and this, according to Plutarch, was also worn by Cato when he was in his villa in winter time, for in the summer he worked nude with his servants. This Cato, even after he had been consul and had enjoyed a triumph, never, we read, wore any garment that cost more than a hundred* denarii, *which equals ten ducats, and that his diet never exceeded thirty* baiocchi *[small Roman coins].*

But to return to the tunic, according to Gellius, no one wore this garment with sleeves without being criticized, though it is true that women wore long, full sleeves as a sign of their chastity. This tunic, it seems to me, was none other than the undergarment, the sottana *or* sottanella *[a long undergown] that we wear over our* camicie *[shifts of linen or silk]. It would not be beside the point to describe the fabric it was made from. Varro*[25] *writes that in the beginning the tunic was a senatorial garment made of wool and that it lasted from the time of Ancus, king of the Romans, up to his own day—and that one had been preserved for a long time, never wearing out, in the Temple of Fortune. From this derived the custom whereby maidens going to be married carried a distaff topped with a skein of wool, along with a spindle wound with thread, in order that, before they did anything else, they wove a tunic and wore it with a toga. So new wives appeared dressed in this ensemble.*

The ungulata, *or rippled robe, was first worn by wealthy private citizens and from it (according to Fenestella*[26]*) was later derived the* sorticolata. *These citizens also wore the garment called the* crebra *and the* papaverale, *which was worn by Torquatus and mocked by the poet Lucillus.*[27] *We also find* the prevesta mentioned, invented by the Tuscans, but it was held in low esteem. The trabea, worn on top of it, was more valued, because it was woven and then decorated with trim in various colors.

The garment worn in a victory procession and later covered with needlework (according to Homer) came from the people of Phrygia, and similar garments were later called freggi. The first man to have one made was Attilius,[28] so they were called Attalican garments. In Babylonia garments woven and dyed in many colors, called polyneces (many-threaded), were worn, and we read that these Babylonians sold one to Nero for eight hundred sestertii. Much earlier, one belonging to Servius, with which he draped the statue of Fortune, cost a great deal of money, and it lasted until the death of Sejanus[29] without ever wearing out or becoming moth-eaten—that is for a period of 560 years. We find writers mentioning another garment called the pallia or palliola, which was worn over other garments in the style of a cloak today, and the Latins called it a pallium. It was worn by both men and women, and went from head to foot. Let this suffice as a description of ancient clothing.

CHAPTER 13
Head Coverings

Now that I have said this much about the clothing of the ancient Romans, it seems appropriate to discuss their head coverings. The tiara, then, covered the heads of royalty in the East. This tiara was a small hemispherical cap, made in two parts, one of which covered the head and the other of which turned upward. There was another ornament called the cidarine, which covered the head entirely and was used among the kings of Persia and Armenia, and this was also called the diadem; it was a narrow strip that encircled and bound the head at its midpoint. It was also worn by queens, particularly Monima Millesia, the wife of Xerxes, a lady highly celebrated by the Greeks. It is said that this king sent fifteen thousand scudi for her to come back to see him, but she would not submit. So, driven by love, he sent her a diadem and named her his wife. Monima, removing the diadem, shaped it into a noose and hanged herself by the neck. But because the diadem could not bear her weight, it broke. So she burst out, like a desperate soul, with these words: "Oh, cursed diadem, that in such a dark hour refused to help me at all!"

To describe further head coverings, the vitta comes to mind, which was a headband worn by married women, which the Vestal Virgins also wore, as nuns do in our day. The causia was a Macedonian cap made of gold and silk and certain other materials. The candis was the head covering of the Medes.

And since it seems to me that I have now shed enough light on the styles of dress that should be presented in this work, I must now begin to speak about the images that I have drawn and had made into woodcuts, at such effort and expense.

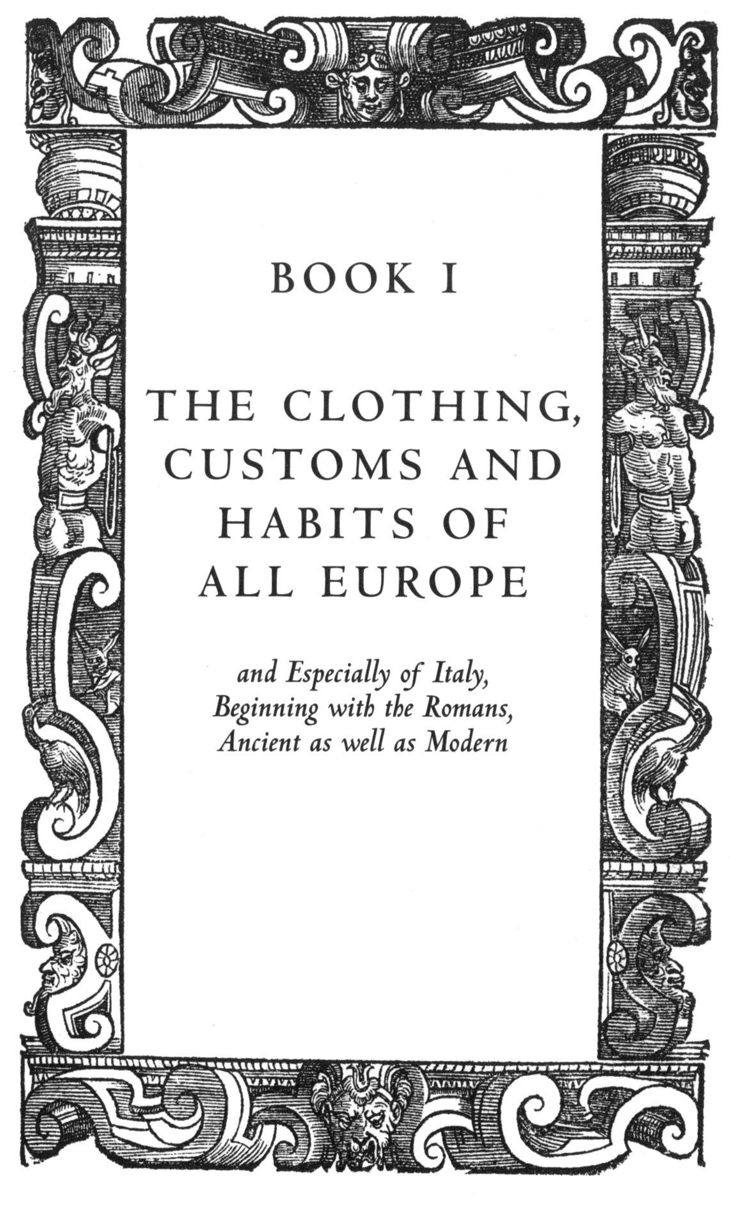

BOOK I

THE CLOTHING, CUSTOMS AND HABITS OF ALL EUROPE

and Especially of Italy, Beginning with the Romans, Ancient as well as Modern

CLOTHING OF AN ANCIENT PATRICIAN OF ROME

Ancient Roman senators were accustomed to wear (as far as can be seen from sculptures of worthy men, and the pages of the best writers) the toga, a full-length gown with a mantle worn in various ways, fastened at one shoulder or unfastened but with one end thrown over the shoulder and the other part under the arm, as is done in our time with the ferraiuolo *[a short cape]. These mantles, moreover, were wide and reached the ground. Such senators, like emperors, were clean-shaven and wore their hair short, and in portraits and sculptures they had themselves portrayed and sculpted bareheaded, as can be seen in every ancient statue and in every medal cast in those times.*

THE EARLIEST CLOTHING OF THE ROMANS, First Worn by the Trojans

It is very entertaining to consider the strange styles of the ancient Romans, and there is no doubt that their clothing gives us more pleasure, because of its distance in time, than does that of modern people, which we have continually before our eyes. Accordingly, those who come to Venice, even if they have seen remarkable things, will not have failed to notice the four free-standing porphyry figures of armed men placed before the door of the cathedral of San Marco. These were brought here to Venice as a group, along with other statues, sculptures, and precious objects, from Greece and from more distant places at a time when this most powerful Republic was enlarging the borders of its Empire with joyful outcries of its name and fortunate outcomes to all its undertakings. It is said, perhaps incorrectly, that these four figures represented the four sons of the kings of Greece and other nations, who, unable to inherit their fathers' kingdoms because of laws of primogeniture and having plundered the greatest part of their fathers' treasuries, embarked together in a ship to seek out a new land and kingdom. The story goes that after sailing through the Adriatic gulf, they arrived by chance in the lagoons of Venice, and here, wanting to rest and refresh themselves, they decided together that two of the princes should look for food here in Venice while the two others stayed on board. And out of ambition to enjoy all by themselves the entire treasure they were carrying, the two who landed to seek food poisoned the food; and the two who stayed on the ship decided to kill the first two as soon as they arrived back on board—which they did, and then began to eat the poisoned food, so that two died of poison and two by the sword. As a result, the inhabitants of

Venice took possession of the ship and found a great treasure in it, as well as the four porphyry figures, which they said represented the council formed by these Greek princes at the capture of Troy.

I wanted to tell this story to let it be known how very ancient this style of dress is, and that it was worn by the Trojans and then by the ancient Romans. It is evident, from the clothing here, that the Trojans and later the Romans wore armor including a corazza [cuirass, body armor covering the torso and hips] and a cortella or storta [a sword with a blade of medium length and a curved handle, carried unsheathed], and that they covered themselves with a long cloak, which later came into use by the Roman consuls. Their shoes were similar to those worn at the time of Alexander the Great, as shown by many medals designed and cast in his time. The cap that covered their heads was round, in the manner of those now worn by the noblest Venetian senators.

Text on page 69

ROMAN CONSULS AND TRIBUNES
Armed for War

It is certain that our ancient Romans established the method and rule for everything that should be done by a well-ordered republic, in peace as well as in war. And since we have been speaking up until now about the government of the Romans in times of peace and war, I do not think it out of place to mention here some of the qualities required in a consul and a Roman general. The Romans, then, elected in times of war a person learned and expert in the ways of the world, believing that a man's prudence overcomes forces greater than his own; moreover, they were less concerned with the beauty of his physical presence than with the readiness of his tongue and hands, two things which, when accompanied by prudence, are of great importance in all undertakings. Once a consul with these qualities and habits was elected, he wore clothing that greatly enhanced and embellished his grandeur. The dress of tribunes and centurions resembled that of the consul, though it was not as rich or intricately worked. The consuls wore a cuirass of steel or iron, or a coat of fine chain mail covered with velvet of cremesino *[a bright red dye], decorated with grotesque faces in the shape of lions' heads or other animals, which served in place of shoulder guards, and they wore elbow-length silk cut in strips. Under the cuirass, they wore a silk cloth that made the armor more comfortable for the body, and above it, from the chest down, a* saio *[a mid-length overgarment] made of certain lengths of brocade of the same color, with golden borders of many different styles, among which stood out small faces modeled in heavy worked gold. They also wore half-length boots, under which they wore* calze di scarlatto intere *[full-length stockings of fine wool] from their feet to their waists, very comfortable for riding on horseback. These boots fastened with laces that were quick and easy to tie. On top of all these garments, they wore a mantle,* porpora *in color, called a* paludamento, *fastened in front with a golden brooch worked in a beautiful style. They carried short swords, hanging from a leather belt enriched with golden buckles. Adorned in this clothing, the consul carried a staff in his hand as a sign of his authority and walked among the centurions and the legions, or cavalry, of the army. The emperors, similarly, wore half-length armor in war time, as is shown in medals and statues, but also fastened helmets on their heads in a beautiful style, and in this fashion they watched over the safety of their country and won immortal fame.*

THE ARMED SOLDIER

The bravery of Roman soldiers, apart from their natural daring, arose from the rewards given for valorous deeds which they had carried out. Soldiers who had performed or attempted some noble act were rewarded very generously by their tribunes, though in the same way if they had behaved in a cowardly way in some engagement they were severely punished. These punishments (like the rewards) were given out in public, in the presence of the entire army, to discipline and stir up, respectively, the spirits of the soldiers. To excite the soldiers to bold undertakings, when one soldier had conducted himself well the consuls had him called up before them and all the others and there, through the loud voices of many public officials, they praised and celebrated the bravery of such men, making their illustrious deeds known to every soldier in the army. After praising them, they also gave them a gift, whose value depended on how well they had fought. Whoever had wounded a foot soldier of the enemy army earned a buckled belt; whoever had thrown a soldier from his horse received as a prize a vessel of gold; and to the armed soldier was given his own equipment for riding a horse. Whoever had preserved the life of a Roman citizen received from the hand of the consul or general a golden crown engraved with oak leaves. From these practices came the custom, when the Senate wanted to recognize and honor good emperors, of making statues and paintings of them wearing such crowns. And such soldiers, the prizewinners, returning from battle laden down and decorated with such splendors, were depicted in the highest places, the most eminent and famous sites frequented by the Roman nobility. Rewards were also given by the consuls to a captain who had carried through some highly important undertaking abandoned in despair by others; and to those who had saved the country from some great danger was given a gem or a crown of greenery cut in exactly the region where the great deed had been done; and in carrying out this ritual, they wanted the victors to be crowned by the hand of the man whom they had conquered. Among those who won this most honored prize were Lucius Dentatus, Publius Decius, Marcus Calphurnius and also Decius Augustus, who received it from the Senate. Enough said on the subject of soldiers' prizes. Their clothing resembled that in the preceding image, so I see no reason to describe it, since I have done so in the preceding chapters.

Text on page 72

THE MAN OF ARMS
on Horseback

I have found it written that the armed men of ancient Greece, in order to be ready and fit for combat, wore lightweight armor, covering their heads with a celata *[sallet, or light, round helmet] of several layers of leather, and that their cuirass, which they called a* saione*, was similarly made of leather. The Romans also used this form of armor, which they covered with* porpora *or* giacinto *cloth. Among military divisions, this was the most honored group of cavalry because, being so lightly armored, they exposed themselves to the greatest dangers that could be encountered. The Persians, too, used these forms of armor over a long period of time, but once they saw that when they were worn in the rain they became very heavy, and that after they got wet they twisted out of shape in the sun (all the more because they covered their horses with the same material), they changed their custom. They began to harness their horses and cover their own bodies with iron plates, and to carry a very large lance in their right hand, and in the left hand a large shield, and they wore a knee-length shirt of chain mail with long sleeves and iron gloves, and* schinieri *[shin-guards] on their legs. On their heads they wore a light helmet, of the kind that fastens under the chin, set off with feathers of different colors. They also wore a cuirass of chain mail covered with silk or leather. So armed, they can be seen painted in various places and sculpted in marble and other materials, showing the grandeur of their plumes, which they used to appear more terrifying to their enemies.*

Text on page 73

LIGHTLY ARMED SOLDIER ON HORSEBACK in Ancient Rome

Lightly armed cavalry soldiers wore the cuirass and the light helmet as did those more heavily armed, and like them they carried their shields in their left hands, but in the right, in place of a lance, they carried a spear, and some carried three in their shield hand in order to continue fighting after having thrown the first. Others, in place of a spear, carried a short lance called the chiavarina, *which resembled the* corsesca *[a pointed lance of middle length, with two down-turned blades at the base] usually carried by foot soldiers. The archers on horseback were outfitted in the same way, and they carried a quiver full of arrows over their shoulders, and in their left hands a bow similar to those used by the Turks, with the right hand always armed with one of these arrows, so as to be ready to strike. At their left hand they had a short, wide sword and at their right a dagger, and for the rest, they were very similar to the foot soldiers, of whom many can be seen on the columns of Trajan and Antony.*

Text on page 74

ROMAN STANDARD-BEARERS

The standard-bearers of the Roman armies, judging from the writings of various authors, were different from one another, though numerous in each of the armies. Some were called image-bearers because they carried the images of princes. Others were called ensigns because they carried insignia; others still aquilieri *and* dragonieri *because they carried eagles and dragons. Their armaments included cuirasses and short swords girt to their right sides. Their clothing was like that of other soldiers and they, too, wore boots. But on their heads, instead of helmets, they wore a hairstyle resembling a lion's head, so that the standard-bearers' aspect would be more terrible and frightening than that of any other soldier. Trumpeters and players of other musical instruments of war also appeared in this style of clothing. And this was also the dress and weaponry of the standard-bearers of the light cavalry, who also carried an eagle at the tip of their staffs, and under this a small banner of taffeta, in the colors of the livery or particular device of their captains. And this is as much of a difference as can be found between the standard-bearer of the cavalry and of the infantry.*

Text on page 75

ROMAN FOOT SOLDIERS,
called Velites

*any sculptures reveal that the foot soldiers of the Roman military belonged to different orders; and the writings of various authors also show that these foot soldiers were called by many names according to their many ranks, among whom some, lightly armed, were called* velites, *such as those who attacked enemies from afar by launching shots from slings against the enemy side. Others were called* lanciatori, *who threw small lances called* zagaglie *and other similar offensive weapons. They had no armor except a sallet, or light, round helmet on their heads. And the rest of their bodies were covered by clothing belonging to their rank, including short capes cinched and fastened at their shoulders, in which they also used to carry stones, to throw at the enemy. They wore a knee-length garment, which they belted, and boots on their legs. And this type of clothing can be seen in very ancient sculptures from the time of the Greeks, and the column of Trajan presents it especially clearly. These garments were of wool, but the capes most often were made of leather, to protect against the rain better. From this we can understand that the* velites *were of three sorts; that is, slingshooters, lancers, and archers, who, altogether, were used more than any other type of soldier in the Roman army because they were the first to enter into close combat. Their clothing was of various colors. The strikers threw a sort of light spear, called* dali *in ancient times. They were equipped with a helmet tied under the chin, as is shown in the drawing here. As defensive weapons, they carried in their left hand a shield three feet wide, and a lance called a* pilum, *similar to a dart, three and a half feet long with a narrow point a palm in length. Once this was thrown at an enemy, it would bend, so it was useless to try to throw it back. At their left side they wore a short, arm-length sword. But in the time of Trajan and Antoninus Pius, they wore* corsaletti *corselets, light body armor covering the chest and back] of metal scales, and many covered them with cloth or leather; and from sculptures it can be seen that they wore boots, and an iron rim around their shoes, which made them more durable.*

ROMAN SLINGSHOOTERS

The slingshooters were of no less importance to the Roman army than any other kind of soldier, and in those times they served in place of arquebusiers [musketeers], since there were no guns of this kind then, striking the enemy from a distance. And these slingshooters dressed for agility and lightness, wearing no iron armor except on their heads, since it is the most vulnerable part of the body. Their garment was very short, and they went almost bare-armed. In their right hands they held the sling, into which they put a round stone of the kind gathered in riverbeds. One end of this sling stayed attached to their right arm and they arranged the other so that after they had spun the sling around three or four times, they could let it loose and throw the stone wherever they wanted. And this militia of slingshooters, which was in use for a long time, were so skillful in this exercise that they kept hitting their target over and over again, no less than arquebusiers do today. They carried the stones at their left side, on top of their short cape or ferraiuolo, *which they tied at their right shoulder, so that while they used the sling, they could move their arms freely. They carried a quantity of stones sufficient to attack their enemies, in order to serve their Roman leaders.*

ILLUSTRIOUS ROMAN WOMEN, Formerly Called Stolewearers

Because I have discussed the clothing of consuls, senators and all the Roman militia above, it seems proper also to mention the clothing of women, not only ancient but modern, noble as well as plebeian and artisanal. So I will begin with the garment shown here, the most illustrious worn in those times, which was worn by the wives of consuls and senators, tribunes and others of the highest rank existing in the Roman Senate. I have discovered, however, that the leading women of Rome imitated their husbands who were consuls and senators by wearing a garment with a stole in giacinto *or* porpora, *along with the long toga, falling in folds to their feet; they wore shoes tied in a way similar to apostolic sandals, with their hair loose and the* palla *or short mantle on their shoulders.*

AN EARLY ROMAN WOMAN'S ENSEMBLE, Worn throughout Italy

The style of dress shown here was worn in Rome and throughout all Italy around the year 1000 after the birth of Christ. As a head covering women used to wear a little cap covered with fine strips of ormesino *[a lightweight silk] in the shape of feathers, more of them in back than in front. They wore floor-length gowns with four arm-lengths of train behind, fringed at the bottom, and these gowns had short, open sleeves, cut in the shape of birds' feathers, which helped to cover the arms of the narrow sleeves of their* camicie. *Around their necks they wrapped heavy chains of solid gold, which they wound several times and criss-crossed on their breast and then let fall behind them and cross again below the waist, in a very beautiful way. And I was given the drawing shown here, along with many other old ones, by the most excellent Messer Giovan Maria Bodovino,[1] the best miniaturist of our time, father of many innovations in this profession and an excellent draughtsman in his own works, to which he gives so much spirit that they seem to come straight from nature.*

CLOTHING OF A ROMAN NOBLEWOMAN
Two Hundred Years Ago

his kind of clothing, I find, was worn in about 1300 among Roman women and also throughout all Italy. It is rather similar to modern dress. These gentlewomen, then, wore a silk undergown, entirely of brocade and without a bodice. They pinned a mantle to their head and let it fall to the ground, trailing a long way behind them, and it was decorated with a border in porpora *or* giacinto. *These women of early Rome also often wore a tunic with a mantle, in* popora *or* giacinto *or gold, with very precious trimmings. And they found it deeply shameful and sinful that any young woman, before marriage, should drink wine, and even married women abstained from it. So much so that the relatives of these maidens used to kiss them not out of love but to find out whether they had drunk wine. And on this subject I remember reading that a Roman gentleman killed his wife because he had smelled wine on her breath as he was speaking with her. Nor was he punished for this; on the contrary, he was pardoned and praised. Another woman, for the same reason, was starved to death.*

CLOTHING OF A BARONESS
and Other Roman Noblewomen

The wives of barons and other Roman lords wear a garment fastened at the head and foot, of silk or some other material, and on top of this, they wear very valuable jewels. From their head a cloth made of silk or satin falls to their feet. Some wear this garment open in front, so that their velvet or satin faldiglie *[a farthingale or hoopskirt], of various colors, can be seen, trimmed very richly. They make a pleasant sight. And when they are in mourning dress, they wear a floor-length mantle on their shoulders. They also wear on their heads a net of black silk full of golden* tremoli *[spangles of silver or gold], along with certain other ornaments; and so they proceed with great dignity and decorum, leaning on some gentleman for the sake of their greater reputation as they walk through the streets. And though they very often ride in coaches, they still are accompanied by many other women, arrayed in very lovely displays of jewelry.*

NOBLE WIDOWS of Modern Rome

Roman widows of our times wear a garment of black Florentine rascia *[a twill fabric of silk or wool] with a white band falling forward in front, and a stole of light yellow cloth over their shoulders. But the women of the highest nobility wear a full-length veil of* buratto *[a lightweight wool and silk fabric], and on their heads, under the veil, they wear a small cap of white linen that conceals their hair. Altogether, they dress in a way that shows great chastity and sorrow for their dead husbands, so that, considering their demeanor, one would say they seem more like nuns than laywomen.*

BRIDES OF THE ROMAN NOBILITY, in Formal Wear outside their Homes

Roman women are endowed with natural beauty, so that even in our time they seem to retain the majesty and imposing presence of their ancestors. They are in the habit of going to many public festivals and entertainments for the sake of pleasure, attending them with due chastity and honorable manners, which bring added splendor to their ancient bloodline. As clothing they usually wear floor-length sottane *of silk or satin, encircled with gold trim, and above this an overgown or* zimarra *[a long, close-fitting overgown] of gold brocade or of silk, trimmed with a border all the way down the front, open from the hem to the waist, belted with very beautiful narrow, long gold bands, to one end of which are attached elegant, well-made fans. From the waist down to below the knees, these* zimarre *are buttoned with fine gold fastenings and buttons of gold, and from there to the ground the overgowns are worn open, to show the undergarment, whose sleeves cover the arms; the sleeves belonging to the overgown or* zimarra *are long and narrow, floor-length, and wide around the elbow. They adorn their necks with several strands of beautiful pearls and other jewels, and wear the hair around their foreheads in beautiful curls; the rest of their hair, tied up with colored* cordelline *[narrow twisted cords] of silk, makes a beautiful sight because of the lovely silk veil, embellished with gold, attached to the top of the head and falling down behind.*

NOBLEWOMEN OF ROME
in Our Time

Young Roman noblewomen at present wear clothing similar to that of the women of Romagna and Tuscany, who like to look both attractive and richly dressed. So their dress includes a very lovely headdress, which they call the canacca *[a snood], which gathers up their hair with strips of golden braid and rises in a cap shape a palm's length above the head, in the style of a* cuffia *[a stiff cap]. Above this, with silver pins they attach a veil of very fine silk, which they let fall down behind. On their ears they wear beautiful earrings made of huge pearls, which they also wear at their necks, along with the small ruffles of their* camicia. *They wear long, floor-length overgarments made of silk brocade, with a pattern of varied leaves, fastened all the way up the front with buttons of gold lace, and underneath they wear long* sottane *with trains more than an arm in length. Their arms are covered with sleeves of golden brocade, sewn to the overgarment, which itself also includes hanging sleeves split in two. They usually carry fans and gloves in their hands, and dressed in this way and accompanied by many women servants and relatives, they go to prayers. This ensemble was taken from life and sent to me by Messer Giovanni Salamandra, an excellent painter who lives in Rome.*

A WOMAN CITIZEN
or Wife of a Roman Merchant

Women citizens, or wives of Roman merchants, dress very sumptuously and grandly, wearing gowns with low-cut bodices that expose their breasts, adorned with many strands of heavy gold necklaces, from which jewels also hang. Their overgarments are of damasco *[damask, a self-patterned, reversible fabric made of silk and linen] or beautifully patterned* brocatello *[a heavy fabric combining linen and silk], floor-length, encircled with borders of gold brocade. Underneath they wear a* sottana *of* ormesino *or* canevaccia *[a loosely woven but luxurious fabric] of silk, and they cover their arms with sleeves of silk netting, under which can be seen a linen or cotton fabric woven with silver or gold. They wear their hair curled, framing their foreheads, and they wear the rest styled under a long veil, which, fixed to their hair, falls to the ground; they take the points of this veil, trimmed with gold, and attach them to a heavy belt of gold. When they leave home, they are accompanied by many ladies-in-waiting, and most often they let their small children, also richly dressed, walk ahead of them, with great elegance in their gloves, flowers, and other refined accessories.*

NOBLE GIRLS AND MAIDENS
outside their Homes

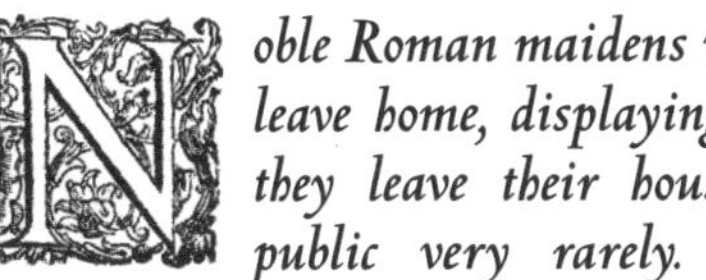

oble Roman maidens walk very modestly when they leave home, displaying their good manners, though they leave their houses and show themselves in public very rarely. They wear a garment of damasco *or silk brocade, patterned with stars or other designs, fastened all the way down with buttons and knots of gold, very long, with trains of half an arm's length, and with long, narrow, open sleeves. From the openings of these sleeves their arms appear, in the same* brocatello *as their* giuppone *[doublet]. They keep their hair bound up under a very thin veil, which hangs lightly and beautifully down their backs.*

ROMAN WOMEN
of Artisan and Plebeian Rank

In the same way that nature creates wide variety among the flowers, grasses, trees, and fruits, assigning a particular virtue more to one than to another, wise human judgment in cities and other well-ordered places has established certain forms and kinds of clothing, as different in cost as in color and cut. So we see that the clothing illustrated here is very different from that of noble and rich women. These wives of artisans wear garments of colored cloth, floor-length, with low-necked bodices, horizontally trimmed in silk and belted with a gold chain. They adorn their necks with strands of coral and other jewels, and with the very white ruffles of their camicia. *They wear curls on their foreheads and a silk veil, which they pin to their hair and let fall to the ground, tying its points to their gold belts.*

COURTESANS RECOGNIZABLE BY THEIR CLOTHING, in the Time of Pius V[2]

*o that they could be distinguished from honorable women, prostitutes or courtesans of Rome at the time of the papacy of Pius V of blessed memory wore a floor-length* sottana *of silk, above which they were allowed to wear an overgament shorter by a half-arm's length than the garment beneath; this* zimarra *was made of black* rascia *similar to what widows wore, and it was fastened crosswise with a strip of white veil. On their heads they wore a half-length veil of white* cambrai *[cambric, a thin linen], arranged into a fold that stood out from the head far enough to cover the entire forehead, and in this way they went through Rome, clearly set apart from honored and respectable women.*

COURTESANS AND PROSTITUTES of Modern Rome

Modern Roman courtesans dress in such fine style that few people can tell them apart from the noblewomen of that city. They wear sottane *of satin or* ormesino*, floor-length, over which they wear* zimarre *of velvet, decorated from top to bottom with gold buttons, with low necklines that expose their entire breast and neck, adorned with beautiful pearls, gold necklaces and ruffles of brilliant white. The overgarment includes narrow sleeves as long as the garment itself, but open, and through their openings the arms of the* sottana *are visible. They make their hair blonde by artificial means, and they curl it and tie it up with silk ribbons inside a gold net, prettily ornamented with jewels and pearls.*

THE PEASANT WOMEN of Roman Territories

*In the villages and hill towns of Rome, and in all the places subject to Roman lords and barons, the majority of women wear a dress of turquoise or green cloth, ending above their feet, with a border of velvet, and with low-cut bodices that leave their necks bare; adorning these bodices with silver brooches, they lace them across a wide opening. They tie on a linen apron with a fringed hem, ankle-length, and they wear a certain kind of shoe, like short boots or half-*bolzacchini *[short, snug boots], which are fastened with laces on the inside of their legs. On their heads they wear a linen cloth, folded back in the style used by Jesuit priests, but the head coverings of these peasant women have needle-worked borders. And as brides, their custom is to wear sleeves of red satin.*

BRIEF DESCRIPTION OF THE CITY OF VENICE
Chapter 1

Quite unlike any other city, the illustrious city of Venice, because of its location, size and magnificence, is one of the miracles of the world. For this reason I will describe it briefly here, to make this book complete. The city is almost eight Italian miles in circumference, and is set in the heart of the Adriatic Sea. An island divided into five sections protects it from the fury of the storms of this sea and offers a safe harbor to seagoing vessels, giving easy passage to ships seeking entry into the mouth of the port, which is set between two mighty castles. Around the city on all sides are twenty-five small islands, almost all inhabited by members of religious orders. The city itself has seventy-two parishes and forty monasteries. It has many, many canals, equal in number to its streets, and its public bridges number four hundred, not counting those belonging to private houses. Its Arsenal is surrounded on all sides by beautiful walls set with battlements, and inside it four hundred men are constantly at work building galleys and other seagoing ships. There are three hundred great galleys, including their fittings, as well as many ships and small boats of every kind. For the use of the city and its commerce, approximately eight thousand boats sail forth, supplying abundant quantities of every sort of food and clothing that could be needed. Near the city is the island of Murano, where glass vessels of all sorts are constantly produced, in quantity great enough to supply the whole world.

In this city there are figures crafted from bronze and marble by the best-known sculptors and statue-makers in the world. There are magnificently built palaces, marvelously painted and inhabited by families of great renown. Altogether, it is a mirror of beauty, a model of good customs, a fount of virtue, the home of good men, a shelter for the industrious, and a warehouse[1] for the whole world of merchandise of all kinds.

THE FORM OF GOVERNMENT AND THE MAGISTRATES OF VENICE
Chapter 2

Now that I have briefly described the city of Venice, I think it would be useful to say something about the different ranks of its nobility, about the magistrates and the governing bodies of the city and all its territories, so that through this explanation, it is possible to understand their customs. All the nobility of Venice, as many as fifteen hundred men, attend the Great Council,[2] in addition to those who govern lands outside the city; together, they create a prince whom they call the doge and give the title of Most Serene Lord.[3] As long as he lives, he retains this office, and he enjoys great authority, which I will not elaborate on here, since it has been described by many excellent writers. In our time, this doge wears a royal cloak, porpora in color, or even of cloth of gold, which might reasonably be compared to the cape of a Roman general.[4] On his head he wears a regal hat, pointed and made of the finest gold cloth, bordered with deep red and encircled with gold; its top resembles an upturned horn. When he enters the

Senate, he finds a royal throne set up for him, and at his arrival all the Senators bare their heads and stand when he speaks. He receives every sign of reverence shown to a king, though his authority is not fully that of a king.

After the doge comes the rank of the Procurators of San Marco.[5] Then a ruling body of six noble senators is elected, one for each Sestiere [urban district]; these officers are called Councillors and they hold power for six months. Next, the Savi Grandi[6] are chosen, along with other officials so numerous that it would be tiresome to list them or define their responsibilities and powers, since they have already been discussed by many famous writers. Altogether, it should be clear that the government of these Venetian lords is almost the same as that of the early Romans.

But because the ceremonies observed when electing the prince are unlike those of anywhere else, I have thought it fitting to say something about them. One must know, then, that after this doge has been elected by those previously elected to the Senate, after the death of his predecessor, new coins carrying his portrait and coat of arms are minted; and then, on an appointed day, he is carried on a platform in great pomp by the men of the Arsenal[7] all around the piazza of San Marco, and everywhere he goes, certain officials on the platform throw money to the people as a sign of joy and celebration. Then, once arrived at a certain spot, he puts on the doge's hat and is carried to his own rooms in the Palace. There he is lodged with all the sumptuousness fitting for the ruler of such a famous and illustrious city, which, after Rome, rightly takes the first place in Europe and is called the Queen of the Sea, untouched and immaculate Virgin, never attacked or put to the sack.

FIRST VIEW OF THE PIAZZA of San Marco, Venice

*The city of Venice seems marvelous to whoever sees it, owing to its location, more than wondrous for its buildings and other features, and more than magnificent in its government—indeed, had it existed in the era that first named the Seven Wonders of the World, it would have been placed first among them. Leaving aside the beauty and nobility of its churches and other buildings, and the sweeping panorama of its many splendid palaces, not to mention the many spacious and beautiful piazzas set in such abundance in front of its churches, I will speak briefly only about the most famous one, that is, the piazza of San Marco, where every Saturday a huge market takes place, equaling and in fact surpassing any great fair whatsoever. To proceed in the best order I can, I will divide this piazza into three parts, according to the three beautiful views one can take of it.*

The first view is available to a person standing near the water, looking toward the famous convent of the church of San Giorgio, inhabited by black-clad Benedictine monks. Turning back toward the magnificent clock, without equal in Italy, he can see, marveling, which astrological sign the sun is in at any time and also the days and minutes of the monthly phase of the Moon. And when the clock makes a complete rotation, marking the hour of the day, the time is rung out on a great bell by two bronze statues resembling Moors, and a beautiful set of the Three Kings, turning around a relief of the Glorious Virgin and led by a Star (which in its motion and shape resembles a star in the heavens); and by an angel playing a trumpet, artfully shown putting it to his mouth so expertly that he seems real. And as each of these Magi arrives in front of the figure of the Madonna, he raises the crown that he wears, honoring this image in a way so lovely that such a sight exists nowhere else in the world.

This piazza is four hundred feet in length and 121 feet in width. This first view includes both sides of the great Palace of San Marco [the Ducal Palace]; both are of the same length and shape, a design that has more in common with German style than with any other. The façades of this palace contain eighteen arches, each ten feet wide, resting on columns two feet thick that support the façades and belong to the Corinthian order, though the capitals of these columns are of earlier fabrication. Below the loggias supported by these arches are many prisons; and on the first floor above them runs another beautiful loggia, containing courtrooms for the different magistrates. This level has another row of columns and a corridor of smaller columns; its walls, from floor to ceiling, are made of alternating red and white Istrian stone.[8] *Above this loggia where the magistrates work one finds two large rooms, one for the Great Council and the other called La Sala del Scrutinio; the walls and ceilings of both are decorated with beautiful paintings by the world's most famous artists and afterward richly embellished with gold. The walls of this palace are 220 feet long on each side.*

Across from the palace the Library building can be seen, designed and completed by the famous Signor Giacomo Sansovino, a Florentine, the most excellent sculptor and architect of his time.[9] *His work belongs to the Doric and Ionic order and is full of beautiful inlays and grotesques in Istrian stone and especially of sculptures of rivers in different poses ornamenting the corners of the first arches, and figures of Victory on the second ones; and at the summit of a balustrade in front of every column is a free-standing statue. All these sculptures are the work of excellent masters of this state, including Girolamo*

This illustration appears on folio 39 of the original book.

Campagna, Titiano Aspetti, Augustino Rubino, Camillo Vincentino, and other young men of great promise, judging from the work they do every day. This building is supported by columns forming twenty-one arches, going from the corner of the Mint to the corner facing the bell tower. From this toward the west lies the full length of the main piazza, extending toward the church of San Geminiano. In front of the bell tower, which is very tall and can truthfully be said to be the most beautiful in Italy, is a little loggia of beautiful sculpted marble, decorated with columns and with four very lovely bronze figures, all the work of the said Sansovino. From this same perspective can be seen three flag-poles, the church of San Marco, and the face of the clock. And although this little description of mine is very brief, I beg my reader to trust in my goodwill and to consider further that nearby, right in front of San Marco at a distance of only eight feet, one sees the bell tower, with a façade forty feet in width on each side and a height of 230 feet; on its top is set a bronze angel, which turns according to the direction of the wind. The pyramidal upper tower is covered with gold, so that when the sun strikes it, it can be seen from far away. At the far end of this view, toward San Giorgio, are two very tall, thick columns, brought here from Constantinople when Venice ruled there; on top of one is the figure of Saint Theodore. Next to them is the canal, on which in 1554 the great wooden boat of the Compagnie delle Calze[10] traveled. In it two hundred noblewomen could comfortably be seated, all dressed in white, in addition to the gentlemen who accompanied them and others making up a total of four hundred, who danced and played music with great merriment and gaiety. And the Companies also had comedies and other lavish entertainments performed.

THE FIRST LEADER, OR DOGE, of Early Venice

Although in modern Venice each doge wears the same kind of clothing and accoutrements as his predecessor, this was not the case for the leaders in the early days of this republic, when each one wore different garments. Proof of this can be found in the church of San Marco, above the door of the Treasury, where there is a portrait in mosaic of a prince accompanied by many nobles and clergymen, showing with what great devotion they all accompanied the sacred body of their glorious protector Saint Mark, to inter him in an honored place. According to what I can make of this portrait, this doge dressed more in the style of the Greeks than in any other. This style is very majestic, as can be seen from the corno *[the doge's cap], still worn today by the doges of Venice, though the one worn now is very different from this one.*

The dress of the early doge shown here, as described by Francesco Sansovino,[11] *was worn by a certain Ordelafo Faliero,*[12] *a man scrupulous and diligent in matters of the government of his republic, whose rule began in* 1085 *and who dressed as we see here. On his head he wore a miter similar to that of the holy pope, round in shape with a pointed top; the top portion was red and around it was a border similar to a duke's crown, and this border, or circle of gold, was full of gems, although other early doges wore a small gold cross at the top of their hat. The rest of his clothing differed only slightly from the modern style except for the way it was worn, because we recognize in it the same mantle and cassock still worn today only by Christian rulers. The mantle was of silk embellished with gold and lined with* vaio *[vair, the pelts of a species of small squirrel with a white belly and gray back], furs held in high esteem in those days; this is the reason that the shields and coats of arms of many noble families today include, among other things, these furs. We also see that early painters, when they wanted to represent someone of great authority, usually painted him with a mantle lined with this fur, visible especially in the portraits of the most serene doges of Venice, very long, enriched with a beautiful border of gold and another strip of gold sewn across them. The untrimmed spaces of these mantles, moreover, were filled with roses of gold, woven with marvelous precision. The doges wore their hair long, and on it a cap of the thinnest white linen or silk, shaped to cover their ears halfway down, exactly as we see today. From their shoulders hung two sable skins, a sign of authority; one covered the right side of the chest, the other the left. The undergarment or gown worn beneath the mantle was the same color as the mantle, woven with gold in the same fashion, and trimmed with a beautiful border, and it was cinched with a rich belt, as we see here, of the same color as the gown. On their feet they wore pointed shoes, almost the same as those worn today but red, and their stockings were the same color.*

Text on page 96

THE CLOTHING OF ANOTHER EARLY DOGE

On the rich and lovely façade of the church of San Marco, above the doors where the life of Saint Mark the Evangelist is portrayed, two other kinds of clothing can be seen, worn by the most serene doges of Venice, who are shown accompanied by a large escort of the nobility, men and women of every rank and station. On the same façade is another mosaic, depicting the body of the Evangelist carried and accompanied by the clergy; among other things we can see a doge in the clothing shown here—it is very different from that of the first doge. He wears a mantle falling from one shoulder, buttoned on this shoulder, open at the right, but closed everywhere else; and as far as we can tell, he wears an ermine bavaro *[broad collar, lapel, or short shoulder cape] similar to those worn by the doges of our time, though theirs are not as large as the one shown here. Even so, this seems to be the same kind of garment—accurately symbolizing the blessed and princely grandeur of this most Christian Republic, founded on the solid rock of the Holy Faith to protect and glorify all Italy, which can clearly be seen from the fact that she has been preserved as an inviolate Virgin up to our time. The garment shown here, then, shares the great dignity and grandeur of this most serene Republic, which encompasses the highest goodness and courtesy beyond words.*

Text on page 97

A NOBLEMAN OF EARLY VENICE

Truly worthy of admiration is the great modesty of dress observed by the first founding fathers of this famous city, a modesty as great as her splendor. You see in this drawing that in those early days the noblemen imitated their prince in their dress and even in their customs, though such noblemen did not wear the doge's hat, which was reserved as a lofty symbol for the leader alone. The nobles, rather, wore a round hat similar to the hat worn by the present-day noblemen of this city, except that the early version had a top with a rounded point. On the front of this hat was a sort of silk trim, sewn in a cross shape, a sign of those with great authority, such as the Procurators of San Marco, the Savi Grandi, the Councillors, the Censors, the Savi of the Terra Firma, the heads of the Council of Ten, the Avvogadori del Commun, and others like them;[13] *and this cross signaled that they were the defenders and maintainers of Christianity. They used to wear their hair shoulder-length, tightly curled, and their beards also long and curled; they wore long mantles decorated with gold, which they buttoned on the right shoulder and let fall to the ground, open on the right side and closed the rest of the way around. Under this mantle they wore a very modest floor-length undergarment, or* sottana, *decorated with different designs and colors but still more grave than grand. This is a garment drawn from various mosaics, but especially the one from which I took Doge Ordelafo Faliero, in the glorious church of San Marco.*

THE CLOTHING OF ANOTHER NOBLEMAN of Early Venice

The clothing of the Venetian nobleman shown here is no different from that previously described, except that this man is wearing a mantle fastened or buttoned in the middle of his chest with a gold pin, while the other man wears his mantle pinned at his right shoulder; and this man's hat does not rise as high. The previous illustration shows an embroidered mantle and a plain sottana, *but the nobleman here wears an embroidered* sottana *and a plain mantle. So we see that styles of clothing have constantly been changing over time.*

A MARRIED NOBLEWOMAN of Early Venice

*n the same church of San Marco mosaics portray the clothing that the noblewomen of Venice used to wear, in a style more religious than worldly. They wore their heads covered with a hat divided into four parts with gold trim, closed at the top like a cap, from which their long curled locks fell down to their shoulders. They wore a kind of collarless, floor-length* sottana *of silk, all of one piece, fitted to their bodies in front, with beautiful embroidery; over this they wore a floor-length mantle with a small train, crossed with lovely strips of golden or silk embroidery, with two sable furs hanging at the front like lapels or a collar. When they went to religious services or elsewhere, they used to take their little daughters with them, dressed in a simple silk gown embroidered on the bodice and tied with a narrow silk braid, and a headdress made of thin gold, imitating a ducal crown. And the style of clothing these women wore, I believe, was also worn by the wives of the early doges.*

48

FESTIVE DRESS OF AN HONORABLE NOBLEWOMAN
of Early Venice

This apparel is very different from the previous one but it is graceful and well made, and was worn by noble ladies when they dressed up for holidays or public ceremonies. On their heads they wore a circlet of gold in the shape of a crown, with metalwork in the center in the form of a round medallion, to which they attached beautiful gems. This circlet was worked all over with lovely decoration, and under it their blonde, curled locks fell down to their shoulders. On top of their heads they tied a very full mantle, which, because of its width, billowed out in a lovely way. This was made of silk embroidered with small golden stars, floor-length, trimmed all around with a golden border and carried over the left arm, around which a corner of the mantle was wrapped; the rest of the mantle they let fall from their right shoulder to the ground. Beneath the mantle they used to wear a collarless sottana, *with a fitted bodice decorated with trim entirely of gold. And dressed in this way, they appeared in public very modestly.*

CLOTHING OF AN EARLY BARON,
also worn in Venice and throughout Italy

Though the activity of this rural baron and early lord appears to be hunting, since he carries a hawk on his hand, his garments are the same as those worn in the city of Venice when men sought recreation, as was also the case elsewhere in Italy, as evidenced in burial monuments in Venice and many famous paintings one can see in the city of Padua, as well as an inscription saying this was the fashion in 1100. It is true, however, that this style was worn more by the high-ranking nobility of the Terra Firma [mainland] than of Venice. The overgarment was made entirely of cloth of gold with various beautiful patterns, and interwoven from the bottom up with rows of silver or golden plates, in the style of body armor, arranged to resemble the feathers of a bird; and when the sun shone on them, they made a beautiful sight. On top of this outer garment, which reached to the knees and was loose and full, they wore a band of either golden cloth or silver decorated with various jewels and precious stones over their left shoulder and under their right arm, where it was pinned with a golden buckle. It was bound with a very wide, beautiful belt, which went very well with the short robe. On their legs they wore full-length stockings and they wore long pointed boots, which curved downward to keep their feet more firmly in the stirrups when they rode on horseback. They wore their hair long, and tied it with a narrow gold band; and in this way, bareheaded, they went out to enjoy the pleasures of the hunt.

LORDS OF CASTLES IN EARLY TIMES in the Venetian State and throughout all of Italy

he lords of castles in the territories of Venice and throughout Italy dressed very soberly, in such a way that their garments revealed the mature intellect and judgment they possessed. On their heads they wore a hat of red ormesino, *with a wide, turned-up brim folded up in front and back, forming a point more than halfway up. This brim was lined with a different kind of* ormesino *or with white velvet. They wore their hair shoulder-length. They wore a floor-length toga of silk and gold brocade, split at the sides, and through these openings could be seen satin or velvet* sottane *with long sleeves, buttoned up to the elbows beneath the half-sleeves of the toga. This upper sleeve was cut very narrow and open, and it hung down behind. They cinched their* sottane *with a silk belt, to which they attached knives visible through the opening of the toga, which was* porpora *or* giacinto *in color.*

This is clothing I have seen depicted in many magnificent and famous places—most recently in a part of Italy called Vico, near the border with Germany on the other side of the Piave river. There, in a very old, small church, there is a chapel dedicated to Saint Ursula decorated with five-hundred-year-old paintings that show the life and miracles of that saint. Among the other things depicted in these paintings, there are two portraits of the lords of that town, who ruled in those days over a very ancient city called Agonia (of which nothing remains today except the foundations of a castle and a bath with sulfur waters, the rest having turned into forest). This famous city of Agonia left behind many writings testifying to its renown, which, preserved over time, are now in the hands of a certain

Messer Odorico Soldano, the chancellor of the town. In addition, near where this city used to be, peasants plowing the fields found certain bronze and silver medals proving that, however mountainous this region (today called Cadore) was, it was nonetheless inhabited by lords and people of great valor and power. This territory is spacious, stretching across forty miles, and it was also full of many castles, which bit by bit have fallen to pieces. Just a few days ago a peasant of the town, digging in the earth, found among other things a small bronze horse covered with a lion's skin, which one could see had been made with marvelous skill. This horse is now in the hands of the Mainardi, a noble family of the town, and I have held it in my hands and looked at it, with great joy at seeing the beautiful style of our ancestors in it, though it is now missing a foot.

In this town today one finds a very lovely stretch of land, as well as many villas inhabited by honorable and ancient families in great numbers, and the castle town is called Pieve, which, along with the surrounding countryside, voluntarily offered obedience to the lords of Venice. The people of Pieve have been so loyal and done the Venetians such good turns that they have deservedly won many privileges from them, including various freedoms—for example, not having to row in the galleys in wartime, not being drafted into the land militia, and other benefits inviolably maintained by the most serene Venetian Senate. To judge their own civil and criminal cases, some families choose their own local representative, and other families are elected judges, called Consuls, to preside over criminal trials. In short, the region of Cadore is very beautiful, enclosing an area forty miles wide; the site itself is lovely, and the land is planted with beautiful fruit trees and wood for building all sorts of houses and ships. It includes as well the navigable Piave river, which has its source within the territory's borders and enriches the countryside with all the goods brought there and the ease with which it allows merchants to send boats in great numbers to Venice.

It is true to say that because of its age, Cadore still contains many noble families, among which the most noble are the Vecelli, which has produced many, many honorable men, full of dignity, temperate, highly courageous, just, and altogether great and excellent in every age and time. What shall I say of a certain Gratiano Vecellio, a man of great judgment and valor, whose dignity was chief among his many virtues and merits? For among the many enormously important responsibilities he undertook because of his great valor, he was appointed judge in weighty, difficult court cases involving the most reverend Patriarch of Aquileia, on one hand, and on the other the illustrious Count of Gorizia, which he resolved to great satisfaction on both sides, proving his great wisdom and being praised and admired by everyone in his time. I shall say nothing of Giovanni Vecellio, who for his great merit and fearless valor earned the position of Castellan [guardian] of Cadore, his native city. And since I have plunged into this ocean of praises for the house of Vecellio, which enjoyed absolute power over a very lovely castle named Bottestagno, I will not linger over a certain Titian [Tiziano], a deeply educated and highly talented man, who proved himself on many occasions, especially when ruling his home town, which gave him all the honor and power that a town can give to its greatest citizens. Vincenzo Vecellio was not only expertly knowledgeable in Greek and Latin, but also richly distinguished in the precepts and rhetoric of philosophy; he showed the beauty of his soul, the loftiness of his speech and the greatness of his judgment to everyone.

What shall I say of Gregorio, the father of Titian, that most excellent painter, who had a formidable mind and exceptional experience, so that the goodness of his soul yielded in no way to the greatness of his intellect?[14] *From this man was born that great, even divine, Titian, not only created by nature herself as honorable, dignified, temperate, highly courageous and just, a great and excellent man, but who surpassed the fame not only of all the men of his time in the art of painting but also all those we can recall from antiquity. For he discovered the true method of excellent painting in oil and knew so well how to imitate nature in his works that the figures he portrayed seem to be actually alive. In addition, he painted things never created by nature. And as a result we see many paintings showing his great skill, in so many copies throughout the world that he has rightly been called the father of drawing, a most skillful inventor, the master of color, and one might say the model of painting. So he deserved to win great rewards from the King of England, from almost all the dukes of Italy, and then a life pension from Pope Paul III, the unconquered King of the Romans, and also the most serene Republic of Venice. In addition, before that, he was created a knight by the Emperor Charles V, who allotted to him three hundred* scudi *a year.*

This Titian had a brother Francesco, also one of the major painters of his region, and hardly inferior to anyone at all in his artistic ability, as his many paintings attest. Another member of this house was Fabrizio, lacking neither fame nor glory for making extremely life-like portraits and painted figures. And no less famous in the memory of men is Tito Vecellio, a man of singular goodness, indescribable courtesy, and great experience in the affairs of his country. His son Marco is a famous and celebrated painter, as can be seen from some of his paintings, which have been placed in the audience chambers of the Senate. Later, this Vecellio was highly diligent and prudent in governing his city, faithful and courageous in negotiating the most important matters, prompt and eloquent in speech, and finally of unusually good character. From him was born the knight Titian a highly educated young man of excellent character and the highest goodness, joined with high spirit, through which he showed the greatness of his courage and the prudence of his intellect. I know that I have strayed from my topic more than I should, but I am certain I will be excused for it—because my love for my country as well as for my family permits me to digress a little more than is proper. Even so, I have left out certain other families, among them the Palatini, Alessandrini, Genove, and Constantine, by whom the greatest part of this region is ruled and governed, not to speak of Giovanni Alessandrino and Pietro, Doctor of Law, his son, both endowed with excellent character and every other virtue.

CLOTHING OF THE WIVES OF THE EARLY LORDS OF CASTLES,
in the Region of Venice and throughout Italy

The clothing of the wives of the lords of castles in the Venetian territories and also in all of Italy was close to that worn by their husbands, as previously shown. They wore a headdress made of a thin silk veil wrapped around their head, with no other ornament. They wore a floor-length toga of porpora *or* giacinto *color, patterned all over and open at the sides, with mid-length outer sleeves that covered their arms, while they let the lower half hang down open; they also wore undersleeves buttoned to the elbow, belonging to their silk undergarment—as far as one can see from the old painted chapel from which the clothing of the lords of ancient castles was also taken.*

VENETIAN DRESS OF EARLY TIMES, WITH THE DOGALINA
[a very full, open sleeve]

In the church of Saint Helena, built on one of the small islands near Venice and inhabited by the reverend monks of Mount Oliveto, supposedly rests the body of the glorious Empress, mother of the Emperor Constantine. Here, one sees early paintings belonging to an altarpiece, in which a cross is set between two figures, one of which, as I was told by those reverend fathers, is the portrait of Saint Helena and the other of Constantine, her son. These figures wear clothing in the Greek style. The saint is dressed in a floor-length robe, unbelted, and the sleeves of her overgarment are split up to her elbow, while the rest of the robe, lined with ermine, falls to her feet, open from the side down, exactly as in another figure that one can see in the baptistery of the church of San Marco, representing Herodias.[15] *Constantine is painted in an overgarment unbelted at the sides, with a crown on his head and a scepter in his hand. Not believing all this completely, I looked all around carefully to see some other clothing, and I also found the kind shown here, which I chose because it seemed to go along with the others. This figure wore a scarlet-colored cloth wrapped around his head, one end of which falls down onto his shoulder. Fastened at his neck, a very wide, long gown in* pavonazzo *[a range of colors from purplish blue to blue-black] falls to mid-calf, bordered with a strip of white near the hem. His sleeves are open and so wide that they can be thrown over the shoulder, and these used to be lined with various furs or with silk, according to the season. The shortness of the gown reveals red stockings and pointed shoes. This dress is very sober and Senatorial, and it can be seen painted and sculpted in many places in Italy.*

EARLY CLOTHING OF A YOUNG NOBLEMAN
Dressed to Go Courting

The clothing in this adjacent portrait I took from a figure sculpted on the capital of a column among those that support the Ducal Palace in Venice near the women's prison; it can also be seen painted and sculpted elsewhere in Venice. The young men of these times wore their hair in a curl on their forehead and the rest of it curled down on their shoulders. They put on an overgarment of silk or gold, brocaded with various large flowers, falling to mid-calf and buttoned with large gold buttons down to a silken belt, to which was attached a sword, at the left side. This overgarment was decorated with lace all around the lower hem. And these men also wore a very long hood of the same material, falling below the belt and hanging down behind, useful in the rain because it took away the need for any other head covering. The upper sleeve of this overgarment covered the arm to the elbow, but the rest of it was open and hung down from the half-sleeve. They wore red stockings and low, pointed shoes.

A MAIDEN OF EARLY TIMES, in Love

The clothing of this young noblewoman in love comes from the same place [as that of the young nobleman dressed to go courting] and is very lovely. They used to wear modest little curls on their foreheads and let their hair, grown very long, fall past their shoulders. They wore beautifully worked gold earrings, and a short string of pearls around their neck. They wore a trimmed overgarment without a bodice, not very full but richly decorated along the breast and the sleeves, with gold or silver studs at the openings, which because of their arrangement seemed like the feathers of birds—a very beautiful and rich style.

THE CLOTHING OF EARLY NOBLEWOMEN OUTSIDE THEIR HOUSES, with the Dogalina

*The clothing of Venetian women of former times, especially when they dressed in the* dogalina *to appear in public, was wonderfully magnificent. On their heads these women wore a* balzo *[a tubular headdress] made of gold wire in the shape of a round garland, which encircled the entire head like a diadem. Their necks were completely bare, without any ornament. The top of their bodice was studded with gems, and it was belted at the waist with a solid gold belt. Most of them wore bodices covered with gold, and the rest of the gown was made of silk, in* pavonazzo *or* cremesino*. They wore open sleeves, calf-length, usually turned up or folded back onto their shoulders, as they often did with the sleeves of their* camicie *as well, exposing their bare arms, whose beauty was increased with gorgeous gold bracelets; and they artificially whitened and softened their hands. For women in those days who had naturally beautiful hands and arms made them even more beautiful, as those with beautiful faces do today. They bound their overgarment with a silk belt and lined it with* ormesino *in the summer and with ermine, marten or squirrel fur in the winter, depending on their preference. Beneath, they wore a* carpetta *[a full-length undergarment] of splendidly embroidered silk. And this style lasted until 1303, when a law decreed that not so much money should be spent on clothing as had been the custom earlier.*[16]

This decree was promulgated during the reign of Piero Gradenigo, the forty-eighth doge of Venice.[17]

NOBLEWOMEN OF EARLY VENICE at Home

In the old days Venetian noblewomen at home, once they had removed their dogalina, *wore a headdress made like a cap or a copper* balzo, *covered with a fine cap of silk and gold, very beautifully worked. Then, on top of their embroidered* carpette, *they wore an overgarment of silk or some other material, without a collar and open at the sides up to the shoulders. This was cut like a tunic, without a bodice, but worn with a belt and trimmed all around. Around their necks they wrapped a thin veil like a stole, whose ends they let fall down their backs. And so, fit and quick to attend to their household duties with the greatest diligence and to care for their children and husbands, they strove to avoid idleness, following the example of the Roman Lucretia,[18] a true model of chastity, whose fame is eternal because of this quality and because of the love she bore for her husband Collatinus, equal to any woman of antiquity in the purity of her soul.*

THE NOBLEWOMEN OF EARLY VENICE
[after 1303]

Since women are in the habit of changing styles frequently, after a while they abandoned the fashion of the dogalina. *But we must not blame them for this particular change since it was the result of a law passed by the Senate prohibiting ostentatious display and excessive spending, which limited how much might be spent on clothing. This law (as Sansovino writes) was followed for some time. But then they began to wear full skirts and an overgarment with a long train; this gown was gradually shortened but cost as much as the first style, in addition to other garments that came to cost even more. Indeed, they wore the* coda, *or very wide, long train, under which they wore a kind of hoopskirt, very similar to the one they now call a* carpetta, *worked and embroidered all over, with a golden strip around the bottom of the hem that kept it standing out in a bell shape, which made it very easy for them to walk and dance. They bound their waists with a gold chain, from which hung a precious sheath with silver knives and a very valuable purse. And the cost of this ensemble reached such a height that it exceeded by far the limit imposed by the law, so the Senate prohibited the wearing of knives, purses, and hoopskirts.*

This way of dressing lasted until the time of Giambellino,[19] *and some such garments are still seen in the hall of the Great Council. This garment was cut rather wide on the breast, and with it, women began to expose their breast and shoulders, as we still see today. At the same time, another style of coiffure arose, of braiding the hair and binding it up with a certain gold coronet like that of a duchess. In this way women avoided the burden of the excessive ornaments and accessories in use today.*

At their necks they wore strings of coral or silver beads, and often a golden band, some real and some false, according to their wealth. The figure we show here is depicted wearing many jewels, and on the hem at the bottom of her gown is a superb border, with a very long trailing skirt or train. Her underskirt is highly wrought, and on her feet she wears (as far as we can tell) very high pianelle *[slip-on shoes leaving the back of the heel bare]. One can see her overgarment, which had no bodice but was trimmed with gold and was so well fitted that it made the woman look very beautiful and shapely. The sleeves stopped at the elbow, leaving the rest of the arm uncovered except by the* camicia. *I have found this kind of garment in various places, and even though excessive spending was prohibited, the style lasted a long time, as can be clearly seen in later portraits.*

Text on page 113

AN ARMED MAN OF EARLY TIMES,
Four Hundred Years Ago

ecause I mentioned previously that the materials used in clothing include not only wool and silk, but also iron, steel, copper and similar materials, it will not be out of place here (as with the Romans) to show those who are curious the armor formerly used by the Venetians. And if ancient burial monuments can be trusted on this subject, I, who have been a most diligent investigator of them, will also be a faithful witness to what I have been able to gather about this matter. Carvings on such monuments tell us that around the year 1200, as a result of the coming of the Goths, men were all armed in this way. The Goths' suits of armor were similar to ours, from which we can conclude that we took our style of armor from them when this fierce race entered Italy so violently and filled it with destruction and ruin until they were driven out by the great captain Narsete. This courageous captain, a great boon to all our towns, remained in Venice for many days, where, before his departure, he carried out certain vows that he had made.

Soldiers in those times wore armor so heavy that it seems impossible to us today, seeing it, that a man wearing such armor could move around—and moreover that even a strong horse could carry a man so armored. And still today, in the church of San Giovanni and Paolo and the Minor Friars and in other places, the armor of the men of those times is seen, which gives me the evidence to discuss confidently what sort of armor they wore. First of all, they armed themselves with a very heavy, thick shirt of chain mail, and this, to protect the head, came down on both sides to form a hood so capacious that it covered almost the entire face. This shirt was so long and loose that it easily covered the body down to the knees. And to protect the head even better, on top of this hood they wore their helmet, which covered the entire head except for part of the eyes and the nose, the result of a narrow opening that allowed them to see but without leaving this part of the face unprotected. This helmet had the thickness of a finger, and at its lower end it formed a wing at each side, allowing it to rest on the shoulders and so protect the throat and the neck. Many of these helmets, with visors, can still be seen both in the Arsenal and in the meeting room of the Council of Ten, where they are freely displayed as ancient and marvelous things; and there, once, wanting to test the weight of one of these helmets, I found I could hardly lift it. From the head down, a cuirass or corselet covered the shoulders and the chest, and, divided in two below the belt, descended to cover the thighs and the legs, having the same function as schinieri. *On top of this armor they belted on their rapier, and I have also seen some cuirasses to which a dagger reaching to mid-thigh was attached. I must not omit that I have also seen a portrait of the Duke of Saxony wearing this armor painted by Titian (at the request of Charles V); while fighting incognito, he was wounded by this Emperors' soldiers and taken prisoner. He is shown wounded in this portrait, with his hand on his rapier. I saw this portrait being painted by Titian himself, whom I followed at the time as a uniquely able man, in order to learn something about this profession of painting.*

THE EARLY DOGALINA, *OR FULL-SLEEVED GOWN,*
Worn in Venice and Other Cities

Looking into the origin and wearing of wide sleeves, or the garment called the dogalina, *I find that it was more popular among young noblemen than among people of other ages or ranks, and that there was great variety in the way it was worn. But I also seem to remember that the women of those times tried to imitate the style, as previously shown. The one shown here is rather different from the others, and I found it painted in an altarpiece in the monastery of San Domenico in Venice.*

EARLY CLOTHING OF VENICE
and other Italian Cities (Young Men)

I have seen the clothing shown here in paintings not only in Venice but also in other famous cities, so I think I am not wrong to claim that there is a certain similarity between this Venetian garb and that of other cities. As far as its origin is concerned, I would say it came from the garment formerly called the giornea *[a loose, usually sleeveless overgarment]. The garment so named can be seen very clearly in this figure of a man, dressed in a gathered mantle and this full-cut overgament, worn with a very low-set belt. And yet though* giornee *resemble each other and are similar to this one in many ways, they can also differ from one another. At that time young men most often wore full-length stockings, a style that lasted for a long time, as old paintings show. Later they began to cut their hair short and to wear overgarments with long sleeves, narrow at the wrist. This type of sleeve pleased the former inhabitants of our city because of the convenience of carrying many things inside it, depending on what they needed, a convenience still appreciated today. I have also found a few paintings that show men wearing a small cap on their heads, with a long piece of cloth tucked inside it, and pointed shoes or low boots in various colors. The quality and cost of the garments of those times, as is always the case, corresponded to people's wealth, nobility, and custom. And these garments were worn throughout all the cities of Lombardy and in other places up to 1250. The style lasted a long time, even though some of it underwent some small changes.*

VENETIAN CLOTHING AND THE BEGINNING OF SLEEVES À COMEO
[sleeves very full beneath the elbow]

I have thought a great deal about when and where this style of sleeve could have originated, for obviously it was worn in a grand way, even though it was made only of wool, once the short mantle (as it was then called) ceased to be worn. I believe that this change of style occurred for no other reason than the weight of the folds in fuller sleeves, which bothered not only old men, tired out by age, but also young men, because it was hard to walk while wearing them.

I have, I think, explained that people of solid reputation and fond of proper decorum wore long robes in the style of a toga, though different from those today. Thinking about this change, I found that many others had written about it in various ways, in the attempt to explain the origins of this style of dress. Some say that the style came from the Romans, having seen exactly such figures on the Arch of Septimius. Others claim that it came from Cyprus, brought from that island by the French, which I am inclined to believe because of the many lilies, among other designs, embroidered on the sleeves. Better support for this opinion consists of the many wooden panels from this era in Venice, whose carvings offer evidence of the same style. But because this isn't very important to us, I will content myself with having said this much and represent this garment to you, so that you may judge for yourselves the true origin of these elbow-length sleeves, which in those days were very short. Perhaps they were more readily adopted because of their comfort by the young and by those who enjoyed the games and dances popular in those days. At this time they began to wear round hats, but much higher than those worn earlier and by the nobility today. They wore belts of the width of three fingers at their hips, as is done today. And following this style of dress, the full-length toga was gradually introduced, which (as seen in our time) won such respect that it was embraced by all noblemen and citizens. And doctors who live in Venice, as well as all those who engage in skillful and honorable professions, still wear it. I will not forego saying, before I finish, that people in those days wore stockings colored differently from their clothing, and their shoes were pavonazzo. *All of this can be seen in the church of San Giovanni and Paolo in Venice, in the altarpiece to the right of the entrance to the choir stalls.*

Text on page 118

THE EARLY CLOTHING OF YOUNG MEN

his clothing, in which a certain purity and simplicity can be discerned, was very similar to that worn by young boys in our time. And truly, one must assume that the young men of that time were so honorable and far from any evil-doing that they refrained from carnal delights until the age of thirty (as far as one can believe) and remained pure and uncorrupted, for the clothing they wore permits no other conclusion. They wore their hair as long as it would grow, and made great efforts to keep it beautiful and shiny, but in a way that imitated the cleanliness and neatness of churchmen rather than the vanity and frivolity of women. And this hair, when it was worn with a circlet of velvet or some other material of silk or gold, was a sign of the virginity of the young man who wore it. They wore a doublet open in front, full on top and narrow below, which was tied with a belt or silk cord, as is done by women in our day. The sleeves of this doublet were wide down to the elbow, then tight down to the wrist. Underneath they wore a gathered camicia *with a wide, round neck, which they let show in front, as is the fashion with our women today. Their stockings, which were called* à brasola *[sewn up behind] because of a certain rear fold or panel set into them, fitted closely to the leg and came up as high as the hips, where they were tied up with* stringhe *[woven, braided or otherwise decorated laces]. And in front and back, where the stockings were still separate and had a space in between, they stretched a flap or crosspiece that covered the exposed parts, a style maintained up to our days in many places in the stockings of young boys. But these stockings were divided into contrasting colors, since they were made of vertical strips, and the doublet was divided into strips in the same way.*

In those times, in certain companies of young men who devoted themselves to dancing, fencing, and other physical activities, each young man wore his stockings and doublet in the colors belonging to his company, just as we see livery worn today. The tradition of these companies has lasted among young noblemen up to our day, and this clothing may be the origin and reference point of the famous company that in former years was called the Compagnia della Calza *[the company or club of tights-wearers]. And here, to say frankly what I believe will be for the pleasure of all, I will digress a bit from my topic. It is said that during the festivities that young men held in those days, dancing was the custom. These parties and dances were also attended and observed by older men, who had not at all lost their taste for dancing, nor the memories of the delights they had enjoyed during their youth. And seeing styles so different from those of their day, they scorned and disapproved of them, and wanting to show the young how much more beautiful and lovely the old ways were, they threw off their overgarments and so, in their doublets, presumptuously tried to re-educate the young (since everyone scorns the customs of others and loves his own). For this they were jeered at by the young men and forced to leave, with kicks ringing in their ears. From this fact originated the masquerades with masks called* Barbachiepi *or* Mattacini *[beard-snatchers or buffoons], which presented these gallant old men's actions and the beatings they gave and received—and their reputation for gaiety gave us this show, much enjoyed by everyone among the other spectacles of Carnival.*

CLOTHING OF A YOUNG MAN
of Early Venice

About the same time there was a custom among young men to wear another kind of clothing, slightly different from the last in that, while their stockings were similarly made, the combination of more than two colors was not seen. On top, they wore a short garment, or gavardina *[lightweight, short overgarment], which was laced up in front with a certain kind of ribbon and had rather fuller sleeves; this overgarment, made of panels of two different colors, covered the rear halfway down. They wore their hair long and cared for it with the same diligence I mentioned earlier.*

SOLDIERS AND BRAVI *[HIRED RETAINERS OR STRONGMEN] of Early Times*

Once the young men had laid aside the activities I spoke of earlier—dancing, jumping, and fencing—they moved to military exercises on sea and on land. And certainly, as experience and annals of the past show us, this earned them much higher praise. They wore (as I far as I can discover) full-length stockings striped in four colors, with the seams and panels running lengthwise. The doublet was similar to the one worn by young men that we saw before, but the neckline ended in a wide collar that came halfway down the breast, and the two sides were tied together under the arm with two laces. The doublet, too, was striped in different colors, as I recall having seen in many places. This clothing had much in common with the German and the Swiss style, with sleeves down to the elbow, a red cap, a long cape, and a hood, as seen in this illustration. They wore a broad sword at their side and, in front, a purse, next to which they also carried a dagger. They were highly trained in the art of swordplay and fighting, to the extent that, standing up, they could seize a man by any part of his body and toss him over with their leg so nimbly that they seemed only to be tossing a feather. And through such skill they made people think of them as brave men of valor.

69

CLOTHING OF THE COMPAGNIA DELLE CALZE
[The Company of Tights-wearers]

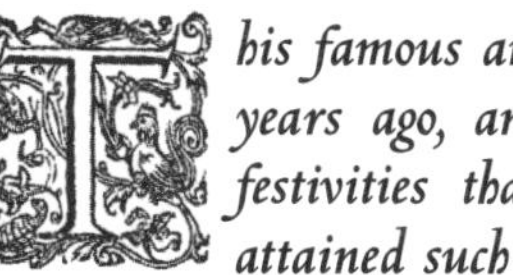

his famous and honored club had its origins many years ago, and it established such spectacles and festivities that no other group of our time has attained such a level of magnificence and splendor; many people still living attest to this fact. The members of these companies, as is still the case today, were all noblemen, but this particular club was much more distinguished and famous than any previous or since, for many sons of great princes are said to have been elected to membership in it. It first appeared in the reign of Doge Zeno, in the 1400s, because at that time many young noblemen from the principal families of the city, having raised a large sum of money and selected a distinguished elite from their ranks, named the group the Compagnia delle Calze*.*

Throughout the period in which this group flourished, each one of its members wore stockings striped in different colors, and they were recognized as members of the club by this shared symbol. But each member also announced his own particular mood and character with some witty and beautiful personal symbol that suited his disposition. In addition, a noble and honorable competition and rivalry arose among them over who was best and most lavishly dressed, each one displaying splendor and magnificence at his own expense, even though they all joined together to organize festivities and public spectacles with money they raised and combined for this purpose. This money was not used only for worldly shows, for they also wanted to demonstrate their liberality and spirituality in religious worship. So they chose a church where they met at certain times and in it, decorated with pomp and royal splendor, they attended a solemn mass of the Holy Spirit, which they had priests perform at their expense. The fame of this club roused the spirit of generosity in the young men of other cities, where they began to do the same thing.

The clothing we see here included, in the lining of the long, pointed hood hanging down the back, the club's insignia, embroidered in gold and silk. And all the members of the club wore another symbol, a slashed red or black hat tipped over the ear, and their hair, grown as long and thick as possible, was tied with a silk cord. They wore doublets of velvet, silk or cloth of gold, as shown in this illustration. The sleeves were attached with very thick silk or gold ties with tips of heavy gold and cut at mid-length, and through this cut the camicia showed through. And for the sake of luxury they used more ties than they needed on these tights in order to show their wealth as much as the shape of their waists, by means of stockings so closely fitted that they showed almost all their muscles, as if they were completely naked. These stockings, as we have already said, were divided lengthwise into various colors, and one section was embroidered with pearls and other gems up to the middle of the leg. The outfit that I have seen portrayed had a siren in the back of the hood, the device, I believe, of the man in the portrait. In this portrait, which I found in the Scuola of San Giovanni Evangelista,[20] can also be seen, painted in an ancient style but by a skilled hand, the custom they had of carrying a perfumed ball. And in this same place I found a picture of many other figures, which I will reproduce in the course of this work.

Text on page 123

DRESS OF FOREIGNERS and of the City of Venice

In all times most new styles of dress, for both men and women, originate with rulers. This can be clearly seen in the beards called Philippine and the French style of curled hair.[21] So it is no wonder that in our time such a great variety of clothing exists.

I recall seeing a style of dress painted by a skillful hand in the church of Santa Maria in Cividal di Belluno [the main town of Belluno], among many other kinds of clothing I saw in the same painting. This was a woman's ensemble, including a very full mantle worn with solemnity and grace over the shoulders. The overgarment was full-length, with narrow sleeves, and bound under the breast, showing great modesty; and in my opinion, this was the dress of a married woman. The color of the mantle I saw was white, covered with needlework, and the overgarment was of other colors, cremesino *or* pavonazzo, *a color much esteemed in those days and in ours. The coiffure consisted of curled hair and golden ties. Next to this figure was another in the same clothing, but with a mantle worn over the head, which, falling to the ground, covered her undergarment entirely, so that she looked more like a widow than a married woman. The clothing I have set here is quite different, because this has very full sleeves, almost in the style of the* dogalina, *but with a second opening below the hand, probably put there in order to allow something to be kept in the sleeve. This seems to be the figure of a maiden, of marvelous beauty, and her posture very much resembles the others.*

The overgarment is porpora *in color, lined with fur and gathered under the breast.*

Text on page 124

THE DRESS OF EARLY VENICE
and Other Cities of Italy

It is likely that this clothing was very popular in its time and that it was worn by a lady of very high rank. And though I have seen it here in Venice and elsewhere, especially in Cividal di Belluno (where it was painted on the façade of a very old house on which portraits like this can be seen, though different in certain ways), I decided to show this one of a woman. Because of the little dog she has in her arms, the antiquity and richness of her accessories, and the graceful appearance she presents, she can be assumed to be a lady of high rank. Her headdress was made of a white veil, bound with finger-wide strips of red silk, and a second veil fell to her shoulders. Her gown was full, and as far as I could tell, open on the sides and gathered in front, covering her at the back, and as it reached the ground, it narrowed down almost into the shape of a sleeve, but a sleeve cut open; and the gown had bracciali *[shoulder rolls] of another color. She also wore a collar apparently made of marten or some other kind of fur, suited to what the season called for.*

In the same place I noticed another portrait, quite different from this, of a lady whose headdress was covered at the top with a veil, which fell most gracefully from her shoulders. She wore dogalina *sleeves, closed and almost floor-length, and her undergarment, too, fitted snugly across her breast.*

Near these two women were two young men clothed in different styles, but I have not illustrated them, to prevent this book from becoming too large; it will be enough to describe them, as far as possible. One of them, then, wore a hat pointed in front, like one that I saw first in the palace at Padua; turned up at the back, it revealed his long, thick hair. Both of them wore the overgarment called a giornea, *but differently. One had the form of a doublet, but wide and full of folds, padding out the chest down to the legs. The belt was a half-foot wide, divided into sections by large studs and slashes all the way around, like those now worn by Frenchmen. I saw that his stockings were full-length, worn with mid-calf boots, which had pointed toes almost a half foot long; and his arms, outside the doublet or, rather, the short overgarment, were clothed with sleeves to the elbow, very beautifully trimmed with a long fold that fell to the backs of his knees. His* camicia *was gathered high at the neck and fastened with five buttons. The dress of the second young man was almost like that of the other lord, including a hat with vertical slashes and a belt with silver clasps, but not so wide as the first. He wore full-length stockings with boots on top, similar to the other man's. The overgarments of both were of different colors, but both ended above the knee.*

THE CLOTHING OF YOUNG AND MIDDLE-AGED MEN in Early Times

I recall having found certain hats an arm's length high, turned up at the back, and altogether of a highly bizarre shape, and also caps made with many pleats, but very wide and tagliate *[slashed]. These existed in so many different styles that they would fill a whole specialized book. But I would like, nonetheless, to shed some light briefly on the subject, first to show that I have some information about it and also to satisfy the curious who would like to know a little more. So I have made a drawing of what I have judged most to the point. These caps were of various colors, as can still be seen in Padua, Venice, Cividal di Belluno, and many other places where I have found them painted, and especially in the house of Signor Pagano Pagani, an excellent doctor and my most illustrious lord, whose clan is truly ancient and noble. I have also seen the same style in other noble and large houses, thanks to the courtesy of their owners, who have given me hospitality and reminded and informed me about many of the early styles of clothing worn in their ancient home territories. Among those worthy of praise are the two brothers Signor Antonio and Tristano Ecchali or Carpedoni, the leading men of their region, men of singular virtue, exemplary customs and mature judgment, and no less rich in their quality of soul than in the goods of fortune. All of these men have given me the occasion for this little digression, as a sign of my gratitude.*

So, returning to our subject, I say that paintings, lost through the passage of time, cannot provide as exact information on these matters as might be wished for. Therefore I must depend on faint records (hints, even) derived from Greek remains. This clothing, then, appeared among many figures of women and young men above certain arches set into cassoni *[low wooden chests], painted and ornamented on the outside, and filled inside with the possessions and clothing of brides, given to them as dowries and gifts. And the image seen here was the portrait of a married man, with one of these red caps. He had a garment of* damasco *with sleeves very full at the elbow, as shown here. But so little detail can be made out in the figure that we can scarcely guess what the rest was. This would not be the case if painting, five hundred years ago, had enjoyed the same status it had had under Alexander the Great, who liked it so much, although it seems that in our time it is beginning to recover the status and win back the honor in which it was held among the ancient Greeks, who refused to let anyone practice the art of painting unless he was noble or at least rich. In this way they hoped to prevent anyone from painting for pay or to earn a living, and anyone who expected to paint had to have the leisure and resources to study and to produce works as excellent as those known to be by Apelles and others. But now painting seems to have attained such a high point that little more can be hoped for. Painters now are so eager to imitate nature that they no longer think it worthwhile to paint a clothed figure; so, concentrating on nudes, they avoid representing any kind of clothing as much as they can. And when they do represent a clothed body, they make every effort to treat it in such a way that under the faint shadows, or rather veils, formed by clothing, we see the nude body distinctly revealed, with all the muscles of the anatomy in every possible perspective—so we almost see what cannot actually be seen. If, then, I have not at the outset systematically described the diversity of the world's clothing, though we must believe it is very great, pardon me.*

Text on page 127

SOLDIERS AND MEN OF ARMS at the Time of the Emperor Rudolph

I have noticed and verified that the armor of soldiers, like the clothing of other people, is subject to change, for some are seen in knee-length coats of chain mail and a hood of mail, and above it a very heavy helmet, with a breastplate and iron greaves, and thigh pieces of metal, buckled on at mid-thigh. Yet I have found other men dressed only in a corselet and a knee-length coat of chain mail. I have spoken of all this elsewhere, so now I will go on to describe and show what else can be discovered on this subject regarding wars of both sea and land. First, in maritime warfare, cuirasses were worn very often because they were a comfortable and manageable form of armor in combat involving many men; examples are preserved in the Arsenal of Venice and in the meeting room of the Council of Ten, displayed as a rare and marvelous thing among the other marvels of the city of Venice, where the armor of the many brave warriors who accompanied Prince Ziani and many other doges can also be seen. The armor there consists almost entirely of cuirasses, richly ornamented, covered with cloth of gold, cremesino *velvet and other fabrics and colors beautiful to the eye, as well as gold brocades enriched with fringes and beautiful embroideries. These cuirasses are molded precisely to the body, not very long, with two wings in front to protect the thighs. The helmets are covered with small caps of velvet and gold, and some are studded with gems.*

To speak specifically of the leaders, they wore corselets, greaves, and armpieces; such armor was not used much by warriors of ancient times, and especially not in naval battles, as can be seen very clearly from the figures created by the hands of excellent painters. So, wanting to discover the truth about this, I looked for and found various suits of armor, some of which resemble those of today. Determined to track down some bust or old breastplate, I finally found, on a tomb in the church of Saint Helena, two armed male figures that I liked a great deal and from them I took this breastplate, similar to a Roman one, but which guards and preserves life better. These figures are of two brothers of the Loredan family, noble Venetians, who, as brave warriors, won so much praise on both sea and land that even today they are still deservedly famous—in the same way the statues that represent them were made by a learned and expert hand so that nothing should be lacking in the immortalization of their name. These two brothers belonged to the family that also produced a doge in our days, the most serene Pietro,[22] from whom is descended his son, the famous Signor Alvise Loredano, who for his skills and generosity obtained all the greatest honors that the Senate is accustomed to give the best men. And from God he received many children of whom much is to be hoped, among whom the famous Giovanni shines for his unique wisdom and exemplary way of life, shown in the dignity and good organization with which he has taken on important political assignments.

THE DRESS OF AN ARMED MAN,
Carefully Painted from Life by Luigi Vivarino

The dress of the armed man shown here is taken from a canvas painted from life by the hand of Luigi Vivarino.[23] *It is the portrait of a certain Giorgio, whose armor is of the style worn two hundred years ago, and it shows an armed man with his lance at rest. Under this armor they used to wear a shirt of fine-gauge chain mail, hanging to the knee; its final touch was a* piccatura *[border] of mail, which equaled in beauty and delicacy those worn by both Roman foot soldiers and cavalry. And just as nations have varied in their styles of armor, and there are also variations within nations, it can be seen that some of these men wore short cuirasses and others much longer ones. So it appears that armor, though different in its details, still tends more or less toward the same form. Other men wore breastplates covered with overgarments displaying the livery and the emblems of their captains.*

EARLY DRESS OF CERTAIN VENETIAN WOMEN

I have found this clothing in different territories and cities, in both public and private buildings, similar in every way except for the headdresses. The clothing I show here, which is more that of a woman of religion than that of a woman of the world, I found in an altarpiece in the Church of the Carmine in Venice, and in the nunnery of Santa Caterina in the same city. I must say, however, that I have found no such style of dress described by any writer. The headdress has the shape of horns and it reaches down over the ears. Some women in these images also cover their heads with a very thin veil and wear a floor-length garment with full, open sleeves in the style of the dogalina, *and as far as one can tell, they wear black. Others are shown wearing a narrow, short mantle, turned back over their shoulders, with narrow sleeves but a colored* sottana. *I still think these were women of the spirit, devoted to piety, though in other places I have also seen the same style of clothing in various colors, enriched and embellished with decorations of silk, with* damasco *especially common. This might arise from the fact that these women, though dedicated to the spiritual life, were of great wealth and rank, which I hope to show later in the proper time and place.*

THE PRINCE, OR DOGE, of Venice

*ince I must speak of the great and venerable majesty of the prince of Venice, I will take as my example the good and virtuous Doge Veniero,[24] who serves as the model from which I have taken the dress I show you here, intending also to mention his successor, Nicolò da Ponte. But to begin with this first man, it can truthfully be said that his virtues raised him not only to the highest rank in his homeland but also earned him the fame of being celebrated by the pens of all writers. This man, unanimously elected as prince to the great joy of all as a sign of favor calling for the greatest admiration and as evidence of the greatness of his merits, followed the custom of other princes and dressed in cloth of gold. At times his clothing was red and at others it was white, according to the ceremonies that he had to honor with his presence, except for days sacred to the glorious Virgin, to whom he was deeply devoted and during which he always appeared wearing white. But this was a custom not so much started by him as by other princes of Venice, for on those days they always wanted to symbolize the innocent purity of the Immaculate Virgin, Mother of Grace, with such clothing. And we know as well that the Doge Celsi wore white not only for these ceremonies, but also at all other times.[25] This fact is mentioned by many writers, to whom can be added the testimony of Sansovino,[26] and together they attest that this Prince Celsi was a man of the greatest piety. Now to speak of the dress shown here, I say that it was the norm from the blessed era of Doge Ziani, when Pope Alexander III was in Venice in the year 1176, at the same time that the Emperor Frederick Barbarossa*

threatened his reign.[27] *At this time the doges wore a floor-length mantle and with it an undergarment of the same length with a train, a style that continued for a very long time. The mantle, the undergarment, and the* corno *were of red velvet with gold trim. But whoever wants to know the whole truth about the origin of their style of dress should read Sansovino in his new book on Venice.*

Here can be seen the shape of the doge's corno, *which is of the same color as his robe, except that when his robe is* cremesino, *his hat is trimmed with gold. And often they also wear a short cape of ermine, which covers their chest and shoulders and is fastened in front with gold buttons, a beautiful sight. The doge's mantle is very full and falls to the ground, and under it he wears a belted undergarment of the same material and length, decorated with gold trim. On his feet he wears* pianelle *of the same kind worn by the noble knights of Venice. And this is the dress worn by present-day doges and past doges in their public appearances, when they are accompanied by large escorts of senators, knights, and their own ministers.*

THE CORONATION OF THE PRINCE OF VENICE

It seems reasonable to me, after having shown what the doges of Venice wore, to make some mention of their coronation ceremony. In this, which includes a great number of rituals, they wear on their heads a corno *of very great value, which is otherwise almost always kept in the treasury chamber. And this* corno, *according to those experienced in such matters, is estimated to have a value of 150,000 ducats. It is carried in procession on the solemn day of Corpus Christi and worn by the new prince throughout the day of his coronation.*

THE DOGARESSA
or Princess of Venice

I cannot find during past centuries that any princesses have left us any record of their dress. I think, however, that their clothing was similar to that already mentioned as worn by ancient noblewomen. The first that I ever saw was Cecilia Dandola, the wife of Doge Lorenzo Priuli,[28] *who made an entrance of great beauty and solemn splendor; in order to witness the spectacle all the guilds converged on the piazza, and the entire palace was decorated with carpets and the finest tapestries and various hangings of silk. With great magnificence, tables were laden with silver and gold vessels. When she entered the palace, she crossed the courtyards with great majesty and visited every place where such tables were set. She walked along accompanied by senators and by her relatives, all grandly dressed. To serve her, 230 noblewomen were chosen, all wearing white silk and adorned with pearls and other jewels. The meeting room of the Great Council was given over to balls, with large musical ensembles and very lovely concerts. At the end of these a sumptuous meal was set out with a great number of different dishes. The princess was dressed in ducal fashion, with a gown of fine gold brocade, on top of which she wore a floor-length mantle with a very long, wide train. The* corno *she wore on her head was studded with a great number of jewels and trimmed with a very thin silk veil, transparent throughout, which allowed the hat it covered to be seen. At her neck she wore a string of valuable pearls, but more wondrous than all the rest was a jewel of inestimable price hanging down to her breast from a gold necklace interlaid with many other jewels. Her belt was in the form of a chain, which, first encircling her upper body, then fell to her feet. Her robe was completely open in front down to the ground and it was completely lined with ermine. This was the dress seen in her solemn entrance, similar to one of more recent memory, that of the Princess Mocenigo, who can be seen now also wearing a cross on her breast. And after her came the Princess Venier, wife of Prince Sebastiano. The clothing that these Princesses wear in private and at home is the* dogalina, *a full-sleeved gown, of velvet or of* cremesino *satin, depending on their preference, under which they wear a similar gown, and a* corno *of the same fabric on their head, but encircled with a golden band.*

Text on page 134

CLOTHING WORN BY THE EARLY LORDS OF CARRARA
and Other Gentlemen of Italy

Because I have seen paintings of the dress shown here in many places, on wooden panels and on walls, I wanted to represent it here and place it among the other illustrations. I do this all the more willingly because I have discovered that this man belongs to the Carrara family, lords of Padua, as far as can be gathered from other portraits of him. This lord wore a floor-length mantle, and in the portrait I saw, he is shown with a hand on a standard. Next to him could be seen another man, in a long-waisted doublet and full-length stockings, which covered his body up to his belt (which was of silk, six fingers in width, with gold and silver buckles). In the same painting are other figures, with long mantles, and caps in the style seen here; they could better be called headdresses, made of velvet or a similar material and wrapped around the head, with one part falling down behind the shoulders. Around the hem of the gown, worn open at the sides in the style used today by the Capitano Grande *of Venice, are decorations in the form of lacework. This was the dress of the lords of Padua, in keeping with their pride and grandeur, a rich and splendid style. And it seems that Ezzelino, too, famous for his cruelty, wore the same garments.*[29]

Text on page 135

PAST CLOTHING OF NOBLE KNIGHTS, not only in Venice and Milan but in all of Lombardy

The proverb says that he who seeks shall find, and the honest desire with which I have set myself the task of researching the variety of clothing has not proved to be in vain. Among other forms of dress I have found this one, common not only to the noble knights of Venice but also to others in Lombardy. I am informed that the dress shown here was also worn by the Latins in many regions of Italy, and especially in Lombardy, by knights, doctors and other men of this kind. To be brief, I found this design sculpted on a tomb, among many others, in the ancient church of San Giovanni and Paolo in Venice, though the figure was so eaten away by time that its form could hardly be made out. I have also seen this dress carved in certain reliefs in the palace of San Marco, and I think I can conclude from these things that it has been in use for six hundred years. In addition I saw it carved on the capital of one of the columns of the same palace, along with many others, which are surrounded by Turkish, Moorish, Saracen, Arabic, Tartar and Latin letters; the Latin figure there wears a headdress like the one shown here. I have seen, too, a knight and a doctor dressed in this style on tombs in the ancient city of Belluno, while in Cadore I was shown a portrait of a knight dressed in this way, and to my eye not only the garment but the cap were pavonazzo *in color. I know that people of similar rank in this time also wore the color* porpora *and vair skins, along with other ornaments, and undergarments of the same color with narrow sleeves, buttoned up to the elbow. So it can be said that this kind of clothing was worn more or less throughout the whole of Italy.*

Text on page 136

EARLY CLOTHING OF VENETIAN SENATORS

The clothing shown here was worn by the senators of Venice more than two hundred years ago. It includes a long gown, toga-style, but not yet with full ducal sleeves, as is the case now. Some people say that only doctors wore this cap with cloth hanging from it, but it seems to me that they are in error, for they were worn not only by doctors but by all noblemen and even citizens. Indeed, we know that such dress was already very common, worn (though with certain variations) by all people of rank. The piece of cloth worn on the cap fell to the shoulders, and I think that it was also worn wrapped around the cap. But because a certain disease of the eyes arose in that time, for which the doctors blamed this piece of cloth, it was removed and separated from the cap as unnecessary, and worn instead over the shoulder, as the stole is now worn in the city of Venice. And because old men are generally of poor health and weak constitutions, they sometimes wore it, especially in times of great cold, on their heads and wrapped around their necks. Images of this style can be seen in the meeting room of the Great Council in the palazzo of Venice. This hood was also worn by the princes, over the corno. *As to the robes of senators, they were always made of velvet,* damasco, *and silk, and were* pavonazzo *in color.*

Text on page 137

AMBASSADORS AND CONSULS SENT TO SYRIA and Other Parts of the World

It was an ancient custom of the Venetian Republic, from the beginning of its expansion, that when they sent their consuls and ambassadors to Syria and other parts of the world, they chose men of a certain seriousness, able to maintain and represent the authority and status conferred upon them by the Republic. In Syria, especially, they were admired, respected and kindly treated by the sultan; and in these regions of the infidel, they dispensed justice and presided over civil lawsuits arising among Christians. To return to our subject of clothing, it is written that when one of these consuls or ambassadors went to see Campson Gauri,[30] *summoned by the sultan himself, he was accompanied by a certain Vittorio Scarpe,*[31] *a most skillful painter of the time; he had the chance to record this clothing better than any other painters had done until then, as he saw it, and as I illustrate it for you in this volume. The ambassadors wore a floor-length gown of light wool, with a full mantle fastened at the shoulder with golden buttons and open all the way down on the left side, with a gold chain at the neck, rich with many jewels. Under the mantle they wore a* sottana *in the style of senators' robes, with open sleeves, especially when he had to speak with the great lord. In those days this was the dress of the ambassadors of the Republic, worn by generals, too, who also wore the ducal cap, as will be seen in the clothing of the modern-day general, taken from the portrait of General Venier, which appears later in this volume. But to return to the consul in Syria, although one is still posted there today, he does not dress in this way, for this grandeur and splendor have been better preserved by those who preside as* Baili *in Constantinople*[32]*—or, more precisely, shifted over to them, because the great lord of the Turks has occupied all those lands, with the result that all the magnificence of all the neighboring provinces has been transferred to Constantinople.*

EARLY CLOTHING OF THE NOBLEWOMEN OF VENICE

From the many kinds of clothing that I have found and copied from paintings in churches and other places in Venice, I have chosen to show you this one, which seems to me to have been worn by noblewomen and in my view is very beautiful. This costume was worn up to the time of the excellent painter Giovanni Bellini. I have seen many examples of the kind of figure shown here, which are of women; it seems that when they left home, they didn't wear veils on their heads. And this woman, whom I have depicted because she is the most beautiful, was dressed in cremesino *velvet and wore long, narrow sleeves almost reaching the ground; her gown is open, but not entirely, and leaves her breast and shoulders bare, but in a modest way, for as much as is revealed by the gown itself is covered again with a very fine, transparent veil of white silk. She wears very narrow short sleeves down to the elbow, made, I think, of cloth of gold, with the rest of her arm covered only by her* camicia. *The gown is pulled back into two folds, which descend into a train two arms in length. The rest of the skirt is full, but the bodice is very closely fitted and belted with a chain of gold. Her head was beautifully dressed in a style very different from the one we use today, because instead of curls, which now stand upright in the shape of horns, we see the hair here falling onto the forehead and some of it tied and braided with colored ribbons, a becoming addition to the loveliness of the figure. In addition to this braiding, the hair is gathered up into a band or circlet of gold, decorated with pearls and other jewels. On their necks such women wore golden chains, but with loops from which hung pearls. I have a portrait miniature of this very style, which is very beautiful.*

VENETIAN CITIZENS OR MERCHANTS in Syria

In Syria and nearby places, Venetian citizens used to engage in more trade than they do today. At that time, then, these places were full of regal-looking merchants who for the most part dressed in a doublet of velvet or cremesino *satin, bordered with contrasting colors and without a collar. They wore red or black or* pavonazzo *stockings with velvet shoes. Their overgarment was of the kind drawn here, with long sleeves lined with velvet or satin, collarless but with a* pettorale *[plackard, or chest covering], which covered the opening and was tied under the arms with silk laces. They wore a gathered* camicia*, a style that lasted for a long time afterward in Italy, and its gathers showed above the plackard. At this time martingale stockings flourished, as well as velvet shoes, and under the gown a belt with silver trim was worn with a knife attached to it with small chains, also of silver. The style of martingale stockings was this: behind, they were left open, as with children, but a piece of fabric broad enough to cover the entire opening was sewn over one thigh and tied with a lace on the other thigh, and this was so well designed that it seemed to be part and parcel of the crotch of the stockings. This way of dressing was very convenient, as anyone can imagine, for once the lace was untied, this piece of cloth fell open and left a man free to do his business while leaving his stockings attached to his doublet.*

CLOTHING AND CUSTOMS OF THE BRIDES of Early Venice

Paintings show the dress of the brides of early Venice decorated in various ways, but no less varied, we may believe, than they were throughout the rest of Italy, for all women naturally delight in outshining others in their dress. But from the many paintings I have seen, I assemble in this volume those that seem worth studying, and especially those in the company or congregation of San Giovanni Evangelista, where I have found many styles drawn from life by skilled and ancient hands. There one sees many brides depicted, wearing a crown in the style of a queen, laden with pearls and jewels, and with a similarly ornamented circlet around the head. Under this crown is attached a thin and transparent shoulder-length veil, and the hair is not curled but worn loose, with part of it falling forward over the ears in a beautiful fashion. On their ears they wore three pendant pearls joined in one earring and set in gold, and at their necks an ornament of gems and gold along with lace. From the same images we can see that their shoulders and breasts were uncovered, since it was then the custom to reveal the whiteness of the skin of that part of the body. From this golden necklace hung a little jeweled chain that fell down and disappeared between the breasts, which were covered with a pettorale *of cloth of gold, which they wore on top of their bodice; and this* pettorale *was needleworked all over with pearls and decorated with other jewels at its center. The sleeves, open at the elbow, matched the* pettorale*, which was tied on under the arms with a hem decorated with gold trim. Some of these* pettorali *can be seen in the treasury of San Marco, displayed during important festivals. They were widely worn in that time by queens and ladies of high rank.*

The gown, according to the woman's rank and the nobility of her blood, was of gold or silver or dyed silk, over which she wore a tunic of very fine, transparent white silk, which also covered her breast. They wore a very heavy gold chain that, though fastened, hung down below the waist and completed the combined splendor and beauty of this style. In this fashion they were accustomed to go to San Pietro di Castello, the patriarchal church of Venice, with admirable propriety and piety, to receive, on a particular day, the blessing of the Patriarch there; then they returned to their husbands' houses.

But this custom of leading brides to San Pietro di Castello reminds me of a similar incident, that of the Sabine women carried off by the Romans, which I think no one will mind my mentioning here. To begin the story a bit further back, in early times each parish of Venice had the custom each year of marrying off one maiden of the parish, for whom everyone was asked to contribute to a dowry. However, in the year 944, or 943 according to the Venetian calendar, it happened that all the brides came together to San Pietro di Castello, on the day of the Translation of Saint Mark, celebrated on the last day of January, according to the custom and with the purpose mentioned above, each one bringing with her for display all the possessions she had acquired from her parish or contrade *[district]. While the brides were being shown to the young men of the city in the piazza of the church, suddenly there appeared a galley and a brig full of well-armed men from Trieste, and they carried off the maidens and all the goods they had with them by force. These men of Trieste left with this booty, while the young men of Venice, who had come to their marriages unarmed and unprepared for battle, were unable to oppose them. The Triestini then stopped in a place not far from Venice called I Tre Porti (The Three Gates) and there they divided up the booty. But the young men of Venice who had come to Castello, each intending to marry the maiden who had most pleased him (for this was the way of placing such maidens), considering themselves seriously offended and insulted, armed as many ships as they could with great speed and set off in pursuit of the Triestini, and after fighting with them, they recovered both stolen goods and maidens. The captain of this undertaking was Doge Pietro Candiano,*[33] *a man of valor who had fought in many battles, and from this one he returned home victorious with his young men, having cut all the Triestini into pieces. And some believe that after this event he attacked the city of Trieste and conquered it, and imposed a tribute of one hundred amphoras of wine per year.*

MARRIAGEABLE YOUNG WOMAN of Those Times

When young women were ready to marry they went about with their chest and shoulders bare, though it can be seen from this portrait that they covered up their breasts. I have seen many similar sets of clothing, though varying in some details, but I have used only this one because I find it more refined in style than the others, especially for its coiffure, and also richer. This maiden wears a very short bodice, which scarcely covers the most beautiful part of her breast; around her bodice emerges the lace of her camicia *in a style that makes the shoulders look very lovely, especially in full-figured, fleshy women. The bodice is bordered all the way around with cloth of gold or some other valuable trim, which is also enriched with gold and jewels; another similar strip, though longer, goes down the middle of the bodice. They wore sleeves of various kinds, and I remember having seen them with gold sleeves and bodices with many pearls; and these sleeves were open behind, embroidered, and fastened with gold buttons, and in these openings the* camicia *could also be seen. The gowns were floor-length and of whatever color pleased the wearer, no one color being worn more than another. The woman I show you here had a* rochetto *[a long, narrow, sleeveless overgarment] of gathered, transparent white silk, divided into two panels tied to the belt; it was woven with designs, which gave it beauty and made it a joy to the eye. I have also found and observed other figures wearing this dress in many places not worth mentioning.*

ANOTHER MAIDEN
in a Different Style of Dress

*hough it is not very different from the clothing discussed above I will discuss this style of dress here because I think it will please you to see it. The portrait in which I saw it was by the hand of Giovanni Bellini, a rare and excellent painter from those times. This costume, however, differs in hairstyle, because in this one the forehead is framed by small curls, made from forward-growing locks. This woman has a* sottana *in the style of a* carpetta*, woven and embroidered with various colors, but with the bodice similar in cut to the previous one; its opening has the shape of a perfect triangle and is full of interwoven patterns, with a border ornamented with pearls. On their shoulders they wore a thin, transparent gold veil, the neck adorned as in the first case, but also with a hanging jewel. It can be seen that in those times they wore gold wires in their ears, with two or more pearls. The gown had sleeves of various colors, open at the elbow and trimmed with various ornaments. I recall having seen these beautiful styles of dress in paintings by Vivarini, in which can still be seen the habit of wearing* carpette *tied at the shoulders and decorated with gold trim, richly embroidered. This* carpetta *encircled the breast, as bodices do today, and it was worn loose, like a nun's* pazienzia *[a long, sleeveless overgown], with an ample, full-length skirt, and open under the armpits, beginning to close at the hips and onward down to the feet. Their hair is seen falling down to their shoulders, and on their head they wear a crown of the kind we see today in paintings of the Holy Virgin.*

REFORMED AND MORE MODEST DRESS

Among the items I have been researching, I find that soon after this [when Bellini painted the previous figure], clothing began to be more modest and not as rich and ostentatious. It is plausible that this change arose from some new prohibition of the kind often passed in our time in order to correct excessive extravagance in dress. My reason for saying this is that I remember having seen an image of the clothing illustrated here a few days after the previous image, or at the same time. I saw this portrait in a fresco—the hair and head were covered with a black veil that fell down the back, just below the shoulders. The bodice was very short, with half-length colored sleeves of velvet or satin or some other silk cloth, although some—indeed many—women wore sleeves of cloth of gold, the rest of the gown being made of some other material, though still colored. The overgarment was black, but I have not yet found out of what material it was made. It was evidently open in front, and through that opening the sottana *could be seen; this lacked a bodice but had a long train, though I have found that in those times trains were not worn long but held up and attached to the belt or to the edges of pockets—which were being used for the first time, though their use continued for a very long time afterward.*

VENETIAN CLOTHING OF FORMER TIMES, From Only a Hundred Years Ago or Slightly More

Women a hundred years ago wore this attire, and I am certain of this because during this time it began to be painted and shown in portraits in various places. This style was worn in Venice and beyond, and though it includes a short bodice it is still more comfortable than our present-day long bodices, which, while they may give women a slimmer silhouette, cause discomfort. And I recall, for this happened in my own time, that these new bodices reached such an extreme that the Magistrato sopra le Pompe *[the committee appointed to see that sumptuary laws were obeyed] had to intervene, for such bodices were being worn long and broad beyond all measure, and with iron stays set into them to hold in the waist more tightly. Warnings were issued that this was the cause of many injuries to pregnant women, and so it was prohibited by law and discontinued, along with many other styles of dress and hair. On their heads they wore a* gabbia *[a high, stiff headdress], as shown in the drawing, of gold or silver thread or plain silk, woven with beautiful designs. Some women decorated these headdresses with pearls and other jewels, but they all wore their hair loose, uncurled, and in its natural color. And for this reason the women of that time are to be commended for their wisdom, as well as for the fact that their complexions appeared whiter. At their necks they wore necklaces and strings of pearls with golden pendants, which hung to the breast in the shape of a rose, and from their shoulders to their elbows hung large, very expensive, sleeves. Their gowns were colored and sometimes multi-colored, with horizontal strips of various hues and with a band of gold or* pavonazzo *velvet at the bottom. The train or tail of the gown was narrow, so that it resembled a lizard's tail, and they fastened this to their waists; and when they left the house, they wore a veil over their heads.*

CLOTHING WORN IN VENICE, and throughout Italy

As far as I can tell, the people of a century ago dressed very differently from the way we do now. This can be clearly seen if we compare this drawing of clothing once worn in Venice and throughout all Italy with our dress today. The reason I say this is that in those times men wore a balzo *on their heads, like that worn by women, made of copper and round, in the shape of a diadem. Covering this they wore a cap of silk woven with gold. They also wore pleated* camicie *with a low collar and small ruffles. On top they wore a* casacchetta *[a wide-bottomed jacket] or a* saione *[a coat or jacket for outdoor wear] similar to those worn by the Germans, with a short waist and a full skirt falling to the knee, and they had full sleeves reaching below the elbow. From there on down the arms were covered only by their* camicie*, with ruffles at the wrist. These* saioni *were trimmed with wide bands in colors different from the main body of the garment, and of cloth of gold or velvet, depending on each man's wealth. And from the same material they made* pettorali*, which covered the chest in front and were tied under the armpits. The doublets, too, were of different colors, and some had horizontal patterns and others vertical. They wore slashed, colored breeches to the knee and tied them with gold or silk ties. Their stockings were colored and their shoes made of velvet, covered at the toes or heels, as I recall seeing them in my house. I describe them to you now as they are still worn in Germany.*

EARLY CLOTHING
of Women and Brides

The clothing seen here is taken from many places outside the city of Venice. It belonged to brides and was first worn in 1090 or 1100. I took it from a print that represented a boat with a bride seated in the center, along with other women. This boat was not as well made as those of today but was more like a fishing boat, and in addition to the boatman, a Moorish boy could be seen. The women in the image wore dogalina *sleeves, almost floor-length and turned back over their shoulders, some* pavonazzo *in color, and their overgarments were belted with gold and silver and lined with a light fabric of the same color as the gown. The* sottana *was worn as shown here, and it appears from the portrait that she is wearing a deep pleat behind. On the bodice and at the neck were large jeweled ornaments. The gown itself was low-necked, open in the front, pulled in at the waist, and cut in a way that exposed the breast. The hair was worn in its natural color, shining and straight; some women wore it unbraided, falling first to the shoulders and then brought back up toward the head and gathered up with ties, as it is now the custom to wear it in some parts of Italy. The women of those times wore their hair down, as I said, but bound up in a gold net of great value that reached down to the ears. And it is evident that they didn't wear long trains, because the Senate had passed a prohibition against it.*

96

CLOTHING OF VENICE
and Other Places in Italy

Wearing of the style illustrated here did not last long among women, though to begin with they had liked it because they thought it was new. In this they were wrong, however, for the same style had been worn long before, though with some differences, since then it was considered richer and grander than other styles. Some wore a balzo like this on their heads, in many diverse colors, and I have seen them in my own day. This was of cloth of gold or silk, patterned with leaves and roses, and decorated with jewels and other trim. They also wore gold chains and belts of great price and carried fans with gold handles, very beautifully worked. On their shoulders instead of a veil they wore a gathered bavero of lawn or cambrai. Their overgarments were most often of damasco, in cremesino or pavonazzo, with a border a half-foot wide at the bottom; their sleeves were very deeply slashed, allowing their camicie to show through, and they wore their bracciali and puffed sleeves slashed, as well. The sleeves were made of velvet or other fabric, with small ruffles that matched the bavero. The bodice was quite a bit longer than usual but of gold, and they had dispensed entirely with the train, open sleeves and dogalina; but underneath, they wore a carpetta. All this can be gathered from the dress of statues and votive figures that hang in the church of the Madonna dei Miracoli, though these figures wear narrow sleeves.

A WOMAN OF VENICE
Sixty Years Ago

It was about sixty years ago that Venetian women began to bring back the use of gabbie *made of copper, covered with caps made of gold net and decorated with diverse and rich ornaments of pearls and other jewels. In those times the bodice ended above the hips, without coming to a point, and it was comfortable and unstiffened, adorned with gold chains. It is quite true that in those times Venetian noblewomen did not have such a great number of pearls as they do now, but they enriched their bodices and gowns with gold trim and wore long, wide, slashed sleeves. In front, their gowns did not reach the ground, but they formed a bit of a train in back. They wore a sable skin attached to a gold chain, and the skin itself was decorated with a head of gold; they arranged it around their shoulders, otherwise wearing few ornaments at their necks. The ruffles of their* camicie *were neither very dense nor very high; they wore their hair loose and natural, and their sleeves were of a different color from their gowns, which were usually* pavonazzo *or* cremesino. *Their stockings were of yet another color, and their* pianelle, *called* zoccoli *in Venice, were low and turquoise or red in color. Some of them wore these* pianelle *divided up into still more colors. On their heads they wore a black veil of transparent silk, which covered their foreheads, as can be seen in the drawing; and this style of dress is similar to that which is now seen worn by the women of Burano.*

GARRISON SOLDIER
without Armor

*his clothing was worn in the time of Charles V, the leader and honor of all Christian militia of the past and present.*[34] *The soldiers wore certain stiff caps or* balzi, *which were popular in the year 1520 and which are still in use today. And because styles are normally set by leaders, and because this emperor wore his beard closely trimmed, everybody else wore theirs the same way—we see the same happening today in beards in the style of Philip of Spain.*[35] *The same can be said of clothing, because as soon as a prince discovers and starts to wear a new style, everyone else tries to imitate it. And what is said of clothing can also be said of all forms of study and customs, so the example, good or bad, that princes set for their followers is very important. This is also the source of moustaches turned up at the ends, for we saw Henri III, King of France, looking this way when he came back from Poland.*

To return to our subject, the clothing shown here included a leather colletto *[a jerkin, or short sleeveless doublet], as still worn in our day, waist-length, worn with colored sleeves with very deep slashes. The breeches, too, had deep slashes, with smaller slashes between them. For the most part, they were made of* scarlatto *[a very fine wool, sometimes colored red] lined with* ormesino, *with a very large* bracchetta *[codpiece], tied in one place with two laces and in another with four, which they used in place of a pocket. Their stockings were tied above the knee, and a few of them wore a mantle or* tabarro *[a short jacket for men], though hooded short capes were more common. They wore small caps that hardly covered their heads, and they decorated them with colored plumes, pins of crystal and small pins*

of gold. Much later they began to wear larger caps, of red or other colors—so large, in fact, that they fell almost to their shoulders—with slashes, in the style worn by the Swiss. This style lasted for a while, until the arrival of small caps of red or other colors, worn by many of them. And at this time they wore mid-length sleeves and long-waisted doublets, which, because they immobilized the waist, did not last long as a style.

Text on page 152

CLOTHING WORN BY THE WOMEN OF VENICE IN 1550

The changeability and love of variety that governs women soon led them to wear curls on their foreheads, beginning at the ears and continuing all the way up the forehead; and they covered the rest of their hair, which they braided, with little caps. They thought that such a hairstyle made their faces very beautiful, and so, eager to increase their beauty further, they began to dye their hair blonde, doing everything they could to turn their hair to the color of gold. Such treatment of the hair came to seem disgusting, however, and instead the craft arose of making little crowns of gold or silver, encircled with lilies and other kinds of flowers and with jewels of great value. All these styles were popular with the noblewomen of Venice. Such styles lasted about twenty years, after which, with the same inconstancy, they began to wear curls differently, trying to make them as shiny as possible, and they also started making cosmetics, not realizing or not caring that with the passage of time, they would ruin their faces. At their necks they wore twisted strands of gold, from which hung and lay on the breast a pendant of very precious gold; in their ears they wore pearls. They wore belts of gold chains, falling to the floor, and their baveri *were embroidered with roses and gold stars and studded with many jewels.*

They wore camicie *decorated with needlework, which spilled down over their breast. These were snug at the wrist and worn with bracelets, or they wore large, slashed sleeves, through which you could see the* camicia, *and adorned their wrists with gold bracelets. Their* sottana *was of velvet or some other fabric, colored, and the overgarment they wore outside the house was of the same fabric, but in black, light or heavy according to the season. Their* pianelle *didn't have soles as high as they do today, and altogether this was a very respectable style, except for the fact that it bared a large part of the breast. This can be excused, however, because it was worn only by young women, for elderly women did not wear crowns but only a gold or silken cap on their braids, and outside the house they wore a thin, transparent black veil, which they also wore to church and to pay respects to the dead; on such occasions they took off all ornaments of gold and silk. In fact, they covered their faces with these veils and let them fall halfway down their breast, as one can see here—though today this custom has been lost and a different one introduced.*

CORTE DEL PALAZZO DVCALE DI VENETIA.

Text on page 154

THE COURTYARD OF THE DUCAL PALACE of Venice

he courtyard of the palace in which the most serene Prince lives is matched by the other courtyard inside the palace, and this corresponds to the piazza of the church of San Marco. Here, every morning, the nobility gathers between tierce and sext [nine and noon], and here the magistrates and officials are expected to carry out their duties. In this courtyard is the entrance to the Great Council, the Collegio and the Signoria,[36] and in the corridors above, seats or courtrooms are reserved for the various magistrates who meet to settle legal disputes. In this same palace the Prince has his rooms, full of grand spaces and great halls, with gilded ceilings richly painted by the most excellent painters in the city of Venice, including Tintoretto, Giacomo Palma, Paolo Veronese, Giacomo dal Ponte, and his son Francesco, among many others. The staircase is made of Istrian stone, and its stucco ceilings are worked in beautiful designs and sculpted figures by the excellent hand of Alessandro Vittoria, famous in our time. The marble statues of Mars and Neptune sculpted by Sansovino stand at the top of the first outdoor staircase, and an epitaph can be seen there recording the visit to Venice of Henri III, at present the King of France. Not far from here, in the stuccoes above the stairs, are other very beautiful paintings, in a small format, by Battista Franco.

This courtyard is square in shape and has staircases on all four sides. Two of these are without a roof, and from these one can see the courtyard very well; the other two staircases are covered, as is shown in the small-scale drawing. The part of the courtyard near the church contains two of these staircases, one facing the entrance, which is the one already described, and the other that goes up to the hallways that, as I have said, contain the seats of the magistrates; this staircase is roofed with lead and supported by columns and octagonal pillars, beautifully made. These pillars also hold up the façade at the eastern end, where the Prince lives. The façade is made entirely of dense stone with many carvings, and it is divided into sections so that it rests on the twenty-five arcades formed by these pillars, each one seven feet from the next. Below, in the section facing south, are prisons built of dense stone; and in the part facing the two wells, which are covered by domes of beautifully worked bronze, are the rooms of the Prince's Scudieri *[standard-bearers]. One enters through two big doors, one on the side of the piazza and the other on the side of the courtyard, both decorated with many beautiful marble statues befitting the grandeur and magnificence of this courtyard; of particular note, above the doorway on the courtyard side, are those two marvelous ancient statues of Adam and Eve, beautiful in their proportion and design. The length of this courtyard is 140 feet as far as the staircases, and the width is 81 feet. Then there are the staircases and a small courtyard that leads to the church; the most powerful senators meet in this courtyard, and from there through a small door one enters the church of San Marco. Finally, into this large courtyard there are two spacious entrance doors, one facing south (where the prisons are) and the other facing the piazza, near the church of San Marco. I do not want to expand on what I have said here, since it is a subject already fully treated by many famous and excellent writers.*

THE CLOTHING OF MEN OF THE NOBILITY and Other High Ranks in Venice Today

A VENETIAN GENERAL IN WAR TIME

This uniform of a general in wartime creates an impression of great majesty and expresses a truly regal splendor. I have taken it from a portrait of Prince Venier depicted in this apparel, which he wore when he was appointed General of the Venetian Republic during the last war Venice fought with Selim, the Great Turk.[1] *And when this unconquered lord took on the office of the Generalship, he was accompanied as far as the church of San Marco by the Governors and* Provedditori,[2] *carrying the silver baton in his hand. There, with fervent orations and prayers to God, a solemn mass, including many ceremonies, was sung by the Patriarch of the city, and Venier was blessed, along with the standard and the baton. After these religious ceremonies, he was accompanied to his galley with the sound of trumpets and drums and many salutes from muskets. This galley was the most beautiful and richly decorated of all, and the best equipped with men and weapons, and was painted red all over. He boarded this galley via a temporary bridge made of the kind of wood called* piatta, *and as soon as he was inside, his bombadiers began to shoot off the guns with which the ship was laden, and when he left this spot, he was accompanied by shots from all the other artillery drawn up there; and at the same time musket and artillery salutes were fired off in the piazzas. But to speak of his clothing, which is our principal topic, he was dressed entirely in* cremesino *velvet, with the ducal cap on his head and a golden mantle, which we have shown elsewhere was the true Roman* paludamentum, *fastened on the right shoulder with massive gold buttons.*

PRESENT-DAY SENATORS AND KNIGHTS of the City of Venice

enators and Knights in our day wear the ducal gown, with full, open sleeves. They do not wear it made of gold, out of respect for the Prince, but on some occasions they wear a stole of gold brocade. Their overgown is of plain velvet, and their stockings and pianelle *are red. But in winter their gowns are lined with very fine and costly fur, such as marten, sable or lynx. In summer they wear gowns of the same style with open sleeves, but of lighter fabric, lined with* ormesino. *While this same ample gown is still worn from time to time by men who occupy certain magistracies during the period in which they hold them, only Knights, the Procuratori and those who have been Savii Grandi and Consiglieri wear them all the time.*[3] *Among such men,* pavonazzo *is the color usually worn. Men who go to govern the most important and noble cities wear this same gown, although once they finish their service, they must stop wearing it unless they have held one of the previously mentioned ranks, which allows them to continue wearing it.*

THE MAGISTRATES OF VENICE

The clothing seen here belongs to the leaders of the Council of Ten, of whom there are three in number, who change every month and are elected by lot. This is an office of tremendous, indeed the greatest, power. These men sometimes wear a red overgarment, which is true as well of the Avvogadori *[state lawyers], another position of high honor and authority, and of the* Cancellier Grande, *who, like the Prince, stays in office for as long as he lives, and whose position is highly respected. The same gown is worn by the* Dottori *who go to govern cities and important places subject to the Venetian Republic. All these officials wear* pianelle *and red stockings.*

EVERYDAY CLOTHING
Worn by the Entire Venetian Nobility

We can confidently say that the dress ordinarily worn by the Venetian nobility is the ancient Roman toga, and its uniformity is perhaps no small reason for the harmony and concord with which this immense Republic has always been governed. Actually, this simplicity of dress can be seen more in men than in women, who through their natural inclination are always attracted to new fashions. The garment shown here is worn in the summer and it has always been worn in the same way—that is, long, of black wool or rascia *lined with* ormesino. *This is not belted but worn loose and is fastened only at the throat with small iron hooks, though some men wear silver ones. Above the collar of the gown they let just a thin border of their* camicia *show, which has very little or no embroidery. Underneath, they wear* braghesse *[breeches] in the style of Savoy, made of* ormesino *or satin, and this is true also of their doublet, which in great heat is usually made of thin linen; and between this and the overgown they wear a very short undergarment also of* ormesino *or some other light fabric. This is the clothing worn not only by the nobility but also by citizens and by anybody else who wants to wear it. Almost all doctors, lawyers, and merchants wear it willingly, since, as a garment of the nobility, it confers great dignity on these others as well.*

FUNERAL WEAR OF NOBLE AND OTHER MEN in the City of Venice

In funerals today, following ancient tradition, it is the custom to visit the relatives of the dead and keep them company until the dead person is taken to church. Two or three days after the funeral, which is carried out at very high cost, the dead person's relatives leave the house wearing a floor-length mantle, fastened at the throat as such mantles habitually are, and with a long train that they let trail on the ground, even if it is very muddy. After a few days, they wear this train pulled up and tied on the inside, and then, finally, they cut off the train and wear the mantle without it for a long time. When the time to put aside mourning comes, which depends on the closeness of their relationship to the dead person, they put on their usual gown with wide sleeves again. But as a reminder and sign of mourning, they wear a belt of leather rather than of velvet for some time, and instead of the usual pianelle *of* rascia, *they wear leather shoes. Sons, brothers, and fathers wear this attire for a whole year; others will wear it for more or less time, depending on how closely they were related to the dead person. This distinction is further marked in that distant relatives wear a simple mantle, whereas when the dead person is a closer relative, the mantle is worn closed from head to foot; and when the relationship is as close as possible, as between a father and son, it calls for a closed mantle and a very long train, as we have said. Men who do not usually wear the gowns habitual to the nobility do wear, on the occasion of mourning, a similar mantle, but their caps are not of the same style, for they cover theirs with a veil. When they stop wearing the mantle, they put on a* ferraiuolo *or cape of wool or cotton or some heavy or light fabric, according to the time of year.*

Text on page 161

YOUNG VENETIAN NOBLEMEN

Young noblemen of Venice, up to the age of fifteen or twenty, wear a short garment; only later do they put on a long gown with full sleeves, since the toga strongly restrains youthful pride and imposes a certain gravity and modesty. But because I said above that the long gown worn by noblemen is also worn by citizens, doctors, merchants and others, I must inform the reader that when the Prince leaves the palace, the secretaries who accompany him wear this long robe in pavonazzo but with a black stole. To return to young men's clothing, under a ferraiuolo they wear doublets and what are called braghesse, mainly in gray, though others also enjoy wearing pavonazzo or some other color, and their fabrics are silk and very delicate. They wear all these colors in as concealed a way as possible, according to the modesty appropriate to this Republic.

Text on page 162

THE WINTER CLOTHING of a Nobleman

Around the beginning of November, depending on whether cold comes early or late, old men stop wearing the open gown lined with ormesino and put on one lined with vaio, which is cinched with a velvet belt that, as I have touched on before, is two fingers wide and has silver buckles. But since these are very light furs, when the cold increases, instead of vaio they line their gowns with squirrel pelts, which are heavier and keep them warmer. They wear these until the weather starts to turn mild and the cold decreases, and then they put on vaio again, until the heat forces them to leave this off and to put on ormesino-lined gowns, which, as we have said, everyone wears open. All outdoor gowns fasten at the throat, but those worn at home have turned-back baveri and they call them Romane [a long, ample overgarment]. No matter how cold it is, they wear hats only of cloth, underneath which those of more advanced age wear an embroidered silk cap.

Text on page 163

NOBLEMEN AND OTHER WEALTHY MEN
Dressed for Comfort at Home

If I have briefly mentioned garments worn at home above, here I will say more clearly that once at home, men take off the gowns already described and in their place they wear a zimarra, a pretina [a man's narrow overgown] or a Romana, as they call it. And the pretine have slightly smaller baveri with a circular cut, while the Romane have larger ones that fall farther down behind, in a squarish shape. These overgarments are floor-length, like those worn outdoors, and the baveri we describe are lined according to the season, as is the rest of the gown, with linings of fur or indoor cloth in keeping with the heat or cold. And in the fur linings of these gowns variations can be seen, not only according to the weather but also to the variety of animals, of lesser or greater value, depending on the wealth of each man. These gowns have half-length sleeves, some cut across and some cut lengthwise, and they can put their arms through them, letting the rest of the sleeve dangle down with a show of elegance. And these overgarments are all worn open but belted, with one side wrapped over the other. Here I speak of the Romane, since the pretine are not wrapped in this way but fastened with buttons, at least down to the belt. And instead of a full-weight cap, especially in the summer, they wear tall, narrow caps pointed at the top, of ormesino or some other light fabric, in black or some other not too bright color.

Text on page 164

HEAD CAPTAIN

The clothing of this captain is very beautiful. The duty of this captain, who is called great because of his authority over other captains, is to command others as seems right to him and to oversee and be vigilant, as do the Bargelli *[police chiefs] in other cities—to stop civil disorder, bring criminals into the hands of justice, post watchmen in certain places and at certain times, and walk the streets regularly at night, accompanied by other men, in order to frighten people of evil intent. He dresses entirely in velvet or* cremesino *satin. This is his customary attire, but he also wears a* pavonazzo *mantle, open in front and at the sides, which he fastens here and there with silk laces, which are tied into very beautiful bows. He cinches his undergarment with a velvet belt with silver buckles, and from this hangs a weapon more like a scimitar than a sword, as long as the gown itself. He wears stockings and shoes of the same color as the undergarment, and a black cap. And the mantle, which we said earlier is normally* pavonazzo*, he wears in red, like the undergarment, on certain solemn occasions.*

Text on page 165

LOWER-RANKING CAPTAINS, *Ministers of Justice*

These lower-ranking captains assist the Capitano Grande *and have the duty of ensuring that the city is cleared of wicked and criminal men; each of them has a certain number of men, called* Zaffi *in Venice and* sbirri *[policemen who make arrests] elsewhere. These all wear the same clothing—that is, a red undergarment and a* pavonazzo *mantle on top—and in addition to the jobs described above, they walk ahead of the Prince whenever he leaves the palace for ceremonies. When they go out into the streets of Venice at night in search of evildoers, they are always accompanied by a certain number of men, who walk with them and assist them in every undertaking. And they, too, wear a black cap.*

Text on page 166

CLOTHING OF THE KNIGHT
of the Prince

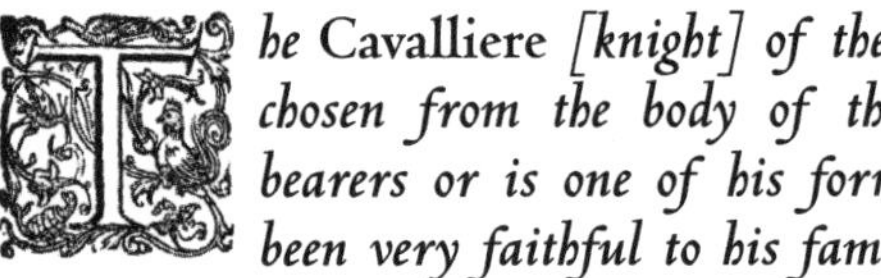

he Cavalliere *[knight] of the Prince is most often chosen from the body of the Prince's standard-bearers or is one of his former officials who has been very faithful to his family; for this reason he is judged worthy of such a benefice and such a title. He always stays near the Prince, ready to attend to his every need, and as the head and superior of all the other standard-bearers, he is fed and housed in the palace. He supports the Prince physically when, going to the Council rooms, he climbs and descends the stairs of the palace. He dresses in* cremesino *satin, velvet or* zendado *[a light and lustrous silk], in an overgarment with sleeves that are open but not very wide, like those of the Senators, though his gown is open in front but not fastened at the throat, as are those of the noblemen. They also wear doublets,* calzoni *[mid-thigh or knee-length trousers] and other clothing of a similar color, such as* cremesino *or scarlet; on their feet they wear* pianelle *of the same color. The knight wears this attire all the time. The musicians of the Prince also dress in scarlet, but only when they accompany him on solemn occasions when he leaves the palace with government officials; after they have taken the Prince home, they take it off.*

This same gown was in use in Venice for years and years among many citizens and prosperous merchants, but now it is used only by those called the Servants of the Heads of the Council of Ten, who wear it in black wool, lined with fur in the winter and with ormesino *in the summer. And the knight of whom I am speaking does the same, except that he lines his garments with furs of greater value than these men do. This garment was also formerly worn by the young men of Venice, who have dispensed with it altogether. The knight wears a round, pointed black cap, as do noblemen, and this cap is also worn in Venice by priests, who also wear a floor-length* sottana *of* pavonazzo, *fastened at the throat and tied with a belt. In the palace this knight wears the* dogalina, *in* pavonazzo, *and he wears the same nobleman's cap in black cloth.*

SCUDIERI [STANDARD BEARERS]
of the Prince of Venice

*he most serene Prince usually employs sixteen* Scudieri *in his personal service, all men of mature age and good reputation. Their duty is to come to the palace every morning and accompany the Prince to the Collegio and to every other place that he must visit; they are paid by the Republic for this purpose. In addition to this required service, they have another one to carry out: two of them must spend a whole week of every month in the palace, guarding the meeting-room. They wear* tabarri *of black velvet, and velvet* bracconi *[wide, padded breeches], and* pianelle *or shoes of velvet. They wear belts of silk and a cap in the style of the Terra Firma, of velvet or some other material depending on the season and their own taste. They are given this position for life, and the Prince never dismisses any of them, even though he could.*

MERCHANTS AND SHOPKEEPERS
of the Merceria and the Rest of the City of Venice

Many of the merchants and well-to-do shopkeepers of the city of Venice wear an overgown with sleeves à comeo *like that of the noblemen, but most wear the short* ferraiuolo *in* rascia, *plain wool,* ciambellotto *[camlet, a fine, longhaired wool], silk* canevaccia, *and other materials, heavier or lighter according to the season. They wear a cap they call a* berretta à tozzo *[a high, full, rounded cap] and some wear it* à tagliere *[with a flat top], with a very narrow folded edge and a surrounding band. This is a style belonging to mature, settled men; the other is worn by young men. Sometimes these older men, though not all of them, under their* ferraioli *wear long gowns called* Romane *or* pretine, *the first (as I have said elsewhere) with open* baveri, *the second fastened at the throat, as you see here. And whichever one of these they wear, many wear the* baveri *showing above their* ferraiuolo *or* tabarro, *and they cinch it with a silk belt. Among them one sees few colors except black, and as far as fabric is concerned, they wear mostly* ciambellotto *or silk* canevaccia. *Their greatest elegance remains more hidden, however, since their overgown covers the upper part of their doublets, which are made most often of satin, meaning that one sees only the sleeves. And these* ciambellotto *gowns are unlined in the summer and in the winter lined with more or less expensive furs, according to the taste and wealth of the wearer. In the summer they wear only* pianelle, *but in winter they add shoes over them and also wear silk stockings on their legs. At all times of the year I have seen Messer Paolo dallo Struzzo look splendid in clothing of this kind, dignified and well put together, a virtuous young man endowed with every rare quality, who has great intelligence and in the profession of druggist yields to no one in his fine selection of goods and making of theriac.*[4] *Nor will I omit Messer Bernardino Pillotto, who, in addition to his famous shop, is a man of the greatest generosity and courtesy, who enjoys many virtues. Both of these men own a great number of paintings and many other valuable objects.*

Text on page 170

COMMANDATORI *OR CITY CRIERS*

he Commandatori or city criers, assigned specifically to the service of various magistrates, number as many as fifty and have various duties inside and outside the city. They are chosen by the Prince. They wear a long, floor-length mantle in turquoise, and on their heads they wear a cap exactly the shape of those worn by noblemen and citizens but red in color, to which they attach a gold medal imprinted with a sketch of Saint Mark. When the Prince and the magistrates go outside, these men are the first in line and they walk two by two in front of all the others, some of them carrying the banners usually carried before the Prince. Their usual responsibilities, beyond those I have mentioned, are to announce, declare, and publicize both proclamations and also what in Venice are called stride *[cries, or legal pronouncements], as well as to be present at the sale of goods at auction. As a sign of all these duties, in past times they used to carry a rod in their hands, which was used until 1523 when they were assigned nstead the gold medal attached to their caps.*

Text on page 171

CLOTHING OF THE ADMIRAL
and Administrators of the Arsenal

If the ancient writers who made such efforts (and rightly so) to describe the Seven Wonders of the World had been able to see the Arsenal of the city of Venice, I am certain that they would have made the number eight instead of seven, since it is more than wondrous. For neither the pyramids of Egypt nor the lighthouse at Pharos nor the walls of Babylon nor the temple of Diana at Ephesus nor the tomb of Mausoleus nor the Colossos of the Sun at Rhodes nor the statue of Jove at Olympus were so great that this could not have equaled or surpassed them. In Venice, then, there is a place called the Arsenal, two miles in circumference, entirely surrounded by crenellated walls and guard-towers. Within this place are four hundred people, constantly working, who receive 1,200 golden florins every week for their labor. The management of this multitude and its provisions is assigned to three noblemen, elected one after the other by the Great Council, and they have the authority to reward the productive and punish the delinquent. They have the duty of choosing a main supervisor, among others, with the title Admiral, while the other, lesser supervisors are called *Proti*, and they oversee the different crafts carried on here. But the Admiral must be a man of great experience in the naval arts, and he is therefore revered by all and provisioned more richly than the other supervisors, who obey him.

His clothing is the one shown here. This Admiral wears a wide gown of *pavonazzo* wool, full-length, with sleeves that also reach the ground and are narrow at the top; this narrow section has an opening through which his arms emerge. He wears a *sottana* of the same color, though sometimes red if it suits him. This, too, is full-length and cinched with a velvet belt with silver buckles. On his head he wears the same cap as noblemen do, and on his legs scarlet stockings. This is a form of dress that makes a beautiful sight and an impression of great gravity.

CLOTHING OF THE ADMINISTRATORS OF THE ARSENAL

We call this clothing Syrian in style. It is worn in Venice by sailors and by Greeks, but it properly belongs to the supervisors of the administration of the Arsenal, who in Venice are called proti, *as being the first in intelligence and worth among their profession. Their gown is black in color, long, and with floor-length sleeves; and under this some wear a* sottana, pavonazzo *in color, but most wear a black one, and a Venetian cap. They used to carry a short sword with silver ornamentation at their side. In addition to the ordinary duties of their craft, they are very faithful to the Prince and serve as guards of the city.*

A SECOND VIEW OF THE PIAZZA of San Marco

This second view of the Piazza of San Marco in Venice is available to a person who stands near the great clock with his back to the north and looks toward the church of San Giorgio Maggiore in the south. On the left one sees the beautiful church of San Marco with these four bronze horses above the door, and on the right, toward the west, the three flagpoles and the bell tower. At the head of the piazza are seen two very large columns of granite, more than three arm-lengths wide, set up here after they were brought from Constantinople; the library building, which is to the right of the bell tower, finished just recently on the side of the lagoon for the offices of the three divisions of Procuratori; and the palace, on the left (to the east), which is next to the church of San Marco. This perspective and view is as lovely and beautiful as any to be had anywhere because one can see an almost endless stretch of open sky and the water with its pleasant waves. In addition, in the morning a large part of the Venetian nobility meets here, and at every hour of the day a great number of men of all nations of the world can be seen, wearing an infinite variety of clothing. And since I am here in sight of the church of San Marco, I think I should say something about it briefly. It is made of very beautiful marbles and decorated with a good number of columns of different colors, with its façade divided into five arches or niches, of which the one in the middle is the largest and more elaborately decorated than the others. This façade is held up by two rows of columns, which are made of very beautiful serpentine porphyry and other marbles, with capitals carved with beautiful, strange shapes, all

gilded; every surface of the largest arch is covered with carvings representing the different crafts, in appealing figures with rich mosaic work. Above this arch is an outdoor corridor where the previously mentioned four ancient and extraordinarily beautiful bronze horses are placed—because of their artistry and their form, they are said to have been taken from the arch of Nero in Rome and brought by Constantine to Byzantium, then taken from there to Venice and set where they are now. Above the location of the horses can be seen, in certain wall shrines, many marble statues, which match the building very well, with its immense set of sculptures and carvings.

This church has five doors leading to the piazza and two at its sides, all made of bronze. The façade is 150 feet long, and the length of the piazza from the clock tower to the columns is about five hundred feet, as we said in the description of the first piazza. We show here in small figures the order that the Prince observes when he goes to church accompanied by the Signoria.

Text on page 175

THE CLOTHING OF BOATMEN
and the Comfort of their Boats

It is hard to believe how comfortable the boats in Venice are until you have tried them. In this city there are a great many ferry routes, each served by many boats with a man at the stern, ready to transport anyone who wishes to cross the Canal or go someplace else. The nobles, and especially the richest among them, each usually have their own boats, with two oars and with salaried men to row them. And truly I must mention the pleasure arising from this comfortable arrangement for those who do not know what these boats are like or perhaps have never seen them. For they offer so much comfort to passengers who have made long trips by horse and carriage and arrive at Marghera or at some other point of embarkation where the calm restores their exhausted bodies and they finish the journey as though they were sitting at home. As a result they forget their sufferings and they are rewarded by the sight, in the midst of the waves, of many beautiful palaces and many people of different nations doing business there. I have experienced this many times myself, having been tossed around in carriages and endured the miseries of riding on horseback. But as soon as I felt the ease and comfort of the boat, in which I could even sleep peacefully, I recovered from the discomforts of the long trip and forgot all my former pain.

Altogether, the comforts and pleasures of such a boat ride are so many and so great that as a delightful pastime in the summer, all you have to do is take one out with good friends, enjoying the coolness of the evening or the morning. Each person can bring his own dinner and musical entertainment with him, and, meeting other boats full of friends and acquaintances, one can ride around the city in pleasant, agreeable company. For even greater convenience and delight, there are various islands and monasteries, and here, or on the shore, people often unload lunch or dinner, and on the grass or under the trees they spend hours in the company of gracious and pleasant groups of friends. And it is no less lovely to be able to travel throughout the whole city either by water or land, with such a great supply of crossing places that even the poor, for a bagattino *[a small local copper coin], can have themselves rowed from one side of the Grand Canal to the other. The nobles of Venice, however, and other citizens and rich or prosperous people, usually have their own boats or gondolas, with various servants; one of them, who controls the whole boat, is called the* Fante di poppa *(the stern-man) and the other is called the* Fante di mezzo *(the mid-boatman).*[5] *He most often attends to other services for his master, while the first one, whose only task is to care for the boat, cleans, repairs, and readies it whenever and however often it is needed. He also has the job of polishing the* delfini*, which are the pieces of ironwork at the prow and stern of the boat, so shiny that they look like silver, and of taking off and putting on the* felce*, which is the canopy of* rascia *or serge; and also of seeing to the seats, which are usually made of wood although many people cover them with padded leather stuffed like cushions. The cover that we have called the* felce *is attached with white silk ropes to the benches and forms an arch over the boat; the whole* *boat is black, except when gentlemen on pleasure jaunts cover the benches and prows of their boats with beautiful carpets. It is also a great advantage that married women and noblewomen, when leaving home, have the convenience of arriving directly at the doors of the palaces and churches to which they are going, and from there of returning to the doors of their own houses.*

Text on page 177

THE CLOTHING OF VENETIAN NOBLEWOMEN
and Other High-Ranking Women of the City

MAIDENS AND GIRLS OF VENICE

The greatest and most remarkable modesty characterizes the method and tradition of bringing up noble girls in Venice, for they are so well guarded and watched over in their fathers' houses that very often not even their closest relatives see them until they marry. And it must be said that many of them, up to the point of marriage, conforming with reverent obedience to the will of their parents, wear no ornaments whatsoever. These maidens, when they begin to grow up, very rarely, indeed, almost never, leave home unless to go to mass or other church services. When they do, they wear on their heads a white silk veil, which they call a fazzuolo, *very wide, which covers their face and breast. At this time they wear a few pearls as ornaments and a few small chains of slight value. Their overgowns most often are rust-colored or black, of light wool or* ciambellotto *or some other fabric of little value, but they wear colored* sottane *and a kind of belt made of silk net, which they call* poste. *But when they are fully grown, they dress entirely in black, with a* fazzuolo *called a* cappa *of very delicate silk, very full and ample, thick and* stoccato *[crimped], and of great value, which covers their face so that they are unseen but can see others. But girls of the nobility and high ranks go out rarely, only on principal festivals and holy days.*

Text on page 178

BRIDES BEFORE THEIR WEDDINGS
in Our Time

Some time back a custom began among the brides of Venice that before they receive wedding rings and take their vows, and only visits have passed between the bride and groom, on one day they are visited by their male friends and relatives and on another day by the women, and then they go out to enjoy themselves, well chaperoned. At this time they wear a fazzuolo *called a* cappa *of black silk that is very thin and covers their face but not their breast, and even though it is not very thick, it still does not allow their covered faces even to be imagined. On this occasion they are richly adorned with pearls and gold, wearing far more of these ornaments than they wore before they exchanged wedding vows. And while this veil covers their face, they wear a bodice and sleeves of colored fabric, most often of white silk, with the opening widely laced crosswise with a silk cord, as seen in this portrait. This opening used to be of gold and embroidered, but now it is plain and without any other ornament. They wear perfumed full-length gloves in the winter, and in the summer their gloves go only halfway down their fingers. They wear necklaces and other ornaments and jewels. They wear a jeweled, floor-length gold belt, and the rest of their gown is black, with a long train.*

Text on page 179

BRIDES OUTSIDE THE HOUSE after They Have Married

Once their weddings have been announced and the parentado (as we call a certain wedding ceremony in Venice) has taken place, they usually dance at balls for several days and appear in public and joyfully receive all their relatives. For this purpose they have dancing masters whom they employ during these days, and these are elderly men. During the time of the parentado, which includes both men and women though they are usually kept separate, these dancing masters lead the brides out of their rooms into the portego [a long hall running down the center of the house, on the main floor] in the presence of their relatives and friends, who are seated there, and they teach them how to bow to everyone and so, to the sound of various instruments, they perform certain dances and then return to their rooms, where there are many women who dress them up, often changing their clothes, and send them forth beautifully attired and so well adorned that when these ornaments are added to their innate beauty, with which Mother Nature has usually been very generous to them, they appear to be so many suns.

In the actual wedding, they go to church with a large group of men and women, the relatives not only of the groom but also of the bride, preceded by musicians. Servants carry torches to be lit as mass is said; this they attend in great splendor, outfitted with carpets and cushions on which they lean and kneel. Once mass is said and the blessing of the priest has been received, they return home and then they are led to the house of their husband, where the festivities start again. For almost a year they continue to wear their hair loose on their shoulders, with golden hair trim and an ornament on their head, such as a circlet studded with jewels of great value, some showing naturally and others by exquisite, careful art all their golden-colored hair, with curls in the style of the day and with so many valuable jewels and pendants at their ears and strands of pearls at their necks, instead of necklaces, that they are a marvel to behold. During this time most of them dress in white satin or some other silk, according to the season, which signals their fidelity and chastity. In the past, they wore simple white, without any decoration, and their hair embellished with curls on their forehead, and baveri and bracciali, trimmed with ruffles at their wrists, too, as you can see here. But for the last six years they have changed all these things completely, with the addition of a new coiffure: they wear two horn-like points artfully made of their hair, attempting to imitate the goddess of chastity.[6] Their garments are white but with beautiful designs woven into them, and their baveri have high lace collars, beautifully constructed of standing openwork lace, as are their bracciali. In a lovely style they pad their bodices, elongated well below the waist, and wear the usual ornaments, of greater rather than lesser value, as can be seen illustrated in the ensemble here. And when they go out, they are accompanied by many older married women of their clan and by a great number of servants, and they wear a long train.

Text on page 179

Text on page 181

BRIDES AT ASCENSION TIME,
or the Sensa[7] in Venice

If ever there is a time that the brides of Venice make an effort to look beautiful and to appear richly dressed, it is during the fifteen days of the Sensa holiday, when great numbers of people from different nations flow into the city. Then the brides set about inventing and adorning themselves in the greatest luxury and elegance they can, because they will be seen not only by their fellow citizens but also by the many foreigners of all ages and sexes who come not only from nearby towns but also from distant ones to see that splendid display of merchandise. During these days, the brides show off the richness of their largest pearls and other most precious jewels, with which they ornament their ears, hair, necks, and breasts. Shining with gold and gems even on their baveri, *dressed in the richest and most fashionable ornaments available to them, and almost a wonder to themselves, to others who observe them they are a portrait of the greatest loveliness and delight that nature and art can offer to the eye. So adorned, they stroll through the Sensa, wafting the scents of pleasant perfumes in the air and revealing their opulent beauty. They wear overgarments of white satin but let their bodices and sleeves show, with all their borders and edges enriched with gold; and they wear gold belts interwoven and studded throughout their entire length with jewels. On their sleeves, instead of* bracciali, *they wear ruffles of a charming and intricate design, trimmed with many golden buttons, which they also use to attach the sleeves to their shoulders. The rest of their overgarment from the bodice down is made of lightweight black silk, either with an interwoven pattern or of a plain weave, and fitted with a train, as we see in the print. In their hands they carry a fan made of cloth of gold and silk, with a beautiful design and a silver handle.*[8] *And from their hair hangs a black veil of very beautiful transparent silk, bordered with charmingly made lace; these veils, falling from their shoulders and gradually becoming wider, almost reaching the ground, stand out around them, covering them very gracefully.*

WINTER CLOTHING OF VENETIAN NOBLEWOMEN and Other Wealthy Women In Our Time

The clothing shown here displays the great extent to which Venetian women wear ornaments of precious gold, rich in pearls and other jewels, and how much effort and care they put into their coiffures. They arrange their hair in a style of curls with certain curls that form a half moon, with its points or "horn" (for they have also invented this name for it) turned upward. They adorn their necks with the greatest splendor, and in their ears they wear little hoops tied with ribbons; some wear pearls or other gems of great value. Every precious thing dangles from them, from their necks to their breast, complementing and embellishing the bodice and forming a necklace composed of large pearls of considerable value. Their belts of massive gold are full of jewels, and on their wrists they wear precious bracelets. Over their camicia *they wear a* carpetta, *most often of* brocatello, *and in the winter it is lined with precious furs. At that time of the year they also wear a muff lined with fur, which protects their hands against the cold. These furs are marten or sable, and the muff is of black velvet or some other silk fabric, fastened shut with buttons of oriental crystal or gold. The undergarment is of brocade or similar fabric. On top of the* camicia, *which is very thin, they wear a lined* sottanella, *and above this a gown of black velvet or other silk fabric with designs woven into it, with an arm-long train; this, because of its great weight, must be arranged and carried by a woman servant. They wear embroidered stockings and high* pianelle; *their veils are of black silk, unpleated, attached to their heads, breasts and shoulders and by one end to their belt, from which it falls to the ground; keeping its magnificent fullness, it makes the wearer look very lovely. Some, truthfully, wear it in a style that covers their hair, and it falls from there onto their breast; but this is a style for mature women.*

Text on page 184

132

NOBLEWOMEN
at Public Festivals

When noblewomen are invited to banquets or spectacles at which some great person will be present, as often happens in Venice, they are allowed, without breaking any law or risking any judgment against them, to deck themselves out and adorn themselves as they please, although outside such occasions their clothing is controlled by the Signori delle pompe [Overseers of the sumptuary laws]. So when Henri III, the King of France, coming from Poland (where he was also king), passed through Venice, he was entertained (in addition to other sumptuous and marvelous spectacles) with an immense gathering in the meeting room of the Great Council of two hundred of the most beautiful principal noblewomen of the city, all dressed in white; and they appeared in such style and with such great loveliness that the king, along with all his entourage, was stunned and astonished. All of them promenaded two by two in front of his royal majesty, and in a graceful manner, sinking low, they gave him the required curtsey. They all had their heads covered with pearls and other jewels, with which they had also adorned their necks, breasts, shoulders, bodices and sleeves, with lovely richness. All these jewels were set in gold and surrounded by very beautiful needlework. In sum, they appeared in such splendor that it was estimated that each one of them was wearing the equivalent of 50,000 scudi. And besides the dances that they performed gracefully before His Majesty, a sumptuous repast was also held, on which many thousands of scudi were spent. But returning to the topic of their dress, I confess that bodices, in that time, were not as long as they are today, and wise and beautiful young women did not curl their hair into such a high shape but wore it as can be seen in this portrait. Their dress was similar to the black dress worn by the woman shown in the previous print, who wears her hair in the shape of a small crown. And the figure I show you here is one of those richly dressed women who were invited to this great party. Now our modern women wear brocades and cloth of gold and silver, with an immense number of jewels and very sumptuous bodices and sleeves. The hairstyle here is modern, as are the sleeves and the bavero, on which jewels are worn; and in their hands they carry very beautiful woven fans with gold handles.

NOBLEWOMEN GOING AT LENT TO SAN PIETRO DI CASTELLO or to Other Services

oblewomen and others of high rank, going to seek pardon at Castello, wear a black gown—for the most part this is of Florentine ormesino, *though some wear satin, and others* ferrandine *[a lightweight silk mixed with wool or cotton] with patterns woven into it; at present, however, they almost all wear patterned silk. At this time of the year most women, as of one mind (perhaps out of respect for these holy days), wear few adornments, though they do not leave aside every kind of beautiful pearl, earring, or necklace buttoned with gold. Some cover their hair almost entirely with a veil, which they used to use to cover their face, but today they turn it back. Their clothing is sober or in the style of mourning wear, of black cloth, and, underneath, chestnut brown or some other dark color. And now, instead of pearls or necklaces, they wear a kind of black amber on their necks.*

WIDOWS OF VENICE

With the death of their husbands, widows in Venice embrace the death of all vanity and bodily ornament. For in addition to wearing black, they cover their hair, fasten a very thick veil over their breast, wear their cappa *low on their foreheads, and go through the streets sadly, and with lowered heads. As long as they want to remain widowed, they wear a train and put on no colored clothing, until the time they may want to marry again. At home they wear a cap on their hair, which covers it up. They always wear black, indoors and out. But if they decide to marry again, without blame they may wear some jewelry, though not of striking appearance, and uncover their hair to some degree, all of which serves to inform others of their intention. This image of dress represents a very modest noblewoman of the* Contarini *family.*

GENTLEWOMEN IN VENETIAN OUTPOSTS AND TERRITORIES, *Indoors and Out*

The wives of gentlemen sent to govern other cities take on their husbands' titles and are called Podestaresse, Capitane *and so on. And certain elegant fashions are also named after these unusual titles, following decorum. For this reason, these women dress very magnificently, according to their titles and rank, and they wear many ornaments, as I show in this portrait. Their gowns are of different colors of brocade of silk, gold and silver. They dress their hair, always blonde (either by nature or by art), very richly with pearls and other jewels. Among others I once saw the famous Gussona, the daughter of the illustrious Barbarigo (the one who died in the naval battle [at Lepanto]), who, in addition to her indescribable modesty and other rare qualities, shone in a most sumptuous gown, because at her neck and on her breast she wore long strands of huge pearls, with a choker of very valuable jewels. From her small and beautifully formed ears hung two very beautiful pearls, set in gold with beautifully worked designs, and she wore a jeweled belt of gold. The veil she wore outdoors was of thin, transparent gold silk, bordered all around with gold lace, and its ground was white. I have seen other women dressed this way, too. At home they wear gowns of velvet or silk, depending on the season, and they go out accompanied by noblewomen of the cities where they are posted, and with them and dressed this way, they go to church and to public festivals.*

VENETIAN WOMEN OF MATURE AGE, AND DISMESSE[9] *[Women Single by Choice]*

Married women who have reached a certain age usually wear this clothing, very far indeed from fancy dress. They have, for the most part, distanced themselves from the vanities of the world, dedicating themselves instead to the life of the spirit, and accordingly they wear this simple, pious dress. Mainly they wear a black gown of ciambelloto *or some other cloth, and a* cappa *on their heads in a way that leaves some of their hair uncovered, and they arrange the rest with similar modesty. Some of them let the* cappa *fall to the ground, and others attach a ribbon to it at the bottom, with which they tie it to their belt, making a sort of sack behind. They wear little in the way of a train, and their* sottana *is most often colored* ciambellotto*; and, dressed in this way, they go about their affairs. As to the* dismesse*, who are also called* disghettate *[freed from the ghetto, i.e., not enclosed], they wear very wide sleeves and gowns of black* scotto *[herringbone wool, of Scottish origin], which is commonly called serge, although they are not necessarily the same fabric. Many of them also wear pearls or gold jewelry, and a muff of fine fur lined with silk, velvet or some other fabric for the winter; in the summer they wear gloves.*

PARTICULAR CLOTHING OF IMMIGRANT WOMEN IN VENICE

Some women wear the same garments but more open in front, with more pearl jewelry: these are women who have come to Venice from elsewhere and who cannot give up their own style of dress right away but do so little by little. This is why courtesans and prostitutes sometimes resemble married women in their dress, even wearing rings on their fingers as married women do—and for this reason anyone lacking experience will be fooled by them. In this portrait it should be noted that they curl their hair and wear their gowns with a deep V-shaped neckline, trimmed with ruffles. And because they are forbidden to wear pearls, at their neck they wear what they call tondini *[round beads] of silver or gold, and other jewelry that imitates pearls. They also wear chains and belts of gold or of crystal, and also golden bracelets and embroidered gloves covering only the upper fingers. Their gowns are cut to form a round belly, in a new style, and are made of silk or other cloth, but decorated all around with rich trim, according to their means. This gown is fastened with buttons of crystal, gold or some other substance. The* sottana *is of silk with decorative strips at the hem, though they also wear it made of* ciambellotto. *As veils, they wear long* cappe *of finely crimped silk with knotted tassels at the corners, and most often they wear white* pianelle *and embroidered stockings. Their* carpette *vary according to the season, and their shoes are in Roman style. The train of their gown is not very long. But very often, some of these courtesans approach men ignorant of their real status, wearing widows' garb very similar to that of Venetian noblewomen.*

COURTESANS
Outdoors

We said earlier that prostitutes who want to win respect by means of feigned modesty wear widows' and married women's styles of dress, especially in the colors worn by brides. Formerly, most of them went about dressed as unmarried girls, a custom still carried out but with greater modesty. So as not to be completely enclosed and covered by the cappe *they wear, yet not being allowed to expose other parts of themselves, they have to reveal themselves in some way, so they cannot fail to be recognized by this gesture. And because they are forbidden to wear pearls, they reveal themselves as prostitutes when they expose their bare necks. To make up for this, these unfortunate women use a* bertone *(as they are called), who plays the role of a husband for them and permits them the use of luxury goods, and under this pretext they can avail themselves of everything that the laws generally forbid them. Their gowns are of* brocatello *of various colors, and embroidered at the greatest expense they can afford. They wear Roman-style shoes inside their* pianelle*. These are the courtesans of highest standing. But those who practice this infamous profession openly and in public places wear silk doublets with gold laces or embroidery of some kind, and also* carpette *that they cover with tied-up cloths or silk aprons. On their heads they wear a short gauze* fazzuola*, and in this style they go flirting throughout the city, easily recognized by all. And everyone sends obscene gestures and words their way.*

WOMEN AT HOME

Women of the nobility and other honorable ranks, when at home, wear gowns of various colors; this is especially true in the summer, when they wear ormesino, cendal *or brocades in many different and beautiful colors, and also cloth woven of four or even six colors, so well made that no brush could paint better. Such lovely fabrics were invented here in Venice by Messer Bartholomeo Bontempele,*[10] *at the sign of the Chalice; when he exhibits these materials of his own design, he demonstrates his brilliant skill, for which, added to his incredible liberality and generosity, he is much loved by the Venetian nobility, and by many princes of Italy, especially the most serene Duke of Mantua. In his shop, to which many great lords and princes send orders (even from as far as the seraglio of the Great Turk), all sorts of brocades woven with gold and silver can be seen. And the noblewomen of Venice wear these a great deal today, in addition to certain hues—pink, pale* pavonazzo, *yellow-green—that look very lovely. They wear their hair in two narrow braids, pulled into a bun at the back of the head and bound with silk cords that are held up with pins of gold or silver, which support the coiffure. Their hair is always blonde, with curls skillfully framing their foreheads, and they go about with such refinement that they look altogether lovable and beautiful. Over their shoulders they wear a* velo *[a piece of thin voile or gauze fabric] in the style of a* bavero, *thin and transparent, and at their necks they always wear their pearls, and at their wrists bracelets of heavy gold, which they never take off, as is also the case with their high* pianelle. *They make every attempt to please their husbands, wishing to preserve conjugal love and to maintain peace and harmony in their homes. They wear very long trains in this shape, but if at home and lending a hand to some work, they raise it up and fasten it to the back of their gown with pins or with a silk tie—this is sewn to the point of the bodice in the back and has a little hook to which they attach their train, or* coda*, as we like to call it.*

Text on page 193

MODERN VENETIAN NOBLEWOMAN

Because women's clothing is very subject to change and is as variable as the phases of the moon, it is not possible in one description to say all that can be said about it. Indeed, it is rather to be feared that even as I am describing a style, women are turning to another one, so that it is impossible for me to capture it all. I had planned not to go any further into the subject of the dress worn by Venetian noblewomen, hoping that what I have said so far would suffice; but in the end I did not want to omit this final figure. Here we see hair curled into the shape of horns so high that it looks very unattractive, not to speak of the energy they put into dyeing their hair blonde with such art and effort and waste of time that it is mind-boggling. The women of our time are also in the habit of making one braid that they gather into a bun in the shape of a coiled snail shell, arranged and pinned in place in the way we described previously. And without leaving aside any of their usual ornaments, they have added others to them, including, to an excessive degree, high-necked baveri *with collars and stiff, upright ruffles that rise almost above the head; these are particularly unsightly, not only because they lack proportion but also because they interfere with the* fazzuolo, *which (to tell the truth) falls down behind them in a very ugly tangle. These collars are made according to very lovely designs and fabricated at great cost, and they are not hidden by the* fazzuolo, *which they wear in black silk so that it will be very light and transparent. They also wear, on top of their gowns, a light* rochetto *of very thin black silk, which, in the same way, allows the colors of their gowns to be seen and makes it possible to tell whether the fabric is brocade or some other kind, a fashion that first began with brides. And in these two portraits, I give the front and back view of this style, which I have described above.*

Text on page 193

Text on page 195

WOMEN DURING THE WINTER, especially Courtesans

In winter many women at home in this city wear long fur-lined Romane, which are very comfortable and allow the wearer great freedom of movement for every sort of task. Many wear them covered with satin, changeable ormesino, or other fabrics, while the linings are of marten, pigskin, and other valuable skins. Some wear these gowns over their camicia, and under them a carpetta of colored silk, also lined with fur and fastened in front with small ties or buttons. These carpette are usually trimmed with different-colored borders, for they have now stopped wearing the finely worked embroidered trim they wore earlier. To return to their overgarments, they have narrow hanging sleeves, floor-length, and they are tied with the silk net sashes they call poste or with silk veli, which have two buttons or tassels at the ends.

This dress is very often worn among courtesans, more than by other women, and courtesans also wear carpette more richly decorated than other women's. Courtesans are forbidden to wear pearls at home but they still do wear them (as I have said), along with very valuable bracelets and long earrings, and they stand continually at their windows, making love to this or that man, as is their custom. With presumptuous shrewdness, if they have been involved for some time with a Venetian nobleman, they usurp his family name; and this is why many foreign men are deceived and believe that they are Venetian noblewomen. And the courtesans' ruffiane [female go-betweens] also make men believe this, for when they lay hands on a foreigner who wants a willing woman, they take such a woman from the street, dress her up splendidly, take her to a secret place and with great fanfare make the man believe that she is a noblewoman. The result is that foreign men, unaware of this trick, brag about what is in fact very far from the truth, for Venetian noblewomen are highly protective of their honor and are models of chastity and purity.

144

VENETIAN NOBLEWOMEN AND OTHERS, at Home and Outdoors in the Winter

Women of high rank, when at home, dress in various colors of silk and brocade, in different styles, and adorn themselves with pearls, bracelets, rings and other jewelry. But courtesans, when at home, present themselves as elegant and well decked out, far more than others. These women, to make their faces more beautiful, treat them with the artifice of make-up and various lotions and bleaches. They can be recognized easily by the way they carry themselves, for at home and outdoors they behave very boldly, showing not only their faces but much of their breast, whitened and painted, and most of the embroidered stockings that cover their legs. But a difference is visible between these women and honorable women in their dress and in their accessories, since courtesans cannot wear pearls, as honorable women do, according to the carefully designed laws in place in the city of Venice (though some of them still do, under the kind of pretext explained above). And they also wear the dress shown here, just as virtuous women of good reputation do.

OTHER VENETIAN WOMEN, *Bleaching Their Hair*

On the rooftops of Venetian houses are certain square wooden structures in the form of open loggias, which, on the mainland, also include walls and roofs, as seen in Florence, where they are called terrazzi *[terraces]. And in the city of Naples, too, on top of the houses there are uncovered areas they call* battuti, *which are made of coarse sand and chalk so well mixed that they resist even heavy rain. But to return to our subject, all women desire to increase their natural beauty through art, and the women of Venice are no different in their eagerness to do this. In doing so, however, they harm more than help themselves because they probably need this art less than other women do. And in addition, when other people recognize the effort they have put into this, they mistrust even the women's natural beauty and judge it as artificial. With this goal in mind, among other artifices, they have the habit of making themselves blonde, and it is for this reason that they spend as much time in the* altana *(as they call the wooden building mentioned previously) as in their bedrooms, or else keep their heads exposed to the sun for days at a time. For this process, in which they are both the served and the servants, they sit on these* altane *when the sun is hottest and wet their hair with a little sponge attached to a wooden handle and soaked in a liquid that they buy or make at home themselves; and over and over again, as they wet their hair, they let it dry in the sun, and in this way they turn their hair blonde so effectively that we think it is natural. During this process, on top of any other clothing, they wear a* rochetto *of very white silk or of fine linen, which they call a* schiavonetto *[a light Slavic gown] and on their heads they wear a straw hat with the crown cut out, which they call a* solana *[sun hat]. This, with its wide brim or flap, supports the loose hair that has been pulled over it and protects the face from the sun while they wait for their hair to lighten.*

Text on page 199

PROSTITUTES
in Public Places

Public prostitutes who work in tawdry places do not have a single way of dressing, for though all of them practice the same profession, their varying degrees of success mean that they cannot all dress in the same finery. Still, all of them have a garment tending toward men's clothing: they wear a doublet of silk or linen or some other fabric, more or less rich depending on what they can afford; and these are decorated with wide strips of trim and padded with cotton, exactly as young men wear them and much like the French style of dress. Next to their skin they wear a man's camicia, *made with as much delicacy and elegance as they can afford. Over this* camicia *is tied, in hot weather, a short or long apron of silk or linen, which reaches the ground; in cold weather they wear a short lined gown either of wool or silk, the best they can afford. The* pianelle *they wear are more than half a foot high but decorated with fancy trim, and with these, on their legs, they wear needle-worked silk; they also wear woolen stockings with Roman-style shoes on their feet. Many wear* braghesse *like men, made of* ormesino *or some other fabric; and by these signs and also by their round beads of silver and their bracelets, they are easily recognized. But there is no easy way to describe how they wear their hair, or how they stand at their windows or even more at their doors and in the street, to draw the foolish fellows who pass by into their webs. They remain there singing love songs with little grace, in keeping with their low status, all noisily making themselves heard with raucous voices.*

Text on page 200

PIZZOCHERE

[Women Who Live in Convents without Taking Vows]

In Venice there are as many types of pizzochere *as there are priests belonging to the Mendicant Friars, whom they match, at least in the color of their clothes. And in this city of Venice, as in other cities of Christendom, there is a certain type of woman, for the most part widows, who, withdrawn from the world through piety or necessity, gather in certain places designed for this purpose. There, secluded from the world, they live on alms and honorable employments, subject to the heads of the religious orders whose habit they wear. These women, because they do not strictly observe the rule of the cloister, cannot really be called nuns; but even so, they live in obedience to some of the rules and orders of their superiors, and they remain chaste and without husbands so that they can serve God, easily visiting the sick and accompanying the dead to burial, and attending sermons and other religious services.*

Text on page 201

YOUNG ORPHAN GIRLS
from the Hospitals of Venice

Great and numerous charitable activities are constantly carried out in the city of Venice, not only in priests' churches and monks' monasteries, of which there are a very great number, but especially in the Spedali[11] *for orphans, who are taken in there as if into a harbor safe from the storms of the evil world. To such places are brought certain young girls who have been abandoned and who have no relatives who might bring them up well and respectably. In these places they are so well watched over and disciplined that they are often envied by girls who have been raised in the houses of their own fathers. Among the many marvelous and praiseworthy things they are seen doing, not least is the sweet choral singing they perform during religious services, with such harmony that many people leave the main churches and go eagerly to their churches to hear them sing. They habitually accompany the dead to burial and leave the house for other reasons as well, but with great modesty and chastity, always in pairs and singing, for it is their duty to pray to God for the first founders of these holy places and for those who still lend helping hands today. And so that such holy work may reach perfection, once they have reached a certain age, they are sent by the heads of these houses to a nunnery or married to a respectable man, and always caressed and recognized as daughters of the places from which they have come. As to their clothing, those from the Hospital for the Incurable dress in turquoise and those from San Giovanni and Paolo in white. And each order does the same thing for boys as for girls, for they dress in the same color once they have reached a certain age, and they are put together with others from whom they can learn some trade by which they can later earn a living.*

HOUSEMAIDS AND HOUSEKEEPERS, *or* Massare, *of Venice*

Women servants in Venetian households have specific duties and they are more or less esteemed by their masters according to the activities assigned to them. This is why wet-nurses, called nene *[colloquial, "breasts"] in Venice because of the duty they have of breastfeeding and taking care of children, are highly respected and affectionately treated, and allowed to eat, drink, and sleep better than other servants so that the milk they give the children is more nourishing and settled. After them those most highly placed are the women who keep the keys to the pantry and the wine cellar, and after them, the chambermaids. And all of these, and the others assigned to housework, usually dress in chestnut brown or* lionato *[tawny brown] wool serge, called* rovano *in Venice, or some other dark color such as* pavonazzo *or another. On their heads they wear a white* fazzuolo *of silk or* bavella *[raw silk], and they cover their shoulders with a plain veil; others wear black, in the form of a long* cappa *or* fazzuolo. *And these women accompany their mistresses to church and wherever they go; they are usually unmarried, so they remain with their mistresses in the house, being (in theory) chaste and free of vice. Other women servants either are married or belong to the category called* dismesse *(women unmarried by choice); each is paid wages according to her duties and what she needs to live on. But those who do other kinds of work in the house, such as cooking, sweeping, and other similar things, wear over their gowns another garment of white or* pavonazzo *cloth, made for hard use rather than finery, and their* sottana *is of colored serge. On their heads they wear white* fazzuoli. *And they attend to all the needs of the household.*

MARKET GARDENERS
of Chioggia

*urrounding the ancient city of Chioggia, as we have said elsewhere, are several villages or towns rich in beautiful orchards and vineyards, full of fruit, especially melons, which ripen very well and abundantly there in their season. From these gardens also come great amounts of vegetables, for they are expertly cultivated, so that in every season they supply everything needed for food, as the most fertile and well-cultivated land usually does. This makes this city of Chioggia very well stocked, and Venice, too, which receives such a great quantity of these crops that it distributes them to all the little islands nearby. These market gardeners of Chioggia, or Palestina, the small island near the city, style their hair in modest little curls framing the forehead, tying up the rest of their hair with narrow silk cords of various colors. They decorate their necks with beautiful coral or silver beads, wrapping a piece of silk* velo *around their necks to cover their entire breast. They wear an undergown of* ciambellotto *or* grograno *[a fabric with a ribbed or corded surface], floor-length, trimmed at the hemline with a border of beautifully needleworked velvet. Over this they wear an overgarment made of black or turquoise cloth, in the form of a* camicia *or* schiavonetto, *cut full without a bodice and cinched with a belt made of* ormesino *or some other fabric, according to their taste. They wear white shoes in Roman style, with raised* pianelle, *not too high. And dressed in this way, with some lovely gift of fruit, they appear before their friends and masters.*

THIRD VIEW OF THE PIAZZA of San Marco

This piazza, which is rightly said to belong to San Marco because it forms something like a large courtyard in front of that magnificent temple, was lengthened and expanded to its present size, with pavement laid down, 433 years ago, according to the plan of Doge Sebastian Ziani (in whose time Pope Alexander came to Venice and peace was made with Barbarossa[12]). Newly instated doges are carried into this piazza from the church of San Marco on a raised platform by the leading men of the Arsenal, who march all around the square. While the doges carry out this public procession they throw coins to the people, and then they are taken to the palace, a custom introduced by this Ziani among many other ceremonies that I will not discuss but that should be models to good princes. All the most solemn processions of the principal Scuole and confraternities during their yearly rituals are carried out in this piazza, as well as all the funerals of the doges, Ducal Counselors, Canons, Knights and Procurators of San Marco, while the bells ring, a custom not observed for anyone else. In addition, every Saturday a general market is held here; during the Sensa, there is an extremely rich display of the work of goldsmiths, jewelers and everything else crafted in metal, with shops on both sides of a wide street covered with awnings. Here for fifteen continuous days more Venetian nobles and foreign lords assemble than at any other time. Many festivities and masquerades are held here at Carnival time—all in all, it is the site of every sort of entertainment.

The length of this piazza, from the west end to the east, is over 540 feet, and the width as far as the bell tower is about 150 feet—though the distance along the offices of the

Procurators, which form a street, to the bell tower, standing on its own, must be about 250 feet. At its back the piazza has the beautiful and ornate church of San Geminiano, and facing it the noble temple of San Marco. On the left are the new offices of the Procuratori, with additional buildings provided for them by Doge Ziani, built to a length of 470 feet as far as the bell tower, divided into fifty-three arches with entryways and shops full of merchandise. On the façade of this building are windows with columns of two orders, 55 feet high altogether, from which it is easy to look out, as though from an observatory. This entire building is made of Istrian stone, arranged into a design by a good man of those times when the art of architecture scarcely existed. In addition, there is the little tower (through whose archway you go from the Pizza into the Merceria), ornately decorated with marbles, sculptures, carvings, mosaics, and gold, but above all with a clock so finely crafted in order to display the heavenly bodies that it has no equal; it is the work of Giancarlo Rinaldi Reggiano, from around the year 1500. At its summit are two giant metal figures that move, striking every hour, and during the Sensa the angel and the Three Magi come forth (moving on a circular platform on wheels) and bow down to Our Lady.

Beyond the clock is the small piazza of San Basso, where a food market is held, and this has at its head the rectory where the priests of San Marco live, on the right side at a distance of 130 feet from the church. We will now discuss this further. It began as a very small building about 830, but it has grown over time, and in 1043 under Doge Domenico Contarini, it attained its present form and decoration. Many consider its structure very solid, and its floor, which is over 200 feet in length and 150 feet across at its apse, has the shape of a lovely cross, above which rest five cupolas, richly decorated inside with mosaics and covered with lead on the outside, as is the rest of the roof. It has a vestibule in front and on its left side, as was the custom with ancient temples, but in its southern corner instead of a vestibule there is a baptistery, which is the chapel and burial place of Cardinal Zeno; altogether it is a very imposing structure. The entire floor of this temple contains various patterns made of colored marble. People estimate the number of columns to be five hundred, of every kind, and admire their rich coverings of sheets of marble, all brought in past times from Athens and other places in Greece, and decorated further in other places with mosaics, renovated from time to time by excellent craftsmen. The façade is divided into five arches, and there are more along each side, in the form of niches into which seven entryways with bronze doors are set, some used and some kept locked. These niches are decorated with columns, marble, and mosaics, but the principal niche has columns of porphyry, serpentine and other multicolored stones of great value, and this niche is entwined with artfully carved festoons. Above these arches runs a railed balcony which opens inward and out; from it rise arches carved in bas relief directly above those below, with points and tabernacles on which statues of saints are set. Above the entry arch are four horses, which, for the rarity of their metal, their masterful craftsmanship, and their lively poses, are unique in the world. For this reason, historians and the backs of medals affirm that they are the ones that Constantine removed from the Arch of Nero in Rome (and which were previously set on the mausoleum of Augustus); he took them to Byzantium and then brought them from there to Venice about the year 1200 and set them in this place.

Among all the other things that decorate this venerable temple (not forgetting altars, pulpits, hanging lamps, rich wall hangings, and other highly valuable things), we must also consider the holy sanctuary that contains so many famous relics of saints. This adjoins the room in which the treasury of San Marco is kept, so called because of the quantity of its jewels and rare, valuable things that have accumulated over many years through gifts to the government and the rule of the Procurators, so that it is considered by foreign princes as being of the highest value. This treasure is displayed on the high altar several times a year. In this temple, as well, is the continual sound of musical instruments, including two extremely famous organs played by the leading men of Europe and a choir of singers directed by Monsignor Gioseffo Zarlino, a man without professional equal in our time and expert as well in every kind of fine literature.[13]

Adjoining the right side of this temple is the great palace where the most serene Prince resides and the Signoria administers all the affairs of state; however, since we have discussed and set down its design elsewhere, we will go on to other matters. In front of the façade of San Marco, on a line with the bell tower, are three very tall poles set on top of bronze pedestals beautifully sculpted with figures and leaves. From these, during certain ceremonies and festivals, hang banners of richly worked silk and gold, as if a sign of the heaven-sent freedom and liberty and power over many kingdoms achieved by so great a Republic; these poles embellish the piazza at all times. Going onward, there is the bell tower of San Marco, encountered again at a corner of the church and the beginning of the library, which was built at the same time as the offices of the Procurators and is so nobly framed and enclosed by a building in the form of a loggia that such a structure has never been so lavishly displayed anywhere else. Its foundation was laid in the year 888 and it is believed to be very deep, set on piles sturdy and thick enough to support such a mass. It began being built above ground in 1148 but its completion was delayed by various accidents. Finally in 1490 it was finished and decorated, though at other times it has been struck by lightning, because, as Horace says,

Saepius ventis agitatur ingens
Pinus et celsae graviore casu
Decidunt turres feriuntque summos
Fulgura montes.

[Most often the huge pine is shaken
By the winds, and, worse, high towers
Collapse; and lightning bolts strike
The highest mountains.][14]

This bell tower is 162 feet in circumference, and 332 feet high in Venetian measure; that is, 164 feet up to its first cornice and from there to the top of its pyramid about 152 feet; the Angel is 16 feet tall, a height that allows it to be a landmark for sailors coming to Venice. In addition to its outer walls, the bell tower has some large inset pilasters, and between one set of them and another is a shallow staircase in Roman style, leading up to the first hallway where the bells serving the church and the palazzo hang, marvelously rich and large.

The building seen at the right of the bell tower is the corner of the library, which faces toward the Ducal Palace. In this library are housed a great number of Greek and Latin books, many of them assembled by the Senate and the rest left by Cardinal Bessarion, a man of the greatest literary erudition.[15] *Most of its foundations were laid in the year 1356, but through misfortunes it was abandoned for many years. In our times it has been finished up to where the offices of the three Procuracies are now being moved, so that the old buildings can be torn down and a view toward the new Procurators' offices can be created, which will be connected to the head of this library and form the right side of the piazza of San Marco. After these three Procuracies, carrying out the will of the Senate and of the most illustrious Procurators, who are responsible for such buildings, had spread the news that such a great undertaking was afoot, almost all the men of good judgment and expertise in the profession of architecture entered into competition. Finally, when all their designs had been looked at and considered several times, the design and artful model of Vincenzo Scamozzo, an architect from Vincenza recently arrived from Rome and staying in Venice, was chosen, which is now considered a wonderful thing.*

With a liveliness of intellect strengthened by years of study and experience in many projects, some already built and others now in the process of being completed, he showed how this piazza could be widened—and indeed it is now unequaled for its great richness. He divided all the land extending to the corner of the library, measuring 500 feet in length, and made another side to the piazza, across from the ducal palace and 120 feet from the broad edge of the canal, into ten palaces to lodge the Lord Procurators who, over time, will be settled here. They have such a wealth of entryways, courtyards, loggias, apartments (giving the Senators space apart from their wives) and rooms that that no one could ask for more. So Scamozzo, as he deserved, was embraced, honored, and rewarded, and finally appointed as the architect for this work, which was begun in the year 1584. And just as the new buildings have a continuous portico, with three orders of columns, each above the other, so too the Procurators' building, laid out a while ago now, will have its own portico of forty-five arches, enclosing shops opening onto the piazza in imitation of the squares of antiquity, but with the Procurators' lodgings located on the inside and on the upper floors. The position of these two buildings, facing one another from the beginning to the end of the piazza, will provide a clear view as far as the main door of the Ducal Palace, with the bell tower a greater wonder still, standing on its own and decorated with further architectural trim. This building will have columns of three orders, the Doric, Ionic, and Corinthian, with so many carvings, grotesque figures, half reliefs and statues of the finest Istrian stone that it can take precedence not only over any building of our time but also equal the most famous ones of antiquity. And I have recounted these details briefly because they are not included in the print of this piazza, as a result of the death of Christoforo Guerra [Cristoforo Chreiger, the German woodcut-maker who worked with Vecellio in Venice], my friend and an excellent printmaker of our time. And because when a new prince of Venice is created, it is the custom to perform a solemn funeral procession around this piazza in honor of the dead prince, I wanted to place these small figures representing men clothed in mourning, with the torches they customarily light as they accompany the body of the dead prince to burial.

CLOTHING OF FOREIGN PRINCES, BARONS OR OTHER MEN
of Other Ranks, often Seen in Venice

he famous city of Venice regularly attracts many princes, who come throughout the year. For their pleasure and to see the great magnificence and famous sites of this marvelous city, they gather here from many different lands, some nearby, some far away, and they dress in clothing of great value. These princes or barons wear a velvet cap, decorated with rich jewels or medals; they wear satin or silk doublets, buttoned with very beautiful golden buttons and embellished with very beautiful trim, also of gold, with gold chains around their necks, enameled and worked with great skill and enriched with costly jewels. They wear a certain type of breeches or trousers of velvet, elaborately made and very richly embroidered, which are lined, like the doublets, with cloth of gold or brocade, visible through slashes in these breeches and doublets, made according to wonderful designs. They wear very thin silk stockings, intricately knitted, most often black or silver, and on their feet they put black leather shoes. And over all their clothing, they wear ferraiuoli *of silk or* canevaccia *or other fabric, and also of very fine black Florentine serge. Clothing more or less like this is worn by nobles and other prosperous and wealthy men throughout Italy.*

RECTOR [OR GOVERNOR] OF THE STUDENTS' SCHOOLS
at the University of Padua

All of the large universities, as an approved custom, elect a head whom they call the Rettore, *a man highly esteemed and admired for his reputation by students and others. The rector in Padua, of whom I will now speak, holds the rank of knight and Venetian nobleman. When he assumes this dignified and solemn office, there are many triumphal processions and festivals, and coins are thrown and banquets and other similar things are arranged, amidst a mighty chorus of voices that shout "Long live the rector!", calling him by the name of his city. This rector covers his head with a cap of black velvet that has small points or horns like a priest's cap, but is a little longer in the back. His gown is of gold brocade and has a hood, lined with marten fur, that rests on his shoulders. Under this gown he wears a* cremesino *satin or silk doublet with gold embroidery and trim or lace also of gold. His breeches are made of the same cloth and his stockings are silk knit, but* cremesino *in color. His shoes are red. And when he leaves his house, he is accompanied by a large number of students. He often dresses with great pomp, all in red velvet,* damasco *or satin. I will not go into the costume that he wears when he is made a knight in Venice and is presented with great ceremony to the Most Serene Prince and his Signoria. The prince gives him a baton and his particular knight puts golden spurs on him; and after having requested from the doge that all of his customary privileges and other things pertaining to his rank be preserved, he returns to his chambers to the sound of trumpets, accompanied by some of the prince's entourage and some of his own, with a large group following behind. And the faculties both of law and of arts follow the same custom I have described above.*

DOCTORS OF LAW OUTSIDE VENICE
and throughout all Lombardy

*he clothing of Doctors of Law or Medicine throughout all of Lombardy is a floor-length toga with open sleeves; it is black in color, of wool,* damasco *or velvet in the winter and in the summer of very beautiful Florentine* ormesino *or* ciambellotto. *Under the toga, these doctors have another gown of silk, and a velvet belt with a silver buckle or a silk belt that falls halfway down their legs. They wear stockings of black wool or silk, and on their feet they wear* pianelle *of black wool or velvet. On their heads they wear a hat of* velluto riccio *[single-pile uncut velvet] or* canevaccia *of silk. This garment is useful to them when they go into Venetian territories or on embassies and into courtrooms because it shows that they are serious men of mature judgment. In our illustrious city of Venice, such doctors dress in a way similar to noblemen, in gowns with the wide sleeves called* à gomito *[long at the elbow], and among them appears in our time the famous and distinguished Annibale Cremona, a marvelous orator, highly learned counselor, noble defender, most impressively skilled, and a man of unique goodness and exemplary manners, affable in conversation and unbelievably hard-working—so much so, that no residence, locale or magistracy has failed to retain the image of his humanity, wise counsel and virtue.*

VICAR, OR DOCTOR, OR ASSESSOR, OR LOCAL MAGISTRATE
of the Venetian State on the Mainland

Among the vicars or assessors or court magistrates or doctors of the Venetian state was a certain Alessando Cremona, brother of Annibale mentioned above, who shone with the radiance of the sun. While serving as Vicar of Bergamo, he died in the flower of his youth; his innate generosity, most noble and innocent, was revealed in the infinite virtue that could be seen in his deeds. And certainly, just as a river springs from its source, a flower from its meadow, and a fruit from its tree, so bravery, prudence, and infinite courtesy flowed from him, anchored by deep roots from which a great number of branches grew, always green and beautiful for their inestimable virtue. Such vicars wear long robes of velvet with narrow sleeves lined with marten or lynx or other furs during the winter; and in the summer, togas of satin, damasco, ormesino *or other similar fabrics in black, as in the figure shown here. I have seen such an ensemble on the person of the excellent doctor Signor Bernardino Barceloni, matching his rare qualities with a toga of this kind, not to mention the noble Doiona family, and also, most famous in medicine, Signor Rhotilio Doglioni. Both of these men most often wear a short undergown with a long* ferraiuolo *rather than any other style, and a shorter undergarment, mid-thigh in length, tied with a* posta, *depending on the time of year. The usual style of dress for most of these magistrates, however, is the one shown here.*

DRESS OF YOUNG MEN OF THE CITY OF VENICE, *and of Students*

he dress of young men or students of the city of Venice and throughout all of Italy is very handsome and elegant, and it allows the wearer to move easily and quickly. In the winter these young men wear a tall black cap, called à tozzo*, of gathered velvet, and in the summer hats of* canevaccia *of silk or* tabino *[a rich watered silk], or* ormesino*, with linings of colored taffeta. Around these hats they fasten a* velo *or a garland of* margaritine *[enameled glass beads], lovely to see, with a medal or precious stone, and a kind of gold braid interwoven with pearls or small crystals. They wear doublets of silk, satin,* canevaccia *or* tabino*, with gold or silk buttons and various trims and laces. They wear decorated, finely shaped, and very white ruffles at the neck, and knee-length trousers of the same fabric as the doublet; and, like the doublet, they pink or slash these trousers in beautiful patterns, and through these slashes they show off their differently colored taffeta linings. On their legs they wear stockings of silk or* stame *[fine hand-knit wool] from Flanders, and their shoes are of Moroccan leather, made with great elegance. It is a custom in the blessed state of Venice that when doges are elected, all of the communities in the dominion of this state elect two orators or ambassadors to come here as their representatives. Since I have seen certain men dressed this way in the company of such ambassadors from Cividal di Belluno, I thought that I should mention here the orators sent to Doge Cicogna from there, one of whom was*

Signor Novello Novelli, a man among whose many virtues nobility, magnificence and unmatched generosity shine brightly. The other was Signor Fioravanti Foro, who, with a divine oration full of new and lofty conceits, in a lovely and agreeable style embellished with marvelous learning and grace, made a speech that caused wonder and admiration, which, along with his brilliance, devoted entirely to virtue, earns him eternal fame.

Text on page 214

CLOTHING OF YOUNG MEN OF VENICE and of Other Places in Italy

Young men going courting most often wear doublets of satin, tabino *or some other kind of silk, pierced or slashed with different patterns in the shape of a cross or stars; through these slashes are seen their colored taffeta linings. On these doublets they wear gold buttons and, at their necks, ruffles trimmed with white lace; and on their heads they wear a cap of* velluto riccio *or* canevaccia *of silk, with a piece of* velo *tied around it and knotted in the shape of a rose, onto which they usually pin a small medal. They wear* braghesse *in the same style as the doublet and needle-worked stockings of silk* canevaccia, *with shoes of Spanish leather; and on top they wear a cape, and they hold a flower in one hand and a handkerchief and gloves in the other. This attire is frequently worn by noblemen, both in Venice and in other cities of Italy, especially by young men before they start wearing sleeves* à comeo, *which they do not put on before reaching eighteen or twenty years of age. Most of them dress in the style I have described, but many wear black, or* argentino *[silver gray], or light* pavonazzo *tending toward purple, especially in their doublets and* braghesse *and stockings, as shown in the image.*

Text on page 215

PRESENT-DAY FOOT SOLDIER
in Wartime

Italian soldiers are very strong, brave, and warlike, as was seen in the year of the victory over the Turks, which occurred in 1569,[17] and continues to be seen every day in their various undertakings. Regarding their dress, I believe that since the world began, there has never been more comfortable or streamlined clothing than this, for in our day soldiers are not encumbered by their clothing, as used to be the case and as we see is still the case in foreign nations, for too much cloth or too voluminous breeches have caused many soldiers to die by tangling themselves up in them. Today we can say that the soldier's uniform fits him well and leaves him free to move, as can be seen in the foot soldier shown here. On their shoulders they carry a long-barreled arquebus [musket], which they are very quick to fire and clean. They also wear two or three other smaller guns at their belt, so that in close combat with their enemies, they can attack them repeatedly. On their heads they wear a morrione [a helmet with a movable jawpiece] or celata with plumes of different kinds of feathers, and on their bodies they wear iron panciere [body armor] or animette with chain mail sleeves. They also wear close-fitting braghesse or knee-length trousers made of chamois, deerskin, colored cloth, satin, or various types of wool. Many such trousers are of patterned silk or brocade, depending on their status, but always rich and beautiful. They wear stockings of chamois or wool or knitted silk, according to what they can afford. They wear leather belts with buckles, and finely decorated pouches for gunpowder, trimmed with silk tassels; at their necks they wear a small powder horn, filled with fine gunpowder, which they put into the touchhole of the musket. And the outfit of this soldier resembles those worn at the time of the naval victory over the Turks in 1571, on the seventh of October.[18] Such a costume reveals the wearer's physical agility and strength in the upper body, which is evident in many noblemen of Italy, who showed such great courage in that war that every trace they left behind and all their deeds richly deserve to be respected and held in undying memory.

A PRESENT-DAY SOLDIER
Off Duty

This clothing is very handsome and comfortable, and it was worn in Italy by the Prince of Wallonia[19] *and the Duke of Savoy—for this reason breeches of this kind are called* braghesse alla Savoina *[breeches in the style of Savoy]. This style of dress was seen in the city of Venice after the capture of Szeged in Hungary,*[20] *when that prince came to Venice; and from that time up to the present, this style has been worn, along with the short beard in Philippine style (as it is called). The attire of this off-duty soldier includes a hat, not very high but wide-brimmed, usually* argentino *in color, with a plume attached to the band. On top, they wear a very beautiful* colletto *of leather, fastened in front with gold buttons; under this, they have a satin doublet with sleeves slashed in a handsome pattern; at the neck they wear* camicia *collars of very white* renso *[a delicate white linen], with small ruffles at the wrist. They fasten their sword and dagger to a leather belt with buckles, and they wear knee-length trousers of patterned velvet and stockings of leather or* stame *and shoes of Cordovan leather; and across the chest, a sash of* ormesino *in various colors, according to their captain's insignia, and a* ferraiuolo *of black or multicolored wool. This is also the present-day clothing of the armed soldier shown previously, although they often change their style of dress, as do the Italians and the French. But I have included this one as most worthy of remembering and most frequently worn.*

BRAVO *[ARMED RETAINER]* OF VENICE
and Other Cities of Italy

In ancient times the same sort of bravi *were called gladiators; today they are known as* bravi *or* sbricchi, *and they serve now one man, now another, for money, swearing and threatening people without cause, causing all sorts of scandals and committing murders. They dress very well, and they like to pick fights for no reason, now with one man, now with another; and such men are called* taglia cantoni *[literally, corner cutters]. They wear a high cap of velvet or some other kind of silk, banded with a* velo *tied into the shape of a rose. They wear ruffles of* renso *and a* colletto *of goatskin or deerskin or chamois, with a doublet of Flemish linen underneath and sleeves of the same fabric. They wear knee-length silk* braccioni *and stockings of leather or Flemish* stame. *They carry a sword and dagger in their belt, and they go around talking about duels and quarrels. On top, they wear a* ferraiuolo *trimmed with gold or silk braid. They change their style of dress, as everyone does, but even so, they always wear shirts of chain mail and* schinieri, *with a* celata *hooked to the back of their belt. They are often favored by prostitutes, who employ them against anyone who might try to do them harm.*

MOURNING CLOTHES
Outside Venice

High-ranking men on the mainland, grieving for the loss of a relative, wear garments similar to the ones shown here, that is, a floor-length black overgarment of rough, brushed, unpatterned wool, or of silk, with a long bavero *made of the same fabric. On their heads they wear a gathered cap embellished with* buratto *or* canevaccia *of silk, trimmed with strips of black* velo*; and they wear black shoes.*

ITALIAN COLONEL, CAVALIER OR CAPTAIN in Mourning Attire

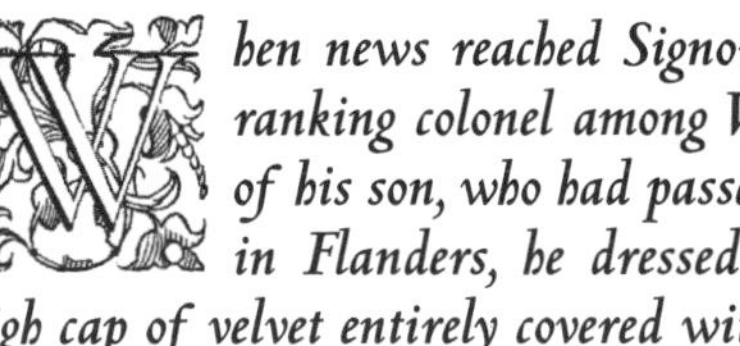

When news reached Signor Scipio Costanzo, a high-ranking colonel among Venetian lords, of the death of his son, who had passed from this life to the next in Flanders, he dressed entirely in black, with a high cap of velvet entirely covered with velo. His undergarment was of wool, and over it he wore a floor-length mantle of brushed plush wool with a hood that reached down to his waist; this hood was sewn from the middle on down with strips of black velo, and he had the edges of this mantle trimmed with the same fabric, in a braided form. And this same attire is worn by many other men in mourning in Italy.

FULLY ARMED SOLDIER DRESSED FOR COMBAT
on Horseback and on Foot

The armor shown here is very protective and useful in times of war, because when it is fired upon by a musket or arrow or other long-distance weapon, the man wearing it cannot be wounded since it is made of very fine, shining steel. On their heads such soldiers wear a large steel celato *with beautiful plumes, and on their backs they wear short* corsaletti *of the same metal, worked with gold, and equally strong thigh-pieces. They carry swords and cover their hands with strong jointed gloves, and they wear visors that keep anything but their eyes from being seen; their horse is similarly armored and covered in steel. But the armed man here is represented in order to show a complete set of modern armor, and how different it is from the ancient. For though the ensemble is derived from the ancient style, new inventions have been added to it along the way, as has also been the case with the discovery of new weapons for warfare. Cyrus was the first among the Persians to find a way to arm both men and horses, but in brass and copper; and he invented chariots with scythed wheels and also the method of setting towers on top of elephants. Since then, following the Persians, such armor has been the custom, but in a better form and in steel and chain mail, which all armed men wear today.*

A PRESENT-DAY MAN AT ARMS on a Caparisoned Horse

The Romans, too, had cavalry of armed men, but very different from ours, because they used the lance and the hobnailed cudgel, or crossbows, with which they shot iron arrows, while our cavalry usually carry a long lance in their hands and four or five muskets attached to their belts, which they handle so well that they put any big army to flight. They wear beautiful plumes on their morrioni *or* celate, *and they set others on their horses' heads, so that they make a most beautiful sight. The horse is entirely covered with sheets of steel and a visor of steel. On top of this armor, such a horse is covered with silk or brocade, according to the status of the horseman, so that he stands out with great grandeur, as does in our days the famous Baron by indirect descent, Signor Pio Obizzi,*[21] Condottiere *[leader of mercenaries] of men at arms, not to mention the beauty of his horses. At the time that the Empress Maria came to Venice his horse was entirely covered in silver chain mail, with very lovely livery.*

A MEMBER OF THE LIGHT CAVALRY
in Armor

Our light cavalry are much better than those of the Romans, for they fought with bows and shot darts, and our men at arms fight with lances and muskets, which they carry ahead of their horses' heads. Our men, too, are very well armored with steel armor in the form of corsaletti*, on top of which they wear a sash of* ormesino *in different colors, and above their* morrioni *plumes made of long feathers.*

SOLDIERS OR SCAPPOLI [FREE GALLEY MILITIA] IN VENETIAN TERRITORIES, *in Galleys Manned by Criminals and Other Galleys*

here exists a certain kind of sea-going soldier, not drafted by the Venetian state but free, who works at times when the galleys of these lords need to be armed. For the most part they are Slavs or Greeks or men from similar nations, accustomed to endure such activity over long periods, brave, strong, and robust by nature. They have rugged faces, being natives of infertile countries, and the majority of them come from these regions, though some are from the Veneto in Italy, and even Venice itself. They wear a woolen burichetto *[short jacket or jerkin] with elbow-length sleeves,* biavo *[sky-blue or bluish] or some other color, without a collar, buttoned down the chest and tied with a striped* posta *a half-foot wide, of linen, silk or striped wool. Below this they wear* braghesse *of linen or fine wool in a solid color, rather wide, tied below the knee; they wear shoes that are not very heavy, and on their heads a red woolen cap with a small plume. They carry broad swords and daggers. And their living expenses are covered by the galley, as is the custom, with the addition of two ducats each month in wages, so they can afford what they need.*

GALLEY SOLDIERS, ALSO CALLED FALILA, *Drafted in Venetian Territories in Time of War*

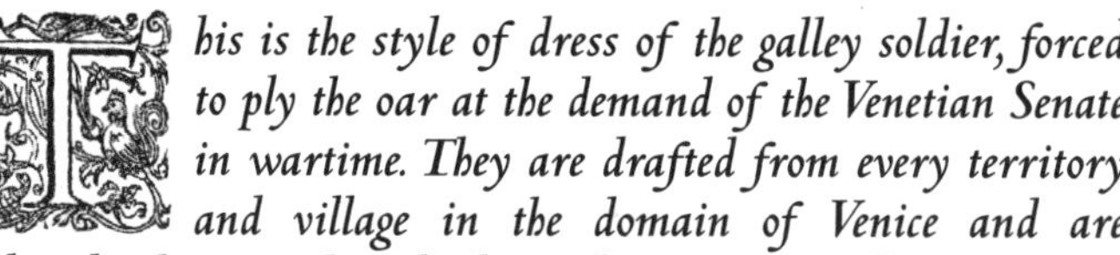

his is the style of dress of the galley soldier, forced to ply the oar at the demand of the Venetian Senate in wartime. They are drafted from every territory and village in the domain of Venice and are enlisted whenever these lords need to arm a galley. They are ready to carry out every command, and their selection takes place every three years among mature and young men most suitable for this task, capable of heavy work because they live from day to day in the fields and woods and easily endure hardships. On their heads they wear a small cap of dark rust-colored felt, with some feather or another, and a short casacca *of wool in the same color but thicker in texture, buttoned in front, with a small collar, and cinched with a leather strap to which they attach a knife. They wear wide, unfitted* braccioni, *with stockings of thick wool tied under the knee; they wear heavy shoes and carry an axe or hatchet. They are strong men, and robust in action. They cover themselves with a* gabbano *[a short or mid-length cape] of* griso *[coarse wool], rust-colored, fit to protect them against both rain and cold, and these also serve them as a blanket for sleeping in because they are lined with another piece of wool, in varying colors.*

GALLEY SLAVES

Because some men, not respecting the law, commit serious crimes, they are sentenced by judges to row for a certain number of years in the galleys, more or less according to the seriousness of their crimes. Some of them are chained with a chain on each foot and bound to the bench on which they have to row; some chains are joined to a crosswise bar with a weight on it, also at the rower's bench. Their heads are shaved and so is their beard, except for a moustache, and they dress in a wide camicia *and an overshirt of* griso*, with a* tabarro *of the same fabric, calf-length, which has a hood behind like the one worn by friars. On their heads they wear a small red cap, and they are given a length of rope to belt this* gabbano*. Dressed like this, they are ready to row and fetch water and wood for the use of the galley; and for sleeping, they have a coarse, inexpensive blanket. They suffer many discomforts as punishment for their misdeeds.*

CLOTHING OF THE CONFRATERNITY ASSIGNED TO EXECUTIONS,
Who Accompany the Condemned of the City of Venice To Death

he clothing shown here is very frightening and horrendous, but all the more charitable because it is worn by rich and prosperous men, who, to earn indulgences for this confraternity, join its other members who accompany evildoers to their death after they have been sentenced by judges. And they are told to dress in this costume by a servant called a Nunzolo *[a summoner] on the evening preceding the day of the execution; then in the morning they are summoned by a bell used only for this purpose. Their attire consists of a sack-like overgarment of black cloth, floor-length, with a hood, which they pull over their heads and use to cover their face, and the rest of it falls over their shoulders. In the middle of their chest they have sewn onto this gown an image of the holy crucifix as a sign of great piety, and there are many large groups of these brothers. They all wear belts and they carry iron chains, which make a noise as they walk along. Grouped in this way, they go to the prison where the sentenced criminal awaits them, and two by two they make a procession, holding a holy crucifix and many tall black torches in front of them, and also a great number of black wax candles. Here they await the guilty man, who, having been comforted by a priest, is accompanied to the place of execution, where he receives the punishment he deserves. Then these brothers return to their church, San Fantino, where they have a beautiful* scuola *[meeting hall], with an altar made of fine, hard black stone and many beautiful paintings.*

GRAVEDIGGGERS OR PIZZICAMORTI [CORPSEBEARERS] *of Venice*

In the city of Venice certain people are assigned by their superiors to dress the dead and carry them to burial and to do everything necessary for this process. Their clothing consists of a mantle, quite long, of berettino *[dark ash gray],* bigio *[dull gray], or* fratesco *[ash gray], open at the front and above and below the arms. Under this they wear a calf-length undergown, and on their head they wear a small cap of the same color as their undergown. This is also the color of their stockings and shoes.*

THE CLOTHING OF THE SHAMEFACED POOR, WHO BEG FOR CHARITABLE ALMS in the Churches and Street Corners of Venice

People who dress in the clothing mentioned here, in which they go around begging, usually were once rich and are mainly Cittadini[22] *who, through bad luck or a change in fortune, have fallen into want; they alone are permitted to wear this clothing. It consists of a loose robe of black cloth, often mended and old, with which they show their poverty. It is floor-length and has a hood, which they wear over their heads and let fall over their faces, with two holes through which they see and yet cannot be seen. In their hand they carry a paper cone to collect alms, which they request with gestures rather than words. They wear black stockings and broken-down* pianelle.

PORTERS OR BASTAGI[23]
of the City of Venice

In various places in the city of Venice certain men called porters can be found, who earn their living by loading and unloading ships and boats and carrying goods on their backs from one place to another. For the most part, they are from Bergamo, the valleys of Trent or Brescia. Ordinarily on workdays they carry sacks of coarse linen cloth, useful for carrying heavy weights, and they arrange them over their heads like a hood and set heavy burdens on top of them. They also wear a gabbano *as their upper garment, which they belt with a rope, from which they hang other lengths of rope. They wear certain loose leggings of* griso*, which end above their feet, and they put on heavy shoes. And they are forced to labor in certain public services, such as putting out fires and unloading salt and working on some days for a daily wage in the Arsenal.*

BASKET CARRIERS WHO WORK FOR BUTCHERS AND FISHMONGERS

There are porters who work in certain places in the city of Venice and in the districts of the San Marco and Rialto fish markets and also in the Butchers' Hall. These men are very familiar with the city and very trustworthy. When they are called for by people who want to send foodstuffs home, they appear with their round baskets with a handle on top, in which they keep a sack of coarse linen to cover the goods that are given to them to carry to people's houses. These men are usually, for the most part, from Brescia or Bergamo. They wear small felt hats or woolen caps and dress in coarse linen with aprons in front, and in knee-length trousers of coarse wool and thick-soled shoes meant for mud and heavy work.

PEASANT WOMEN IN THE REGION SURROUNDING VENICE,
Seen in Venice on the Day of the Ascension of Our Lord, a Venetian Holiday and Fair

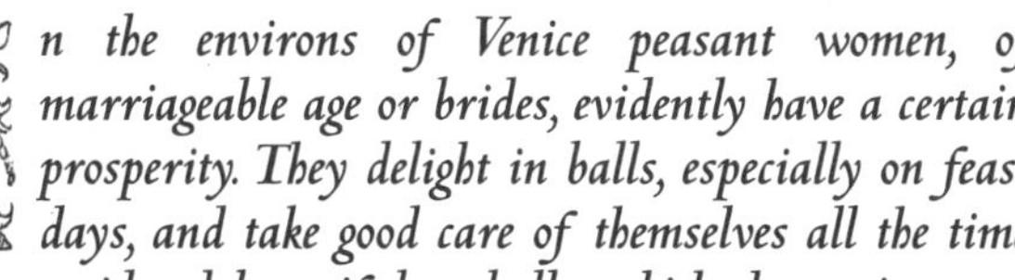

In the environs of Venice peasant women, of marriageable age or brides, evidently have a certain prosperity. They delight in balls, especially on feast days, and take good care of themselves all the time so as to be considered beautiful at balls, which they enjoy very much, and to entertain the owners of the land on which they work so that these men will be generous to them. On their heads they wear hats of very fine straw, made with beautiful skill. Under these, they wear their hair very well arranged in a net of gold threads; they wear gathered baveri *in the style of a* camicia, *and on top of these a veil of silk or some other thin fabric. They wear overgowns of fine cotton or wool in various colors, with silver-gilt brooches on their bodices, which are trimmed with bands of velvet or of some other kind of silk, and corals or silver beads around their necks or on their breast, as well as down the seams of their sleeves. Over this gown they wear a circular apron of silk or some other very thin material, arranged with small fasteners in the form of needle-worked rosettes with narrow silk ties. They wear belts of* cremesino *or black velvet, with silver studs. They wear needleworked stockings with white embroidered shoes and* pianelle *covering them. They dress very neatly and look very lovely. On their hats they wear feathers of different colors and bands of beautiful silk in different colors.*

YOUNG PEASANT PLANNING TO MARRY, ON FEAST DAYS IN PADUAN VILLAGES and Other Places Near Venice

In the villages outside Padua and other nearby places are peasants who practice the art of agriculture, and on feast days they spruce themselves up carefully, to look handsome at holiday dances where some of their girlfriends meet. On their heads they wear hats of fine straw, banded with silk poste *in different colors like those of their beloveds, but a little higher at the crown. Their* camicie *are trimmed with white ruffles, and they wear doublets of thin linen with* braghesse *of wool or other colored fabric and stockings of the same cloth; they wear shoes of Cordovan leather and on their hats feathers of various colors. As weapons they carry spears and staffs and certain knives, which they wear at their belts and sometimes use to wound their rivals in love. When they take a wife, it is their custom to lead her to church for a marriage ceremony, which is also attended by her mother-in-law and other relatives. They present her with slippers and ribbons for her hair, and they arrange them on her head and feet in the presence of all the relatives, while reciting some lovely words.*

PEASANT WOMAN FROM THE TERRITORY OF TREVISO AND OTHER PLACES, *Who Come on Saturday to Markets in Venice*

*he clothing shown here belongs to peasant women who come to Venice for the Saturday market from villages in surrounding areas. When they enter the city, they take off a large, broad-brimmed hat, which they wear outdoors and carry in their hands; it is made of thick straw and banded with a strip of red or* cremesino *silk. They wear an overgarment of a different fabric in sky-blue or* biavo, *with a fairly close-fitting bodice, which they fasten with silk ties wide enough to allow their white* camicia *to be seen underneath. On this bodice they wear silver gilt studs, and wrapped around their head and neck they wear a white veil of cotton or some other fabric, which holds their hair in place. And because they come from outside the city, where there is a lot of mud, they fasten up their overgarment a palm's width above the ground with a leather belt three fingers in width, above another garment that they wear underneath. Over their shoulders they carry two baskets, with chickens and hens in one and cheese, eggs and fruit and everything that can be produced in villages in the other. They wear high-cut shoes covered with thick leather to protect them from mud and water.*

A PEASANT AT THE MARKET
in Venice

Peasants who come to Venice at the season of All Saints' Day, to sell geese, eggs, and other edibles, wear the clothing shown here. It consists of a rough hat of thick straw and an undergarment, mid-thigh in length, of wool, rust-colored, berretino *or* fratesco, *while on their feet they wear shoes of heavy leather for the mud. Onto their legs they tie high leather boot tops, and on top of their short undergarment, they put on a* ferraiuolo *of coarse wool, rust-colored or* berretino, *with a long* bavero *from this* ferraiuolo *down over their shoulders. And so dressed, they rest a staff on the ground, with a goose or two for sale.*

THE CLOTHING OF LOMBARDY

EARLY CLOTHING OF MILAN, IN LOMBARDY

The province of Lombardy has had many different names, but in the end it kept the name it had taken from the Lombards, who ruled over it for a very long time. This is the richest province of Italy, not so much for its lovely setting and its beauty as for its good fortune of producing everything that can be desired for pleasure. Milan is the largest and most populous city of this province; this is why it is called "Milan the Great." It abounds in everything necessary for human food and clothing, and the people here work at making everything that can be desired.

The clothing of the women of Milan in early days resembled what is portrayed here. In the past, these women gathered their hair into a net of gold or silk, leaving some loose on the sides to hang down at their temples; they tied the net on with a thin cord of colored silk, which was quite long and which, because it was knotted at the back of their heads, fluttered about. Around their necks they wore a string of pearls, or round silver beads, or coral, according to their rank. They wore an overgarment of ormesino *with bands of gold embroidery at their breast, halfway down their gowns and also at the hem, and this gown was covered all over in little flowers of gold. At the back there was a small train; in front, the gown was open from the middle down, allowing the* sottana, *of velvet or beautifully patterned* damasco, *to be seen. With this overgarment they wore wide sleeves in the German style, but tied in many places with silk ribbons, perhaps red or some other color and very long, which were formed into bows with the ends left free to the wind. At the bottom of the sleeves of the overgarment appeared other sleeves belonging to their* camicia, *but very wide; because of this width, they hung down from the wrists from the waist to the knee.*

Text on page 237

NOBLEWOMEN AND WIVES OF MILAN AND OTHER CITIES OF LOMBARDY,
Seen in Venice

he noblewomen and wives of Milan arranged their hair in a lovely, graceful style: framing their foreheads they wore charming little curls and their tresses, crimped and curled in rings, beautifully framed the tops of their heads. Onto their hair they pinned a veil shaped like a lily, with a lovely point reaching down toward the forehead; the rest of this veil was pinned to the collar of the overgarment, which was of fine damaschetto *woven with designs of large flowers and roses. The overgarment was floor-length and fastened all the way down the front with shiny gold buttons. They wore strings of beautiful pearls at their necks and gold chains, with very white ruffles. At their backs, they attached veils of very thin silk, which fell all the way to the ground. And this is exactly the style of noble dress now worn by women of Milan, as seen in Venice during the feast of the Ascension of Our Lord.*

Text on page 238

MARRIED NOBLEWOMEN OF MILAN
and Other Places in Lombardy

This is a style of clothing belonging more to the married noblewomen of Milan than to others. These noblewomen wear a cloth of ormesino *on their heads, colored or black according to their preference, which leaves visible only small curls framing their foreheads and ruffles at their necks; this cloth of* ormesino *is so large that it covers their shoulders entirely. They wear a three-quarter-length* Romana *of patterned* damasco *or patterned velvet, fastened with gold buttons down to the waist. These* Romane *are worn open from the waist down to the feet, revealing floor-length* sottane *of* ormesino *with bands of patterned velvet or gold brocade. Their* zimarra*, on top, has open, short sleeves and the wearer's arms emerge from them, showing the sleeves of the* sottana*. They wear* pianelle *but not too high, and this is how they walk about.*

Text on page 239

CLOTHING OF THE DUCHESSES OF PARMA and of Other Noble Ladies throughout Lombardy

The clothing shown here is taken from life, in a sketch sent to me by Messer Erasmo Falte, a bookseller; the image was made most skillfully by the hand of a good painter of Parma, and Messer Falte sent it to me along with many others, and this is a print of the picture. These ladies wear a coiffure including curls and braids beautifully arranged around their foreheads, with jewels and silk flowers most delicately worked. To the back of their hair they pin a beautiful veil in a very charming fashion, made of silk with stripes of gold, and trimmed all around with lace also of gold; this veil falls from their head and covers their zimarra *or overgarment completely. One end of this veil is drawn up under the left arm and pinned on the breast with a little mask of heavy gold. The* zimarra *or overgarment they wear is of striped* rasetto *[satinette] or printed velvet, adorned with gold trim, floor-length and fastened with a single gold button on the breast; they wear the rest of it open, but with gold buttons all the way down to the hem. These overgarments have half-length sleeves, or* bracciali, *below which is seen another narrow sleeve as long as the* zimarra *itself. These undersleeves, too, are loaded with heavy gold buttons where the arm emerges from the half sleeve, covered with the sleeves of the* sottana, *which is of gold brocade or silk patterned with large flowers, attached to a very tight-fitting bodice in the style of a doublet, fastened with gold buttons. On the front of this* sottana *they wear a gold band, set with many different jewels, which reaches down to the hemline. They are accustomed to wearing the* verducato *[a farthingale, or hoopskirt], or* faldiglia, *which shapes their full-skirted* sottana *artfully into a bell, very convenient for walking and dancing. This previously mentioned* faldiglia *has now become the fashion throughout Italy. Around their necks they wear magnificent chains of gold and jewels, and very white, broad ruffles trimmed with embroidery, gold lace, and beautiful needlework. They wear earrings with pearls or other precious stones, and* pianelle, *though not very high, and also gold bracelets with jewels and pearls. This style of dress, as well as others that will follow in order after this one, has been adopted recently by noble and rich women throughout all of Lombardy and Italy, including Ferrara, Mantua, Milan, and other large cities.*

MARRIED WOMEN AND LADIES OF THE CASTLE TOWNS IN THE REGION AROUND PARMA
and Other Places in Lombardy and throughout Italy

he clothing in this image is not very different from the previous one. The coiffure worn by these women includes curls framing the forehead, and they braid the rest of their hair and wrap it around their heads in a lovely design, decorating it with silk and golden ribbons formed into a rose at their hairline; from this some suspend a little veil striped with gold and lace, fluttering in the breeze, while others wrap it around their head. They wear gold earrings set with jewels and pearls around their necks, from which fall the beautiful ruffles of their camicie *prettily embroidered and trimmed with* merletto di opera di aco *[needle lace], enriched by handsome gold necklaces set with various jewels, which rest on their breast. They wear a* zimarra *of* ormesino, *white or some other color according to their taste, made of masterfully needle-worked fabric. This they wear open from the breast down, floor-length, and heavy with buttons of gold or crystal, with long, open sleeves from which their arms emerge, covered with the sleeves of their bodice. This is styled like a doublet, coming to a point that gives a rounded shape to the belly of the* sottana, *over the* verducale; *this undergown is of* rasetto *or* brocatello *and is floor-length. On top of the* zimarra, *behind their shoulders, they attach a veil made of silk woven with gold, which hangs in front of them, pinned together at the bottom and trimmed all around with gold* merletto al fuso *[bobbin lace] or* di opera di aco. *At their wrists they wear very white cuffs, finely worked, and around their necks they wear very beautiful pearls and heavy chains. And they also wear thick gold bracelets.*

THE CLOTHING OF PRINCIPAL LADIES OF THE STATE OF MILAN
and the Region around Parma

The principal noblewomen of Lombardy, especially Milan, Parma, Ferrara, and Mantua, wear their hair in pretty curls around their foreheads and tied with silk and gold ribbons. They arrange jewels, including pearls, in the shape of a rose, and place one large pearl in the middle of their forehead; the rest of their pearls they wrap around their head like braids, which they gather together under a lovely veil of gold or silver, knotted in a lovely way at the top of their head. They let the ends of this veil fall onto their shoulders and down their backs to the ground and on into a long train. They wear earrings of large, beautiful pearls, and a wide lattuga *[ruff] at their necks; on their breast they wear gold chains. They wear a gown of* pavonazzo *velvet or some other silk patterned with elegant foliage or some other hand-worked design—this is floor-length with an arm's length train, and has wide, open sleeves, not very long, and fastened with buttons of gold or crystal. They also wear half-length sleeves, or* bracciali, *with the same kind of buttons, from which their arms emerge in the sleeves of their* sottana, *in* damasco *or* ormesino *or some other kind of fabric. Their overgown is a very close-fitting* zimarra *with two openings in the bodice, which has gold buttons, and the gown is fastened all the way down with similar gold buttons and unified from head to toe with bands of patterned brocade of velvet or silk, which go all around the hem and also down both sides.*

CLOTHING OF PRIVATE NOBLEWOMEN
of Lombardy

Certain noblewomen of Milan, Parma, and other cities of Lombardy wear a very elegant coiffure: they curl some of their hair around their foreheads and gather their braids around at the back of their heads in a beautiful design, with artificial roses made of silk ribbon; on top of this they arrange a small veil that gives a mushroom shape to their hair, which they decorate with lovely flowers, natural or of silk, and this veil falls to their shoulders behind their head. They wear attractive ruffles at their necks, of fine renso or cambrai, very white and decorated with the finest needlework; these are supported by the collar of their overgarment, which is of satin or some other fabric, floor-length and patterned with marizo ad onda [wavy lines with a shimmering effect], and with gold buttons and very beautiful gold fastenings from collar to hem. This overgarment has wide sleeves, in a fabric different from the fabric of the gown itself and lined with colored ormesino; they are of a length similar to that of the dogalina, and are fastened to the bodice with gold buttons. The arms emerge from these sleeves covered in the same color as the sottana, with very elegant small slashes. Such women also adorn themselves richly with chains and necklaces and with modest trains. And I saw this style of clothing at the Ascension Day fair in Venice.

WOMEN OF MIDDLE RANK

The custom of these middle-ranking women is to wear a floor-length overgarment of black silk or ciambellotto *or wool, belted at the waist with a silk binding and then open down to the hem; through this opening can be seen a woolen* sottana, *embroidered with wool or silk thread in a contrasting color. On their heads they wear a piece of black* ormesino *tied under their chin, covering their whole head in the style of a hood, and they let this fall down behind them and blow in the wind.*

GIRLS OF THE PEASANTRY AND ARTISAN CLASS in Parma

In Parma and other regions of Lombardy both peasant girls and girls from artisans' families adorn their heads with colored silk ribbons, which they tie to their hair and top with a pretty veil; this veil covers the rest of their hair, and because it is very long at the end, they let it flutter in the wind. At their necks they wear round beads of silver or coral, and they have ruffles, not very high, on the collars of their camicia. *They wear an apron of thin white linen, decorated with colored bands of silk needlework, and a stiff, sturdy bodice. They wear sleeves of the same fabric, with* braccialetti *trimmed with* velo. *They wear* pianelle *in various colors but most often white, and velvet belts with silver gilt buckles.*

ANOTHER STYLE FROM THE STATE OF MILAN and Other Places in Lombardy

During the days of the Sensa in Venice, I saw another style of dress, too, which, because it was so chaste, I think worth adding to the others. For some time I studied a woman, among others from this region, dressed very modestly. She wore a sottana *of silk* brocatello, *closed in front with buttons down to the hem, with a high, snug bodice and collar with beautiful, bright white* lattughine, *needle-worked with very beautiful designs that I am sure were done by hand. She also wore an overgown of black silk trimmed with velvet, open in front and not very long; at her neck and on her breast she wore a gold chain, along with bracelets and pendant earrings at her ears. Her coiffure was very elegant and modest. She also wore a mantle similar to the Venetian* cappa *(as it is called), of thin, crimped black silk. This fell from her head midway down her leg, but it was pulled up a bit around her shoulders; it was tied in front with a ribbon. To some extent this style of dress resembled that of Venetian women. She wore small* lattughine *at her wrists and carried a fan in the Neapolitan style, with a very modest train all around her.*

A MARRIED WOMAN OF FERRARA IN FORMAL ATTIRE, Outside her House

Ferrara was named after the iron that it once used to pay tributes to the Romans, just as Argenta was named after the silver that it paid in tribute. The city of Ferrara is beautiful and large but has a bad climate because its location is rather swampy (though this is improved by the fires kept burning there). It is situated on the banks of the Po river, which flows through it to the east and the south. It possesses large territories, and though they are swampy, they are fertile in wheat, wine, and fodder of all kinds. It has always been loyal to the popes of Rome, who gave it as a feudal holding to the House of Este, who still possess it.

The married women of this city go about in a very neat and modest way. They wear an elegant headdress, braiding their hair and wearing a few curls at their temples. On top of their heads they set a silk veil, light yellow or black, woven with gold thread, which they draw very gracefully into a point over their foreheads; the rest hangs to the ground. They wear low-cut overgarments, floor-length, with a short bodice of patterned velvet or rose-patterned gold brocade and a train of modest length. They wear a sottana *of lightweight* rasetto *or silk* broccatello, *with silk and gold trim. They adorn their necks with a gold chain containing jewels and precious stones, and with a ribbon of colored silk from which they hang beautiful medallions and jewels.*

The title on this print is incorrect in the original book.

UNMARRIED GIRLS of Ferrara

The unmarried girls of Ferrara are usually naturally beautiful, slim, and of very fine intellect. They wear their hair neatly arranged, pulled up into braids, with pretty curls around their foreheads, and they cover the rest with a silk veil that they let fall to their knees. If they notice that some man is gazing at them too intently, they cover their faces with this head-covering or veil. They wear overgarments of silk, floor-length, with a bit of a train and a bodice in the Venetian style, closed in front and tied with a thick gold cord. Beneath this they wear an undergown of ormesino *or satin, trimmed with many bands of gold brocade or patterned velvet. At their necks they wear silk* baveri *and pearls, and at their wrists gold bracelets. Now, however, they are gradually changing their style of dress, and they wear* zimarre *and various coiffures resembling those of Lombardy, which I have already described.*

MARRIED WOMAN OF MANTUA
in Formal Attire

Mantua is a very ancient city, built five hundred years before Rome by a certain Ocno, King of Tuscany, who gave it the name Mantua after Manto, his mother. It was conquered by many kinds of people, but finally it came under the control of the House of Gonzaga, to which it is now most happily subject. Its married women have a graceful and beautiful appearance. They wear a floor-length overgarment of velvet or damasco *or some other silk fabric, with a tight-fitting bodice in the style of a doublet, and long, slit sleeves through whose openings their arms emerge, covered in* damasco *or whatever other silk their* sottana *is made of. They wear high ruffles at their necks, a gold chain of several strands with a beautiful medallion or valuable jewel, and belts of gold. They usually curl their hair and wear a silk veil on top of it, which they let flutter in the breeze down to their shoulders. In their hands they carry fans of lovely feathers.*

MARRIED NOBLEWOMAN OF MANTUA
in a Different Style of Clothing

his is another kind of attire worn by the married women of Mantua, in a very different style from the one previously shown. They wear their hair curled at their temples, with a lovely veil that they draw into a point over their forehead; the rest of their hair they arrange on top of their heads in the form of little mountains. At their necks they wear ruffles attached to their camicie, *beautifully needle-worked and made of very thin white linen. They wear a calf-length overgarment of velvet, satin,* ormesino *or some other silk, with bands of gold or silk brocade at the hem, and with long, open sleeves from which their arms emerge, clothed in silk of another color and trimmed diagonally with gold bands and braid. Beneath this they wear a floor-length undergown of gold brocade or silk, with a train an arm in length; and at their necks they wear scarves of* ormesino, *colored red or pink, with a gold medallion hanging from it to the middle of their breast. Now, though, they are gradually changing their style of dress, imitating the other regions of Lombardy.*

198

NOBLE GIRLS OF MANTUA

When they attend public festivities, the girls of the city of Mantua curl their hair around their foreheads and enclose the rest in well-made nets of gold. They wear pearl earrings in the form of little stars, and at their necks baveri of renso needle-worked with gold, small ruffles, and necklaces of precious stones. Over their baveri they hang silk ribbons down to their breast, to which are attached medallions of gold. They wear low-cut gowns, floor-length, of damasco, silk, or gold brocade, with foliage patterns and rather long trains. They wear satin sleeves, pinked or slashed in the shape of small crosses, with ruffles at their braccialetti. Dressed in this way, they look beautiful, graceful, chaste, and splendid. They go to many balls and parties, more perhaps than in other places in Italy, where many young people, women as well as men, meet; they are very agile and skillful in dancing and live joyfully under their peaceful prince and his rule.

NOBLE GIRLS OF BOLOGNA, *Going from Home to Church*

he city of Bologna is situated on the slopes of Mount Appenino, in the midst of the Via Emilia. Mount Appenino itself is to the south, while to the east is the Savena river; on the west the Reno river and the stream called the Avesca flow through the city's center. It spreads over five miles, and it is full of magnificent churches, spacious palaces, beautiful streets, sheltering arcades and loggias. It has many cardinals, archbishops, bishops, learned men, and valiant soldiers, and it has had three popes. It is abundant in wheat, wine, meat, oil, and dairy products of all sorts, and for this reason it is called "Bologna the Fat."

When the girls of Bologna go to church, they look very modest and lovely. They wear curls framing their foreheads and cover their hair with floor-length silk veils, which they also pull over their faces, covering themselves in a beautiful way. They wear silk gowns, most often white, with differently colored silk trim and needle-worked bands around the hem; they wear low pianelle *and hold their veils tightly at their breast and waist. They hardly ever appear at a window or at the door of their houses but are almost always shut up inside, doing needlework.*

WEALTHY NOBLEWOMAN OF BOLOGNA

Bolognese noblewomen are gracious and well mannered. They wear their hair in the style of the women of Milan, with curls framing their foreheads, which they adorn with a large pearl and a pointed veil of white silk net. This they pin halfway back over their hair in a lovely fashion that allows them to form several folds, and then they let the rest of the veil fall gracefully to their shoulders. At their necks they wear ruffles four fingers high and finely needle-worked. They wear high-necked, floor-length overgarments of black silk woven in patterns with marvelous skill or needle-worked, and high bodices fastened at the sides with metal eyelets, a lovely sight. Under this they wear a gathered undergown of elegantly patterned white silk. They adorn their breasts with beautiful, valuable jewels, which hang from heavy gold necklaces; at their necks they wear pearls, and they wear gold chains as belts. Their sleeves are white, but they wear them tied with gold ribbons woven with pearls. On top they wear a mantle of silk buratto *or* ferandina, *in the Lombard style. And I saw this attire in Venice, and then it was drawn and incised by Cristoforo Guerra [Chrieger, or Krieger], a German from Nuremberg and a most excellent maker of woodcuts.*[1]

This is the wrong woodcut in the original book, since it duplicates that which appears overleaf.

COURTESANS OR CONCUBINES of Bologna

The courtesans of Bologna, for the most part, dress in white satin, in floor-length overgarments with an arm's-length train. These overgarments have sleeves open all the way down the arm but are tied with silk cords and fastened near the wrist with gold buttons, which also fasten the gown over the belly. On their heads they wear a piece of black ormesino, *which they pin to their hair at their foreheads, making a beautiful point, and then they close it at their breast with a gold button—trimmed all over with gold, it covers their head, their breast and their shoulders. They wear gold earrings with small pearls, and on their foreheads they wear their hair very elegantly curled.*

A WOMAN OF ANCONA

*hen the Lombards entered Italy after the death of Eunuco*[2]*, they decided to destroy the power of the Roman Empire completely; to do this, they also decided to change the names of the provinces and magistrates. And when they sent a new magistrate into the province of the Marches formerly called Agro Piceno, they renamed it the Marca, which in their language means "perpetual rule." Others claim that this region was named by the French, in whose language it means "province." Whatever the case may be, it is a very fertile region, rich in wheat, wine, oil, meat, fodder, and dairy foods of all kinds. It produces many literary men and strong captains and brave soldiers, who do not like one another much but prefer foreigners to people of their own nation. In this March there are many former Roman colonies, of which the principal one is Ancona, a very populous and lovely city, situated near a mountain that slopes toward the sea; it is called Ancona because in Greek ancona means "bend," that is, a slope. Here there are a beautiful port and fortress.*

The women of this city dress similarly to the married women of Rome: that is, as women of importance and mature age, but not too lavishly. They wear a full, long mantle of silk or patterned ferandina *or some other thin silk, similar to* buratto*. This mantle is black in color, and they arrange it and tie it back in such a way that when they pull it upward, it appears to be made of two separate pieces. These mantles are worn in many parts of Italy and Spain by noblewomen of high rank. These women of Ancona cover their heads with a thin* velo*, which looks light yellow in color. Under this mantle, they wear black overgarments of velvet or satin or some other kind of silk, depending on the season, and accordingly, they also wear satin,*

brocade or ormesino. *The young women adorn themselves with pearls, jewels, gold chains, and other similar ornaments. And though it may seem that I have digressed, since this attire has nothing to do with my subject (that is, the dress of Lombardy), I still wanted to set it here, because it is worn only in the March of Ancona and differs from the dress I have presented up to now. In other ways their clothing differs little from that of Lombardy and Romagna, the women's as well as the men's.*

Text on page 256

MARRIED WOMAN
of Piedmont in Turin

*Piedmont is a densely populated province. Its name means at the foot of the mountains [*al piede de' monti*] because of the mountains that separate it from France. It has beautiful cities and many castles and towns. The principal city is Turin, which, as with all of Piedmont and Savoy, is ruled over by the house of the Filiberti. The high-ranking married women of Turin wear mantles of silk with various patterns woven into them, similar to those of Spanish women; their undergowns are of silk brocade in very fine colors, and very expensive. They cover their heads with a large, costly hat of very fine straw, intricately woven and very delicate. Their hair is hardly visible because it is gathered under this hat into a gold net, but it can be seen through the opening at the top of the hat, which is similar to the type used by Venetian women to bleach their hair. The bodices of their overgarments are high-necked. Their oversleeves are open and tied at the bottom; in them they keep their handkerchiefs, and these sleeves are lined with silk of different colors. Their belts are of gold in a beautiful style, and long. Their* camicia *collars are trimmed with ruffles, and at their neck they wear pearl necklaces and other jewelry. And this is exactly the style of dress of the married women of Piedmont as it was sent to me by Messer Christoforo de Maganza, an excellent engraver and an inhabitant of that region.*[3]

Text on page 257

GIRL OF TURIN

he girls of Piedmont are very pleasant and modest. They wear clothing similar to that of Milanese and French women, and have similar hairstyles. But their hair is completely natural, without any kind of artifice. When they go out, they cover their faces with a piece of ormesino *or a veil or some other thin fabric, and in this* ormesino *or other fabric they make two holes for their eyes and another for their mouth and for their nose, which they look through like people wearing masks. They are very narrow at the hips and at the waist, enough to cause wonder in those who look at them. The bodices they wear are close-fitting and high-necked, with a rather long point or V-shape at the navel. Their over-garments are of satin, velvet, silk* canevaccia*, or* ciambellotto*, and floor-length. They carry fans in their hands, and they make themselves up a good deal, to look beautiful. They are friendly and pleasant in conversation, but also very chaste.*

Text on page 258

THE CLOTHING OF LIGURIA OR GENOA

CLOTHING OF A LADY OF EARLY GENOA

iguria is a large region that begins beyond Marsia and extends from the Varo river to the Magra river. The territory is divided into the western and eastern coasts of Genoa, with Genoa, the principal city, at the center; hence the names of the two coasts. The beautiful and powerful city of Genoa is situated on its grand port, so that the onlooker feels as if the city is being embraced by it. This port looks toward Africa and faces southward; it is protected by a quay artificially constructed as a shelter for ships. In our time this city was sacked for three days by Signor Prospero Colonna and was then liberated for the most part by the Emperor Charles V in 1520, at the time he came to Italy to be crowned by Pope Clement VII. From that time to this, the city has grown so much that it is a marvel.

The early clothing of women of Genoa, from 1200 on, consisted of two overgarments, one short and knee-length and belted under the breast, the other floor-length, like a carpetta or a sottana, without a bodice, of silk, and bordered all around with velvet in different colors. Some women also wore an apron on top of this gown, either of the same fabric or of a thinner one, with similar borders. The sleeves of these gowns were similar to the large sleeves of early clothing worn throughout Italy at the time, but very full and gathered at the elbow. From here to the wrist, they were narrow but open underneath, so that the white sleeves of the camicia came through, and because these were so wide, they hung down in folds. They wore their hair loose on their shoulders, but gathered and tied up some of it so that not all of it fell free; in their hands they carried a hat to protect themselves against both the sun and the rain. From their belts, which were quite wide, hung a purse in which they carried spending money and other small things necessary to women, such as needle cases, thimbles, silk thread, and whatever they most needed for their housework. Their legs showed because their gowns were shorter than those worn in our days, and they covered them with stockings of thin, colored wool; their shoes were low-cut, pointed in a way similar to those the Turks wear today and, like theirs, of various colors. And they were very affable and courteous, speaking frankly and freely, and they have preserved something of their former character up to today, though with great modesty.

MODERN CLOTHING OF A GENOVESE NOBLEWOMAN

These are the most affable and most pleasant-spoken women of all Italy, because they do business in public with such skill and friendliness that they seem to be the sisters of all those with whom they exchange and sell goods. They go about buying and selling without any loss of reputation because women who buy and sell at the greatest profit are very highly esteemed, so they are shrewd and sharp-witted. The noblewomen of this city wear their hair all in curls, and their locks are decorated with beautiful nosegays of flowers, which grow abundantly here at all times of the year. They gather their hair under a thin veil of transparent yellow silk striped with gold, which forms a very lovely point at the top of their head, and they let the rest of their hair fall freely from their head down to their shoulders. They wear a bodice, or rather a doublet, of white silk or of very fine, thin linen, pinked all over and woven with gold and bordered with trim of silk and gold lace; this bodice or doublet has sleeves open down the arm, tied with ribbons of gold and silk. They wear the ruffles of their camicia high, and these are very well made. They wear overgowns that are not very long, with silk bands of different colors at the hem, richly embroidered in gold. They wear rather low pianelle and almost always wear a purse hanging from their belt, and a thing embroidered all over with gold and various patterns that is used to hold sewing needles or other objects.[1] On top of this overgarment, they use golden brooches to fasten mantles or sbernie [short mantles] of dyed silk in colors

different from their overgowns, which they let fall to the same length as their gowns. The girls dress similarly and go in twos or threes wherever they please, holding hands with one another and being seen by everyone. I received this drawing from the excellent painter Messer Antonio Zappello, who spent a long time in Genoa and completed many works there.[2]

Text on page 261

PLEBEIAN WOMEN OF GENOA

Other women, whether non-noble, poor, or of any other low rank, have the same manners and present themselves in the same way as the noblewomen, but they dress rather differently. For when they leave the house, they usually cover their head with a piece of silk cloth, very thin, such as ormesino *or taffeta of various colors, depending on their preference; they wear this cloth in a point at the center of their foreheads so as to cover their hair and shoulders. Then they wear a high-necked doublet, fastened under the chin, which they embellish with the small ruffles of their* camicie. *With a row of silk buttons in different colors and the snugly fitting waist these doublets have, they make a pretty sight. Their sleeves are open in front but tied with silk cords in different colors. Their overgarment falls from their waist to their ankles, so that their* pianelle, *no more than four fingers in height, can be seen. This overgarment is embroidered and patterned, with silk trim and bands different in color from the gown itself. From their belts hang a purse and a* gusellaro, *as they call it, in which they carry sewing needles. And because it is always spring in* Genoa, *the women always carry fragrant flowers in their hands, and also wear them at their breast and on their heads.*

Text on page 262

THE CLOTHING OF BRESCIA, *Verona and Other Nearby Cities of Lombardy*

erona is a very noble and ancient city. It was one of the twelve cities built and governed by the ancient Tuscans, and it was given its name from "Vera," a very ancient family of Tuscany. Now it is situated and counted among the cities of Lombardy. It is built on the River Adige, which flows through its center, and it has many beautiful hills not far to the south; it has a beautiful amphitheater and is full of grand, noble buildings. It abounds in everything necessary for human sustenance and in merchandise, and it is rich. And for this reason, in our days, they say it is called "Vera una" [truly one], meaning that it is a unique city.

Noblewomen of Verona arrange their hair in a beautiful style, with braids so well plaited and so artfully encircling the head that they resemble snail shells or spirals; over these braids, they attach a veil, pinned into so many loops that when they catch the wind, they stand up like a crest and look very elegant. At their necks they wear ruffles of very white, thin renso *and* cambrai*, so well needle-worked and starched that they make a lovely sight. On top of their overgarment, attached to their shoulders and falling gracefully from there to the ground in a long train, they wear a mantle of silk,* ferandina *or silk* buratto*, skillfully woven with elaborate designs, so that it looks like those that Roman noblewomen used to wear. They wear a beautiful overgarment of colored silk, in whatever color they prefer, with a skirt also of decorated silk, fastened with golden buttons; the bodice of this gown is in the style of a* colletto *[a short, snug doublet] with slashes, through which another very lovely kind of silk can be seen. The sleeves are also of silk, but with gold trim, open along the arm but tied with silk cords in different colors. They adorn their necks with imposing pearls and gold chains that fall onto their breast and wear very valuable belts, also of gold, that confer dignity and beauty upon them, as was seen in Venice on the Day of the Ascension of Our Lord.*

THE CLOTHING OF MARRIED WOMEN of Verona and Brescia

Married women of Brescia, Verona and other nearby places wear their hair curled at their temples and their forehead; they braid the rest of it and cover it with yellow silk, which they wear with a pretty point at the center of their foreheads. They wear an undergarment most often of yellow damasco, *and above it another of black satin, with a bodice in the style of a doublet, closely fitted to the breast, fastened with gold buttons and very high-necked; above this bodice the beautifully needle-worked ruffles of their* camicia *show. At their necks they wear a gold chain with many strands, and at their waist a chain of the same metal. On top of their overgown, they wear a cape of black silk* buratto *or* ferrandina, *which, falling from their shoulders, covers them entirely, and which they fasten at the bottom in front. They wear low* pianelle.

CLOTHING OF A WOMAN OF VICENZA

Vicenza was one of the twelve cities built by the Tuscans. It has been governed by many different peoples; among them the last to sack it was the Emperor Frederick II, who, pretending to offer a treaty, entered the city, set it on fire, and plundered many of its neighborhoods. And this Frederick remained in the city for as long as the attack on it lasted, in the year 1258. After his death, the city returned to its former liberty. But then it was sacked by the tyrant Ezzelino da Romano[3] *in 1275. It was attacked again by Paduans under Mastino dalla Scala, the first Lord of Verona, who was fleeing from Verona, which had surrendered to* Giovan Galeazzo, *first Duke of Milan.*[4] *At that time, Vicenza, following the advice of a certain Lady* Catherine, *surrendered to the rule of the lords of Venice, who have governed it up to the present day with the greatest generosity and justice.*

The clothing of the young married women of this city includes a coiffure of curls framing the forehead, and braids arranged under many flowers made of silk and gold; these braids are tied together high at the top of their heads with these silk flowers, so that they look like lovely, pleasant hills in bloom. To this coiffure they also pin a very thin, white silk veil, which they let fall to their shoulders in a graceful style. They wear overgarments of satin with high collars, from which the beautifully embroidered and very thin ruffles of their camicie emerge; *the bodices of these gowns are cut like doublets, with wide sleeves open along the arm and fastened with gold buttons; the bodices themselves have the same ornaments going down the sides of the breast. Then the overgarment falls from the bodice to the ground, with an opening in front through which can be seen a* sottana *of silk* brocatello, *with a gold strip all around the elegantly embroidered hem. Their stockings are of very thin wool, embroidered all over, and their* pianelle *are not very high. At their necks they wear gold necklaces, and as belts they wear chains of gold buttons—to the end of this belt they attach a very beautiful feather fan that they hold in their hand.*

Text on page 266

CLOTHING FORMERLY WORN BY MEN AND WOMEN in Padua

After his city of Troy was set on fire and ruined, the Trojan Antenor, accompanied by many people, came to the farthest reaches of the Adriatic Sea and built Padua. This city then became so powerful that it assembled an army of twelve thousand soldiers against its enemies. It has always been friendly with the Roman people, so when discord arose among the citizens of Padua, it was Rome that sent them Marcus Emilius to make peace. Later the city was destroyed by Attila,[5] king of the Huns, but rebuilt by Narsete Eunuco, a captain of the Emperor Justinian and of the people of Ravenna. And then a hundred years after it was put to ruin by Attila, it was burned down and totally razed by the Lombards; then, restored again after the tyranny of Ezzelino, it became a possession of the lords of Carrara with the title of patronate, and these men of the House of Carrara, inheritors of a fortress named Bassano, came to live in this city of Padua and became citizens there. Then, driven out by Ezzelino again, the lords of Carrara returned with Ansedino (a legate of the Church of Rome), and were made rulers of the city. Their first lord was Marsilio Carrara, who, unable to withstand Can Grande della Scala, the lord of Verona, handed the city over to this Can Grande and fled. Following the death of Can Grande, Marsilio returned to power. After ruling for ten years, he finally died in 1340 without heirs, and left as his successor his cousin Ubertino. Then the city came under the rule of other people, most recently the lords of Venice, who from 1509 to today (in spite of some disputes with the Emperor, who occupied it for a short time) govern the city with the greatest generosity and justice.

Because this city of Padua is so ancient, I will not hesitate to say that in order to acquire detailed information on early dress there, I went to Padua and saw, painted by very skillful painters on the walls of the Palazzo Pretorio, the dress of men and women of former times. As far as I could see, their clothing was very bizarre, for some men of those times wore shaggy hats with an arm's-length point jutting out in front and turned up toward the sky. They wore knee-length overgarments with very many folds, called giornee, *which they tied with long belts. They wore full-length stockings of various colors, with pointed shoes. In the women's attire that I liked most the woman was wearing a single, simple gown like those worn indoors by noblewomen of Venice. It was collarless, red in color, and its sleeves were floor-length but slashed down to the elbow, so open that she could put her arms through them. This style, I think, was worn throughout almost all of Italy, because similar examples can be seen in many places today. This woman appeared to have been of high rank, because she wore a heavy, jeweled gold chain diagonally from her left shoulder to her right hip; at her neck she wore lovely pearls and at her ears beautiful earrings of gold and jewels. Her gown was so long that it trailed far behind her, and she was adorned with a jewel at her neck and a gold* balzo *in the style of a diadem with gorgeous pendant pearls.*

BRIDES OF PADUA,
Friuli and Other Nearby Places

At the time that the most serene King of France was in Venice, a great number of people gathered in the city in order to see the sumptuous structures built to welcome his majesty and the grand festivities held here,[6] *attended by beautiful Paduan brides, who looked very splendid in their dress and carried themselves very nobly. And they were accompanied by large numbers of relatives, servants (both men and women), and by married women. They had decorated their heads with many small, well-arranged curls, and they wore the rest of their hair braided and covered with large pearls. They also wore a strand of pearls at their white necks, which were decked with a beautiful needle-worked* bavero, *trimmed with ruffles of very thin fabric; and on top of this* bavero, *they wore a jeweled gold necklace of great value, which hung to the middle of their breast. Their overgarments were of brocade woven with different types of colored silk, with long bodices cut low in front and fastened with magnificent gold buttons from the breast down to the waist. From the waist their skirts fell open down to the ground, and through the opening could be seen a* sottana *of green velvet. The overgown had double sleeves, one open and lined with colored* ormesino, *the other covering the arm and trimmed with gold buttons, with small ruffles at the wrist. In their right hands, they carried a very thin fan with a silver gilt handle. At their waists they wore a heavy gold chain set with precious stones, down to the knee, and to this was attached a very beautiful sable fur, with a head of gold that seemed the living picture of a sable, and for eyes it had two rubies.*

MARRIED WOMEN OF PADUA

The married women of Padua also dress in a way suitable to their rank. They wear their hair in curls framing their foreheads and bind the rest of it into lovely braids, which they wrap around the crown of their head. To this coiffure they pin a very thin and beautiful silk veil, which, because it is so wide, falls behind them to the hem of their overgarment, though they take up the ends of this veil and pin them to their belt in front. They wear an overgament or zimarra *of black velvet, somewhat shorter than their undergown, with a fine strip of needle-worked gold brocade at the bottom. They also wear floor-length undergowns of silk brocade; often these are of* ormesino, *satin, and velvet in different colors. At their neck they wear ruffs of very fine white linen and a gold necklace of several strands. They close their gowns with golden buttons and belt them with very thick gold chains. They resemble Venetian noblewomen in their customs, especially the unmarried girls, who are shut up at home with all the care and restraint appropriate to their status. And when they go out, they wear rust-colored garments, or some other sober color, and few ornaments. They also cover their faces with white silk veils, as Venetian girls do. The non-noble and plebeian women attend festivities with greater freedom and less surveillance, as is the custom in many places in Lombardy. In that region, girls stand at their windows to see the men they love, while the men, as they pass by, greet them in a very familiar way. And when they go to parties or entertainments, they give precedence to one another according to their age and rank.*

SPOSA DEL FRIVLI.

BRIDE OF FRIULI AND PLACES NEARBY

he province of Friuli is located in the Marches of Treviso. It is bounded on the east by Istria, on the north by the Giappi Mountains, on the west by the Vindelician and Norcen Alps, and on the south by the Adriatic Sea. It was named Friuli from the Latin Forum Julii, *referring to Julius Caesar, who led many legions and squadrons of soldiers from here across the Alps. It was also called the region of Aquileia after its largest town, Aquileia, a patriarchal city*[7] *and the principal city of the area. Finally it kept the name Patriarca, as it is still called today, because its people, leaving its heights and coming down to its low, marshy lands from fear of barbarians, built dwellings there and when they wanted to speak of their villages and of that province, they called it Patria.*

This area was ruled by fourteen dukes of Lombard descent and two of Gallic descent, and when they died the province came into the possession of Louis III for as long as Charlemagne's family line lasted. During this time Berengario of the Lombards began to grow in strength and made himself its duke; and when he died, he was succeeded as duke by Berengario II, and after him came Berengario III, and finally Adalbeno, his son. When he was imprisoned by the Emperor Otto,[8] *this province came under the rule of this emperor, who donated Aquileia to the Church, along with Udine, Fagana, Gruanio, Bugara, and Graitano and all the land between the Livenza and Piave rivers. The Patriarch of the church of Aquileia was then Rodoaldo XLIX [sic], to whom the Emperor Corrado presented the entire Duchy of Friuli and the Marquisate of Istria, along with many other holdings. From these the church of Aquileia took more than a hundred thousand gold florins annually, which it continued to enjoy until the year 1509, when the province came under the rule of the Lords of Venice.*

And since the people of that province dress in the style of Lombardy and of the regions of Padua and Treviso, I will say no more about them except to mention some brides of this region of Friuli. They wear their hair in many shapely little curls framing their forehead and temples and gather the rest of it under a gold net, laden with jewels and precious stones; around this net they tie a strand of large pearls, which they also wear in earrings and necklaces. They wear very well made ruffles of renso *or* cambrai, *and an overgown of white satin with a high-necked bodice, buttoned with gold and decorated with a strand of pearls and a thick gold chain. These gowns have open sleeves with strips of gold brocade all over them, and through the sleeves the brides' arms can be seen, similarly clothed in white satin or cloth of silver or of gold. They wear a gold belt, and the bottom of their gown is banded with gold lace or strips of brocade, with a small train. The clothing shown here is worn in all the Marches of Treviso, Padua, and Udine and the entire region of Friuli. There, there are many countesses and chatelaines and other married noblewomen, who wear mantles of silk with* zimarre *or overgowns of velvet or black satin, and* sottane *of gold and silver brocade in various colors, according to their rank.*

Text on page 271

THE CLOTHING OF NOBLEWOMEN
of Cividal di Belluno

ividal di Belluno, though a small town, is very beautifully sited, ancient, and adorned both with beautiful buildings and with even more piazzas with fountains of fresh water. It is located near the Piave, a fast-moving river that rushes headlong toward the sea, but which is convenient and abundant in every sort of goods for Venice. It is made lovelier by beautiful terrain with flowering hills, shady woods and delightful valleys. The city itself is full of noble families worthy of every kind of praise, among whom the House of Piloni is one of the principals, because it is very noble and a haven of all virtues—on its members it seems that the heavens, with the help of nature and God, have conferred all the wealth and happiness that a mortal being can hope for.[9]

And truly, whenever I consider what a magnanimous soul might be, my thought soars up and I call to mind the character of Signor Odorico Piloni, a most upright and admirable scholar, whose virtue deserves to be praised, proclaimed, and honored with every honor the world offers. For in his speech he is most learned, weighty and brilliant, and in his judgments and opinions there is never anything trivial, so that all his actions, proceeding from his sharp intelligence, are directed toward virtue through long practice and many kinds of learning, enriched by his perfect and firm judgment, and, above all, begun, followed through and concluded with perfect order. And these are trustworthy proofs of his worth, which he has demonstrated in the many important and respected magistracies and offices he has undertaken and from which he has earned no reward except praise and glory. Altogether, he is a man who possesses every virtue, large and small, and who enjoys many rewards of fortune and many possessions.

Among these possessions is Casteldardo, a place six miles from the city in a most lovely setting and blessed with unending spring—it displays such high excellence that nature seems to reign like an empress here and, ruling over every pleasant part of it, seems to rejoice and laugh. Within it is built a palace on a beautiful site, lovely inside and out, high and well proportioned, in which Odorico has a study. In addition to many different kinds of books, this study is full of every ancient object one could desire, including ancient medals, portraits of heroes, and marble and bronze sculptures, as well as wondrous natural objects in substances of every noble kind. Throughout the region it is called "Noah's Ark," a name chosen for it by the most illustrious Cardinal dalla Torre, with the result that everyone passing through the region wants to visit it as a marvelous and unique thing. There is also a garden that he has artfully built so that it contains fragrant flowers of every sort, plants green at every time of the year, lovely paths, well-watered bushes, and tall and lofty trees bearing fruits of every kind and of exceptional excellence, which, because they are so perfect, are given as gifts to the most important men of the region.

Not far from this is a little wood, set on the top of a lovely hill, skillfully planted with saplings, green and pure and so similar in size that they seem to have been painted by the most excellent painters; these, through the variety of fruit they offer in every season, are a perfect lure for every sort of bird, which gather here in great numbers. Here, too, are paths attractively made, set with small ponds over which traps of transparent horse skin are ingeniously stretched, in which great numbers of every kind of bird are caught in every season, in a delightful and infinitely useful way. Also in this wood is a little house, decorated with architectural details and painted green all over outside and with every sort of animal, which excels every other *lovely and delightful thing in the wood. Here, as a pastime, it is a pleasure to enjoy the sight through certain openings of the birds being caught in these traps.*

In addition I will say that this Signor Odorico had three sons, among whom each one is a mirror of good manners and a shining ray of virtue. The first is Lord Giorgio, a university scholar, to whom it seems that Bartolo and Baldo[10] rightly yield their place in the discipline of law. And the other sons are Lord Antonio and Lord Cesare, who, following in their father's footsteps, faithfully maintain his virtue and model of good customs, for they themselves have many other pleasant and delightful estates. He also has three daughters-in-law, the wives of these three sons, Ladies Dignamerita, Faustina, and Doretta, very modest in their dress, welcoming in their speech, wise in their behavior, clever in their responses and chaste in their demeanor. They wear silk and gold brocade, depending on the time of year, as do the other noblewomen of the regions of Padua, Treviso, and Friuli; they wear their hair neatly arranged, with curls at their temples and the rest braided and pinned to a very thin silk veil that falls down their back. On top they wear an overgown of velvet or satin, buttoned in front to the waist and open from there down, through which can be seen another floor-length gown of ormesino *or* damasco. *Their overgowns have wide sleeves but these are narrow at the wrists; on their arms they also wear the sleeves of their undergown. They wear gold necklaces at their necks and matching valuable chains at their waists.*

Text on page 273

CLOTHING WORN AT HOME BY NOBLEWOMEN of Cividal di Belluno

This most fortunate city, among its other famous families, is still the residence of the Miara family, very noble and ancient. Among its members is Signor Cavaliero Miaro, whose fame in these parts is well known on account of his excellent liberality. Great generosity can be clearly seen in him, combined with high daring and the greatest skill, through which he demonstrates the grandeur of his spirit and the prudence of his intellect in every enterprise. He has as his wife the excellent and most worthy Cavaliera, who was born to the noble Carpedone family and who grew up, cared for, tutored, and educated, in a way that makes her not inferior to her husband but, indeed, superior in intelligence, goodness, and liberality to anyone alive. She is no less industrious than her peers, and in learning inferior to none of the famous women of ancient or modern times, nor in sobriety to any man of the church. In her demeanor and habits shine the virtue and goodness that can also be seen in her actions and in the demeanor of the Ladies Vittoria and Cecilia, very beautiful and gracious young women, wise and modest, equal to any other young woman of their age. Also belonging to this very noble family are the Lords Felix and Antonio, distinguished by all the virtues necessary to free men, who are as sharp-witted in discussing matters of law as they are firm-minded in making decisions and learned in giving advice.

The clothing worn by these noblewomen of Cividal at home resembles that of other women around Padua and the rest of Lombardy. It consists of a coiffure including little curls at the temples and braids tied with very beautiful silk cords in different colors. And at their neck they wear the neatly arranged ruffles of their camicie *and gold chain necklaces. They wear doublets of silk, striped with gold, and others of different colors, forming a rounded belly with a very pretty point; to this they attach a* carpetta *of satin or some other silk, decorated with gold trim. And here young girls speak freely but still chastely with the men they love.*

FORMER CLOTHING OF THE CITIZENS OF THE MARCHES OF TREVISO AND CIVIDAL DI BELLUNO

and all of Lombardy and Many Other Places in Italy

From 1576 onward, young men of Italy used to wear the clothing shown here. On their heads they wore velvet caps à tozzo, *though not as high as today, and some had them made of* tabino *or thinly woven silk, as is the case today. They wore short black capes of wool or* rascia, *waist-length, with long hoods the same length as the capes. They wore wide trousers, not very long, reaching just to the knee, and silk doublets, slashed in patterns, with very large silk buttons; they put on long stockings of wool or* rascia, *tied below the knee. They wore shoes of black or white Cordovan leather and attached a sword to their belt.*

PEASANT WOMAN OF CIVIDAL DI BELLUNO and Other Cities and Neighboring Lands

he peasant women of this city dress as do the others of Friuli and other places nearby, especially when they are ready to marry or are wives already. They wear clumsy, unbecoming curls framing their foreheads, with nets of colored silk, under which they gather up their hair. They wear camicie *of rather coarse linen with small ruffles and strands of coral beads. They wear an overgown of* pavonazzo *wool with velvet trim, and velvet sleeves with buttons or beads of silver gilt; and they go about in the sleeves of their* camicie, *wearing the velvet sleeves hanging down behind. They wear a belt of black velvet with small silver plates and they usually wear silver gilt brooches on their bodices, similar in size to a* reale *coin. Many wear stockings without feet, turned up at the bottom as you can see in this figure, with wooden clogs on their feet. They go to many parties and balls until they marry; they attend these in the company of their male companions, talking about love; but soon after they are married, most of them stop all this. In summer they dress in white cotton and other lightweight fabrics. They wear aprons of Holland linen with a particular black wool trim, and their gown is trimmed with strips of the same wool. These gowns are most often made of* bigio *wool.*

THE CLOTHING OF NOBLEWOMEN from Conegliano

Treviso is a strongly defended city, located on the plain. It is rich and noble, full of beautiful palaces and endowed with very fertile land, full of fruit trees of every kind, and watered by the Sile river; this last fertilizes and cleans out this city, which abounds in wheat, wine, meat, dairy products, and oil in great quantity. As a result, all the Marches of Treviso, which contain many estates and castles, have been ruled over by many different people, but most recently by the Emperor and now by the lords of Venice. In its jurisdiction it has many castles, towns, and lands, among which is the very noble city of Conegliano, named in ancient times Colle Iano, after Janus, a great nobleman of Troy, who, having fled Troy with Antenor (the founder of Padua), built the city called Conegliano in 1143 BC. It is set between the Piave and Livenza rivers, almost at the border of Lombardy and the region of Friuli. It has a large fortress built on top of one of the highest hills of this territory, which was used for warfare in ancient times since its two sets of walls made it unconquerable. Its patron saint is Saint Leonard, and in its piazza it has a beautiful fountain of fresh water; it abounds in everything needed for human sustenance. Because it is so ancient, it has many noble families, among whom the most important and noble is the Montalbano clan, which has produced many gentlemen rewarded with many honors and rich in fame for their heroic deeds and adventures abroad, which have been so increased by the illustrious Signor Cavaliero Pietro Montalbano that he has raised the family name to the stars with his magnanimity, courtesy, valor, and every rare quality that can be desired in a man of accomplishment. As a result, he has had the extraordinary honor of being decorated by the pope, the invincible Emperor, and the most serene and Christian King of France, who, united and agreed in recognizing his intrepid valor and singular goodness in addition to the skill on horseback with which he is endowed, graciously honored him with rewards for his virtue. The city also has the most noble house of the Coderta, in which today can be found Signor Giovan Battista, worthy of every praise for his rare qualities and the gifts of his unconquerable spirit.

The clothing of the gentlewomen of this noble land consists of a closed floor-length overgown of velvet, either cremesino *or black, which, fitting closely over a doublet of satin worn underneath, makes a beautiful sight. To this doublet, which is bordered with gold and silk trim, they attach another gown of* tabino *or* brocatello, *and under this they wear* faldiglie, *which make it possible to walk easily and quickly. Their overgarment has long, floor-length, open sleeves, through which the arms can be seen, adorned with gold brocade and gold bracelets. They also attach to their shoulders a mantle of very thin silk, which they let fall behind them, fixing one end of it to their left shoulder. They wear a high coiffure of braids, decorated with lovely pearls that shimmer behind them, and under these braids they attach a veil that falls to their shoulders. This style of dress resembles that worn by many other noblewomen of Lombardy and the area around Treviso.*

Text on page 278

THE CLOTHING OF TUSCANY

CLOTHING OF A WOMAN
of Early Tuscany

he province of Tuscany is full of beautiful, big city-states and so many villages, towns, and castles that, being inhabited everywhere, it can truly be said that the entire province is one city. And since Florence is the principal city of Tuscany, I must say that it had an ancient origin, but opinions vary about this. Leonardo Aretino claims that the soldiers of Silla were its founders, seeking peace and quiet there, as they also did in Fiesole, at that time a large city; to refresh themselves after coming down from the mountains near Florence, they built a town of houses between the Arno and Mugnone rivers nearby. Beginning to enjoy the comfort of the place, the inhabitants of Fiesole gradually began to come down to the town below, so in a short time they made it into a large city; by means of four very beautiful bridges, they crossed from one river bank to the other, where there was space to expand as much as they wanted. Raphael of Volterra in his Commentary on Cities claims that the founders of Florence were from Fiesole, and that they enjoyed its smooth terrain after their descents from the mountains. But Ennius in Book 7 of his Commentaries argues that the founder was the great Janus (according to Cato, who also held that Florence was first called Arignano). Whatever the case may be, it is enough for us that today it is called Florence the Beautiful. After it was rebuilt by Charlemagne, the city had the custom of electing two consuls every year to its governing body, adding them to a Senate composed of a hundred Padri, wise and experienced men. Then, thinking they should change their mode of government, they began electing ten citizens whom they called Anziani [Elders]. This system lasted from 1254 to 1287, when the city gained its freedom from the Emperor Rudolph by paying him six thousand gold florins. Then the Florentines changed their magistracy and elected eight men, whom they called the Priori delle arti (the heads of the guilds) and a Gonfalonier of Justice—these were required to stay in office for only two months. But this system was changed three times: the first was in 1343, when the Florentines bought Lucca from Mastino della Scala for fifty thousand gold florins; the next change occurred in the time of the Frenchman Gualtieri, called the Duke of Athens, who began to take possession of Florence; and the last change came when Pietro Soderini was elected Gonfaloniere for life in 1535. Then Alessandro di Medici was made Duke of Florence by the Emperor Charles V, and he took as his wife Margarita, the illegitimate daughter of this Charles V. When this Duke Alessandro was killed in 1537 by Lorenzo, the son of the late Pierfrancesco di Medici, Cosimo, the son of Giovanni di Medici, was made duke. He then acquired the title of Grand Duke of Tuscany from Pius V of blessed memory in 1569, and passed on to a better life in 1575. He had a son, Francesco di Medici, who died in 1588 and had as his successor Ferdinando, his brother, who governs the city piously today.

The dress worn by women in Florence three hundred years ago consisted of a short overgarment open in front, but fastened with buttons of gold or silk; this garment was made of the same silk as the buttons; it had wide, knee-length sleeves embroidered with thread or lace of gold or silk, of the same kind used in the overgarment. Under this they wore a floor-length undergown with a train of colored silk half an arm in length. At their neck they wore pearls or gold beads, and their hair, unstyled, fell down onto their shoulders. They held tambourines in their hands, which they played most harmoniously.

CLOTHING OF THE PRINCIPAL MARRIED WOMEN OF FLORENCE

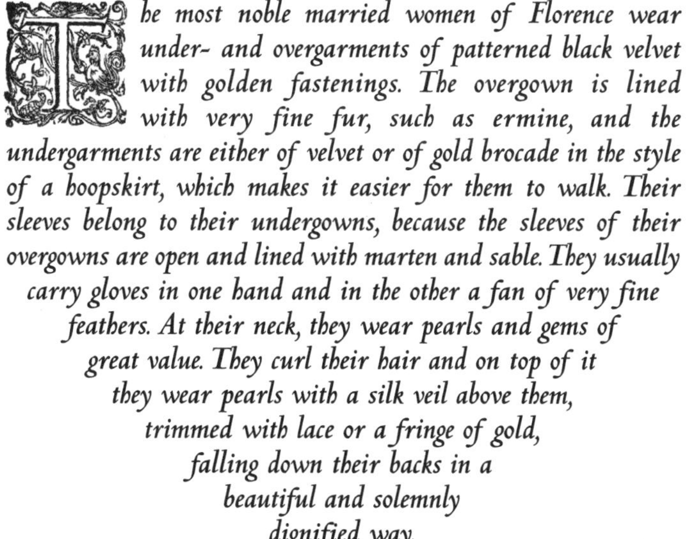

The most noble married women of Florence wear under- and overgarments of patterned black velvet with golden fastenings. The overgown is lined with very fine fur, such as ermine, and the undergarments are either of velvet or of gold brocade in the style of a hoopskirt, which makes it easier for them to walk. Their sleeves belong to their undergowns, because the sleeves of their overgowns are open and lined with marten and sable. They usually carry gloves in one hand and in the other a fan of very fine feathers. At their neck, they wear pearls and gems of great value. They curl their hair and on top of it they wear pearls with a silk veil above them, trimmed with lace or a fringe of gold, falling down their backs in a beautiful and solemnly dignified way.

THE CLOTHING OF RECENTLY MARRIED YOUNG NOBLEWOMEN IN FLORENCE
and Other Places in Tuscany

ewly married brides in Florence wear overgowns of gold or silver brocade or of silk, richly patterned and ending just above the feet; they are fastened with small gold clasps, which have a gold button on one side and on the other a loop for the button, and these clasps make a splendid sight. The gowns have open sleeves, slightly shorter than the skirt of the gown, and the bodice of the gown is buttoned to conceal everything but the neck, which is adorned with a beautiful bavero *of lovely* lattughine, *and several strands of pearls of great value. They wear their hair curled, and for two years after their marriage they wear no veil on their head. Under their overgown, they wear* faldiglie *over wooden hoops, which make it very easy to walk, and their undergowns are of* damasco *or patterned brocade. To their overgowns they attach sleeves of velvet or some other silk, trimmed with lace in a pretty design and with woven trim of gold or silver. And in their hands they carry gloves.*

CLOTHING OF A YOUNG FLORENTINE WOMAN Married for Several Years

After Florentine women have been married for two or three years, they wear a silk veil on their elegantly arranged hair; this veil, made of net and trimmed with tremoli, *falls from the head to the shoulders. They wear sleeveless* zimarre *as their overgarment, of silk in various colors and patterns; these are floor-length, high-necked, and buttoned only on the breast. Under these they wear another gown of gold brocade, buttoned all the way up and pinned to a doublet worn underneath, made of cloth of gold or silver, with sleeves that show beneath the* zimarra, *worked with very beautiful crosses or stars or other similar designs. They wear a* bavero *at their neck with lovely ruffles and strands of pearls of great value, and a gold chain with many jewels that is very grand to see.*

CLOTHING FORMERLY WORN BY FLORENTINE GIRLS
Outside the House

This dress was worn over a long period some time ago by the unmarried girls of Florence, but today it seems that it is no longer in use. They wore silk, floor-length gowns with beautiful trim and bands of needlework, and these gowns had a rather long bodice and sleeves of the same material. They wore a rather high-cut white bavero *with very delicate ruffles. They curled their hair and on top of it they wore a very wide white silk veil, which they let fall to their shoulders. At their necks they wore handsome gold chains, with valuable medallions and jewels.*

CLOTHING OF NOBLE UNMARRIED GIRLS of Tuscany

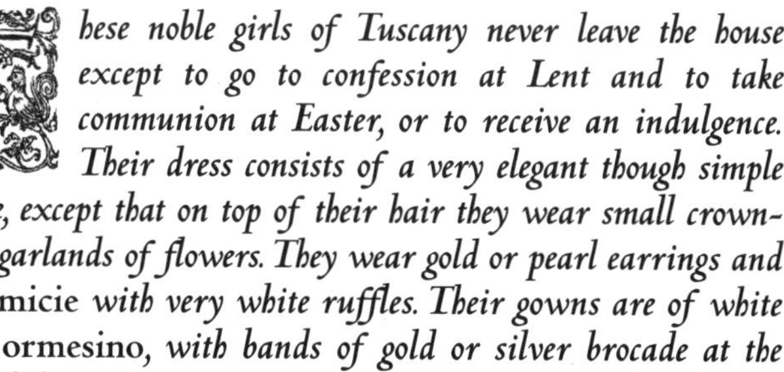

These noble girls of Tuscany never leave the house except to go to confession at Lent and to take communion at Easter, or to receive an indulgence. Their dress consists of a very elegant though simple coiffure, except that on top of their hair they wear small crown-shaped garlands of flowers. They wear gold or pearl earrings and thin camicie *with very white ruffles. Their gowns are of white or red* ormesino, *with bands of gold or silver brocade at the hem and down the center of the front. These gowns, floor-length, are attached to a doublet-shaped bodice of damask, satin or brocade of various colors, with sleeves slashed or pinked in the modern style. Their bodices are trimmed all over with gold or silver lace and fastened with protruding gold buttons. They usually carry handkerchiefs of very white* renso *in their hands, superbly needle-worked.*

MIDDLE-AGED WOMAN
of Tuscany

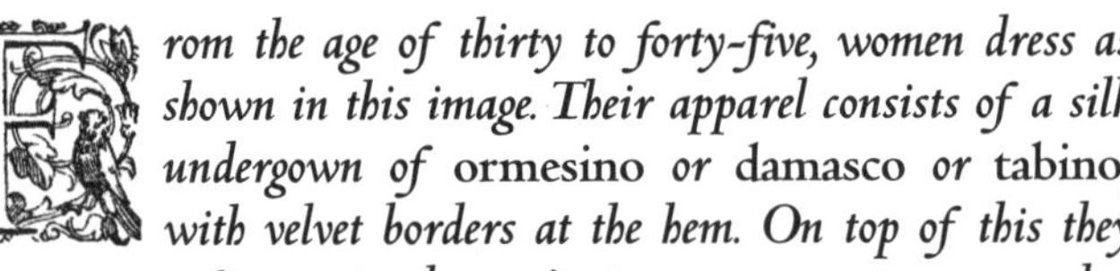

From the age of thirty to forty-five, women dress as shown in this image. Their apparel consists of a silk undergown of ormesino *or* damasco *or* tabino, *with velvet borders at the hem. On top of this they wear a gown of very simple* rascia *in* pavonazzo *or some other color, with a strand of pearls at the neck and a piece of silk or of* velo *that they tuck into their belt at the bottom of their bodice, in front. On their heads they wear a cap of velvet, black, or some other color, with a white veil underneath that falls down their back.*

WOMEN'S CLOTHING WORN WIDELY IN FLORENCE and throughout Lombardy

he dress of the woman shown here is not exactly a Florentine style but it was introduced by the ladies-in-waiting attending the Grand Duchess of that city,[1] *or by the wives of the courtiers to the Grand Dukes. Framing their foreheads they wear small, flat curls and they gather the rest of their hair into gold nets, over which they arrange a beautiful loop of* velo, *which they let fall onto their shoulders. As overgarments they wear* zimarre *of cloth of gold or silver, with long sleeves that reach their knees; they use only the small upper part of these sleeves, down to the elbow, to cover their arms. The sleeves are buttoned with gold or silk buttons and beautifully needle-worked all over with gold or silk. This* zimarra *is high-necked and worn with a high collar, and they wear* ninfe *[small, fine ruffles] or* lattughe, *very white and small. And at the back of this* zimarra, *to their left shoulder, they pin a veil or silk* fazzuolo *that they drape under their left arm.*

EVERYDAY WEAR OF A NOBLEMAN of Florence

Men of Florence usually wear a short gown or casacca *of black serge or* rascia, *and their trousers and stockings are of the same fabric. On top of this they wear a black mantle of* rascia *or wool, floor-length, which they fasten at the neck in front and let fall to their feet. They wear ruffles at their wrists and neck, and on their heads they wear hats of felt or* ormesino. *On their feet they wear shoes and* pianelle, *and dressed in this way, they go about the city doing business, in which they are very shrewd and hard-working, and, as a result, rich.*

CLOTHING OF THE PRIMI, *Magistrates of Florence*

Those in public office in the city of Florence wear a garment called a lucco, which resembles a mantle, open at the sides and in front and completely lined with black. Under this they wear a sottana of stamped rascia or some other kind of patterned cloth, of which their sleeves are also made; their arms emerge from the side openings of the gown. When it rains, they wear hats of ormesino on their heads, and when it is cold, hats of felt. Under their overgarments they wear a silk posta or black tie. They wear stockings of stame and black shoes inside velvet pianelle. In the summer the Lieutenant of the Grand Duke and his counselors wear this lucco in satin or in cremesino velvet, with an undergarment of the same material and stockings of the same color, with pianelle or shoes of black velvet. Then in the winter they can wear it made of wool, rascia or serge, in the same colors. On duty, they wear a black cap on their heads, and the Lieutenant of his Highness and the Counselors also wear a hood of pavonazzo silk on the left shoulder. And as long as they are part of the magistracy, they must wear this lucco whenever they leave the house. If the weather is rainy, they have it carried behind them on the street and are allowed to wear a long wool ferraiuolo, below the knee, but once they arrive at the palace, they wear this colored lucco as long as they are indoors. When he leaves his house, this Lieutenant of the Grand Duke takes two mace-bearers with him; the Counselors are each accompanied by *only one. The magistrates of the Forty-eight always wear this* lucco *in wool or black* rascia, *lined with red or* pavonazzo *silk, each one taking a servant with him. And a similar outfit is worn by* Cavalieri *of any denomination, as long as they are Florentine citizens and receive benefits from the city; and on this garment they wear the symbol of the denomination they serve.*

Text on page 289

CLOTHING OF WIDOWS AND OTHER WOMEN IN MOURNING

The dress shown here is for mourning and so is more appropriate for widows than for other people. These widows wear a shoulder-length veil of bisso *[very fine linen] on their heads; old women wear a veil of linen. They wear a mantle of Florentine* rascia *or* ferrandina *or* ciambellotto. *They wear a floor-length sash two fingers wide. And it is important to know that widows in Florence who do not wish to remarry wear their* fazzoletto *[a piece of fabric used to cover the head] on top of a mantle of black Florentine* rascia, *which they tie to their belt in their first year of mourning. When that year has passed, they wear this mantle longer, through the second year; and at the end of that year they wear it floor-length, and keep it in this style.*

Text on page 290

EVERYDAY CLOTHING OF PEASANTS
of the Villages around Florence

Peasants in the villages around Florence usually wear an undershirt of linen, white or colored, on top of which they wear a short overgarment that they call a salt'imbarca *[a jump-in-a-boat] of* griso *or some other coarse cloth; this has a collar four fingers in width, completely open at the sides under the arms and usually without sleeves. If they do have sleeves, they are only half-length and allow the sleeves of the* camicia *to show through. On the sides of this* salt'imbarca *are sewn ties an arm's length long and this is how they belt the garment. On their heads they wear a straw hat and sometimes a wool cap. They wear full-length trousers down to their feet and heavy, coarse peasant's shoes, in order to stamp down on farming tools while turning over the soil.*

Text on page 291

UNMARRIED PEASANT GIRLS
of Tuscany

he peasant girls of Florence and nearby regions wear some of their hair in curls, while they cover the rest with a silk or silver net, which they decorate with silk flowers in the winter and real flowers in the summer. At their neck they wear a strand of small round beads of silver or gilt, and their white camicie *have* lattughine. *They wear long, full gowns that they call* guarnelli, *of thin white linen, and a close-fitting, neat bodice that they bind with a sash of red or green silk. Over their gowns, they wear a white apron of very thin linen; from their waist down, this apron is decorated with red or black silk, beautifully needle-worked. They decorate their breasts and shoulders with flowers, which they can also smell, and they carry an elegant handkerchief in their hands.*

Text on page 292

THE CLOTHING OF SIENA,
a City of Tuscany

MARRIED NOBLEWOMEN OF SIENA

Some people claim that Siena was built in the year of our Lord 382 by Sienese Gauls in the time of Breno, who was passing through Italy at the time. Others claim, though, that it was built by the Romans for aged senators, who went to live there because the climate was better than anywhere else. This city was always an enemy of Florence, for Siena sheltered the Ghibellines when they were chased out of Florence by the Guelfs. It is one of the principal cities of Tuscany, because it is rich, pleasant, and situated in a very lovely place, distinguished by a beautiful university and abundant in every kind of food. This city, in order to remain free of certain factions, gave itself over to the Emperor, who sent a body of Spanish guards there; however, the Sienese drove them out in 1552 and called on the French to defend them. From this it came about that Peter of Spain, being commissioned by the Emperor Charles V, led a war against them that ended by order of Pope Julius III with the help of certain laws, but because the Sienese did not observe them, war began again. So finally Pietro Strozzi, general of the Sienese, was defeated by Medichino, the Marquis of Marignano; and thus the city of Siena, which had been free, became subject, along with all its territories, to the Emperor. Then, in the year 1557, with the agreement of the Emperor's son, King Philip, it came under the wise rule of Cosimo Medici, the Grand Duke of Tuscany; and at the present time it is ruled by Ferdinand, formerly a Cardinal and now Grand Duke as the result of the death of his brother Francesco.

The married noblewomen of Siena wear overgarments or zimarre *of* damasco *or patterned velvet in different colors, according to their taste; many of their gowns, however, are decorated at the front with golden needlework and also at the hem, and are floor-length. Under these they wear a* sottana *of silk or gold brocade patterned with foliage, of which their sleeves are also made. And they have a close-fitting bodice, not very long but cut low. Over these gowns, they wear a long silk veil, which, falling from their head (which is covered with a smooth velvet hat) reaches the same length as the gown. At their neck they wear very beautiful strands of pearls and rich gold chains, and they wear ruffles at their wrists and very close-fitting silk* baveri.

THE CLOTHING OF SIENESE NOBLEWOMEN
Married to Highly Placed Officials

Certain gentlewomen, wives of the principal men of Siena or of officials of the Grand Duke of Tuscany, wear a floor-length gown of cloth of gold or of brocade, richly decorated with a short, low-cut bodice that exposes the entire neck, and bracciali *sumptuously bordered with woven gold trim, with which their hems are also decorated. They wear silk* baveri *with very pretty ruffles, and at their necks they wear beautiful strings of pearls, with valuable jewels hanging from their center. They also wear necklaces or gold chains, finely worked, with pendant diamonds or rubies at the center. On top of their gown they wear mantles of silk* velo *with gold lace, which are attached to their heads and fall to the ground with great magnificence and splendor.*

THE CLOTHING OF A WOMAN OF PERUGIA

Perugia is a beautiful and noble city. It is situated on top of the Appenine range of hills and has many castles, towns, and lands beneath it. Its territory is full of lovely hills, which produce very delicate wines, delicious figs, great quantities of oil, and excellent fruit. The people of Perugia are brave and noble and belong to many famous families. The city is subject to the Roman papacy and it has a large university, sumptuous buildings, and many beautiful churches.

The women of Perugia wear a thin veil or a piece of cambrai *on their head, which covers their curls, ears and entire neck and ends gracefully at their shoulders. They wear overgarments of silk, velvet, satin or* tabino*, with short bodices fastened with colored silk ties. They adorn their necks with gold necklaces supporting a single jewel that hangs at their breast. And they cinch these gowns with a gold chain. Their gowns have wide, open sleeves, from which their arms emerge, covered in the same fabric as the* sottana*, which is of figured velvet or* damasco*, and floor-length.*

MARRIED NOBLEWOMEN of Pisa

Pisa is a city of Tuscany, two and a half miles from the Tyrrhenian Sea. Through its center flows the Arno river, as in Florence, but the river is also navigable outside the city and nearby. The people of Pisa were very powerful, especially at sea; among their other undertakings, they subjugated Carthage in the year 30. They captured the king and took him, bound, to the Roman Emperor. They also subjugated the island of Sardinia, killed the king of Mallorca, and took the queen to Pisa, along with her young son, to whom they later restored power. They have been friendly and faithful to the Roman Church. They brought the tablets of the law—which are now in Florence—from Constantinople; and after many long wars, they were finally defeated and became subject to the Florentines. They have a very beautiful university, where the order of the Knights of Saint Stephen was founded.

The dress shown here is exactly the one worn by noblewomen long ago. They wore a very beautiful coiffure with modest curls and gold earrings with beautiful pearls, with which they also adorned their necks; from their necks a necklace of very fine and valuable jewels also hung down onto their breast. They wore an overgarment open in the front, floor-length, needle-worked in gold, silk, and silver, with various foliage patterns; under this they wore a second, lighter gown, different in color from the other but much richer, for this one was decorated with small roses, pearls and other beautiful jewels, and it was bordered at the hem with tremoli *of precious stones. These gowns were cinched with jeweled gold chains of several strands, which they attached to their right shoulders and then let fall, ending in fine trim, down behind them to their feet. At their necks they wore a silk sash like that of soldiers, and* baveri *and ruffles at the neck. In one hand they carried perfumed gloves and a pretty flower, and in the other a fan of fine feathers.*

Text on page 297

YOUNG UNMARRIED GIRLS
of Pisa

The girls of Pisa, in the style of Tuscany, usually wear ornaments of middling value such as jewels, and gold at the neck and breast. They wear their hair uncovered, satisfied with a few modest curls and neat braids tied with colored silk ribbons. On top of a bavero *made with* ninfe *they wear a sash of* ormesino *in various colors, like the ones soldiers often wear. They have two gowns, that is, one underneath, long and floor-length, of silk, red, white or turquoise, and another on top, knee-length, of fabric of a different color from the one under it; the two together fall into many folds, because they are both very full. They cinch these gowns with an amber or crystal belt. They are almost all beautiful and well-mannered.*

Text on page 298

THE CLOTHING OF THE KINGDOM OF NAPLES

THE CLOTHING OF A NEAPOLITAN WOMAN in Early Times

he Kingdom of Naples is very large, rules over many famous provinces, and is very fertile in wheat, wine, oil, meats, fruit, and other things necessary for human consumption. The capital of the kingdom is Naples, which means "new city" (nova polis), *because after being destroyed, it was built again. It is situated by the seashore on several lovely hills. It has a beautiful port, full of all sorts of vessels, very grand houses with lovely gardens, and a large population. It is abundant in all good things, and now it is subject to the King of Spain.*

The women of this city, two hundred years ago (according to the way many excellent painters of the time depicted them), wore a floor-length overgarment without a bodice, with narrow sleeves cut above and below the elbow and tied together with silk cords; from these sleeves hung down the sleeves of the camicia, *very wide and white, which were tied at the shoulder with long silk cords that fluttered from their arms. Over all their clothing they wore a silk mantle, draped from their right shoulder down to their left side and then pulled up onto the right shoulder with its end left loose, a lovely sight. They wore their hair loose in front and made a thick, long braid of it in back, tied it with colored silk ribbons, and let it hang down full-length, as German women do. They wore their side hair loose, falling from their ears to their necks; they covered the rest of their head with a* cuffia *or a veil of silk, with a ribbon around their forehead holding the entire coiffure in place.*

A MARRIED WOMAN OF NAPLES

People often say "Naples the Gracious," which is confirmed by the beautiful manners of the noblewomen of that kingdom, and especially of that city. Their clothing consists of a very elegant coiffure of shapely curls. In the middle of their foreheads, the point of a thin, small veil falling down behind is set with a beautiful diamond or ruby or sapphire or some other precious stone. These married women wear very white fine ninfe or camicia ruffles, high and well shaped with starch, letting nothing but the face show. Below, they wear floor-length gowns of gold or silver brocade, or of silk, with a short train and with woven gold trim all around the bottom. Their overgarment is in the style of a zimarra of satin or velvet, high-necked and fastened all the way down the front with gold or silk buttons. Its sleeves are open, and the arms come through clothed in the sleeves of the sottana, with ruffles at the wrists. In their hands they carry fans and beautifully needle-worked handkerchiefs. They also wear many gold necklaces at their necks, lovely to see and very valuable.

A NEAPOLITAN BARONESS

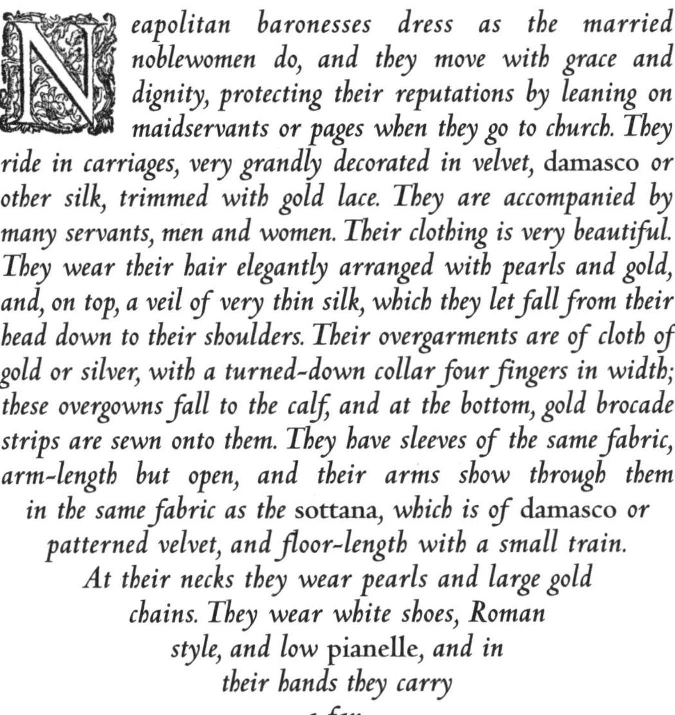

Neapolitan baronesses dress as the married noblewomen do, and they move with grace and dignity, protecting their reputations by leaning on maidservants or pages when they go to church. They ride in carriages, very grandly decorated in velvet, damasco *or other silk, trimmed with gold lace. They are accompanied by many servants, men and women. Their clothing is very beautiful. They wear their hair elegantly arranged with pearls and gold, and, on top, a veil of very thin silk, which they let fall from their head down to their shoulders. Their overgarments are of cloth of gold or silver, with a turned-down collar four fingers in width; these overgowns fall to the calf, and at the bottom, gold brocade strips are sewn onto them. They have sleeves of the same fabric, arm-length but open, and their arms show through them in the same fabric as the* sottana, *which is of* damasco *or patterned velvet, and floor-length with a small train. At their necks they wear pearls and large gold chains. They wear white shoes, Roman style, and low* pianelle, *and in their hands they carry a fan.*

CLOTHING OF A WOMAN OF NAPLES,
No Longer Worn

*lthough the image here is of a costume that few, if any, Neapolitan women wear nowadays, I nevertheless saw a woman of rank dressed in this way in Venice. She wore her hair beautifully curled in front, and in back it was wrapped in veils of very thin silk, part of which belonged to her coiffure while the other part fell down onto her shoulders. She wore an overgarment of black* ormesino *lined with red taffeta. It was floor-length with a short train, and the sleeves were of the same fabric, but slashed or pinked. The bodice of this gown was high-necked and close-fitting, fastened all the way down with gold buttons. At her neck she wore a necklace of round gold beads, with a very white* lattuga*. This overgarment was open from the belt down, and under it was a* faldiglia *skirt with wooden hoops inside at the bottom and circles of gold brocade on the outside, with bands of needlework. In one hand she held a beautiful fan with an ebony handle, and in the other, perfumed gloves.*

NEAPOLITAN GIRLS

eapolitan girls usually wear a lovely coiffure, composed of many curls and decorated with a string of pearls. They wear camicia *ruffles, high and beautiful, and a floor-length overgarment of white* damasco, *with a strip of gold brocade at the hem. The overgown has open sleeves, through which the arms appear covered in patterned silk. They wear a small train and in their hands they carry a fan. They do not use much make-up or many artificial beautifiers, and they rarely appear in public. For some time now they have worn long overgarments in the style of the* zimarra *(but with open sleeves, similar to the ones shown in the dress presented here), with a small veil blowing in the breeze, especially when they leave the house. Artisan and plebeian women dress similarly, so that they cannot be told apart from noblewomen.*

PRESENT-DAY MARRIED WOMEN of Naples

Married Neapolitan noblewomen of today wear a coiffure in which the hair is pulled back without curls, tied with silk ribbons and knotted with a very thin silk veil, which they then let fall loose behind them. They wear very high camicia *ruffles. They wear an overgarment with a high-necked bodice, on top of which, in the center of the breast, they pin a strip of thin silk* velo, *the ends of which they let fall behind on their shoulders in a dignified style. This overgarment is made of silk* brocatello *in beautiful patterns. It is floor-length, open from the bodice down, with long sleeves that they pin behind them; these sleeves are open halfway down, with openings through which their arms emerge, covered with the sleeves of the* sottana, *which is of satin or colored velvet, according to taste. Rich women still often wear this style of dress, but gradually they are yielding to the styles of Spain, for this style has been corrupted by the Spanish who continue to live in the city.*

THE CLOTHING OF A WOMAN OF ROMAGNA
and the Territories of the Marches

The province of Romagna is very rich and populous. It was given this name for being faithful to the Roman pope and to Charlemagne at the time that the Lombards were masters of this region, so that this pope and his Imperial Majesty, wanting to reward such loyalty, wanted the region to have this name in return for having helped Rome. And because Romagna shares a border with the Marches of Ancona, it has a similar style of dress.

The dress of the women of both these provinces consists of a tightly bound coiffure of modest curls and very blonde hair, on top of which they wear a silk veil decorated with gold tremoli, which falls from their head onto their shoulders and makes a pretty sight. They expose their white necks and their ears adorned with various jewels. They wear floor-length overgarments of silk in different colors, with long, floor-length, slashed sleeves through which can be seen the lining of cloth of gold. Under these gowns they wear silk brocade faldiglie with wooden hoops inside, which allow them to walk freely, and these faldiglie are bordered in a lovely way with strips of gold brocade. The overgown is in the style of a zimarra, with gold buttons from top to bottom; at their neck they wear necklaces of gold. They then wear a silk veil, very elegant, pinned at the right shoulder, which, passing under the left arm, makes a beautiful sight from the back. Around this veil is very finely placed gold lace.

THE CLOTHING OF A PRESENT-DAY NEAPOLITAN NOBLEWOMAN

Because there are seven provinces in the kingdom of Naples, speaking of those that belong to the mainland—that is, Abruzzo, Capitinata, the Territory of Otranto, Calabria, Basilicata, Principato, and the Territory of Lavoro—the dress of the women of this kingdom is very diverse, as has been confirmed for me by Messer Francesco Curia.[1] *This most excellent painter of the city of Naples sent me drawings of many styles, among which, in addition to those already shown, the following four seem to me to be the most beautiful and commonly worn. The noblewomen of that kingdom go about with their breast closely covered, as do the women of Spain, with very heavy, sumptuous overgarments of colored silk, adorned all over with woven trim of gold and silk or silver and with needlework, according to their rank and wealth. Under these gowns they wear a hoopskirt, which they call a* verducato, *perhaps because they are most often of green* [verde] *cloth. This is very tight and narrow at the waist but wide and full at the hem so that it has the shape of a bell, resulting from the stiffness produced by many small cords sewn in at the bottom. On top of this* faldiglia *they wear a belted gown of silk, black or in color, which they call a* gonella, *decorated at the hem with three or four bands of colored velvet, with patterns woven into it. Instead of a bodice, they wear a doublet with wide, comfortable sleeves of cloth of gold or silver or of white silk, with the waistline coming down to a point and fastened with buttons. They also adorn their necks with very beautiful* lattughine, *which they call* pizzelli, *and these are made of very white* cambrai, *four fingers high, decorated with elegant lace, which must be of needlework. On top of this doublet they wear a long robe of velvet, satin or* damasco*; they call this a* robba*, and it is made in the style of a long, floor-length* zimarra*, with wide, split arms, not very long, with* spallacetti *[shoulder rolls] at the top of the arm; this* zimarra *is open in front and decorated with woven gold or silk trim, and it has long slashes at the front of the bodice. When these women go outside, they wear a mantle of very thin black silk, like that worn by the noblewomen of Venice, with this difference: it is trimmed around the edges with padded silk lace, and with black enamel ornaments in the shape of little daisies, gilt above and below. This mantle is fastened at both shoulders, tied under the arms and fastened in front with a gold buckle or narrow silk sash. They usually wear* pianelle *in the Spanish style, high and round-toed, slashed in a thousand pretty ways along the sole so that various colors of silk and patterned brocade can be seen. They wear stockings of silk or* stame*. Most of their hair is coiffed in the Spanish style, high and round with a certain puffed look, lovely to see, and they usually put beautiful flowers in their hair and pin to it a very thin silk veil of various colors, striped with gold and silver, which they allow to fall behind onto their shoulders. They wear gloves or half-gloves, and gold, pearls, gems, and other jewelry.*

Text on page 307

CLOTHING OF A MODERN HIGH-RANKING NOBLEWOMAN of Naples

Although we include no image of a gentleman of Naples, it should be noted that in this kingdom, men of rank dress very sumptuously, wearing velvet, satin, and other silk fabrics in great quantity, and all their garments are snug-fitting, narrow in cut, and richly trimmed. They wear doublets, trousers and stockings of silk, as we now see every day in our own regions, and they take great pleasure in weapons and horses.

To explain the image included here, I will say that there are many gentlewomen in the city of Naples who most often wear a gonella *with many bands and trims of black silk, with a doublet with a slightly rounded belly that ends in a point or with a bodice reaching up over the breast, decorated with woven trim. At their necks they wear a* bavero *that they call a* cozzetto, *of* cambrai *or thin* renso, *which, tied with narrow strings or pinned at their neck, covers their shoulders yet leaves a part of their delicate breast bare. When they are widows, they always wear a mantle of black wool, very ample, which covers their head and shoulders, falling down to the ground at the back in a full, gathered shape with a bit of a train, and a veil that covers their head under this mantle, which is like the* Romana *but has wide sleeves in the style of a nun's gown. And such noblewomen, in a pretty fashion, wear a gold chain around their necks, which falls to their knees, and to this, in the summer, is attached a fan in the form of a peacock's tail, made of the finest straw and decorated with* tremoli *of gold or silk. In the winter, they attach to this chain a muff lined with the finest furs. Otherwise, they dress as the lady in the print that precedes this one.*

The gentlewomen of Naples are notably refined and luxurious in their dress because they value adornments that they can wear on their backs more than any furnishings for their houses. They use silk very abundantly in their clothing, which they decorate with beautiful lace and trims of woven silk, with margaritine *made of enamel or crystal, whichever they prefer. However poor a woman may be, she never leaves her house without a servant, and if she cannot take anyone else out of the house with her, she will use her husband or brother or sons, on whom she leans to go to church. And because spring lasts forever in Naples, the women almost always wear flowers, with which they adorn their ears and hair in a very lovely way, so that they look just like nymphs; and as a result of the herbs they carry wherever they go, a gentle and pleasant scent of perfume follows after them. They also habitually dye their hair blonde with artfully distilled waters, so effective that their hair appears to be silver. They also make up their faces with various powders and mixtures; it is frequently the case among them that a woman who does not wear make-up is the target of jokes and derision. Most often they wear high collars, adorning their necks with lovely* lattughine *of* renso *or* cambrai, *trimmed with needle lace in beautiful leafy patterns. But there are many gentlewomen, who, being very devout as a result of the teachings of the Jesuits, go about dressed more modestly and more thriftily, in a white veil that covers their heads and falls down over their shoulders, as can be seen in this print.*

SUMMER CLOTHING OF MARRIED NEAPOLITAN NOBLEWOMEN of High Rank

Because Naples is a city bathed on one side by the Adriatic Sea, it has a port where ships arrive from many parts of Italy and other places in order to exchange merchandise. In this port a beautiful jetty can be seen for the convenience of the ships that come here. These days, the city is surrounded with strong walls and three castles: Il Nuovo, Il Capuanno, and Sant'Hermo. It has a university where all disciplines are taught, to which students come in great numbers from all over the kingdom. The surrounding territory has a mild climate and a pleasant location, and it is rich in fruit trees and abundant in all necessary things. From every part of the kingdom princes, dukes, marquises, counts, barons, knights, and noblemen gather here, and they delight in pomp and spend so much money on their horses, servants, liveries, and decorations that it is a wonder and a marvel to behold. There are also many elaborate churches, charity hospitals, luxurious and well-designed palaces, and beautiful decorative gardens. Altogether, it is a center for everything that can be desired for use, comfort, and the pleasures of a well-ordered life—everything that comes from nature or is produced by the artful mastery of the many brilliant minds that flourish here.

All the women of Naples carry a beautiful rosary, including round gold beads decorated with silk; going to prayers, they also carry a handsome rope in the style of Saint Francis. In the summer, over their hoopskirt they usually wear a gonella *of* cremesino *silk or some other light fabric, and less often of satin or* damasco*; this gown has a half-length bodice with a point in front, which is prettily trimmed. They do not wear doublets in* *the summer, but they do wear* baveri *at their necks, with ruffs of* cambrai *or very fine white* renso, *embellished with lace and other needlework, beautiful to see. They also cover their shoulders and breast with these* baveri *and wear many herbs and flowers of the season on them. On top of this gown they wear an overgarment of* ormesino, *in the same color as the undergown, prettily decorated with lace and other needle-worked trim like that on the undergown. The front of their overgarment has long vertical slashes, and their sleeves, called* à persuto, *have a slash down the middle, out of which they can easily move their arms. So in that season they go about in* camicia *sleeves of very finely needle-worked* renso *with small ruffles at the wrist. And on top of the overgarment they also wear a mantle, similar to those described above. In this season they wear their hair rather high, following the Spanish style of today. They pin a veil to their hair, with some left over at the top, which lends them a graceful air, and the rest of it they let fall to their shoulders. In the other details of their clothing, they dress as other women of the city do.*

Text on page 310

THE CLOTHING OF NOBLE GIRLS
of Naples

he gait of Neapolitan women is dignified, lovely and very modest, so they appear quite graceful to those who see them. They enjoy large retinues composed of pages and ladies-in-waiting and large numbers of their neighbors and relatives. The ladies-in-waiting wear neither hoopskirts nor gonelle *and instead of a* robba *they wear a simple floor-length gown fastened at the neck and closed all the way down, most often of colored wool because this style is rarely made in silk; these gowns are bordered all around with needle and bobbin lace and woven silk trim of the same or of a different color from the gown. This gown has* braccialetti *from which hang sleeves that cover the arms. In the winter these unmarried girls wear a doublet and in the summer they wear* camicia *sleeves of* renso *or of some other delicately thin needle-worked linen, and very elegant* lattughine *at their necks and wrists. They wear their hair in a style in between high and low, and they attach a short veil to it, which is let loose to the wind so that it is almost always fluttering about. They wear beautiful silk stockings and* pianelle alla Romana, *as do the other women in this kingdom. They usually carry a lovely rosary in their hands, and a handkerchief. And they delight in flowers and other scented plants.*

Before I end this discussion of Naples, I will make some mention of men's clothing. I will say that Neapolitan noblemen dress very sumptuously and fashionably, perhaps more than other lords and noblemen of Italy, for they wear a great deal of velvet, satin and every other sort of black silk fabric and very fine serge, with gold and silver silk lace and with other richly decorated trims. As to the cut of their clothing, they wear long and short garments closely fitted to the body. Rather than short stockings, they wear them full-length, of very fine silk, and their short, slashed breeches are of soprarizzo *or* tagliato *velvet, with embroidery or lace of gold or silk, depending on the time of year and their resources and taste. Under their overgarments they wear a doublet of satin or some other silk fabric, with a rounded belly, trimmed with lace and pinked in patterns. On top of the doublet they wear a* casacca *of velvet or serge, but in the summer it is made of a lighter fabric, with the sleeves hanging behind, stylishly fitted; from this jacket the sleeves of the doublet emerge. They cover their heads with a cap of* velluto riccio *decorated with gold medals. And sometimes they wear a lovely cap with beautiful, valuable feathers. They wear a cape of very thin serge, lined with* tagliato *and* velluto soprarizzo, *but in the summer they wear it in some other elegant fabric. And since they all devote themselves to arms and chivalry, they carry swords embellished with gold and velvet-lined scabbards. They wear shoes in the Spanish style, most often of velvet, and low boots in the winter, with* pianelle *outside them. They ride very handsome, valuable horses, caparisoned in velvet and gold or silk embroidery, and they are accompanied by a large number of pages, grooms and servants, all dressed in livery.*

CLOTHING OF CALABRIAN MEN

alabria is a large province in the kingdom of Naples, very populous, and fertile in everything useful and necessary for human food. It is full of fruit-bearing hills, rich valleys, and precious wines. This province produces sugar, honey, wax, mineral salts, sea salt, gold, silver, wool, cotton, saffron, and other similar things, such as linen and hemp and silk, in sufficient quantity to supply all the other regions of Italy—and manna rains down from its skies! This region is full of groves of cedars, apple trees, oranges, and lemons.

The clothing most commonly worn by the men of Calabria is like the one shown here. That is, they wear a woolen cap on their heads in the winter and in summer one made of silk, with a small folded-back brim and a lining of ormesino*; and a thigh-length overgarment of black wool, with a border of velvet or woven trim at the hem. They wear full-length leggings cut of coarse wool down to their feet, and high shoes for the mud. On top of this, they wear a long, floor-length mantle of black wool bordered with woven trim, without a collar or shaped neckline, but fastened with a button in the center of the chest, and so they go about, dressed at little expense.*

THE CLOTHING OF WOMEN OF GAETA

Gaeta is a very ancient city of the kingdom of Naples. It is built on a mountain, which is bathed by the sea on three sides. It is called Gaeta after a woman of that name, who was the nurse of the Trojan Aeneas and who was buried here. It has a very secure port and is an invincible fortress because of its setting and because of the thick walls that surround it. Its territory is full of splendid gardens, which supply all of Italy with apples, oranges, limes, and lemons. The women are beautiful but not very rich. On their heads they wear kerchiefs that cover their heads and shoulders completely. They wear an overgarment of mixed or pure wool, without a bodice but floor-length, which they cinch with a linen band. On top of this, in back, they tie on a red or pavonazzo *cloth with a band of colored velvet at the edge. In front they wear an apron of white linen, skillfully needle-worked with black or red silk. And on their shoulders they wear a* casacchino *of* pavonazzo *or red wool with sleeves, which ends a quarter length below the waist.*

THE CLOTHING OF WOMEN OF THE ISLAND OF ISCHIA

he island of Ischia is set in the Ligurian Sea. It is not very large, but is very strong and rich in excellent wines that are called, in Naples and Rome, Greek wines from Ischia. On this island Ferandino, the son of King Alfonso II of Aragon, took refuge when King Charles of Sicily entered the city of Naples in triumph.[2] *This land is so strong and naturally fortified that the city can be entered only through a very narrow pass, for it is encircled by cliffs. It is an island eighteen miles in circumference, and the city is inhabited by a thousand families, and it is strong—indeed, invincible. And below it are eight villages, one of four hundred houses. It produces a great deal of wine, amounting from year to year to 16,000 barrels.*

The women of the city and of the villages are usually beautiful and graceful, and because there is no craft of silk-making or wool on this island, most of the women spin; they also attend to cultivating the land. On their heads they wear a fazzuolo *or a piece of white linen, which, after forming several folds, falls to their shoulders, trimmed with fringes of red or black silk. They wear an overgarment of thin linen, floor-length, with very full sleeves bordered with finely made lace. At their back they tie on a piece of colored silk brocade, and in front, a white linen apron needle-worked at the hem with red or black silk. At their necks they wear silver or coral beads. And they are rarely idle.*

A MARRIED SICILIAN NOBLEWOMAN
Dressed for Public Festivities

icily is located between the Tyrrhenian Sea, Africa, the Adriatic Sea, the Ionian Sea and the Siculian Sea. That is, on the east it has the Ionian Sea and the Siculian Sea; then on the south and the west, the African or Libyan Sea; and on the third side, the Tyrrhenian Sea. It is an island in the shape of a triangle, with a circumference of 550 miles. It is very rich in wheat, which ends up throughout all of Italy, and fodder, fruits and other things necessary for human use. There are also gold and silver mines.

The dress of the women going to public festivities includes a hairstyle with little curls framing the forehead; the rest they gather into a gold net, which, at the top of the head, is set with a little rose made of pearls or small rubies. They wear a long, floor-length overgarment of thin cloth of gold or silver, woven in the style of brocade, with a high-necked bodice rising to the throat, at which they wear very white camicia *ruffles. They wear a padded bodice, which is not unbecoming, and they cinch their waist with several gold chains. They wear the sleeves of their* sottana, *and those of the overgarment fall to the floor. This gown has a border of gold embroidery at its hem. At their necks they wear gold chains of two or three strands, and they fasten their bodice with gold-enameled buttons.*

A SICILIAN NOBLEWOMAN
in Church

When going to public festivities, Sicilian noblewomen dress very splendidly, but when they go to religious services, they dress in a much more restrained way. In the winter, they wear a long woolen mantle, floor-length, which they tie at the neck and let fall to the ground; in the summer this is made of ferandina *or* ormesino. *When they fasten it at the neck, they bring it far enough forward that it reaches their head and covers it completely. Under this they wear a* sottana *that they keep on at home after they have returned from church and have taken off the cloak.*

A NOBLE GIRL OF SICILY OUTDOORS,
Going to Church

When girls leave the house they wear a mantle of ferandina *or woolen or silk* buratto, *which, placed on their heads, forms a small point at their foreheads and then, falling down, covers their entire body. They use no make-up or other frivolous things, but go about very modestly and piously. They are very amiable and virtuous, and they take great pleasure in music and songs; and many know how to compose learned verses.*

THE CLOTHING OF THE KINGDOM OF FRANCE

THE CLOTHING OF FRANCE in Early Times

Because I intend to speak of Spain immediately after France, it seems like a good idea to explain some of the contrasts that exist between these two kingdoms. The Spaniards invented the custom of piercing their ears and wearing gold earrings, with valuable gems, a style abhorred for a time by the French. Now not only French women but also French men wear them. France is much richer in bread and wine than Spain, but not in abundance and flavor, in which Spain exceeds her by far; this is because it rains very, very often in France, while in Spain it is necessary to carry water by aqueducts far from the rivers that are its source. In Spain there is a greater abundance of apples, wax, saffron, rice, wheat, sugar, broom, rosemary, lemons, capers, dates, citrons, quinces, and other aromatic fruits, though France imports all these things, in the same way that it imports wool from Flanders and Italy. The constitution of the Spanish is hotter and drier and their skin is darker than that of the Gauls, who are colder and moister and have softer and whiter flesh.

The women of France are more fertile than those of Spain. The French are taller, but the Spanish are more robust and narrow at the waist; the French fight with more ferocity and strength, but the Spanish with greater acumen and skill. Spain has always been praised for its nimble, swift horses and its men ride with short stirrups and are very skillful; the French, on the other hand, ride heavy horses and are good with weapons.

The French are voluble and the Spanish are taciturn. The Gauls are merry by nature and in company they are never solemn, but the Spanish are serious and are less easy-going drinking companions. The Spanish drink wine mixed with water and the French drink it straight. The speech of the Spaniard is more sober, but the Gaul's is smoother. Among the Spanish, the Castilians speak the best language, but in France no differences can be discerned, to the extent that it is impossible to know which city speaks the genuine Gallic tongue. Spain has more land, but Gaul has more people. Spain sends many, many goods to France, as has been said, and France sends wheat, linen cloth, thread, books, and other small goods, such as knives and mirrors, to Spain. Spain has a greater number of titled princes, and France more noblemen. In Spain there are two dukes, whose annual income is fifty to sixty thousand ducats; there are also two hundred marquises, each of whose income almost equals that of a duke. There are also sixty counts, whose average income is ten to twenty thousand ducats per year, though some among them have an income as high as fifty thousand. There are still others, viscounts, barons, and leaders of the militia, called Adelantados *in Spain; there are also viceroys, governors, masters of the horse, and heads of local government. There are also high masters of knightly orders, such as that of Saint James, of Alcantara, of Calatrava, of Saint John of Rhodes, of Montesa, those they call the Knights of Christus, and others called Davi. The income of each one of these is fifty thousand ducats or more. As far as ecclesiastical positions go, France has more of them, for they have twelve archbishops and sixty-six bishops, whereas Spain has only nine archbishops and forty-six bishops. But the income of those in Spain is much higher than of the French ones, for the church of Toledo alone gathers and saves two hundred thousand ducats every year, of which the archbishop by himself enjoys eighty thousand, and all the other bishops have at least eight thousand ducats in income per year.*

And because the clothing of France should be discussed first, it seems right to me to talk about the country in some detail. The powerful and warlike kingdom of France was formerly divided into many parts, that is, into Belgian Gaul, Narbonne, Aquitaine, Provence, Burgundy, Picardy, France, Normandy and Brittany; Aquitaine still retains its ancient name. During the period from then to now, Neustria and Austrusia have been forgotten, though they were familiar to the people of early times. This large kingdom expanded to include all of Italy and it was highly loyal to the Roman Church. It repaired and restored, we might say, everything that the rage of the barbarians had destroyed, so that the Italians owe a very great debt to the French, or the Gauls. Gaul, the third region of Europe, took its name from Galate, the son of Herod of Egypt, who came to the region of Gallia before the fall of Troy and built, in Celtic territory, a city called Alesia, which was much later destroyed by Julius Caesar, the first Roman emperor. This Galate ruled over that kingdom so it was called Galatia, but the Romans subtracted a syllable and called it Gallia. The region expanded so much that they divided it into two parts, that is, Cisalpine and Transalpine Gaul. Cisalpine Gaul today is called Lombardy, that is, on this side of the Alps; and Transalpine Gaul is France, whose principal city is Paris, which was founded by Julius Caesar and today has a flourishing university and a very large population.

In early France, which has always been a very Christian country, women's attire used to include a large, beautiful rosary, now called a Cavalier, *made of fine bone, which they always carried in their hands. They wore their hair loose on their shoulders, and on top of it they placed a beautiful piece of ormesino or thin white linen, decorated all over with different strands of beautiful pearls (with which they also adorned their neck and breast) and also with valuable jewels. They wore a low-necked, floor-length overgarment, with a small train, lined throughout with sable and other very fine furs; and under this they wore another gown of patterned velvet or damasco, with narrow sleeves though very full at the wrists. The sleeves of the overgarment were wider still and revealed the furs with which they were lined. They wore gold chains, and, dressed in this way, they went to church.*

Text on page 320

A NOBLE BRIDE
of France

Before they marry, noble girls throughout France have the custom of speaking and chatting very intimately with the young men who love them, who behave very familiarly with them but very chastely in their homes. This practice lasts until they take them as wives, and once they have married them, they take them to a thousand entertainments and parties among friends and relatives for a long period of time, and many dowry gifts are exchanged between them. These women of France are very gay by nature and very sanguine, and they are mostly fair-skinned and blonde. And while they are unmarried and their lovers are close beside them, they often caress and welcome the men who love them, never revealing whom they love the most; passing their time in witty conversation, they entertain many suitors, who are equally welcomed by their fathers and mothers.

Their clothing includes a small cap of black velvet trimmed with jewels set in gold, with a feather laden with beautiful pearls; under this they arrange their hair very prettily in braids decorated with pearls. At their necks they wear beautiful camicia *ruffles, very wide, white and well-formed. They wear a long floor-length overgarment of velvet or satin or brocade or colored* ormesino*, according to their taste, with a medium-sized train. This gown has a very close-fitting bodice, pointed at the waist and high-necked, with small slashes on the breast, which is rich with gold chains and many strands of jewels. They wear open sleeves, slightly longer than their arms, with* braccialetti *trimmed with jeweled gold, from which their arms emerge covered in gold brocade. They wear a gold chain as a belt, and instead of buttons to fasten the gown, they wear gold brooches, decorated with well-set precious stones, which make a rich and lovely sight along the opening at the front. When they go out, they are accompanied by their noble relatives, servants, and married women with maidservants in a large company, in a very honorable fashion.*

THE MARRIED NOBLEWOMAN
of Paris and Nearby Places

When married noblewomen of Paris and places nearby, married for a number of years, leave their houses, they conceal their faces because they wear a mask-like piece of silk or black satin, with two holes, over their face; when they see a relative, they reveal their face to greet them but then cover it back up. Their headdress is called the attifet, *and it forms two arches above their forehead; this is covered with a little veil attached to the point of the headdress on their forehead, covering their hair and then falling to their shoulders; under this little veil, you can see prettily shaped curls. They wear high* baveri *with beautifully formed ruffles, and at their necks they wear pearls and gold chains. They wear a long, floor-length overgarment of velvet,* damasco *or satin, open in the front but tied with silk or gold ribbons. Their sleeves are open and from these openings their arms emerge, covered in the sleeves of their* sottana. *This attire is also worn by widows, but in black and without any ornaments. At the deaths of their mother or father, the daughters accompany their bodies to the grave, in the company of other relatives; but wives do not accompany their husbands, nor husbands their wives.*

MARRIED FRENCH NOBLEWOMAN of Orléans

he married women of Orléans, a noble city of France, wear a headdress that they call the chaperone (chiapparon), *set on top of their hair in the style of a round cap or snood with edges gathered up with woven gold. This is fitted around the hair, which is turned back and puffed in the shape of a little mushroom, as shown here. From this hangs a stole of black velvet, a palm and a half long, in three folds that fall down in back. The overgarment is of black velvet, very wide, with a stiff bodice belted with gold links. They wear* baveri *with white ruffles. They cover their faces and uncover them only in the houses of relatives or friends. They are corseted tightly at the hips and waist, and to look wide-shouldered they wear little circles of copper or some other metal at the shoulders of their gowns to puff them out, and their sleeves are very full. These women usually wear black on top and other colors below. And they are used to going freely wherever they like, because they are respected and held in high esteem.*

A FRENCH NOBLEWOMAN
from Avignon, a City of France

queen of Naples named Giovanna[1] *found herself owing the Holy Seat of Rome a large sum of money in past taxes, which she had not paid from this feudal kingdom. So to cancel this debt to the Roman pope, she decided to cede her own city of Avignon to him, in the year 1360, which she indeed did, in perpetuity, to Pope Clement VI. This city is situated on the Rhone and it is of marvelous antiquity. So Pope John, inspired by some good reason, moved his residence here, where it remained for sixty years.*

The clothing of the noblewomen of this city is very modest. It consists of an ankle-length black velvet robba *or* sbernia *with sleeves that cover their arms, and* braccialetti *lined with green* ormesino. *They wear as a* sottana *a gown of silk* brocatello, *embellished with large gold flowers. They wear ruffles and* baveri *embroidered with gold and silk. Their coiffure consists of hair wrapped in a gold or silver net, on top of which they pin a* fazzuolo *of* renso, *linen or* cambrai, *wide but not very long, which they let fall to their shoulders. Some women, instead of this* fazzuolo, *pin on a piece of* ormesino *or* taffetano, *and so, in a dignified way, they go about their business.*

NOBLE GIRL OF FRANCE

It is a particular custom of the French to train their daughters from an early age in the study of literature, music, and needlework, so they send them to school, though with their faces covered, and well turned out. Their attire consists of beautiful blonde hair, with curls on the forehead and temples, which they enclose in a beautiful net of gold or silver or silk. They wear overgarments of velvet, satin, ormesino *and* damasco, *in lovely and diverse colors, but no black. These gowns are very high-necked and narrowly cut, so that just a little of the white, very fine* camicia *ruffles can be seen. The sleeves are slightly shorter than the gown and open near the shoulders, and through their openings the arms appear in the sleeves of their* sottane, *which are usually of* brocatello *woven with large flowers in different colors. They wear no other ornaments at their necks, but they fasten their strands of pearls or golden chains with certain silk cords and gold rings high on their bodice, and this makes a pleasant sight. They do not wear trains but their custom is to have beautiful borders of woven gold sewn all around the hems of their gowns.*

MOURNING CLOTHES OF A NOBLEWOMAN of France

When their husbands die, noblewomen in mourning, especially widows, do not go to the burial but do nevertheless leave the house to oversee the funeral rites. They wear the style of dress shown here for a full year. It includes a floor-length overgarment, completely black, of buratto *or* ciambellotto, *closed in front and unbelted. On their heads they wear a white or black veil, whichever they prefer, which falls here and there to their feet. The sleeves of the gown are slit and open halfway down the garment, and through them they can bring out their arms, covered with the black sleeves of their undergarment. They cover their breast with a white veil, gathered and tied crossways with a cord, and so they go about, sad and grieving.*

FRENCH NOBLEMAN

French noblemen are very magnanimous by nature and skillful in every profession, as much in literature as in music; they devote themselves to the practice of arms, both on foot and on horseback. They have good health and they are very friendly, but also prone to rage and quick to be angry. They keep their promises, and they go to war well outfitted. The French people never keep or maintain one style of dress but change it according to their caprice; this is the result of their wealth, originating in the fertility of the country, which is abundant in all good things.

Their usual style of dress is to wear silk or any other beautiful rich fabric available. They wear short capes of fine wool and also of velvet, but very badly made. They curl their hair and cover their heads with a velvet cap with precious plumes. Sometimes they wear long ferraiuoli *of very thin wool. They wear velvet* colletti *trimmed with gold lace and gold buttons, and underneath a doublet of* ormesino *in white or other colors, with long, rounded bellies padded with cotton. The sleeves of these doublets are very wide in the arms but narrow at the wrist. They wear short* bracconi, *very tight on the thigh, which practically reveal the veins of their flesh. They wear their knees uncovered, and silk stockings. They used to belt on long, narrow swords but today they carry them three fingers wide.*

CLOTHING OF A FRENCH NOBLEMAN,
No Longer Worn

*rench merchants and traveling salesmen from Picardy and other provinces of France, especially when traveling, usually wore a* robba *of velvet or wool with open sleeves, and with huge silk and gold buttons, as many as they wanted, which they fastened there and down the front. This robe was calf-length, and they wore it over their shoulders, hanging open all the way down. On their heads they wore a cap of colored velvet bound with a strip of silk or* buratto*. At their ears they wore earrings of gold or pearls, as they do today, and around their ears they curled the hair of their temples, which they let grow quite long (as they do now). They wore a* colletto *of very beautiful leather, perfumed, with buttons of either gold or crystal, very elegant and decorated all over with gold or silver woven trim. They wore* bracconi *much fuller than those worn today, of patterned velvet and other silk. But today, instead of caps, they wear very wide hats, high and pleated. And on their feet in the summer, they wear velvet* pianelle, *four fingers high but very narrow; in the winter they wear them with shoes of soft leather, most often white.*

276

CLOTHING OF A PRESENT-DAY FRENCHMAN

At the present time, Frenchmen usually wear clothing extravagant beyond all measure, as can be seen throughout Italy, especially in Padua and here in Venice. They wear felt hats with brims so wide that they cover their shoulders. They usually wear doublets padded with cotton at the stomach and very long, reaching the bottom of their stomach or belly. They wear short bracconi, which they attach to their belt and use to cover their legs down to the knee, but fitting so snugly to the thigh that they reveal almost all their muscles and sinews. They wear stockings of stame from Flanders or of silk, up to mid-thigh, which they either fasten to their bracconi or wear tied and gartered above the knee with the tops folded back over and hanging down to mid-shin. They wear woolen or silk ferraiuoli, calf-length, some with sleeves, some decorated with woven silk trim and others not. They also have the habit of wearing earrings, some of pearls, others rings of gold, and they let their hair grow so long at the temples that it reaches from behind their ears almost to their shoulders. On their feet they wear white shoes inside velvet pianelle four fingers high but narrow; and so dressed, they travel throughout Italy.

CLOTHING OF A NOBLEMAN
of Burgundy

Burgundy is a duchy that shares a border with France and neighbors on Flanders and the region of Lorraine; it is subject to King Philip of Spain. Men's attire there is very splendid. On their heads they wear velvet caps, enriched with beautiful feathers and gold and silk cords, and at their necks beautiful, deep camicia *ruffles. They wear velvet* colletti, *slashed up and down and decorated with woven gold trim, and through these slashes can be seen their colored satin doublets with matching sleeves. Over their shoulders they wear a short* tabarro *of satin or velvet, waist-length, with sleeves diagonally trimmed with many strips of the same fabric. They wear* bracconi *of patterned velvet or* damasco, *with small cuffs that cover their knees, and stockings knitted of worsted silk or* stame; *on their feet they wear shoes in the French style. They adorn their necks with long, massive gold chains in several strands, which they also drape under their right arm, and with a silk sash, in the manner of soldiers. And they are rather haughty in nature.*

CLOTHING OF A WOMAN OF VERDUN, *in Lorraine*

Verdun is a principal city of Lorraine, and it is very rich, noble, and abundant in good things. Its women, however noble they may be, are not ashamed to do everything necessary for a household, even though they have many servants, men and women. They wear a very high headdress, of velvet or wool or Florentine rascia, *in a style that can be seen in the preceding print. They wear* baveri *with thick, high ruffles but open in front, with pretty needlework. Their floor-length overgarments are of velvet or silk or* damasco. *In their houses they wear aprons of* renso, *and in public they wear them made of* damasco *or* ormesino, *cinched with leather belts with silver or gold buckles, and with a chain also of gold, with a jewel at its center. On their ears they usually wear beautiful earrings of gold or pearls.*

CLOTHING OF THE WOMEN OF LOTTHARINGA, in Lorraine

Lottharinga is an area of Lorraine, of middling wealth, so its women work hard and dress modestly in wool and ciambellotto. *They wear a headdress of white veils that covers their hair entirely, and over their shoulders they wear a circular* bavero *of silk with only a few small ruffles, but beautifully needle-worked in front. Their overgarments are most often of* ciambellotto, *floor-length, with a rounded bodice but open in front. They tie on a linen apron with a velvet, silver-buckled belt. And on their feet they wear low* pianelle.

CLOTHING OF VALMONT,
near Lorraine

Valmont is a place on the border of France near Lorraine, a very large duchy, and subject to the King of France. The women of this area wear this headdress of black wool, and long overgarments of serge or Florentine rascia, *as can be seen from the preceding illustration of their clothing. They dress very modestly and are sharp-witted in their behaviour; they wear clothing of different colors. They speak a dialect different from any other language in France. These lands are rich and fertile, and they have many pastures for their animals; for this reason, this place is rich in meat, dairy products, and oils of all kinds.*

THE CLOTHING OF THE KINGDOM OF SPAIN

CLOTHING OF A LADY OF ANCIENT TIMES in Spain

pain is a large kingdom, bathed by the sea on every side, except the one that separates it from France by means of very high mountains called the Pyrenees [born of fire], so named for the frequent bolts of lightning that fall from the sky there. Spain was formerly divided into three provinces, that is, into Bettica, today called Granada; Lusitania, today Portugal; and Aragon, which today comprises Catalonia, Castile, Navarre and Galicia. The first king of Bettica was Jubal, the nephew of Noah, who built a city there and called it Jubal after his own name; next, Ibero succeeded to this kingdom, from whom the River Iber afterward took its name. The tenth king who came to power in this kingdom was named Hispalo, from whom the entire kingdom of Spain took its name; today this is owned by the most powerful Catholic King Philip of Austria, son of the Emperor Charles V of beloved memory. The Spanish people are grave by nature, shrewd, and very thrifty, given to lust, sober in eating and moderate in drinking, of middle height and dry rather than otherwise in their bodily humors, satisfied with little food, and vainglorious in many matters. They dress in black more than in any other color. The Spaniard is astute, brave in warfare, and able to endure every sort of discomfort when necessary.

The women are brown in complexion, and the girls go out covered up; they are very withdrawn in social exchanges and rarely seen at public festivities, though when they do go out, they adorn themselves with many ornaments. The clothing shown here is from former times and was customary a hundred and forty-four years ago, though it is true that it is still worn in some parts of Spain. And in some elements it imitates our Italian style, as in the headdress and arrangement of the hair, which they wore covered with a veil pinned on top and falling down to their shoulders. They wore a pleated, floor-length overgown of satin or velvet, with a round-necked low-cut bodice allowing the camicia *underneath to be seen. This gown was sleeveless, but they covered their arms with linen sleeves, quite full, which they tied around their arms; and these sleeves were snugly bound at the ends, near the hands. This gown had a train of some length, embroidered all around the hem at the feet, with various trims. In their hands they used to carry large, round feather fans, and in this way, without further pomp or ornament, they went out in public.*

Text on page 335

CLOTHING OF A SPANISH NOBLEMAN
at the Court of the Catholic King

Spanish men, especially those who mingle at the Catholic court, usually wear Italianate clothing—that is, short—but different in style since at court one moment they wear trousers, but the next they wear bracconi *with full-length stockings. On their backs they wear a* saio *similar to those worn in Italy twenty-five years ago and now retained by scholars or old men. On their heads they wear a rather high cap of silk, and around their shoulders they wear a cape of serge or silk* rascia, *similar to those of Roman women. They are careful, from a sense of great propriety, to wear their caps when they wear these capes, and to wear hats when they wear* ferraiuoli. *They do not change the style of their clothing according to the season, but they do change from wool to silk and from silk to wool or* rascia. *They all normally carry swords, even shoemakers and tailors and other craftsmen.*

Text on page 336

AN UNMARRIED SPANISH GIRL

Spanish girls usually go out covered with a mantle, as Venetian women do, but with their hands they skillfully arrange an opening for their eyes in this mantle, to allow them to see through it. Outside the house, they all dress in black, except the brides; on their feet they wear certain wooden clogs, or very high pianelle, *but made with little charm, which they fasten over their feet, like the Clogging Friars. They rarely wash their heads, and they wear their hair black and as it was made by nature, drawing it high off their foreheads almost as women beyond the mountains do. Such Spanish women are quite given to lust, but they are moderate in eating and most often they drink water. They usually eat simple food, without much enjoying the delicate dishes made in Italy.*

Text on page 337

A MARRIED WOMAN OF SPAIN

he married noblewomen of Spain, and especially those of the regal cities, wear a very grave style of dress, especially outside their houses. They wear a wide black mantle of silk or ferandina, like those worn by the women of Rome and also in many other parts of Italy; placed over their heads, it falls to the ground, ample and very comfortable, and is then held closed at their waist. Underneath they wear a floor-length gown of gold brocade or of silk or damasco, and on their feet certain high pianelle, which are tied as are those of the Clogging Friars; these ties are of velvet, and they are visible because the gown does not reach down to the pianelle themselves. But as soon as they take off their mantles, they appear in gowns with bodices so narrow at the sides that it seems impossible that their bodies can fit into them. They become accustomed to such narrow waists as little girls, so they remain in this shape as long as they live; but the fact is that they grow all the more in their chest and shoulders, where they appear to be very plump.

Text on page 338

CLOTHING OF A LADY OF TOLEDO

Toledo is a principal city of the kingdom of Spain; it is rich and noble and full of superb buildings. Among its churches is one of an archbishop, with an income of two hundred thousand scudi. *The women of this city dress as follows: they wear their hair neatly arranged under a piece of white felt shaped like a Turkish turban, but widened at the top, which is very useful. Their overgowns, of* ciambellotto *or wool or silk, are short, not reaching below the ankle, and they wear low-cut bodices open in front, but they tie them together with silk cords. Their sleeves are very wide, without any trim or pleats. They tie on aprons of cotton or silk, woven in various patterns. On their necks they wear strings of very large pearls, and on their feet shoes or short boots in various colors.*

Text on page 339

A WOMAN OF SANTANDER,
in Biscay

The clothing of this woman of Biscay is graceful and beautiful, no less lovely than chaste, no less chaste than practical, no less practical than affordable. Her headdress is a little hat of felt or velvet, high enough that she can wrap a large piece of very thin renso *or a silk sash around it. Under this little hat she puts a piece of* ormesino *or* taffetano, *which reaches down to her shoulders and beyond. Her* sottana *is of wool, and is ankle-length. Her overgarment is of* ormesino, *without proper sleeves, though with the beginnings of them, which she fills out with the sleeves of her* camicia. *She usually wears at her waist a belt of* velo *or silk, or a silk or linen apron, and some plebeian women wear this apron richly needle-worked.*

Text on page 340

A WOMAN OF BILBAO,
in Biscay

his is a woman's attire both lovely and sober, demonstrating her noble status, and it is suitable for winter. It is rather different from the garments worn by women of the main cities of Spain, because they all keep their faces covered with a mantle, while the woman shown here goes uncovered. On top she wears a calf-length robba *or overgarment of* damasco *or patterned silk, lined throughout with very fine lambskin or marten or wild fox. Underneath she wears an ankle-length gown of satin encircled with bands of gold brocade, which she cinches with the silk ties of an apron of needle-worked silk. She adorns her neck with large pearls and her head with a bizarre headdress, as the preceding print shows. On her hands she usually wears gloves or some other refinement, and so she goes about, meeting relatives and friends.*

Text on page 341

CLOTHING OF A WOMAN OF BISCAY

Biscay was formerly called Numantia, and it produces excellent sailors, who, when the rage of the winds roars at its peak, climb the mast all the higher and raise the sails. The land around this city is sterile and lacking in what our nature requires so the women dress in a very simple manner. The clothing of the woman shown here is a little cap of velvet, quite tall and pointed at the tip, which these women put on their heads and narrow or widen as required by loosening or tightening a band of silk at the base. They also wear a piece of ormesino, *which they tie over their heads and let hang down in front under their chin, covering both the chin and also their breast. They wear ankle-length undergarments of wool, and overgarments of the same fabric, unbelted and without any other ornament. And they wear shoes of soft white or black leather.*

Text on page 342

DRESS OF A PLEBEIAN WOMAN of Biscay

Plebeian women of Biscay practice demanding and tiring crafts, because their lands are sterile and not supplied with the things that human nature requires. Their headdress is very simple, of felt or white wool, and covers their head and the whole back of their neck; it is stiffened with small wood or copper hoops that they put inside it. They wear an ankle-length gown of fustian or cotton, with a low-necked bodice and long, wide sleeves, which they tie halfway down and attach to their gown with woven ties. They wear belts of rope or leather, from which they hang a sheath containing a knife. On their feet they usually wear zoccoli*; and they always go around spinning.*

Text on page 343

DRESS OF A WOMAN OF GRANADA,
in Spain

ranada is one of the eight kingdoms of Spain, of which the others are Aragon, Portugal, Castile, León, Toledo, Galicia, and Navarre. In this kingdom of Granada, among others, are two famous cities, Hispali [Seville] and Cordoba, which was the home of Seneca, otherwise called Lucius Annaeus, a Stoic philosopher who was the teacher of the Emperor Nero and the uncle of the poet Lucan. This Seneca was held in high esteem in Rome because he was the teacher of Nero, and he was believed to be a man of great learning, as is shown in the letters he wrote to the Apostles Saint Peter and Saint Paul. Finally, he was condemned to death by his student, the Emperor, two years before the martyrdom of the said Apostles, because Nero remembered the beatings his tutor had given him. This tutor Seneca chose to die in a warm bath, where his veins would be cut open; and so it happened.[1] *Granada was also the home of the most learned Averrhoes,*[2] *and of many others.*

The clothing of the woman shown in this print is very strange, and in my opinion it resembles the clothing of the Moorish women of Barbary more than any other, because the two are similar in color. This woman wears a very simple hairstyle, with long hair that waves down to her shoulders, on which she sets a round velvet cap with a small medallion on its band. Over her head she pulls on and lets fall over her shoulders a garment of wool, very full, made in the style of a priest's surplice, which has neither bodice nor sleeves, as is visible in the drawing. She is shod in unusual boots slashed at the knees; over these boots she ties cords, with which she fastens wooden soles under her feet, which serve her as shoes.

AN UNMARRIED GIRL
of Spanish Granada

Certain girls in the Kingdom of Granada go nude from the waist up. As a headdress they wear a circle of wood or copper padded all around with cotton, holding in place a piece of wool or linen which they wear on their heads and which falls down to their shoulders. Under this piece of wool or linen they wear a short, thigh-length cape, open in front and trimmed along the hem with embroidered bands of another type and color of cloth. Then they wear a pair of white braghesse *or trousers of linen or wool, very snug, which they tie to their belts. They wrap their legs with bands, as we do with children. And because they are poor, they go about in this fashion, spinning.*

THE CLOTHING OF GERMANY

THE CLOTHING OF HIS IMPERIAL MAJESTY THE EMPEROR

Germany is a very large region of Europe, separated from France by the Rhine river. But the German people, because they are excellent in arms and not satisfied to stay within their own borders, passed beyond them; and today in addition to their original territory, they hold Rezia, Vindelizia, Norico, Pannonia north of the Alps, and part of Illyria as far as the borders of Trent, as well as almost all of the nation of Belgium, formerly under the jurisdiction of France. All the territory the Rhine passes through has taken on the name and language of Germany, which is now understood as consisting of all the land found between four bodies of water: the Rhine, the Danube, the Vistula, and the North Sea. And to mention some facts about the Empire, I will say that Pope Gregory V, formerly named Bruno and the Duke of Saxony, gave the scepter and imperial diadem to Otto II,[1] his relative, who had taken Rome by force from the hand of a certain Crescentius Nomentanus, a Roman consul, whom he cruelly put to death. He assumed the imperial authority in perpetuity in Germany, to the dissatisfaction of the Gauls, because this power had up to then been in their hands. But because Charlemagne had left no successors, the Emperorship went to Ludwig, the son of Lothar, and then to Hugh Capet—and so, without struggle, it remained in Germany.

After he had been crowned by the said Gregory V, Otto II, returning from his coronation as Emperor in Germany, called together the princes and consulted with them about how the next emperor should be elected. Because this multitude of people gave him differing advice, each one wanting to favor his own family, he informed them that however great a number of them there were, equal numbers would have to be elected from ecclesiastical and secular men; and to these men was given the duty of organizing these elections and of being officials of the Empire, as the people most fit to decide who was most suited to this highest government. To this all the princes and barons of the kingdom consented, and they nominated three bishops of Germany, spiritual and temporal lords, who would also be Chancellors of the kingdom. They were as follows: the Elector of Mainz would oversee the affairs of Germany; the Elector of Cologne those of Italy; and the Elector of Trier those of France. Their duties were to be carried out in the Imperial Court. To these were then added four Princes, who serve equally closely to the Emperor and recognize him as the temporal lord of the world. They are as follows: the Duke of Saxony, the leader of those who follow the sword, and for this reason he carries a sword in front of him, signifying that he is the source of justice; the Margrave of Brandenburg, who attends to the Emperor's bed and is called the Master of the Bedchamber; the Count Palatine of the Rhine, the Sutler [provider of food]; and the King of Bohemia, who serves the Emperor with drink. And all these care for the body of the Emperor. To them belongs the authority over elections, so that no one can usurp the Empire as happened in the past through claims to hereditary right, which were the cause of great unrest.

The first Emperor to be elected, following the Golden Bull of the Emperor Charles IV, was Saint Henry, the founder of the Bishopric of Bamberg, when he was not yet the King of Bohemia but only a duke. Then to stabilize the Empire even further, good and useful ordinances were passed, including the following: that to the seven Electors should be added four dukes, four margraves, four landgraves, four burgraves, four counts, four soldiers of the nobility, four villagers and four peasants, and many other things not relevant here. This ordinance was made in the year 1001.[2]

As to the clothing of His Imperial Majesty, it should be noted that there was a great difference between what His Majesty wore in public on his imperial throne and what he wore as a private man off the throne. So it seemed more worthwhile to me to include an image of his usual emperor's garb than of his other, private wear, so as to discuss his appearance on the throne. When His Majesty is in public on his imperial throne, he is surrounded by the following retinue: the Archbishop of Trier, as Chancellor of Gaul, sits opposite him; the Archbishop of Mainz, as Chancellor of Germany, sits on his right; the Archbishop of Cologne, as Chancellor of Italy, at his left; and to the right and left of the Archbishop of Cologne sit the King of Bohemia and the Margrave of Brandenberg, respectively. In public processions, they observe the same order, because the Archbishop of Trier precedes the Emperor, the other two Archbishops accompany him on either side, and the King of Bohemia follows behind. All the clothing worn by the Emperor demonstrates his great majesty, and we cannot even estimate the value of his diadem, which he wears in the style of a miter, and which, closed on top, is encircled by the crown. The gold scepter that he holds in his right hand signifies his rule and justice. Next, in his left hand, the orb denotes his dominion over the world, and the cross on top of the orb signifies his rule over Christians. The lamb that hangs down as a symbol of the Holy Fleece is not usually worn by the Emperor, because Charles V founded this order, and it is worn only by a man who has had it conferred on him by King Philip of Spain, Charles's son.

As far as the rest of his clothing is concerned, he looks like a ceremonially robed priest wearing a surplice and a cope, because he sings the Gospel in the presence of the pope at his coronation. The mantle that he wears on top is of gold in the style of a cope, embellished and enriched with many jewels and full of pearls on every surface. His robe is giacinto *(that is,* pavonazzo*) in color and made of velvet, bordered at the bottom with gold and with trim also of gold. His* rocchetto *or surplice is very precious and closely resembles the garment of a priest.*

Text on page 348

CLOTHING OF ECCLESIASTICAL ELECTORS of the Empire

The ecclesiastical Electors of the Empire are three archbishops, who are also secular lords: the Archbishop of Trier, Chancellor of Gaul; the Archbishop of Mainz, Chancellor of Germany; and the Archbishop of Cologne, Chancellor of Italy. All three of these wear the clothing visible in the print shown previously when they are at court in the presence of His Imperial Majesty. On their heads they wear a cap of cloth of gold, lined with very white ermine fur, turned up in the shape of a crown. They also wear a rounded bavero*, almost mid-arm in length, lined with the same fur, similar to that of our Prince of Venice. Under this they wear a long, floor-length gown of* porpora *velvet, lined with ermine, with sleeves of cloth of gold. In their hands they usually carry books and gloves.*

Text on page 349

CLOTHING OF SECULAR ELECTORS
of the Empire

There are four secular Electors of the Empire: the Duke of Saxony, who carries a sword signifying that he is the source of justice; the Margrave of Brandenburg, who oversees the bed of the leader and is called the Master of the Bedchamber; the Count Palatine of the Rhine, the Sutler; and the King of Bohemia, who serves him drink. And these men are seated in great majesty, showing that they are highly diligent in their duties. Their clothing is very rich, and they still wear a floor-length overgown, open in front with rather full sleeves, cremesino *in color and lined with ermine, as previously mentioned. And above this they wear a* rocchetto *or* bavero *that covers the chest and is lined with the same fur. On their heads they wear a cap similar to that of an ecclesiastical Elector.*

Text on page 350

CLOTHING OF GERMAN PRINCES or Barons

In the time of Emperor Ludwig, which began in the year 903, and even before him, there were not many titles of nobility or so many different kinds of them as there are today, because only the titles of king, prince and baron existed; there were no dukes, margraves, counts palatine, or other counts and knights. For in those times, such men were more readily named according to the office they held and performed than to the cities or states they ruled and possessed, and none of these titles were inherited after their death. So dukes were merely the leaders of legions of soldiers and armies, and the margraves and counts were deputies to the government from geographical regions and land-holdings, so that rule over all these regions and lands belonged to the Emperor and the Empire and to no one else.

The clothing of German princes and lords consists of a velvet cap, not very tall, with different-colored plumes, and on their shoulders they wear a cape of damasco *or black velvet, lined with marten or sable, slightly more than waist-length, with sleeves decorated with velvet or other fabric. They enjoy wearing very thick gold chains of many strands, which they wear on their chests, low down on their doublets. These are made of* pavonazzo *silk, trimmed all over in woven gold and silver, and fastened with massive gold buttons. They customarily wear* bracconi *of cloth of silver underneath and of slashed cloth of gold on top, embroidered everywhere with pearls and other beautiful needlework. They wear full-length, knitted silk stockings and shoes of soft leather. Usually their stockings are* pavonazzo *or green in color, and they often wear swords attached to their belts. But recently most of these German lords have started dressing in the Italian style, especially those who have spent time in Italy and as a result are much more courtly than the others.*

CLOTHING OF TITLED GERMAN LORDS

The name "Count" in the ancient language of Saxony means judge, but because there are different kinds of judges, different kinds of counts also exist. In Germany, for example, are found some called Landgrave counts, that is, erratic judges who give ill-considered sentences, so that on occasion what they declare in the morning they will rescind in the evening. Others are called Dingrave counts, judges of the peasants. Others are called margraves, and they have jurisdiction on the borders of a region because the name Marca *is a German word meaning "border" and these men have jurisdiction over the boundaries of cities, districts, and fields. There are also Palatine counts, who have judicial authority over conquered lands; and finally, from this word "Marca" is derived the word marquis.*

These titled men of Germany, then, usually wear ample tabarri *of velvet or satin or* damasco*, lined with other silk fabrics in different colors, and these* tabarri *have* baveri *or very high collars and end four fingers' length below the belt. They wear very beautiful satin doublets with long slashes, fastened in the center with gold buttons, which also close the front of the doublet; their sleeves are very full. They wear wide, knee-length* bracconi *of patterned velvet with long slashes, needle-worked all over with gold or silver along every decorative strip, and they are lined with green* ormesino *and worn with knitted silk stockings that they pull up snugly on their legs. They wear black shoes in the Spanish style. They adorn their necks with high* camicia *ruffles, and on their heads they wear a rather high cap,* *with beautiful plumes and medallions. They belt on swords and daggers, beautifully decorated with silver. And this clothing can often be seen on gentlemen who come to Italy through the Cadore Pass at our border, and who sometimes encountered a certain Hettor Vecellio of Cadore, a man of great authority in his region, who was expert in the German tongue because of public and private business and visited very frequently by these men on various occasions.*

Text on page 353

CLOTHING OF GERMAN WOMEN
in Early Times

The women of Germany, in early times and now, were and still are renowned for being very chaste and faithful to their husbands. The clothing shown here was worn by women of this large region two hundred years ago, and it was very chaste and full of modesty. None of their hair was visible under their headdresses, not even curls; rather, they were satisfied with a net of silk or gold thread, into which they gathered their hair. They adorned their necks with pearls and wore a floor-length undergown of red satin, with many folds and without a train, but with full sleeves. On top they wore a silk mantle that they pinned to the net of their headdress, and, held at the waist, it fell down to their undergown halfway down the leg. They showed part of their breast by wearing a low-cut, flat bodice, and they also wore white leather shoes.

301

Text on page 354

CLOTHING OF A WOMAN
of the Tirolean Countryside

he Tirol is a county called Enipente or, in the vernacular, Spruch, because of the rule the princes of Austria have here, and it is not very far from Carinthia [Karnten]. It was left to the House of Austria by a man who was its hereditary lord as an act of ill will toward his uncles, the Princes of Bavaria; the Austrians then governed it until they exchanged it for the Duchy of Karnten. The attire of the noblewomen of this county includes a headdress of white silk or renso *or* cambrai, *very well arranged, which covers their whole forehead and all their hair, wrapped around it in a beautiful style. They wear a full, floor-length gown of wool, at the bottom of which are sewn on many bands of another wool or silk of another color. They wear small ruffles of white linen around their necks and snugly fitting bodices. They wear no trains. They are very devout, and both the unmarried girls and the married women of that country enjoy riding beautiful and well-caparisoned horses. They also like to hunt with sparrow hawks in the company of their relatives and friends.*

Text on page 355

UNMARRIED NOBLEWOMAN of Augsburg

ugsburg is a city of great importance, full of riches, and it is very ancient, located among rivers abundant in fish. It has sumptuous buildings, many large, clean piazzas, and beautiful walls with strong bastions and impassable moats; the circumference of its turreted walls is nine thousand paces. It was named Augsburg by the decree of Drusus,[3] who captured it and surrounded it with beautiful towered walls; and even though it has endured the greatest suffering and destruction, nonetheless it has no hostility at present toward any city of Germany. Its women enjoy good health, so they are fair-skinned and pink-cheeked, and very friendly to foreigners. Even if they know a foreigner only slightly, they invite him to their house and welcome him graciously, and the unmarried girls are the first to take his hands and greet him warmly and ceremoniously with chaste kisses.

Their clothing is nearly always entirely black. On their heads they wear a small cap of velvet or wool; after they braid their hair into two braids, the cap covers the rest of their hair, which they wear loose down to their shoulders, with curls of false blond hair like threads of gold at their temples. They wear bodices of black wool, bordered with velvet and high-necked, pulled in so snugly at the waist that they seem to be wearing very tight belts. The sleeves of their bodices are also very tight. They usually wear floor-length carpette *or overgarments of wool, which they attach to their bodice and cinch with the silk ribbons of their aprons, which are made of patterned* damasco *or figured velvet. They wear small boots of cordovan leather or suede, laced up their legs with bootlaces and buckled. They delight in being clean so they bathe frequently, at home or in public baths. They also wear purses containing money, attached to their belts with little chains of copper wire.*

PATRICIAN GIRL
of Augsburg

For many years now, present-day nobly born girls of Augsburg have begun to change their style of dress, as a result of the regular presence of foreigners who go there continually and wear different kinds of clothes. They wear a circular headdress of many veils, tied here and there with gold threads or silk and gold cords and with beautiful medallions, which form very attractive puffs on their heads. They wear overgarments of silk in different colors, floor-length, with trim from top to bottom and borders of gold embroidery. These overgowns are pavonazzo *in color and open from the waist down, and through this opening can be seen a* sottana *of* ciambellotto *with a moiré finish or of patterned* damasco. *They usually wear white* baveri *with rather high ruffles, and around their ears curls of artificial hair. They adorn their necks with pearls and wear gold belts. These girls usually dress more elegantly before they are married than after, some wearing golden snoods as a headdress and others small caps of velvet.*

MARRIED NOBLEWOMEN of Augsburg

The married women of Augsburg display great sobriety in their clothing; they wear clothing similar to that which I have seen worn by Queen Maria, the sister of Charles V.[4] *They wear overgarments with long, narrow* ciambellotto *sleeves, lined in the winter with the most beautiful furs they can find and in the summer with* ormesino. *When they leave the house, they cover their heads with a cambrai veil, which they let fall in front like a stole. They wear little boots of tightly fitted leather. They are accompanied outdoors by maidservants carrying baskets, and in this way they go to buy food for the day. Their noble husbands almost all wear clothing in the Italian style. Having said this, many of these women dress without fur-lined garments, but they wear the same headdress and tie on an apron similar to the ones that unmarried girls wear; dressed in this style, they go informally about their business in the city.*

MARRIED WOMAN
of Bavaria

In the time of Strabo,[5] Bavaria was a very infertile province, but today, because it has been well cultivated, it is fertile. It is full of many villages, landholdings, and noble cities. Its territory produces no wines, but they are brought here in quantity from other regions. Otherwise, it is abundant in everything necessary, and it is rich in iron mines and watered by many rivers full of fish, almost all of which flow into the Danube.

The married women of this region wear an overgarment of velvet or black wool, very high-necked, with narrow, tight sleeves and very large short oversleeves, and with beautiful bands embroidered with gold or silk, four fingers above the hem. They wear another undergarment of pavonazzo silk, with a band of gold needlework placed at the same height. They do not wear trains, and they dislike make-up and pianelle that are too high. They adorn their head with a veil that they shape into a point in front of their forehead, and they wear the rest of it gathered into a gold or silk net, on top of which they put a close-fitting cap of velvet. They also adorn their necks with gold necklaces in many strands, and in their hands they usually carry perfumed gloves.

UNMARRIED GIRL
of Nuremberg

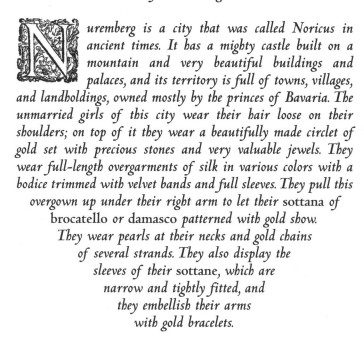

uremberg is a city that was called Noricus in ancient times. It has a mighty castle built on a mountain and very beautiful buildings and palaces, and its territory is full of towns, villages, and landholdings, owned mostly by the princes of Bavaria. The unmarried girls of this city wear their hair loose on their shoulders; on top of it they wear a beautifully made circlet of gold set with precious stones and very valuable jewels. They wear full-length overgarments of silk in various colors with a bodice trimmed with velvet bands and full sleeves. They pull this overgown up under their right arm to let their sottana *of* brocatello *or* damasco *patterned with gold show. They wear pearls at their necks and gold chains of several strands. They also display the sleeves of their* sottane, *which are narrow and tightly fitted, and they embellish their arms with gold bracelets.*

BRIDE OF NUREMBERG
Dressed for her Wedding

The brides of the city of Nuremberg are better dressed than all the others of Germany. They wear a high hat of gold leaf, intricately worked, with beautiful jewels attached to it, and under this headdress some of their hair falls gracefully at their temples. They wear an overgarment of silk, giacinto *or* porpora *in color, with a very tight-fitting bodice, from which come narrow sleeves lined in very white and refined furs, as are the upper sleeves of their gown, which come halfway down the arm. They wear* sottane *of gold or silk brocade woven with large patterns, and belts of very heavy gold chains, beautifully made, which they let hang from one end down to the hem of their gown. They adorn their necks with large pearls in many strands and wear decorated borders around the bodice of their overgown, which leaves the neck bare.*

FORMAL CLOTHING OF A NOBLE BRIDE of Nuremberg

When brides of the upper-ranking nobility in Nuremberg go to church to perform their marriage rites, they dress very splendidly and are accompanied by many processions and sweet and harmonious music. Two of the leading Senators flank the bride on each side in the procession, and, formally offering their arms, they escort her to her holy vows. These brides wear a headdress made of gold, decorated with very beautiful foliage patterns and with precious jeweled lace at the top; this headdress is higher at the front than at the back, and their hair shows underneath it in a lovely fashion. They wear overgarments of pavonazzo *satin with many pleats and a collarless bodice that exposes their entire neck, adorned with beautiful pearls. The sleeves of this gown are rather full and long and can also be used as a muff, when they put each hand into the sleeve of the other arm. Underneath they wear a gown of red* ormesino *and, out of propriety, they tie on an apron made of the most beautiful furs that can be found. And so, with a gracious and beautiful face, they are accompanied by a great crowd of people, each of whom, to signal their joy, wears a garland of silk flowers or real ones over a green cap.*

FORMAL CLOTHING OF A MARRIED NOBLEWOMAN of Nuremberg

Married noblewomen of Nuremberg wear a headdress consisting of a white veil that, after wrapping their hair in it, they tie in two or three places with gold trim, drawing the veil into a point at the center of their foreheads. They wear overgarments of cremesino *velvet with high-necked bodices, banded across the middle with gold trim and with four or five gold necklaces, which they let hang from their neck onto their breast. The sleeves are those of their rich* sottana*, which is worn very close-fitting with a high neck, above which their very modest* camicia *ruffles can be seen. These* sottane *are made of silk or* damasco*, very elegant. For greater splendor, on their right arm they carry a very long fur, which they let hang down in front in the place of an apron. At their wrists, rather than bracelets, they wear gold chains in many strands.*

A WOMAN OF FRANKFURT
Outside the House

rankfurt is a rich mercantile city of Germany, in which large numbers of merchants from every country gather, especially from Italy, and deal in merchandise of great value. The women wear a silk veil on their heads, which they shape into a beautiful point in the middle of their forehead, and on top of it they place a large, floor-length mantle of black silk; because it is so full, it covers them almost completely. And they hold it in front in such a way that it partly conceals their beautiful sottana *of moiré* ciambellotto, *which has a high-necked bodice, crossed with very wide velvet bands. In front, they tie on an apron of* ciambellotto *in black, a color much worn in Germany; and so dressed they go about their business.*

NOBLEWOMAN OF THE PALATINATE of the Rhine

his region of the Palatinate produces the best wines to be found along the Rhine, where the great snows that fall make it very, very cold; yet in spite of this, it is a rich region, and its women are bony and thin, but with beautiful pink and white complexions. Married women and high-ranking ladies wear black velvet in floor-length overgarments, open from the waist down in a way that allows their sottane *of* damasco *or patterned satin to be seen; snugly fitting sleeves cover the arms and emerge from the cap sleeves of the overgarment, which is cut very narrow at the sides and decorated with massive gold chains, looped several times around their necks, around which emerge their beautifully made* camicia *ruffles. They cover their heads with a gold* scuffia *[small, stiff cap], on top of which they wear a small cap of black velvet with plumes of very fine feathers of every color.*

NOBLEWOMAN of Cologne

Cologne is a large city near the Rhine, and the river, watering the territory, makes the city very rich in every necessity. It is governed temporally and spiritually by its archbishop, who is one of the Electors of the Empire. Many relics and bodies of saints can be seen here, including the body of Saint Ursula and many of her virgins, and the Three Magi. On their heads the women of this city wear a small velvet cap, on top of which they pin a very wide veil that, puffed out by the wind, has the appearance shown in the preceding image. They wear a floor-length overgarment of moiré ciambellotto *or very thin linen; the bodice is of a different color from the gown, and they wear their bodice fastened with silk cords. The sleeves that they wear are those of their* sottana, *and in front they wear an apron of* ciambellotto. *They usually wear beautifully needle-worked* baveri *and finely made neck ruffles.*

MARRIED WOMAN
of Cologne

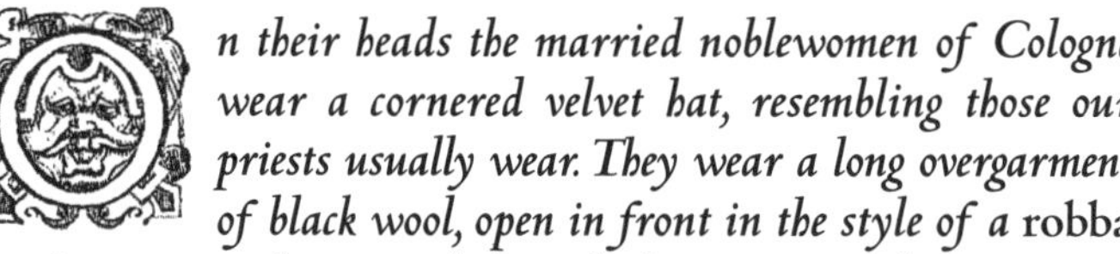

On their heads the married noblewomen of Cologne wear a cornered velvet hat, resembling those our priests usually wear. They wear a long overgarment of black wool, open in front in the style of a robba *or* zimarra*, with a very high neck that supports their* camicia *ruffles. Through the opening of the overgarment can be seen their undergown of* damasco *or silk and gold brocade, bordered all around with beautifully embroidered velvet bands. At their necks they wear gold necklaces of two or three strands.*

MARRIED NOBLEWOMAN of Alsace

Alsace is a very fertile region, so its people are abundantly supplied with everything they need; and among other things, it produces a great quantity of wines, and of good quality, which they take to the regions of Switzerland, and there they are sold to Swabia and southern Germany, and also to England. In these regions can be seen many bodies of saints, brought here by the Emperor Charles V. The mountains of this region contain many, many mines. The women, when one of their close relatives dies and they are in mourning, wear a white band on their forehead, which they let fall from their shoulders to the ground; and having wrapped these bands almost entirely around their faces, they accompany the body of the deceased to burial, which is usually in a place selected away from where the person died. They carry the deceased, covered in black, on a carriage pulled by horses covered from head to foot in black, followed by the grieving and sorrowful relatives, in tears. And should the husband of one of these women die, the wife then finds black bands and sends them to her relatives, who bind their heads with them, and the husbands do the same thing if their wives die. More precisely, the bands worn by the women are of thin white velo *and those worn by the men are black. And as the period of mourning goes on, they gradually shorten and cut off these bands so that when the mourning comes to an end, so do the bands. This is the custom followed in many places in Germany.*

The dress of the women of Alsace includes a small cap or hat of black velvet, richly decorated with pearls and jewels, under which they wear a scuffia *woven of gold that covers their hair, and at the sides near their temples some curls can be seen.*

They wore an ample robba *resembling a cape but short, no more than waist-length; it is of black velvet and very wide. They wear full-skirted gowns of silk or* damasco *without gathers or pleats and with a long train, and these gowns are trimmed with embroidery all down the front and around the hem. The sleeves are of the same fabric as their overgown, with puffed, richly trimmed short oversleeves. This gown is very high-necked, and around their necks they wear ruffles and large pearls and gold necklaces. They wear short boots of soft white leather. Some unmarried girls wear caps and earrings, and they tie on a* ciambellotto *apron.*

BRIDES OF SAXONY AND MAINZ

It is a custom in the German parts of Saxony that when brides go to church to take their vows, they are accompanied by two of the leading Senators of the city, who, meeting these brides halfway to the church, hold them under the arms, making walking easy and smooth for them; they are also accompanied by all their relatives and also by those of their husband. These people, as a sign of joy, wear green garlands of beautiful, fragrant flowers, and they follow the bride in an orderly, dignified procession; in front of them march many musicians, playing the sweetest harmonies on various instruments. They are also accompanied by a great number of unmarried girls and ladies-in-waiting, and by their relatives and friends, who are carefully and elegantly dressed. Once married, they go for the wedding party to the houses of friends or to inns, and there everyone contributes to the cost of the ceremony with presents they give the bride after they have eaten; and this festivity lasts almost all day and through the night, with wild revelry, during which many stay drunk on wine. But the brides themselves stay sober and hardly touch the food. And because the party is supposed to last all night, with dancing for the relatives all the way through, the husbands sometimes retire to bed with their brides before the festivities are over.

On their heads these brides wear scuffie *of gold cloth, which keep their hair in order and are trimmed with very beautiful needle-worked flowers, interwoven with jewels. They wear a floor-length overgown of the finest wool, very full and with needlework all around the hem and a bit above it; the bodice reaches all the way up to the neck, and from it emerges a hand's width of very well formed* camicia *ruffles. At their necks they wear many gold chains with medallions or valuable jewels. They also wear an apron of very fine linen or white* ciambellotto, *beautifully needle-worked, reaching their feet. On their shoulders they wear a short, sleeveless velvet vest lined with the finest furs, which makes them a beautiful sight to see.*

A GIRL OF MAINZ
in Formal Dress

All of the unmarried girls of Germany, and especially those of Mainz, dress very chastely when they go out: they cover themselves up and show none of their skin except their face and hands. They wear narrow, close-fitting bodices, by means of which they keep their breasts white and firm. They have the custom of bathing every week and washing their entire bodies, because there are baths in almost every house and many in public places that separate different sorts of people, so that women are not seen by men or men by women. But it is also the case that women of high rank do not go to public baths on the days they are reserved for men but only on the days they are reserved for women. These women are very affable in conversation with men and embrace and kiss them in a very chaste and friendly way. Some women, in the winter, gather in these public baths to spin and sew, and when men come into these places, the women judge ill-mannered those who fail to embrace or kiss them, though chastely and fondly. And if by chance, as they are sewing or spinning, one of these girls should drop a thimble or a spindle, whichever young man picks it up from the ground and gives it back to the girl can kiss and hug her as a reward.

The clothing of these women includes a scuffia *enclosing their hair, woven and needle-worked all over with little stars and roses. They wear a gown of fine wool or silk, closed and buttoned all the way down, with a narrow bodice fitting snugly at the hips and bordered with bands of velvet in front, behind, and at the sides, as are their* spallacci*. And at the end of their* *sleeves, near their wrists, are further bands, and in their hands they often carry beautiful flowers, either carnations or roses or some other kind. They adorn their necks with white ruffles and with gold chains of many strands, and they trim the hems of their gowns with long bands of velvet two or three hands in width; these gowns are very full and pleated. On top of them they tie a floor-length apron of* ciambellotto *or silk* canevaccia.

Text on page 372

A NOBLEWOMAN
of Mainz

Mainz is located in the most beautiful part of Germany, toward the bottom. Since ancient times it has always been Catholic and full of great theological scholars, but now it has been reduced to such a state by the bad counsel of Martin Luther and his followers that no one there, or only a few people, are not sullied with heresy. It is ruled by and subject to a duke, who is ordinarily one of the Electors of the Empire. Formerly, this country was called Alsatia, but now it is known as Saxony, so that it is necessary to know that when Alsatia is spoken of, Saxony is meant.

The married noblewomen of Mainz wear on their heads a hat of velvet lined with very refined and precious fur, with a very wide scuffia *of gold net that they use to cover their hair, though they let their hair show on the side, at their temples. They usually dress in a floor-length overgarment of scarlet or of fine* pavonazzo *wool, with many pleats and with gold trim, beautifully made and needle-worked. Over this they wear a short velvet cape with woven trim at the bottom, lined with marten or some other similar fur. This cape has a collar or* bavaro *so high that it covers the entire neck and protects against the sharpness of the great cold that exists in these countries. They adorn their necks with white ruffles and with several strands of gold chains and a pretty medallion or jewel, which hangs from the chain and makes a beautiful sight.*

Text on page 373

WOMAN OF LIVONIA

ivonia shares a border with Lithuania, Muscovy and Germany, and also with Swabia, all very cold places. This region of Livonia is very rich in saltwater and freshwater fish and in animal skins of different kinds—squirrel pelts, ermine, wolf, fox, and other similar animals. The attire of the women includes a silver headdress in a triangular form, almost resembling a bishop's miter, and it is almost all overlaid with gold in leafy patterns. They wear an undergarment of colored wool with an open bodice; this is tied with silk laces, some above the waist, as can be seen in the preceding print. On top of this gown they wear a floor-length mantle with a very high collar that covers their entire neck and part of their head; it is of red wool lined with very beautiful marten or sable furs, and it is embellished outside with cords of green silk, which make the mantle beautiful and also reinforce it. In this region the common people live poorly; men wear coarse wool in various colors and boots of animal skins with the fur still on them.

Text on page 374

NOBLEWOMAN
of Livonia

*he rich noblewomen of this region, like the men, usually eat food without any added flavoring, enjoying the taste the food naturally has. They follow a German way of life but have been subject to the Poles from the time of King Sigismund*[6] *to the present. When this country was Catholic, it enjoyed every prosperity; but from 1527 to the present day, it has embraced the sect of Martin Luther and the people have gone from bad to worse. This province has many forests for hunting, in which a great number of bears, foxes, martens, beavers, and other animals can be found; especially highly valued are the skins of polar bears caught in the cold mountains, where hares change the color of their fur according to the season. The clothing of wealthy and noble women consists of a cap of velvet or wool, very large, with a pointed top in the shape of a pommel and an oblong canopy, lined all over with squirrel pelts on account of the great cold, which continually produces ice in these regions. This hat is very high and broad and covers their entire head and part of their face, protecting them very well against the cold winds that prevail there. They also wear a short mantle in the style of a cape, without sleeves, of red or green wool but lined throughout with the most beautiful furs that can be had. This coat is quite full, and in its seams are silk cords attaching balls of amber or silver to its surface. They also wear a floor-length, gathered woolen overgown, lined with very fine ermine, which is also displayed down the front and around the hem. This is also the clothing of brides when they go to the house of their husband, but they wear a headdress of silver gilt in the style of a crown, and they take with them a large crowd of married women and girls, all dressed in red mantles. Finally, the married women of that region are almost all devoted to the arts of magic and to incantations.*

A BRIDE OF SILESIA
When She Goes to Church

Silesia is a province of Germany under the rule of the Emperor, and it is governed in the manner of a republic. It is very abundant in meat and other animals and animal skins. It borders Bohemia and Hungary. All the men and women of this region are very pleasant and courteous. The unmarried girls are hugged and kissed, though chastely, by their lovers, and they keep company with them very familiarly, dancing together and talking about their love for one another. They do this without raising distrust in their fathers or mothers; this may perhaps be the result of the great penalty imposed by the law against adultery. And so in these regions there are no prostitutes. As soon as the girls become brides, they go to the church together with their husbands to make their vows in public and, accompanied by two young men who walk between them with garlands of various flowers on their heads, they take all their guests to the wedding party, as is also the custom throughout Germany. These brides, accompanied by the two men previously mentioned and by a great number of unmarried girls who walk in front and behind them, go together to the church. The brides wear a headdress made of a piece of heavy worked gold, which resembles a crown because it is embellished all over with different jewels, and from it their hair descends, knotted with colored ribbons interwoven with gold thread, and falls down their back. They wear a floor-length undergarment of satin or tabino*, in whatever color they like, with many heavy folds; and over it they wear an apron of*

zendado *in the German style, in a rosy pink color. On top of this, they wear a very wide, calf-length mantle made of different squares of fur of the same size, which is very beautiful to see. Once the wedding ceremony is over, they go back home in great joy, accompanied by sweet, harmonious music. And here they dance and eat sumptuously.*

Text on page 377

A WOMAN OF MIDDLE RANK
in Silesia

The women of middling rank in Silesia are very expert in business, so they go throughout the city buying and selling what they need. On their heads they wear a cap of marten or fox fur because of the great cold typical of the region. They wear sottane *of red wool, with many pleats and folds, which, since they are made without bodices, they close and fasten with velvet or leather belts, very broad, from which they hang a purse and a sheath with knives. They also wear an apron of* ciambellotto *or linen, and on top of these gowns they weara fur mantle, according to their rank. They usually take their daughters with them, also dressed as they are, whom they teach from an early age to buy and sell and barter, so that they become skillful and experienced in business.*

325

Text on page 378

UNMARRIED GIRL
of Silesia

These girls wear a crown on their head, made of silk, and most often of needle-worked velvet. Under this crown their braids show, tied with colored silk ribbons so that they fall to their shoulders in two sections; gold beads are arranged around these ties. The bodices of their dresses are of various colors. They wear high-necked camicie *with high ruffles, and their bodice is fastened at the center of the breast and decorated with different kinds of trim. The sleeves are very full but narrow at the wrist and bound with a long strip of velvet trimmed with many clasps. Since the gown is open in front, it reveals the* sottana *of turquoise satin with a very wide, decorated band at the bottom. They do not wear trains or high* pianelle.

Text on page 379

BRIDE OF DANZIG

anzig is a mercantile city a league's distance from the sea, to which many ships come from different countries, loaded with many kinds of grain and merchandise. These are brought into the city on a river, and on this river, at the point where it meets the sea, is a port with a fortress called Diminde. The river is called the Bissolo in the local language, and it flows through Poland and is navigated and traveled along by rafts laden with goods. This area is very rich in fish, meat, and bread. Some of the people here are Catholic and some Lutheran. There are many beautiful women with fine manners, and they have the custom of going out to amuse themselves in the company of their young lovers without fear of losing their reputations. This city, because it is situated in the north, endures very great cold, so they wear furs in great quantity and of various kinds. Brides, as can be seen in the print here, dress in the style of Silesia, wearing a headdress in the form of a crown or a doge's hat; this is made of heavy gold with a jeweled band all around it, worked with intricate patterns. They wear their hair loose on their shoulders. These people are absolutely self-ruling and to retain their freedom, they pay tribute to the King of Poland. They also share a border with Bohemia. The young girls wear an overgarment with a short bodice, closely fitting at the breast, which they decorate with gold chains. Their overgarment is made of silk and colored wool according to their taste; it is also very often found made of moiré ciambellotto. Their arms emerge easily from the sleeves of their sottane. The sleeves of the overgarment are very long, diagonally trimmed with strips of velvet or satin. They wear a very long belt of red silk cord, from which they hang a sheath with knives and keys. Some wear fur mantles with many gold buttons around the collar and also down the front opening of the overgarment. Altogether, this attire is praised as one of the most beautiful in Germany, as the preceding image shows. These people usually live in the Saxon style. They are rich in grains, meat, oil and every other foodstuff they need because of the many ships that arrive there all the time. They have the finest fermented beverages in all of Germany, which are so precious that they are on a par with malmsey. As to religion, they follow their own path, for some of them are Catholic and many others are Lutheran.

THE WOMAN SERVANT OR HOUSEMAID *of Danzig, Pomerania or Denmark*

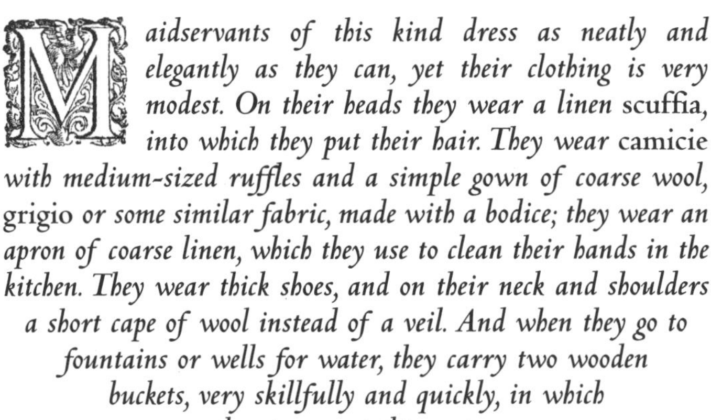

Maidservants of this kind dress as neatly and elegantly as they can, yet their clothing is very modest. On their heads they wear a linen scuffia, *into which they put their hair. They wear* camicie *with medium-sized ruffles and a simple gown of coarse wool,* grigio *or some similar fabric, made with a bodice; they wear an apron of coarse linen, which they use to clean their hands in the kitchen. They wear thick shoes, and on their neck and shoulders a short cape of wool instead of a veil. And when they go to fountains or wells for water, they carry two wooden buckets, very skillfully and quickly, in which they transport this water.*

DRESS OF A SWEDISH BRIDE

Sweden is full of north winds, and among the lands that face north, it is very fertile and abundant in fodder and apples, rich in silver, copper, lead, iron, and livestock. It has no shortage of fish, rivers, seas, and game. In sum, Sweden's population is greater by half than that of Norway, and it is richer in metals and other things. But in many places it is rough, mountainous and marshy. Stockholm, though small, is the royal seat and a merchant city. This city is strong by nature and human design, and it is built on marshes like Venice; the sea enters it in two branches, so deep and wide that ships can come in with hoisted sails. The brides of this country wear a headdress of velvet, made in the form of a papal miter, with various gold bindings, which at the top form something like a little crown. They wear a fur cape with a very high collar, trimmed with a border at the hem. This cape covers both their shoulders and their arms. On their heads, under the miter, they wear a short fazzuolo *of linen or* ormesino*, which, worn under the chin, resembles the* soggolo *of our nuns. Their ankle-length undergarment is of black wool, deeply pleated but without needlework. And such brides wear lovely little boots; and they are very chaste.*

A MARRIED WOMAN of Sweden

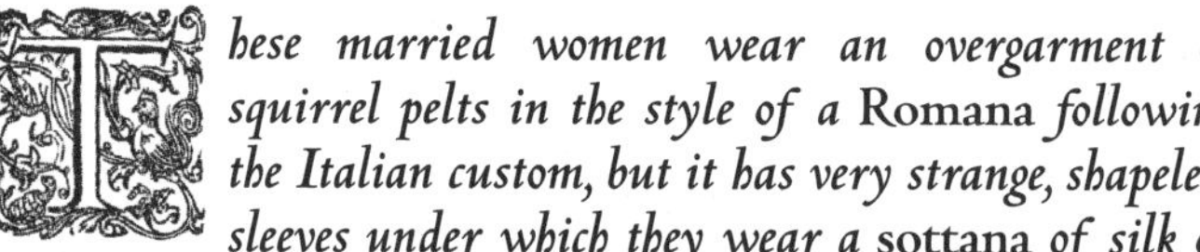

These married women wear an overgarment of squirrel pelts in the style of a Romana *following the Italian custom, but it has very strange, shapeless sleeves under which they wear a* sottana *of silk or wool, with a very high-cut bodice. They do not bother with trim at the neck, but, wearing their gowns long and plain, they content themselves with a cap of vair, rather high, and they wear their hair gathered up without braiding it. Such women have good health; they are fair-skinned and very pretty. In those regions are woods full of game. There are many ice fields on which loaded wagons travel. People of that country wear* zoccoli *and hobnailed shoes, and they carry walking sticks on their climbs, using them to go about a half mile at a time. Many animals are trapped in those regions, such as squirrels, beavers, sables, and ermine, and the people are very industrious in capturing such animals, whose pelts they go to sell in Muscovy and Tartary.*

GENTLEMAN of Bohemia

Bohemia is located in Germany and is surrounded by the Black Forest; two rivers—the Elbe and the Moldova—flow through it, and on the steep bank of the Moldova is situated Prague, a large city and the capital of the kingdom. All of its rivers flow into the Elbe, which has its source in the mountains that divide Bohemia from Moravia. Even though this region is very cold, it is still rich in fish, livestock, birds, wild animals, fodder, and wheat, but it has no oil. Excellent cervosa *[a fermented beverage made from various ingredients] is made there and taken to Vienna, in Austria. Its people love novelties and for this reason the city of Prague is full of brawls and heresies. The common people of the kingdom are much given to gluttony because the country is so fertile. This nation accepted the Catholic faith under Bořivoj, the son of Nestoric, in 900. The men of this region wear large hats of heavy wool. Their overgarment is lined with the fur of wolves and bears and is not very long but has wide sleeves. Under it they wear* burricchi *of colored wool, which they keep pulled in tightly with the leather strap of their swords; since they are all men of arms, everyone wears a sword at his waist.*

332

MAN OF THE LOWER RANKS
in Bohemia

Most of the inhabitants of this region generally wear a high, shaggy wool hat like those of the Uskoks. They dress in blue or red wool, lined with fur. Their tabarri *have sleeves that they can put their arms into if they need to. Their undergarment, similarly, is of wool lined with fur that they tie with their sword belt. They all wear tight* bracche *made of a single piece of cloth, and on their legs they wear boots of soft leather. They have a shoulder guard made of furs, in the shape of a rounded* bavero *that protects them very well against cold, wind and heavy rain.*

NOBLEWOMAN
of Bohemia

This is a type of noblewoman who is very chaste because she shuns all vanities. She wears a wide cap of velvet decorated with golden pins, with a colored feather and a rather wide band, under which she gathers up her hair in a gold net. She also wears quite high chemise ruffles, with a rounded bavaro *of velvet or some other kind of silk covering her shoulders. She wears a gown with a snug bodice, bordered with velvet, with pretty lacings at the side, and sleeves tight down to the wrist, where she wears small ruffles. She belts this gown with her apron strings, and the apron itself is of* ciambellotto *or some other kind of silk or wool, also trimmed with borders at the bottom. This gown has no pleats; rather, its skirt is round in the style of a* faldiglia *as worn in Lombardy. Such women, however high they are in rank, perform every kind of menial housework. They also always wear very valuable gold chains. And they wear shoes like those in Germany.*

A BOHEMIAN WOMAN of Low Rank

Plebeian women of Bohemia wear gowns of wool with horizontal trim of satin or velvet; the wool of these gowns is coarse or they are made of linen. They wear a hat of shaggy wool with a white veil that hangs down and wraps the chin, in the style of a half-mask. They wear a short mantle on top of another short overgown, lined with fur, under which is still another full undergown of wool, to protect them against the cold. They walk along all bundled up in their clothes, with quick steps, as they do in Germany. They wear boots of leather and suede, without any pianelle. *They do a lot of business, both buying and selling, in contrast to the women of Italy.*

THE CLOTHING OF HELVETIA

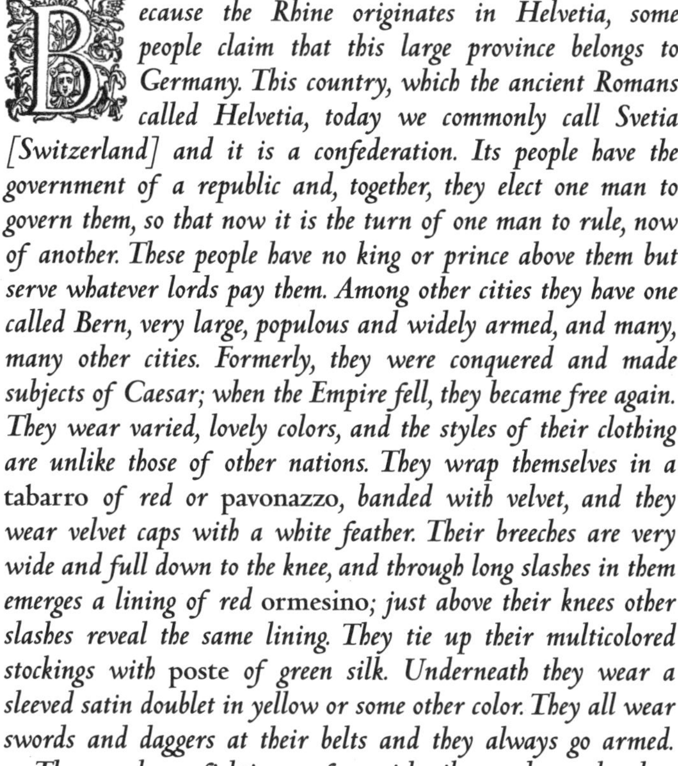

CLOTHING OF THE LEADERS OF HELVETIA

Because the Rhine originates in Helvetia, some people claim that this large province belongs to Germany. This country, which the ancient Romans called Helvetia, today we commonly call Svetia [Switzerland] and it is a confederation. Its people have the government of a republic and, together, they elect one man to govern them, so that now it is the turn of one man to rule, now of another. These people have no king or prince above them but serve whatever lords pay them. Among other cities they have one called Bern, very large, populous and widely armed, and many, many other cities. Formerly, they were conquered and made subjects of Caesar; when the Empire fell, they became free again. They wear varied, lovely colors, and the styles of their clothing are unlike those of other nations. They wrap themselves in a tabarro *of red or* pavonazzo*, banded with velvet, and they wear velvet caps with a white feather. Their breeches are very wide and full down to the knee, and through long slashes in them emerges a lining of red* ormesino*; just above their knees other slashes reveal the same lining. They tie up their multicolored stockings with* poste *of green silk. Underneath they wear a sleeved satin doublet in yellow or some other color. They all wear swords and daggers at their belts and they always go armed. They are brave fighting on foot with pikes, and very loyal to whomever they serve. They wear velvet shoes in the old style, but also in leather. And in their eating and drinking, they resemble the Germans.*

AN UNMARRIED GIRL
of Switzerland

*ormerly, girls of these regions of Switzerland dressed more modestly and inexpensively than they do today, because, wrapping a white linen kerchief around their heads, they thought that was enough to suit their rank. And dressed in this simple way, they went out in public. But little by little they have so distanced themselves from this custom that now there is little difference between them and the girls of Germany. They braid their hair and tie it with red silk ribbons; the braids hang down full-length. On their heads they wear a piece of jewelry or a garland made of a narrow band of gold or silver and full of rubies and other jewels, which fits tightly to their head and keeps their hair neatly in place. Their gown is of red* ciambellotto, *sometimes with an open bodice, trimmed with strips of yellow velvet, and their arms come through it covered and adorned with the narrow sleeves of their* sottana. *These gowns are very full, like those of German women, and with two yellow borders at the bottom. They wear a beautiful apron of green linen tied below their pretty, modest bodice. They wear low* pianelle *in red or* pavonazzo. *They dislike make-up for the skin and other cosmetics. They encouraged their rulers to make a law that all women who wear make-up or curl their hair should have their heads shaved and never grow their hair back again. But they do tie on a hanging purse and a sheath with knives.*

A MARRIED WOMAN of Switzerland

Married women of Switzerland wear fur hats on their heads, covered with velvet in the shape of a corno. *They wear a small, close-fitting bodice, short and modest. Their arms are covered only by the full sleeves of their* renso camicie, *which are narrow at the wrist with ruffles and flawless needlework, as is also the case at their necks. Their gowns are of* damasco *if they are noblewomen; for lower-ranking women, they are of thin or thick wool. They like them to be as high-collared as possible, floor-length, and very full, and at their hems they like to have a velvet band of whatever color they want as long as it does not clash with the gown. They wear very beautiful* sottane *with satin borders. They also wear a large hanging purse with knives and other things. They wear aprons of* ciambellotto *or thin linen, needle-worked at the hem. At their necks hangs a strip of colored silk, like a necklace; and so, contented with this simple style of dress, they go everywhere on their own. They walk, as in Germany, with short, quick steps. They do business in every sort of merchandise, and they make an effort to leave their husbands at leisure, conserving their energy for war and other more important activities. They are strongly blamed if they are not clean and neat in their cooking.*

GERMAN COACHMAN

oaches are widely used in Germany to transport people and goods to the places they need to go. Most of them are driven by coarse rather than civil men, who swear whenever they like and behave without any courtesy. On their heads these men wear a hat of shaggy cloth, very wide, and some of them wear it with a brightly colored cock's feather. They wear a sleeved guarnaccia *[a full-cut, sleeved, mid-length cloak] of frieze or some other coarse cloth, rust-colored or red. Under this they wear a* burichetto *of leather or of the fabric of the jacket, fastened with a thick lace. At their sides they tie a pouch of leather or coarse cloth in which they carry everything they need for their carriage and horses. In their hand they carry a horsewhip with cured knots in it, to beat the horses if they do not keep going. They wear coarse, simply made* bracconi*, rather wide at the thigh. Finally, they wear heavy old boots, easy to put on, in which they walk through the mud and dust. Then, arriving at an inn, they shout out obscenities and water their horses.*

SENATOR AND REGIONAL AUTHORITIES of Leipzig

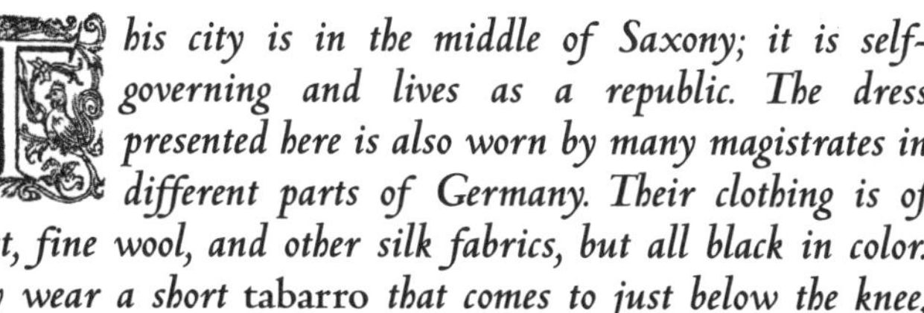

This city is in the middle of Saxony; it is self-governing and lives as a republic. The dress presented here is also worn by many magistrates in different parts of Germany. Their clothing is of velvet, fine wool, and other silk fabrics, but all black in color. They wear a short tabarro *that comes to just below the knee, fur-lined and bordered with fur at all the edges. Their* bracconi *are slashed lengthwise, in the Italian style. They wear quite high velvet* berrette à tozzo, *but with a band of gold cord around them. Underneath they wear a velvet, fur-lined short* buricchino *with loose sleeves. At their neck they wear large chains of heavy gold, and this is because they are proud and fond of display. They drink too much wine, shamelessly, so they get drunk, and when they want to show affection to an Italian friend, they encourage him amiably to drink too much and get drunk, though some men of that region do not participate in this or in lust or lascivious love.*

A PRUSSIAN MERCHANT

Prussia produces industrious men who do business and travel throughout Livonia, Lithuania, Germany, and Poland to all the markets and fairs. They make large purchases of furs, and because they are nearly always traveling, their clothing is simple and allows them freedom of movement. On their heads they wear a leather cap or hat in a fantastic shape, and furs according to the style of all these regions. Underneath they wear a calf-length undergarment of leather or heavy workman's wool, also lined with furs, more practical than showy, and fastened with tin or leather buttons and braided trim. Their guarnaccia *is of wolf or bear fur, which is water- and wind-proof. This attire also belongs to other countries, such as Russia, Poland, and Tartary. They wear boots made especially for walking and riding on horseback.*

A MERCHANT of the Low Countries

Since people of various countries come to these regions, the men's clothing combines Flemish and Italian styles. Against the cold they wear a short, knee-length overgarment of animal skins and fur, and under this a fitted casacchetta, *mid-thigh in length, of rather coarse wool, which they fasten with buttons. They cover their heads with a woolen hat lined with fur. And dressed in such short attire, they walk everywhere. They wear tight-fitting suede leggings and shoes with three lines of stitching. Their* bracconi *are padded with cotton and more practical than showy.*

CLOTHING OF THE NOBLEMEN OF HUNGARY AND CROATIA

ungary is bordered on the south by the Drava river, while today its northern border is Sarmathia, which we call Poland and Wallachia. Austria is to the west, and to the east is Reziano (Retz in the local language). This country yields to no other in the bravery of its men, the fecundity of its animals, the richness of its farmland and the abundance of its fodder. And it peacefully combines three categories of people: priests, warriors, and peasants. The country as a whole is divided into villages and into country districts called counties, which, if they were safe from robberies, would be more populated than they are. Compared to all other countries, this one has a good climate and a beautiful setting. There are many, many cities. The clothing of the people resembles that of Croatia, as I will explain in greater detail below.

The main style of dress of the noblemen of Croatia, and this might also be said of the Poles and the Hungarians, is that they wear a small hat of fine wool, but thick like felt, colored or black, with a feather above their forehead and a turned-up brim slashed at each side. They wear long overgowns with long sleeves, with large, square baveri *that cover their shoulders almost completely and are lined with fur. They usually wear very beautiful buttons of silk braid. Their overgarments are floor-length, as are their sleeves. They wear a scimitar on a silver or iron chain. The colors of their gowns are* porpora *and every other beautiful color. They wear full-length, wide woolen stockings that have an opening in the back and can be fastened with copper, brass or silver eyes or loops, which allow the leg to be tightly covered from the knee down. In their hands they carry an iron-covered mace in the shape of a pike, trimmed with silver. They are mostly tall and strong, with robust, ruddy faces.*

343

Text on page 396

THE CLOTHING OF CROATIAN MEN

The clothing shown here is worn not only by the Croatians but also by the Hungarians and by most of the Poles. The Croatians are Christian but subject to the Turks. Because of the cold, they dress in garments lined with fox, wolf, and other elegant animals such as martens and others of similar breed. They have a noble ruler, who not long ago in Venice was very well treated by the Croatians here. He wore garments of fine wool in scarlet and other colors, and also of satin, damasco, velvet, and other fabrics. He wore a hat or cap of velvet, with fur, to ward off the cold. The back part of the Croatians' overgown is longer by a palm and a half than the front. It is open up to the knee and through the opening can be seen hanging a sword, three fingers in width but not very long. These Croatians shave their heads, leaving only a lock of hair on top in the middle; they fasten their overgarments down the middle of their chests with many buttons of gold or other metal. Their undergown is usually as long as the front of their overgown. This undergown they cinch only with a sword belt. They are handsome men, bearing arms and very skillful on horseback. They very often wear boots and other heavily made footwear.

Text on page 397

A HUNGARIAN
in Genuine Hungarian Clothing

Hungarian men wear long garments, especially in red. But since not all of them can wear reddish porpora or other fine fabrics, they wear whatever they can, but longer in the back than in the front. All of them wear buttons fastened with braided trim, some of silk mixed with gold and some of crystal. Their overgarments are sleeveless and not very long, and they wear the sleeves of their undergarment instead, which are so long that they serve them as gloves, which are not worn in those countries. They usually shave their heads and also their beards, keeping only a moustache. Their hats are of fine red wool, lined with fine fur, with the brim turned back in a dashing way. They rarely leave off their daggers. They are warlike and active men. They wear high-arched shoes with soles of iron or of colored leather, and short, colored boots.

345

Text on page 398

SLAV
or Dalmatian Man

This country produces men and women who are tall, robust, and healthy, but in their behavior and speech they are usually coarse. They dress in colors and rarely wear black, except when they mourn their dead. On their heads they wear a cap, red or some other color, usually of felt, with an upturned brim. The nobles and high-ranking men among them wear velvet, damasco, scarlatto, *and other fine wools of different colors. They wear a short* casacca *and under it another similar one, and green or red stockings, full-length but tied under the knee. They belt on a scimitar in Turkish fashion and many of them carry an iron-covered mace. They wear rather high felt shoes with a covering of leather, which they lace up their leg above the foot. They are Catholic and pious, arms-bearing and hardworking.*

346

Text on page 399

A DALMATIAN
or Slavic Woman

The women of that country have very good health and are tall and active. They wrap their heads with a fazzuolo *of silk or white linen and with this they keep their hair in place but styled in an attractive way. They wear many different colors and fine wools, and their gowns are long and without bodices; rather, they wear them belted with sashes and very wide wool ties. These gowns are richly pleated but at the hem they are bordered with silk bands. On top of these gowns they wear a short garment of fine wool or satin or* damasco *with half-length sleeves that they call the* ghellero, *which is open and roomy and makes them look very graceful. They adorn their necks with pearls and gold chains, and they walk about freely. They wear red stockings and low white* pianelle; *and they are very pious.*

Text on page 400

A DALMATIAN WOMAN
from the Island of Cres

Every year on the day of the Ascension of Our Lord, beautiful women from Cres, a part of Dalmatia, come to Venice; their headdresses resemble the type nuns wear more than those of other women. They wrap their heads with a kerchief or veil of thin silk or linen. They wear ankle-length gowns of thin, colored wool with a short bodice and rosettes of gold or silver at the top. They wear thin camicie *without ruffles and usually their sleeves are those of their* camicia, *but they are drawn in at the wrist. They tie an apron of linen high up under their breasts and cinch themselves at the hips with leather belts and silver buckles. At their hems their gowns are bordered with one or two bands of satin or velvet, or with fabric of another color, and they go around without* pianelle *so as to be more comfortable as they work. But they wear white leather shoes to be able to dance better and to walk quickly.*

Text on page 401

THE LEADER OF THE USKOKS

This is a very ferocious tribe, daring and terrifying, subject to Prince Charles of Austria.[1] They inhabit steep, mountainous places and they live in a region called Senj. They make their living by constant robberies and raids, and share a border with the Turks, with whom they are always fighting. They use small, armed boats to sack large ships and boats loaded with goods. Altogether, they are a fearsome people, sharing borders with various other groups, brave, bellicose, and constantly starting fights. Their territory is in Dalmatia. Their leaders wear silk of all kinds and fine wools; in battle, they wear coats of fine-mesh chain mail. Their overgarments resemble those of the Slavs, long in the back and short in the front. Their sleeves are made of a single piece of cloth and are elbow-length. They use hand weapons, especially swords, in order to be more agile in sea battles. They fasten their overgarments with gold or silver buttons, which they often leave undone. On their heads they wear a small cap of velvet or other fabric in a fantastic shape; it comes down to the middle of the neck in back, and in front it is turned up with a slash on each side. They are so nimble and fast when they run that they move through those wild mountains as quickly as chamois. They wear full-length red or green stockings and heavy work shoes.

Text on page 402

YOUNG WOMAN
of Ragusa

Ragusa was formerly called Epidauros by Ptolemy,[2] *but it is not the same city today, for the old city was destroyed by the Goths; on the ruins, the present city was rebuilt on the shore of the Adriatic Sea in the region of Slovenia. Ragusa's port is man-made, lying under a high, steep mountain. The city has many fountains, which have their source in the nearby mountains and make the city very abundant in fresh water. It is very populous and has rich merchants and large ships. It is governed like a republic. Many of its people dress in the Venetian style and the rest dress as they wish. Their language and way of speaking is usually Slavic. The women typically are not very beautiful. They wear a headdress consisting of a gold or silver net into which they gather up their hair; they wear earrings of pearls and other jewels and they adorn their necks with pearls of great value. They wear a floor-length* sottana *of cloth of gold or silver or of patterned velvet, with some sort of trim at the hem. The bodices of their gowns are short and decorated with a beautiful jewel, attached to a gold chain that hangs around their necks. On top, they wear a floor-length mantle of silk or* buratto *or some other fabric, but always black, open at the sides in a way that allows them to put their arms through the openings if they want to. They rarely leave their houses but are very willing to stand at the windows. The woman in the print here is a bride of the nobility. She belts her dress high and wears a very modest bodice. And their gowns are far enough from the ground to reveal their white shoes in low* pianelle.

Text on page 403

A NOBLEWOMAN
of Poland, Russia, and Muscovy

ecchо [Łódź] was the first place to have its people subjugated in the region of the kingdom of Poland, so the Poles were first called Lecchiti. The first seat of the government in Leccho was Gniezna, a citadel that is still standing in greater Poland and is located in a low plain; because of this location, Poland took its name, as if to say "the Plainland." Earlier, the country was called Sarmathia. Some claim that "Poleia" in the Polish language means flat, because the entire region is flat. It is has many forests but few mountains. The country is cold so it lacks wine, but it is rich in grains, in great quantity, and in other sorts of fodder. It has plenty of fish, animals, game, milk, butter, wax, horses, and wild asses. It is a very large and fortunate country; it has a large quantity of apples, and because they do not know where to put them all, they are forced to keep them in underground caves in the mountains. The Poles are good Christians, and above all they honor Saint Thaddeus the Apostle,[3] being certain that he baptized their country, and they also venerate Saint Bartholomew, claiming that he gave them many articles of faith.[4]

The clothing shown here is also worn in the part of Russia called Ruthenia, and in Podolia, which is an area of Poland. Its eastern border is Muscovy and it is as fertile as Poland, in which very great cold is the norm, but because it is so rich in wood and animals, they make huge fires of the wood and clothe themselves with the furs of the animals. These three countries—Poland, Lithuania, and Prussia—are very similar in their style of dress. The women of these countries cover their temples, ears, and chins with a fazzuolo *tied on their heads; they cover the knot of this cloth with a velvet cap lined with fur, high and comfortable for the ears because it is cut long enough to cover them, in a charming way. They wear overgarments of velvet, satin or other fabric, lined with furs according to their status; and they wear these in the style of a* pretina, *very wide and with long sleeves. Under this they wear floor-length* sottane *of fur-lined wool, richly pleated with a border of trim at the bottom, and they add an apron of linen or* ciambellotto, *also trimmed. They decorate their bodices and sleeves with strips of velvet, and at their necks they wear gold chains. On their* camicie *they wear neck and wrist ruffles as German women do, and their shoes are also like those of German women.*

WOMAN OF POZNAN
in Poland

Poznan is a large, beautiful city in greater Poland, abundant in all good things, which is also true for the rest of the region. Since the women there are very different from others, I have included a print here that represents the area as a whole; this is based on descriptions by Messer Angelico Fortunio, a knowledgeable young man I recently met who has returned from this region, where he lived for three years. The women of this city wear a cap of wool or velvet, lined with fur, much more practical than many seen so far in my book. They wear a floor-length gown, as long in the back as in the front; it is of different colors of silk, wool or other fabric, but it is always lined with fur and has many pleats. Even though the region is fiercely cold, the women wear only their simple camicia *sleeves in every season, with nothing else; these have many pleats and are made of silk or of linen, but so starched and polished with a stone made for this purpose that they become very lustrous and look more like paper than cloth. They also wear a* tabarro *lined with fur and covered with silk or some other colored cloth, as suits their taste. Some of these capes are open at the sides so that they can bring their arms out of them. In the summer, they wear simple shoes and most go bare-legged; the less noble wear little boots of lightweight leather. They pull their waists in tightly with very tight-fitting bodices. At their necks they wear elegant small ruffles, shaped with great skill. The unmarried girls wear garlands of roses, which they preserve in salt all year so they can wear them whenever they leave the house to go to church. Such garlands are also worn by brides and by men at weddings, and on holidays. They carry knives attached to gold and silver chains. They walk with short, quick steps. Around their necks they wrap a white* fazzoletto *and they wear gold chains with a beautiful small jewel.*

Text on page 406

THE NATIVE CLOTHING
of Polish Men

Polish men are bold in war and brave on horseback; all the soldiers are noblemen and able to endure hardship very easily. The horses of that country are small and most often geldings. The people are very devout Catholics but given to gluttony. They usually eat rye bread and drink very good cervosa.[5] *They never eat young goats or small game birds. Their overgarments are almost floor-length, and they usually wear valuable fabrics such as silk and very fine wool, in wintertime using furs of various kinds including fox, wolf, hare, rabbit, squirrel, wild dogs, marten, lynx, and sable, as well as other less well known kinds. They also wear vair and squirrel pelts, especially the women. Men wear full-length stockings of colored wool, very loose above the knee, which they tie to their belts with a cord that goes round and round the waist and pulls and gathers the fabric up snugly. From the knee down, these stockings fit tightly because they are fastened at the back of the leg with small silver clasps or hooks. Their shoes are very bizarre in shape: their toes point upward and then they widen toward the middle of the foot; and at the heel, under the sole, they have a circle of iron that grips to allow the men to stop safely on the ice. And for this purpose they also put sharp studs on the soles; these also serve as our* pianelle *do because they wear a pair of thin, simple shoes fitting snugly inside them and they wear the overshoes on top. The inner shoes are made of yellow or red or* pavonazzo *leather. Over their* sottana, *they wear a floor-length gown, and on top of this they belt on a sword. They shave their heads, and in the center on top they wear a lock of hair that they let grow very long; they also shave their beards, leaving only a moustache.*

Text on page 407

A NOBLEWOMAN of Muscovy

uscovy is a very large region, whose principal city is called Mosca or Moscow; this was built along the Moscow river, and has a circumference of fourteen thousand feet. They do not use minted coins in this city. In the center of the city square is a square rock, and whoever succeeds in climbing to the top without falling off becomes the leader of the city. These people hate the name "king" and prefer the term "duke," which they accept more willingly as being closer to the people. The man who is duke of the region wears a hat taller than those of other men, but otherwise he dresses as they do. The custom of that region is that women wear pearls in their ears, and men, as young boys, do the same. They consider women who marry a second time to be virtuous, but not those who take a third husband, and the same is thought of men. These people are greatly given to drink and to lust, which they think of as an honor as long as it doesn't threaten marriage. As to their religion, they follow the Greeks. They are great farmers because their country is very fertile in everything except wine, but they drink a beer made from millet, barley, and hops. The country is flat throughout, full of animals and rich in fish; it is four hundred miles wide and rich in silver, and it is defended and surrounded on all sides with strong guardhouses, so that not only foreigners but also people of the city cannot leave without permission from the duke. The city contains wooden houses and many squares, but these are set far apart, because wide fields are positioned in the midst of the city and the Moscow river flows through its center. In the main square is a fortress with sixteen turrets and three very strong and beautiful bastions, seemingly without equal. This province of Muscovy contains many duchies within its borders, each of which can muster many thousands of armed men for warfare for its own purposes. They have no fruits except cherries, because the north wind prevents others from growing, but the land is very fertile in every kind of fodder and legume. Here the bees make honey in profusion in the hollows of the trees. The people celebrate mass in the Greek Orthodox style, including offerings made from the pulpit; they read the miracles of Christ and the Epistles of Saint Paul.

The women of this region dress like the men, but they wear sleeves of the same length as their overgarments, which are of silk or some other fabric according to their rank. They wear small velvet caps, lined with fur. The sleeves of their sottane *are narrow but so long that they almost cover their hands, so they need no gloves. Both unmarried girls and married women wear this style of dress. They live without any education or training in manners. Their maidservants dress in red wool. The noblemen are very eager to protect their honor and they rarely allow their women to leave the house to see anything. They are very devout Christians, and whenever they see an image of Christ, they stretch out and bow their heads to the ground, whether in church or elsewhere. The women wear their hair in a very modest style and they wear short gowns with short boots. They fasten their* casacche *at the breast with gold braided trim. At the entrance to their houses they have small painted images of Christ, and when they go inside, before anything else they prostrate themselves on the ground to honor these icons.*

A NOBLE AMBASSADOR
from Moscow

mong the men of Moscow it is considered a great sin to cuckold other men or to commit rape, although there are no prostitutes. When their prince intends to marry, he informs the entire empire that in every city under his rule the most beautiful and virtuous girls should be chosen and brought to him by men eligible for this duty and by trustworthy married women, who watch over them very carefully. Then they choose one to please him and recommend her to him with no regard to her rank, and the others are married to his principal barons and lords. The clothing of the highest noblemen (as seen in our time in Venice, worn by an ambassador coming to visit Pope Gregory XIII, accompanied by the Reverend Posevino of the Jesuit order[6]) is of silk, satin, damask, velvet, and other types of fabric. Their hats are of sable and so are their overgarments, and they are lined with other kinds of fur, from martens and other animals. Their sleeves are long and they like to use them to cover their hands. Under this they wear a garment in the style of a Greek casacca, *belted and somewhat shorter than their overgown. The colors they wear are black,* pavonazzo *and* rovano. *Some men, however, wear a different kind of hat, pointed and tipped with gold, in the shape of a loaf of sugar.*

CLOTHING OF A MUSCOVITE FOOT SOLDIER

Foot soldiers wear loose-fitting, comfortable clothes, including a short, ungathered garment of thick felt, open in front, over their other clothing; though it is the same length as their other garments, this one is padded against any blow. They wear leggings of tanned leather that end in thin leather soles, worn, as we do, as shoes. As a belt they wear a striped silk sash, to which they attach their scimitars or knives. They all carry a bow, which they are expertly trained to use. Their custom is to wear hats of different shapes, lined with furs, rather like those worn by the Armenians and Georgians; these are exported from Moscow to Persia and other countries. These Muscovites are very hostile to Jews, and they refuse to be in their company or even to look at them. Their houses are made entirely of wood, taken from the famous Black Forest, but they are well divided into beautiful, well-arranged rooms. They live luxuriously on many delicate foods, such as pheasant and other game birds, and on wild and domestic animals, though they suffer from a scarcity of wine, which they drink only at large banquets and on holy days. They use malmsey as medicine. They hunt falcons and eagles, and they drink a cervosa of cherries, morellos, and other delicious flavors.

MUSCOVITE SOLDIER
on Horseback

These Muscovites are men of low height but with shapely, muscular bodies. They have blue-green eyes, big bellies, and short legs. They practice the various arts of war, riding horses at top speed, wrestling, and shooting with the bow. In their kingdom the laws are very simple but very fair. Their horses are low to the ground and they have various gaits. Instead of armor, these soldiers wear garments padded with cotton that protect them against blows. Their weapons include an iron-tipped lance, a bow and arrows, an iron mace, and a curved sword. They ride with stirrups drawn up short. They are very skillful at shooting arrows, which, even as they are fleeing, they turn around and use to wound their enemies. For some time now, they have been wearing celate *and* corazze *and using arquebuses and artillery, though not in great quantity.*

THE CLOTHING OF FLANDERS

A GIRL OF BRABANT
and Other Places Nearby, Especially Antwerp

This large region begins in the north with the Schelde river, following its turn toward Antwerp as far as the new dike built near Saint Odomer in order to expand the kingdom; a messenger could hardly make this trip on foot in three months. But from east to west, the country can be crossed in a day, from the River Lisa to the sea. The part of the region nearest to France is called Gallic Flanders, and it contains many very famous cities. The land is better suited for pasturing animals than for growing wheat, so the Flemish export a great amount of cheese and buy great quantities of grain. For oil, they use linseed and turnip oil. They have no wine (though they import it from France and Germany) so the Flemish peasants drink beers. This region has many woods near the sea. They keep their fires going with wild grasses mixed with dark, damp earth; they also burn straw and ox dung dried in the sun, and from this they make fire. When certain winds blow, the country suffers greatly from floods. Queen Mary inherited the kingdom from the last Count and Lord of Brabant, and from Flanders she married Prince Maximilian of Austria,[1] who became the Lord of Brabant and then of other areas and cities. With this wife, Maximilian had Philip and then Charles V and then Ferdinand. Charles V then sired Philip, today absolute ruler of Brabant.

The women of this country are very pleasant and friendly, because it is the custom for unmarried girls to play many games with their young lovers at every time of year. So in the winter they do this on the ice and in the summer in lovely gardens.

They embrace and kiss one another, keeping company at home intimately and familiarly, without damaging their reputations. The girls of the city of Antwerp wear a headdress made of thin white silk into which they gather their braids, which they also let fall down their backs. They also bind their hair tightly with a gold garland resembling a crown, and they make small curls that they arrange around their foreheads and temples, though very modestly. They wear overgarments of silk and velvet or some other fabric, according to the season, and these gowns have very snug, one-piece bodices, untrimmed and cut low. Their gowns are long with little decoration at the hem and not many pleats. They wear small spalletti *[shoulder rolls], very prettily needle-worked, and their sleeves come out of them, very close-fitting, so that they look altogether charming, trimmed all the way down with white silk veils. They usually wear a belt, hanging all the way down to their feet. They wear* baveri *with elegant, high-cut neck ruffles, fastened with gold buttons. These young women are very pleasant and extremely chaste with their lovers. They wear aprons of silk,* ciambellotto *or linen, and tie them on to be quicker at their household tasks.*

Text on page 413

A NOBLEWOMAN of Antwerp

In this city, women of a mature age go out alone. On their heads they wear a hat of fine straw in the shape of a bowl, which they take off when they greet someone, as we do with our caps. They wear a high bodice, fastened up to their chins so that the ruffles of their camicie *barely show. They also wear a silk head-covering with a stole, of velvet or some other fabric, that falls down behind and keeps their hair in place. Their overgarment is of silk or some thin, colored wool, floor-length, with a* sottana *of silk or some other fabric. They wear aprons of linen or* ciambellotto *and shoes without* pianelle*, or with low* pianelle*, in white or red. They avoid curls and make-up and they wear no gold at their necks. More than in any other country, the women here enjoy fine* renso *linen, which they decorate elegantly with needlework. They work at painting on tapestries and wall panels, in quantity. They are more involved in business than the men, and they buy and sell very adroitly.*

Text on page 414

A NOBLEWOMAN
of Brabant, or Antwerp

When women wearing the preceding dress in Antwerp leave their houses, they wear a thin, high mantle lined with wool, which they pin above their foreheads; then, with a copper wire or circlet of wood, they shape it into a large curve that leaves their face uncovered. Their sottane *are of silk, not closed at the top but with a lovely opening here and there. The overgown has a rounded bodice and is fitted in such a charming style that it makes the wearer look very graceful and slim at the sides—so much so, in fact, that it seems impossible that her hips could be so narrow, but she learns as a child to move in such a tightly fitted gown. Their beauty comes from the narrowness of their hips and the whiteness and perfection of their faces. Their bodices are decorated with gold trim down to their waists. They wear beautifully needle-worked* baveri, *because they can boast of being more skillful at this craft than any other people. And on top of this* bavero *they wear another layer of the same type of wool or silk as their overgarment, in the style of a high-necked doublet. They wear close-fitting sleeves, narrow at the wrist, with gracefully formed ruffles. Under their gowns they wear* faldiglie *in the Spanish style, and at the bottom of their overgarment they wear narrow bands of fine fur as a decoration. The fabrics they wear include serge,* ferandina *or* ciambellotto, *and many kinds of silk and velvet.*

Text on page 415

WOMEN OF BRABANT

The clothing shown here is very beautiful and modest, and it more or less resembles clothing of the past in many ways. The headdress they wear, like a cap or hat, is very comfortable, with a small circular brim similar to the French atiffet *with its point at the forehead. This is then covered with* cambrai *or black* ormesino, *and above their coiffure, adorned with modest curls, they wear the point seen here, shaped in a stylish way. They also often wear the overgarment shown previously, and under it a gown of silk or some other fabric, with a bodice in the style of a doublet—this is chin-high, in a very chaste style, and they enjoy gracefully shaped ruffles at the neck. Their sleeves are plain and of the same fabric as their overgarment, which is open from the waist down, without buttons; and under it can be seen a* sottana *of a different color, also of silk. These women have fair complexions and are usually pale. Those who have ruddy skin are not much admired, for people suspect them of not knowing how to drink wine properly; in this sense they are like the Romans, who, if they were related to some woman and disapproved of their drinking wine, frequently kissed them in order to tell, by smell, whether they had been drinking that liquor; and if they found them guilty, they would punish them. So they drink* cervosa. *And all the members of a family sleep in the same room. They all eat from the same pot and drink from the same cup. They are very neat, quick, dedicated to every kind of honorable task, and very quick-witted; they apply themselves very much to the art of embroidery, and their needlework is sold throughout the world. It is admired in our country today for its charm and beauty.*

363

Text on page 416

A GIRL OF METZ, in Flanders

The city of Metz, in the region of Mediomatrix,[2] is very ancient and is the principal city of that region; it is located in the midst of the area, between the cities of Toul, Verdun and Trier. Trier is at the north, Toul at the south and Verdun to the west. This region is fertile in fruit and beautiful for its meadows and vineyards, which are watered by two rivers, the Moselle and the Seille. Some inhabitants speak French and some speak German. The city was besieged by Charles V, but because of its great cold and bad climate, it was not conquered.

The clothing of these girls includes a mantle, which is lovely to look at because it is not very long and is full of pleats. It is made of ciambellotto *or black* moccajarro *[a fine fabric of silk mixed with hemp] and it allows a bit of the coiffure to be seen; they wear this mantle instead of a hat when they leave the house. They wear overgowns of silk or fine wool, colored and sometimes in black, with a short bodice and a very narrow border; and if it weren't for their* baveri, *which they wear with high neck, their breasts would be visible. Their gown is richly pleated down to their feet. They wear no jewelry at their necks, and because they are busy housewives, they wear an apron of moiré* ciambellotto *or* rovano cendal.

THE CLOTHING OF ENGLAND

This is an island of Britain, formerly called Albion because of its white cliffs,[1] which appear to sailors and from which we receive very fine white chalk for writing and drawing. Britain was named after Brutus, the son of Sylvius, the last king of the Latins; he was the captain of certain Trojans who, with a number of armed men, arrived on this island and killed every person they found there. The noble forest called Caledonia already existed here, from which the island also took the name Caledonia, then Albion, and finally England and Scotland. Beyond this, that is, to the north, is the island of Thule, now thought to be Ireland, which owes obedience to the King of Denmark. Near here, too, are the Orkney Islands, which number thirty. England and Scotland, then, occupy the same island, which King John gave as a protectorate to the Roman pope through a legate named Pandolfo, who was in his kingdom as an envoy from Pope Innocent III; at the same time the king of Ireland committed himself to paying a tribute of seventy gold marks a year to this pope. Then Andolph, the English monarch, reaffirmed that England would pay tribute to Pope Leo IV; and after him, King Henry, who had Thomas the Bishop of Canterbury killed, tried to have the kingdom recognized as a feudal territory of the Roman Church.[2]

AN ENGLISH NOBLEMAN

he English nobility has a long and ancient ancestry. They wear wool and black silk. The toga shown here is of patterned velvet or of very thin black wool. They wear the same fabric underneath, and their undergarment has a high neck worn with ruffles. On their heads they wear hats of velvet or of felt if they are counselors or men of some official rank. Their overgown is lined with fur, because of the great cold that the winds create on this bare island. They cinch this robe with a belt of silk or some other fabric. They wear shoes lined with soft black leather. They are very fond of red-haired men; when they see a foreigner with hair of this color, they say, "What a pity he isn't an Englishman."

A MARRIED ENGLISH NOBLEWOMAN

The women of this island are very courteous and friendly to foreigners whom their husbands invite home. They dress grandly, displaying their magnificence. Their gowns are often a sensible, restrained black. On their heads most do not wear gold or jewels but small hats of black velvet, though some wear them in red, with splendid feathers. They wear sottane *of silk, with few pleats and with a border of gold or silk embroidery at the hem. They do not usually wear belts of gold, but of colored silk. On top, they wear a* zimarra *of velvet or some other fabric with a patterned weave, lined with fine furs because the island is so cold, and this* zimarra *is open from the waist down but close-fitting in the bodice, in the style of a doublet. Their* sottane *are high-necked, with ruffles and every sort of refinement, and at their necks they wear gold necklaces in many strands, with jewels or precious metals hanging from them. Their sleeves are made of skillfully needle-worked* sessa *[gauze]. Their overgowns are floor-length, without trains. They have beautiful complexions, and in a modest and gracious way, they are very kind to foreigners.*

A GIRL
of the English Nobility

Englishwomen are usually beautiful, graceful, attractive, pleasant, and modest in their manners. The young girls easily fall in love with men of the same rank. They go out freely and in a modest fashion. They greet and are greeted and shake hands indoors and out, and they are gracefully attractive. Almost all of them have lovers, who keep company with them in a familiar way, and when one of them longs for a certain girl, he asks her father and other relatives for her as his wife; once the marriage has been agreed upon, the bride to be, going to church, walks between two well-dressed little boys with a large following, and the bridegroom does the same. On her head this bride wears a velvet cap or a very modest hat. Her overgarment is of velluto ad opera *or of some other silk or brocade, with a rounded bodice cut low; it has a border of velvet or of a different color from the bodice. This gown is not very full but is decorated with small gold brooches. Their sleeves are narrow and beautiful, and the gown is floor-length with a rounded skirt. They also wear richly needle-worked* baveri *of* sessa *or some other thin fabric, but with high necks and ruffles. Only a few girls wear a strand of pearls at their neck. Their hair is gathered into a gold net and can hardly be seen. They have the custom of carrying flowers in their hands and especially of wearing them at their breast in a very lovely way.*

A YOUNG ENGLISHMAN

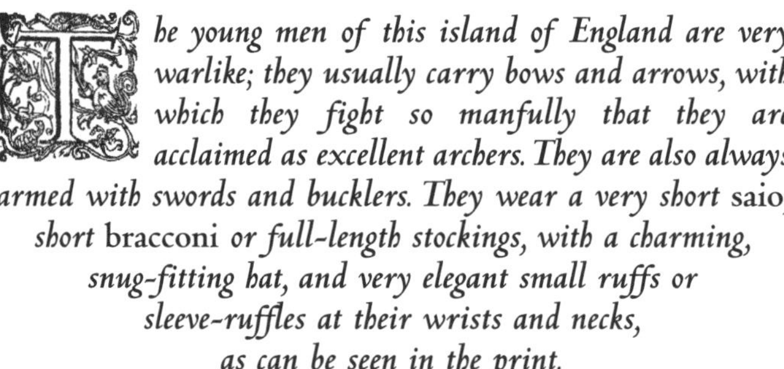

The young men of this island of England are very warlike; they usually carry bows and arrows, with which they fight so manfully that they are acclaimed as excellent archers. They are also always armed with swords and bucklers. They wear a very short saio, *short* bracconi *or full-length stockings, with a charming, snug-fitting hat, and very elegant small ruffs or sleeve-ruffles at their wrists and necks, as can be seen in the print.*

AN ENGLISH NOBLEWOMAN

This noblewoman looks much more splendidly dressed than most others. However, as far as her coiffure goes, she is satisfied with a beautiful veil, dexterously arranged and tied under her chin, falling a half-arm's length down her back, and a scuffia *of* ormesino *or of linen; this holds in and covers her hair in an attractive way, lifting it higher in the middle of her head than elsewhere. She wears very modest earrings and a close-fitting bodice. She wears a* camicia *trimmed with small ruffles and an open silk* bavero *with ruffles of its own. The bodice of her gown is cut low and has a pointed shape down at her waist; the gown is made of* brocatello *or patterned velvet, closed in front down to the hem. From her belt hangs a small leather or velvet pouch, in which she carries money to spend for shopping, bargaining, and giving alms, and other similar necessities.*

ENGLISH WIDOW

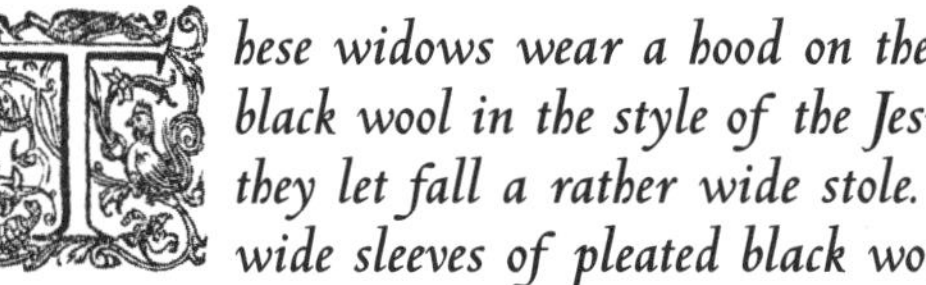

These widows wear a hood on their heads, made of black wool in the style of the Jesuits, behind which they let fall a rather wide stole. Their mantle has wide sleeves of pleated black wool and reaches the floor. They wear nothing white except a fazzuolo, *which they tie around their neck and let fall a bit onto their breast. The married noblewomen of this island go out on horseback, dressed in velvet and accompanied by maidservants. Other women of lower rank wear wide black caps, or green ones. Finally, the women on this island do every sort of work, such as butchering meat to sell in public and minding the shops, while the men go out to enjoy themselves.*

SPOSA DI LIVELLANDIA.

A BRIDE OF SJELLAND,
Gotland, or Oland

These islands are in the region of Gotland, on the border with Sweden.[3] *They are very rich in butter and cheese because of the many pastures for animals, which they have in very large numbers. In particular they keep a kind of white horse of small size that they train to do many tricks, such as dancing to the music of a tambourine or trumpet, going around in circles like a mill, jumping through iron hoops like a dog, and other tricks. They are very strong and agile. These islands are naturally surrounded by marble cliffs that seem to be man-made. They have very safe ports and a great abundance of fish. A bride's attire in this region includes a little crown of gold or gilt on her head, according to her status; as an overgarment she wears a piece of wool similar to a nun's* pacienza, *or even of satin or some other very thin and very white fabric, signifying that she is chaste and pure. She never looks a man in the face without the permission of her mother until she is married. During the marriage process, they are very circumspect and do not sleep with their husbands until they have said their vows and received the blessing of the church. These marriages take place between equals and are finalized when the father of the bride, in the presence of witnesses and relatives, say to the husband, "We give you our daughter as an honor, to be your wife and to share your bed, to become mistress of the doors and the keys and to possess a third of your wealth," and says to both bride and groom that if they should violate the marriage, they will never have peace with their relatives. Then all the men mount beautiful horses and, guided by an able leader, they go to the cathedral; the women do the same, also led by a wise woman. Once everyone has arrived at the church, carrying many torches, the brides are wed, with a richly decorated crown on their heads. After the ceremony is over and the ring has been put on, it is the custom that the couple hit each other on the back with their fists, to confirm their vows. And this is done to the accompaniment of much music and merriment. These brides are simply dressed, as we see here, and so clothed, they return to the house and sit down on the bed to eat with their relatives and friends, who usually treat them with great courtesy; a particular custom is to give them an ox, a horse, and an ax, meaning that they must be faithful in good and bad times and support one another in hardship and danger. The following day, they have another banquet, and the bride, with her hair loose on her shoulders, goes around the table with many pleasantries and carries silver cups full of wine in her hands, which she gives to each guest, one after the other, signifying that she has become the mother of the family. The people of these islands, finally, are healthy, robust, tall, ruddy, and well mannered.*

Text on page 425

A GIRL
of Livellandia, or Gotland

*he unmarried women of these islands wear a simple dress with narrow sleeves, cinched with a woven belt of gold or of silk, from which they hang beautiful knives and a square purse. In front they drape a needle-worked shawl, as can be seen in the preceding print. They wear a small cap, richly trimmed, with a little plume. Other girls wear mantles attached in front with silver pins and a gown, not very long, of wool or fine cloth, thin linen and also silk. In these regions, they have six months of the year of days without nights, and six months of nights without days. These regions border on Denmark and on northern countries such as Muscovy, Lithuania, and Livonia.*

Text on page 426

A WOMAN OF MIDDLE RANK
in Sjelland or Gotland

ear these islands are some smaller ones, gentle and pleasant, to which people go in small boats to amuse themselves. These islands have a friendly climate, so the people sleep uncovered without suffering any harm or risk to their health. The middle-ranking women of Sjelland and Gotland wear short mantles with a rounded bavero. *Under these they wear a gown without a bodice, in the style of a belted* casacca, *crisscrossed with trim and some decoration at the bottom of the hem, and a rather short* sottana, *decorated in the middle with a small inset square of a different color. These women wear their hair cut short in a style of long ago, with a cap divided into different colors. They wear shoes in a style of years past, and small boots of deerskin or some other animal. They carry a bronze container along with them, in which they put every kind of food.*

THE CLOTHING OF TURKEY

he Ottoman clan began with a certain Osman, a ferocious man, who was given this name by the Galatians after the place where he was born.[1] However, it should be noted that four families came out of Persia with their armies in 1250: that is, the Ottomans, the Assembreni, the Candelori, and the Caramanians; they separated one from another, and went to different parts of Asia and Europe, until finally each one of them conquered particular lands. The Caramani took Cilicia; the Candelori took Pontus, near the Black Sea; the Assembreni took lower Armenia and Cappadocia; and the Ottomans, led by Osman, made themselves masters of Asia Minor and gradually subjugated the other clans. Osman was from a low-ranking family, poor, and little known among ordinary people, and he was born to peasants, but through his military prowess, he became famous and renowned among the Turks because he was a hardworking man and eager to wage war. Then he assembled a great many soldiers and began to rob both Christians and, even more, his Turkish people; and in addition to his subjugation of them, it then happened that his captains began to fight among themselves, competing over who would rule, and such disagreements ensued that they faced each other with banners flying. Since fortune had presented Osman with a perfect opportunity, so well suited to his desires and his habits, he began to plunder other peoples and to conquer many of them. As a result, he won such power over them that he began to attack their territories and to seize some of them by force, sacking some and making treaties with others and destroying many cities in order to terrify everyone, so that it seems that this was the principal basis of his state. In these actions he was greatly favored by disagreements among the Christians; taking advantage of them, in ten years he took Bythnia and all the provinces around the Black Sea. Finally, after ruling for ten years, he left the kingdom to his son Orcan, who showed the same capacities as his father. With him, then, the Turkish Empire began. Because I want to speak of the varieties of dress rather than their family line, court and army, I will describe the variety of dress of the people who serve the Great Lord in times of peace and in war.

Nor will it be beside the point to speak of Constantinople, the city where this Lord usually resides;[2] *and since I have to speak of the Seraglio, the port, and other places, I will describe them briefly. Modern writers locate this great city of Constantinople in Thrace and call the region Romania,*[3] *near the canal that divides Europe from Asia; the region was first called Lico. But after being destroyed, it was rebuilt by Pausanias, and he named it Byzantium, making it the capital city for seven years and considering it part of Thrace. Later, it was conquered by the Athenians and then by the Lacedaemonians. This final subjugation lasted until the time of Constantine the Great, who, inspired by the saints and by the pious motives (I would say) of stopping the onslaught of the Persians and restraining the Parthians who were attacking the Roman Empire in the east, moved the imperial seat there and enlarged it with everything belonging to a great city, calling it Constantinople after his own name.*[4] *Because the site seemed so lovely to him, he plundered Rome and other cities of many ornaments, solely for the purpose of embellishing and enriching his beautiful new Rome. In addition, near the sea he built a very beautiful palace and fortified the city by enlarging and reinforcing its walls, decorating it with churches and many other sites. Altogether he accomplished so much that his city won the name of New Rome and his country was called Romania. The Turks today call Constantinople Stamboul, meaning "great city". The city is an artillery shot away from Pera and is triangular in shape; it has two sides facing the sea and one on land. Its fame and grandeur were so great that Mehmet, king of the Turks, unable to bear the fact that such a great city was not subject to him, decided to conquer it; he pushed himself to do this in order to surpass the glory of his predecessors, who had been aggressively driven back when they had attempted the same thing. So he had a castle built at the mouth of the Bosphorus and started attacking the Empire, not caring whether he violated truces or treaties that had been agreed on; he accomplished so much that he finally became the ruler of the city. The result was that all the Christians who survived the massacre fled to Pera. In this way this ancient empire, which had existed for 1,159 years, perished. It fell and was captured on May 5, 1453. But I will mention here a remarkable thing, informing you that Constantinople, restored and rebuilt by Constantine, the son of Saint Helena, was conquered and subjugated under the rule of another Constantine, the son of another Helen.*[5]

THE LORD OF THE TURKS

[The print is a portrait of the Sultan Murad III]

*The Turk usually resides in the Seraglio, in a section of the city that the Greeks call Saint Dimitri but the ancients called Point Chrysochera; it looks from the east directly into the face of the port. This Seraglio is surrounded by strong walls and it occupies two square miles. In the middle of it, on the top of a hill, a beautiful and delightful garden can be seen, which, beginning in the middle of the hill, slopes down toward the sea. There are very many different dwellings within it, and a portico supported by columns, similar to a monks' cloister, and around it are two hundred rooms, in the last of which the Lord sleeps during a large part of the summer. But Bazajet II had them divided up and set a group of houses in the middle, protected from the north wind and every other discomfort, in which he lived during the winter. In this cloister the Sultana also lives, about whom more will be said in the proper place. In addition, inside it there is a beautiful, large stable, where the Lord keeps forty or fifty horses for his own use. The main gate of the Seraglio, through which one enters it, is on the side of Santa Sophia, and very high, and carved and sculpted in gold letters and leaf patterns in different colors. Through it one then enters a great and spacious untiled square, at the far end of which are two big towers, guarded by a large number of doorkeepers and Janissaries, who arm themselves here because they are not allowed to enter the court of the Great Lord of the Seraglio before dismounting and disarming; from here one walks into another courtyard, very large, where the Bassas [pashas] hold audiences three times a*

week. In this place no one dares even to cough or spit in order to avoid making noise, so that however great the throng of people, the silence is greater still.

It is impossible to say or imagine how very rich and more than beautiful the clothing of this Great Lord is. As far as color is concerned, he appears now in one, now in another. Still, I will say what he usually wears: a dulimano *[loose formal overgown] of gold and a* sottana *of velvet, in whatever color he prefers. He wears many* broccatelli *and other kinds of silk, such as* zendado, *and very often white satin woven with silver. The sleeves of all his gowns are made of the same fabric as the body of the gown. On his head he always wears a turban of very beautiful* sessa, *and when he goes out, he wears two feathers in it, one on each side, laden with pearls and jewels. He wears buttons of heavy gold and adamant. He wears short boots and always rides a horse equipped with a rein and bridle, as suits a man of his stature.*

Text on page 430

A MUSTI

A Turkish Musti is similar to a Patriarch for the Christians. He is the man who administers and controls all spiritual matters, especially Turkish monks and above all those of Constantinople. He always wears green moiré ciambellotto, *though sometimes it is white. He wears a turban much larger than any other, but with a low* corno *[baton around which the turban is wound]. As far as we can tell, these men are alike in age, and they have wives and children.*

Text on page 431

AN AGA,
the General of the Janissaries

his title belongs to the General of the soldiers, and particularly of the Janissaries. They are assigned this post by the Lord, usually at an age between thirty-six and forty. They are very highly esteemed. Their wages are a hundred aspri *per day and six thousand ducats for each of them per year. An Aga receives clothing five times a year, of cloth of gold and silk. Every Aga also has a food allowance, for himself and his entire family. And so that one man alone does not command the Janissaries, he has a lieutenant to help him, called a Chechaia, that is, an overseer, who is paid two hundred* aspri *per day, in addition to thirty thousand* aspri *in yearly salary. For greater magnificence, he also is attended by four* Giannizzeropegi, *meaning chancellors or scribes, who are paid a hundred* aspri *a day. But they have no official form of dress. This Aga has three to four hundred slaves in his service, and he is a person of such high rank that he often becomes a brother-in-law or son-in-law to the Great Lord. Twice a week he holds open court, and on those days he is required to give a meal to the Janissaries, including bread, rice, mutton, water, and wood. And every time the Lord leaves his quarters or goes to the mosque, the Aga rides alone behind him at the head of a squadron of Janissaries; his horse is richly caparisoned. He wears brocade, velvet, satin or other fabrics, trimmed with gold. His buttons are of heavy gold, and he wears his overgarment open at times and closed at others. He wears whatever colors he likes. On his feet and legs he wears short boots, red, yellow or* pavonazzo. *His turban is large, like that of the Great Lord, with a* corno *of* cremesino *velvet and trimmed with one or two very valuable feathers.*

Text on page 432

BALUCHI BASSI
[Great Pashas] of the Janissaries

If nature did not maintain a firm and stable order in her creations, who can doubt that the world would be full of confusion? So we find, not only in our own country and all other populations but also among the Turks, military leaders below the rank of general and colonel given different titles. These serve as the hands and the eyes of the Lord from one rank to the next, all the way up to the Great Lord. And since we speak here of the government of the Turks, under the General of the Janissaries there are captains of a thousand Janissaries each, called Baluchi Bassi. They are paid 100 aspri *a day and supplied with a horse. They wear particular hats, some rather like those of the Solacchi or like those of the Janissaries, but broader at the top. They wear silk, satin,* damasco, *and red and green* ormesino, *but in dark shades. In the winter they wear the finest furs of every kind, such as lynx, sable, and marten, with gold buttons, short boots, and colored shoes in the Turkish style, depending on whether they are riding or not. These men number three or four hundred; their duties include accompanying the Great Lord into the countryside or to the mosque; when they do, they ride in a beautiful marching order, grandly seated on their horses in front of their squadron of Janissaries, carrying a small lance and, attached to their saddle pommels, a small round shield and a* busdegnano *or iron-clad mace. They make such an impressive show that whoever sees them from a distance in this formation would estimate that four hundred of them were a thousand of our horsemen, because of the large standing feathers they wear on their heads. Sometimes, instead of these plumes, they wear one white feather. When these Baluchi Bassi are old and no longer fit for combat, they are appointed guards of castles and fortresses and paid as they were before.*

Text on page 433

CADIL ESCHIER

There are two Cadils Eschiers, great doctors of law and the heads of the Turkish legal system. One oversees the laws in Greece and the other those in Anatolia.[6] *They are admired for their religion, as the metropolitans are among the Greeks in their church, and among the Christians, the Patriarchs of the Roman Church; and similarly, as legal judges, they resemble the Chancellors and presiding judges in France. They rise to this rank by being chosen from among the leading and most learned men of law. Both are taken from the pool of men considered so learned in the law that it is thought no one knows more than they do. They are of a mature age, rich in knowledge and judgment. As a result, the status of these Cadils Eschiers is very high and honorable. They usually follow the court, which they call the Porte, and in honor and reverence they take precedence over the Bassas, although they have less authority. They enforce the law, and with the cooperation of the Bassas they hear testimony from the Cadis, who are the judges of the provinces. They review the sentences imposed by the Cadis of the provinces under their jurisdiction, that is, of Greece and Anatolia, which make up the true Turkey. Their pay for administering the Church and the law is about seven thousand ducats a year, not including extra pay. They each have two or three hundred slaves to maintain and serve them, and in addition, at the expense of the Lord, they are assigned and provided with ten secretaries and two Murluc Bassas, who oversee the management of their horses. They wear* ciambellotto, *satin, and* damasco, *but in subdued and modest colors such as* berrettino, *brown, and* pavonazzo. *The sleeves of their* casacche *are very long and narrow. Their turbans, or* Dulipani, *are large, like those of the Musti—that is, of an amazing height and thickness, with a point in the middle that they call a* Mogevisi, *usually lower than those others wear. And if they occasionally wear the color green, they wear it in a dark shade, out of respect for the descendants of Mohammed, who wear light green. They usually ride mules or geldings, with a crupper of* porpora *wool trimmed all the way around.*

A HIGH-RANKING TURK at Home

In the same way that among many plants and flowers, one is more highly esteemed than another, so too among men in a republic, though we are all of the same species, one, through some accident of fortune, has a higher status than many others. Coming specifically to the Turks, I say that they do not all have the same rank or status, but there are distinctions of all kinds among them, including not only what they wear but also how they live. Turks of high status (as is also the case with us) live in large and very beautiful houses, but white and simple, without much decoration. They use few chests, but rather two or three rods on which they hang their clothes. For sitting, they use neither benches nor chairs as we do, but spread out a fine mat from Alexandria, and on top of that they set a fine carpet, and on top of this a large cushion of velvet or gold, and on top of all this they sit down; however many people there are, there are an equal number of cushions. When they eat, they cover the table with ox skins or raw deerskin with the hair still on, in a round shape, four or five palms wide, around which are sewn many iron rings, so that certain straps, running through the rings, open and close the leather like a purse; after they have eaten, they hang it from a hook. And since we are on this topic, let me say a few words about what they eat. Their diet is totally different from ours, for it is more frugal, spare and coarse, without many condiments or seasonings, that is, sauces or gravies. They eat a great deal of meat; their greatest delicacy are sheep's feet, sold in many shops in Constantinople. They prefer roast to boiled meat, and they roast it in this way: they take a big iron pot, as large as a cauldron, and at the bottom they put hot coals, and on top they set the meat, which they roast by the heat of the charcoal—which cannot be good for them or well flavored. As to their drink, they usually drink water, though they have other man-made beverages; even though wine is prohibited to them, they gulp it down anyway, especially when someone else is paying for it.

Text on page 436

HOW THE TURKS RIDE HORSEBACK
in the Rain

Because the Turks pay great attention to cleanliness, when they are on horseback and it rains, they are very careful not to get wet or dirty. So on top of their turbans, which they wear with great elegance, they wear a certain kind of hood, usually of red felt, pleated in such a way that when it is opened, it looks like an umbrella. On these occasions, on top of their overgarment they wear another garment of coarse wool, which they call felt, which protects not only their clothing but also their bodies from any kind of rain, no matter how heavy.

Text on page 437

GATEKEEPERS OF THE TURKISH LORD,
Called Capuges

Certain men who belong to the army of Janissaries are stationed at the gates of the Lord of the Turks; they are called Capuges. Depending on how they have conducted themselves, once they are no longer fit for war because of age or some other disability, they are assigned a salary and made guardians or gatekeepers of the Lord's Seraglio. They are highly respected, so no one can enter any place in this Seraglio without their knowledge, and their rank rises the more closely they are stationed to the rooms of the Great Lord. They wear the same clothing as the Janissaries, that is, a felt hat, but without the metal sheath and with no feather. They stand at the gates with a red staff in their hands. They wear fine wool, and, underneath, satins of every kind and velvets and also brocades, according to the rank they hold, resembling the noblest Turks. Most of them are mature in years. They receive many presents from those who enter this Seraglio; such gifts provide them with very good incomes.

Text on page 438

A PEICH,
or Staff-bearer of the Sultan

The Lord has forty staff-bearers, usually Persians by birth, called Peich *and* Peiudur *in their language. They receive a salary of eight to ten* aspri *a day, and they are given clothes twice a year, of satin or woven in various colors, but in a pleasant, short style; their overgarment in front has a round, half-length skirt, knee-length in back, and under this they wear a* camicia *and stockings of thin silk. On their heads they wear a cap of thin silver gilt, which they call a* siuf, *and in front a sheath of the same metal, embellished with fine stones, though some of them are false. At the top of their cap, some wear a plume, along with small colored feathers of various birds. They wear a wide sash of striped silk that they call a* Chochiach, *long enough to wrap three times around their waist. Attached to this they wear a beautiful dagger called a* Beciach, *decorated with ivory and fish bones. They are very adept at running; indeed, it is said they give themselves stitches in their sides. They go leaping ahead of the Lord, running non-stop on the soles of their feet without pausing, and as long as the route is level, keeping their eyes on him as they run backward, continually shouting, "Maù Deicherim," or "God keep his Lordship in long-lasting power!" The Lord also employs these men for more important matters, for they carry letters with great speed; they go around shouting "Sauli! Sauli!" that is, "Make way! Make way!" and leap among the people like deer. They move so quickly that they match the trot of a good horse. In one hand they carry an axe that they call an* Angiach *and in the other hand a handkerchief full of white sugar.*

386

Text on page 439

JANISSARY SOLDIER

he Janissaries are usually taken from the hands of their fathers and mothers and then persuaded by caresses and lures to forget their own faith and take up the false teaching of the Mohammedans. There are a great number of them, sometimes as many as twelve or fourteen thousand, and they are the ones who have given the Lord his stupendous victories. Most of them carry a scimitar, a dagger, and a small axe, hanging from their belt. They also carry rather long muskets, and they use them very skillfully. Others use half-length pikes. To seem more ferocious, they let moustaches grow on their upper lips, shaving off the rest of their beard entirely. Twice a year they are given clothes of turquoise wool; it is their privilege to wear a high cap of white felt on their heads rather than a helmet; they call this a zarcola, *and it is decorated in front with a garland of spun gold lined with silver gilt, rising at their foreheads and enriched with rubies, turquoises and other fine, valuable stones. At the very top they place a feather, which they wear constantly as a mark of distinction recording some heroic deed in war, so that not everyone can wear it. They march in divisions of tens, hundreds and thousands; every ten Janissaries going into battle have a tent and a Bedouin to attend to it, who serves all ten men. They also have Great Pashas, captains of a hundred men, and a Cechaia or Protegero, who is the leader of a thousand men or the lieutenant of the leader of them all; and then the Aga or captain. All these leaders and captains and corporals ride on horseback, and they dress differently from the Janissaries. As to their salary and provisions, some receive more and some less. But from the lowest to the highest, it never falls below or exceeds four to eight* aspri. *To increase this salary, favor is not important, but merit is. These soldiers have reached such a point that, knowing how valuable they are, they refuse to swear loyalty to the Lord unless they are first given the right to sack the possessions of Jews and Christians. Other details I will omit, for the sake of brevity.*

SOLACCHI,
Archers of the Sultan's Bodyguard

The court of the Turkish rulers is wonderful to see. Besides a great number of armed Janissaries and staff-bearers, the Sultan also keeps three hundred specially chosen archers, selected from the boldest, most skilled Janissaries, all of whom he has wear colored livery, either of white damasco *or silk. These men's garments are long in back and hitched up in front, and belted with wide, rich belts of gold and silk in the Moorish style. They also wear a high hat of white felt, with a large and very valuable plume. Their weapons include a scimitar and a gilded bow and arrow that they keep in their hands, drawn as if they are always ready to shoot; on their shoulders, they wear a quiver. When the Sultan goes to the mosque or out of his territories, they accompany him two by two, surrounding him completely. The left-handed archers walk in the group on his right, and the right-handed archers on his left, so that if on some occasion the Sultan should ever have to flee or they should need to come to his aid, they would not have to turn their backs on him. Also, when the Sultan is traveling outside his territories and needs to cross a river or body of water, they must get him across it. And if it should happen that the water comes up to their knees, they will be rewarded with fifty* aspri*; but if it should come up to their waists, then they will be given a bonus of 100, and if it comes higher still, another 100 will be given to each of them. And if the water should be deeper and faster, they will cross it on horseback. But they are rewarded with this bonus only the first time, even if they should find it very deep. Their daily pay is from 12 to 15* aspri*, and they are given new sets of clothes twice a year, as are the Janissaries. They have two leaders, called the* Solacchi Bassi*, who receive a salary of 60* aspri *per day, along with their clothing, like other captains, and they ride on horseback.*

A TURKISH WOMAN AT HOME

It seems to me that everything Turkish women do has something graceful and splendid about it. They usually dress like men, more or less richly according to their status. Married women wear certain miters (so to speak) of velvet or some other fabric with veils on top of them, arranged in such a way that one part hangs at the left and the other falls to the right, that is, behind; and when they go out, they cover their faces with this. When they are at home, they usually sit on cushions or pillows covered with silk or some other fabric; these are set on very fine carpets, more or less beautiful according to what their rank permits. On their heads they wear a gold or velvet cap with feathers. Their overgowns are luxurious, long, and open in front. They wear their hair braided down their back in a very modest way. At their necks they wear gold chains of many strands and one, larger and longer than the others, across their breast. Their overgowns are long, open down the front and buttoned down to the belt with gold or crystal buttons. There's no set color for their garments; they wear every hue except black. They wear braghesse *or trousers of* ormesino *or* sessa. *They sit barefoot, keeping their little* pianelle *near them. Their trousers are very rich, especially around the bottom, which some of them have trimmed with jewels. They tie on very fine sashes woven in the Moorish style, full of gold and marvelously lovely. They wear the sleeves of their gowns very long.*

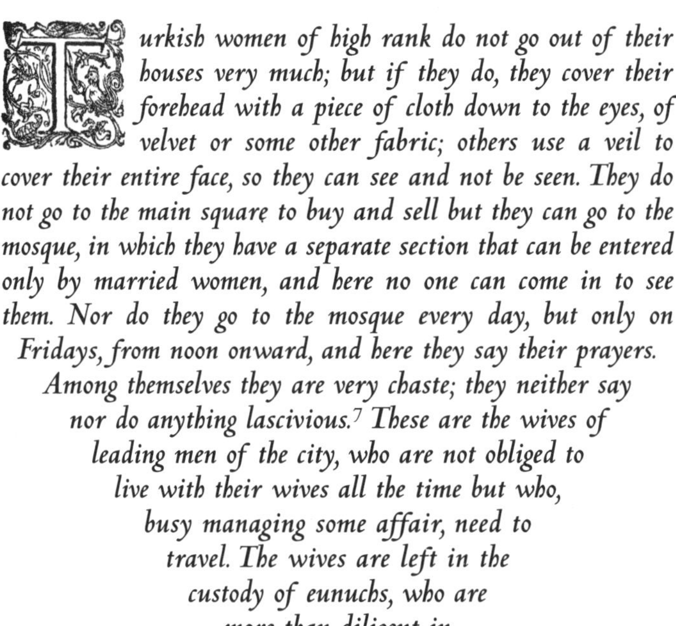

A HIGH-RANKING TURKISH WOMAN outside the House

Turkish women of high rank do not go out of their houses very much; but if they do, they cover their forehead with a piece of cloth down to the eyes, of velvet or some other fabric; others use a veil to cover their entire face, so they can see and not be seen. They do not go to the main square to buy and sell but they can go to the mosque, in which they have a separate section that can be entered only by married women, and here no one can come in to see them. Nor do they go to the mosque every day, but only on Fridays, from noon onward, and here they say their prayers. Among themselves they are very chaste; they neither say nor do anything lascivious.[7] *These are the wives of leading men of the city, who are not obliged to live with their wives all the time but who, busy managing some affair, need to travel. The wives are left in the custody of eunuchs, who are more than diligent in their duties.*

A TURKISH BRIDE

Turkish men may have several wives, but one is the principal wife, with whom they usually sleep on Fridays, the day of their religious celebration. When this woman goes to be married, she is accompanied to the house of her husband or to the mosque in this fashion, and when she travels through the city to some amusement, this form is observed. She rides a well-caparisoned horse under a baldachin carried by four servants, with curtains around it that cover her down to her knees, so such brides can see other people but cannot be seen themselves. But even though these brides proceed in so concealed a way, they wear the most beautiful clothing they can, of brocade or patterned silk, very expensive, and they wear large jeweled ornaments and many valuable pearls on their heads, necks, and breasts. A man marries his other wives with less ceremony. Should a Turk be going through the city and meet an unmarried woman who pleases him, he asks her if she will be his wife; if she answers yes, he asks her what man will give her to him. Once they have all agreed, they will go to a judge and take each other in marriage; then the husband will lead her to his house. Some husbands, to avoid quarrels that might arise among their wives, keep them in different places, but some keep them all together. They also marry without making vows and they take wives without dowries, so they are almost forced to buy them, in contrast to the Roman custom, according to which men bought a son-in-law, not a daughter-in-law. The Turkish husband is also obliged to pay his father-in-law for every piece of finery that his bride is to wear. They divorce their wives for infidelity or sterility; to do this, they seek the opinion of judges. Even so, the man must pay the woman whatever he promised her, and the sons of all the wives inherit from their father.

THE FAVORITE OF THE TURKISH SULTAN

Very lucky is the woman who, among others, receives from heaven or her own good fortune the status of being the woman most favored by the Turkish lord. This happens either because of her close consanguinity with him or the influence of the stars or her exceptional beauty. This favorite of the sultan lives in the same Seraglio as he does when he is in Constantinople—that is, in the part of the circular complex containing almost two hundred rooms, in the last of which he resides for most of the summer. In this circle or cloister, there is another Seraglio for the sultana, his wife, which is full of magnificent baths, and there is also an area where the pages live, of which there are usually at least five to six hundred, raised in the Mohammedan faith and trained for every sort of service, especially in the military arts. As to the clothing of the sultan's favorite, we must imagine that the gold and purple[8] *she wears pale by comparison to the pearls and jewels that adorn such a lady. Her* cidari *is very high, with very beautiful trim and a thin veil that falls from its peak to the ground. In her apparel she wears whatever colors she fancies.*

Now that we are on the subject, it should be noted that in the center of the city there is another old Seraglio, formerly inhabited by Mehmet II, surrounded by walls two thousand feet in circumference. These walls are very thick and two canne *[about fifteen feet] in height.*[9] *Inside them are many small houses with their own bedrooms and kitchens, where the wives or concubines of the sultan live. These normally exceed two hundred in number, the majority being daughters taken from Christian parents. They are confined to the close care of eunuchs, and each group of ten has a woman who rules over them. The Lord makes use of these women whenever he likes. If he should impregnate one of them, he immediately has her separated from the others, increases her prestige and economic status, and adds her to the number of his wives, so that, should she give birth to a boy, she can, within her rank, reach the highest level of power. Any other women who seem to be sterile the Turkish lord then marries to his Solacchi and other officials.*

393

Text on page 446

LADY
of the Seraglio

Because so many wives or concubines are chosen to serve only the Turkish lord, they are considered worthy of equal treatment in the way they live and dress. So only one style of attire will be shown here, as representative of what all these women wear. All of them receive clothing from the Lord two or three times a year, according to the season; in the nobility of their dress they demonstrate the nobility of their service to him. They wear high-necked undergowns and style their hair only by combing it and letting it fall down their back. Their caps, which match their gowns, are of velvet or satin, trimmed with gold embroidery but not very high.

Text on page 447

A TURKISH WOMAN
of Middle Rank

All Turkish women wear long gowns, as do the men, without veils or kerchiefs. Those of middle rank wear a small cap of velvet or some other fabric, from which a square veil is hung, falling to their mouths and covering almost the entire width of their face, so that they see but are not seen. Their gowns are buttoned down to the waist, and they never allow themselves to be seen by anyone outside their houses. They wear short colored boots, like men's, and over these they wear trousers of very thin white sessa or silk. And no one molests them in word or deed.

Text on page 448

BEGLIERBEI,
or Armed Men

Nothing about the Turks causes such wonder as the speed of these Beglierbei *in warfare, for they are quick to face danger and to obey their commanders, especially their Lord. They swim across deep rivers, make their way over steep mountains, and march through difficult terrain, risking their lives in obedience to him. There is no sedition or unrest among them. They endure sleeplessness, hunger and thirst exceptionally well, and in battle they emit quavering shouts rather than any other cry. At night they maintain such silence in their quarters that, if need be, they would rather let prisoners escape than make any noise in the camp. It is claimed that they fight with greater military strategy than any other nation. So it is no wonder that the empire and rule of the Turks increases every day, and it can truthfully be said that this nation has been undefeated for almost two hundred years. No soldier rides armed but has his weapons and baggage carried behind him. Instead of banners they carry lances with variously colored threads hanging from them, which identify the captains. To stir up their courage for battle, they use drums and flutes. In every religious gathering, they pray for the soldiers, especially those who have died in battle. They write down the noble deeds of their heroes. No one, however worthy, expects to be seated on a chair; but with a sort of skirt that they make out of their garments, they sit on the ground like children.*

Text on page 449

BEGLIERBEI
and Armed Men

It seems appropriate to me here to offer a brief commentary on the good government of the Great Turk, not so much in the military (for I have already described that) but rather in the civil context. Let it be known, then, that all his realms are divided into two nations, one called Natolia and the other Romania. Natolia is the name of the provinces beyond the Hellespont toward the east, such as Bythnia, Asia Minor, Cicilia, Phrygia, Galatia, Pansilia, Cappadocia, Paphlagonia, and Caria, together with certain islands including Polia, Zonia, Lesbos, and Smyrna. In Natolia the following languages are spoken: Greek, Italian, Scythian, Armenian, Wallachian, Ruthenian. In this region are thirteen cities with Turkish Governors, whose names I will omit for the sake of brevity. Romania, the other nation, includes Dacia or Serbia, Thrace, Dardania, Achaea, Morea, Arcanania, Macedonia, Epirus, Russia, and part of Slavonia. In these regions live twenty-five Presidents, and also in the most notable cities, of which there are many. All these Presidents are ruled over by two princes, one in Asia or Natolia, the other in Europe, that is, Romania, whom they call a Bassa *or* Beglierbei, *and these, after the emperor, have the greatest power. They also have a large number of soldiers, on horseback or on foot, always ready when needed. The* Beglierbei *are held in the highest esteem, because immediately after the Aga, the head of the Janissaries, leaves office, he is made a* Beglierbeo *or a naval Commander. After these are only two men, shown here in two prints, one after the other. The second figure placed here is the* Beglierbeo *of Natolia; he, too, is a person of great power and most excellent judgment, who goes armed, as we see here, in white armor; and their horses, too, are armed in white. Such men were called* cataphracts *[mail-wearing soldiers] by the Romans.*

Text on page 450

AZAPPI,
or Galley Archers

It has always been the custom among the Turks to train as well as possible in the use of the bow. So they arm their galleys with many Azappi. *These are soldiers who, as long as they serve, are paid a salary of five* aspri *per day. They wear a short* dulimano, *knee-length, in whatever color they like, open in front up to the belt to allow greater freedom of movement. Their sleeves are slightly more than elbow-length. They attach a scimitar and a quiver of arrows to a strap that hangs from their neck to their hip, and, as can be seen here, they also wear a bow. On their heads they wear a small cap in the same color as the* dulimano, *in felt or some other fabric, and trousers and shoes in the Turkish style.*

Text on page 451

IOPEGI,
or Bombadiers

here is little or no difference between the Bombadiers and the Azappi. They receive the same salary. They wear whatever color they choose, though to distinguish themselves from the Azappi, they wear a strange headdress on their heads, usually in red.

Text on page 452

SLAVES AND PAGES
of the Sultan

In the Seraglio where the wife of the Great Lord lives (as I have already described) are found magnificent and sumptuous baths, and also a very large number of children who have been taken or offered and handed over as payment for taxes to the Great Turk, called pages by us and by them. In any case, they are all slaves. They are always ready to serve and to carry out their master's will. In this place they are raised, fed and educated in the law of Mohammed, and also in horseback riding, archery, the handling of weapons, and other military and civil duties. Taken all together, they range from the ages of eight to twenty; their number, as has been said before, is usually five or six hundred. Their style of dress is unusual and splendid, for their gowns are floor-length. They carry no weapons, and on their heads they wear a small cap of velvet or light gold or silver cloth, turned up in front, with a single feather.

Text on page 453

TURKISH STRONGMAN,
called Roncassi

In Turkey, as in other nations, can be found men who are truly brave and high-spirited, and others who try to seem so but who are really cowards. These, however, are called strongmen among the Turks. In these regions, they follow behind the Bassas, Sanghiacchi, *and* Beglierbei *and are employed by them; and because they make a career, in a manner of speaking, of being warriors, they are called* Dellì, *which in Turkish means crazy or daring; for without provocation or any just cause—indeed, for no reason whatsoever—they challenge anyone to compete with lances on horseback or on foot and in single combat. The weapons of such men are scimitars and daggers, and in their hands they carry sharpened hatchets or hammers on one side, and on the other many pointed weapons. On their heads they wear these two wings or many feathers to show that they are mad, fierce, and impulsive. And no one is allowed to wear wings of this kind except a man who has done something on foot or horseback to make himself famous and distinguished. So such wings and feathers are highly valued, as the ornament of a valiant cavalier. Their garments are short and closely fitted, suited to combat, and more or less valuable according to how much their masters give them. They wear doublets and leggings in the Turkish style, and short boots in yellow, red and turquoise or studded leather in their particular style. Their weapons are of iron in the manner of other nations, especially when they ride horseback; and they behave in a bold, arrogant way, as if wanting to warn everyone to flee and beware of their terrible rage.*

Text on page 454

STRONGMAN
of the Cassi

This is another sort of strongman, but of a nobler kind, for they do not follow anyone, however elevated, for the sake of gain, but they stand upon their own reputations and make great efforts to win esteem. The style of dress shown here, on top and bottom, is strong, soldierly, and efficient. They also wear hobnailed boots, so that if, in combat, they need to flee from the enemy, they can run easily. They cut into a small piece of the flesh at their temple to create a calloused slit into which they put feathers, inserted between the skin and the toughened flesh. They wear little armor, but they do wear a small cap or round helmet and carry a hammer in their hand or a scimitar. And they act in so bold a manner that they convince people that even their shadow can kill.

Text on page 455

SLAVES
of the Bassas

After being captured at sea or on land by the Turks and being subjected to them, great numbers of people are made the slaves of the officers of the Great Turk and his Bassas, which he has in the hundreds. These send their slaves out to perform various tasks, both for their own affairs and as mercenaries; and in the evening, when they return from their work, these unfortunate slaves have to give whatever they have earned during the day to their masters. They live on bread and water. Their garments are of grigio *and other rough, cheap fabrics. On their heads they wear small caps of finely pleated felt. They wear shoes and stockings in the Turkish style and many also go barefoot. Every time the Great Lord needs soldiers, the masters set them to row in the galleys and they are paid five* aspri *a day or a thousand for the entire voyage (which in our terms would be twenty* scudi*), and these voyages last for five or six months. They lead a very strange life; and their dress is shown here.*

Text on page 456

AGIAMOGLIANI

here are two different manners and ways in which many Christian regions become subject to the Great Turk, with enormous misery and ill fortune. The first is that their own sons are taken by force and given to certain Commissioners, who, once taken, up to the number of three per father, present them to certain higher officials, who choose the best-looking among them and put them into the Seraglio; there they are educated and brought up in the law of Mohammed, trained in military arts, and assigned to masters of fencing, riding, reading, and other skills. Those who are found to be completely unfit for military service and lacking in intelligence are set to learn some other skill suitable to their capabilities, and those who are incapable of any skill are set to carrying water and wood to state offices and to keeping the Seraglio clean. Many of them are made into gardeners or cooks or the servants of Janissaries, Spachi *or other Captains. This is the first way Christians enter into the affliction of slavery.*

The second way is that some Christian regions and lands are conquered by the Turks but given certain privileges and exempted from this tyrannical requirement of giving their children to the Turk. But the people are so oppressed and overwhelmed by taxes and unbearable demands that finally, unable to make inflated, impossible payments, they resolve to hand over their children in order to suffer less themselves. Many of these children, as soon as they become slaves as previously described, receive clothing of light blue fabric twice a year; on their heads they wear a high, yellow cap made in the shape of a loaf of sugar. They receive two or three aspri *a day in salary and they are placed and set under the control of a Captain who is paid thirty* aspri *a day himself, and outfitted by the Lord. These Agiamogliani are clothed as previously shown, but the coarser ones are sent into Natolia or Asia Minor to look after animals and work the land. And they do this in order that they should learn the Turkish language. They spend four years there, until other unfortunates are sent there. Accustomed to such hard work, they are sent to Constantinople and given over to the Aga of the Agiamogliani or Janissaries, who assigns and distributes them to serve these Janissaries, or, seeing that they are unfit for war, teaches them (as I have said) some trade.*

The offspring of these people are so hostile to Christians that they have no worse enemy than this breed. They wear coarse fabric in turquoise or white and on their heads a small cap, usually in red.

CLOTHING OF A TURKISH PIRATE

The behavior of the Turkish pirate is tyrannical, rapacious and violent. And many histories say in particular that this overwhelming army of pirates had its beginning at the time of Alexander the Great in the East as follows: at the time that Rome reigned supreme, there was an uprising among the Caramanian people,[10] *formerly called the Cilicians, who lived around the Sea of Marmara, and they began to live on the water and became expert in sailing; and in order to obtain what they needed, they began to prey on, rob, and murder people who had done them no harm. And realizing what benefits the attacks they made brought them, many of them became pirates and corsairs on the Mediterranean, and providing themselves with brigs, light galleys or* groppi *(small sail-powered transport vessels),*[11] *they occupied many sea coasts in order to have the easiest access to evildoing. They caused so much damage, altogether, that people could no longer cross the sea in safety, so ports were shut down, along with exchanges of food and other vital supplies needed by many regions of Italy. So the great Roman Republic began to experience every kind of shortage and scarcity. Needing provisions, they commissioned Pompey*[12] *to oppose the pirates with a naval fleet. He undertook this task, and, as a valiant captain, he defeated them in under forty days, took control over them and sent them to live in places far from the sea; on the seacoasts and cities and villages near them, he established new colonies.*

Few words are needed to describe their clothing. It is comfortable and well suited to working on board ships. As far as the overgarment goes, it resembles that of the Turks, but it has a wide bavero *and long, full sleeves. Their caps are of red wool and so is most of their overgarment. Their stockings are of various colors, but mostly made of wool. Then they wear a* burricchetto, *belted with a striped sash over their* camicia, *which hangs outside their* bracche *like a pleated skirt or apron and has wide, hanging sleeves of very thin linen. The rest of their attire is similar to the Turks', though different sorts of men wear this style of dress. But it is usually worn by people who live by the sea, and also by prosperous men and other soldiers.*

Text on page 459

A TURKISH SLAVE

Not all the Turks have slaves, but those who need service discuss the price of certain slaves and agree on a price, as we do ourselves. Their clothing is humble, short, and fit to work in. They wear stockings of linen or coarse wool, more often white than any other color, but all in one piece and without feet, and shoes in the Turkish style. They wear their camicie *outside their* bracche. *They wear colored shoes and go around in their* camicia *sleeves and in* burricchi *longer in the back than the front, but of coarse wool, like a striped pilgrim's cloak. They wrap their heads in coarse white* velo, *and usually buy their own food and carry it in colored, striped* fazzuoli. *They wear hobnailed shoes, similar to those worn by others, as we said earlier.*

Text on page 460

A TURKISH WOMAN

We have already seen, in our previous descriptions of clothing, much of the attire worn by Turkish women, but I thought I should add this figure as an example of how lovely it can be. In general it can be said that all the women of these regions are very modest and respectable as far as showing their hair is concerned. This woman, whom I will describe first, wears on her head a fazzoletto of silk, in various weaves and colors, on top of which she puts a small cap, rather high, of velvet, satin, cloth of gold or silver, without any trim. As to their clothing, I have said that Turkish women usually dress as men do, except for their heads and feet. But they dress in a close-fitting and elegant way in gold and silk, as far as is possible, though they still wear a certain form of dark-colored bodice rather than any other, leaving it open enough at the breast to show a string of pearls, which, hanging from the neck, has a beautiful jewel sumptuously attached to it, resting on the breast. They wear silk or very fine cotton sashes, woven in the Moorish style, and long sleeves in the style of a jacket but actually belonging to their sottane. They wear braghesse of sessa and stockings of fine wool without feet, and many wear pearls and other jewels down at their edges. They wear pianelle with narrow strips of red or turquoise velvet, full of jewels, and most of their feet show, white, bare and elegant.

But since we are speaking of married women, I will add, as further information, that the Turks can legally have four wives, whom they can marry with no obstacle or consent from relatives except their mothers and sisters. They choose as many as they like, as long as they can support them. Whatever happens, the children of all these wives inherit equal shares of their fathers' goods, with only one difference: two daughters inherit the portion of one son. For the sake of maintaining peace among them, the men do not keep all these wives in one house, or, to avoid the contention that would always arise among them, even in the same city. The husbands can divorce and take them back three times, and those who have been repudiated can live with whatever new husband takes them. To conclude, I say that when women leave the house, they cover their faces with a veil, and both men and women dress in long clothing, and they do this so that when they answer a call of nature, they do not reveal their private parts, and what they are doing cannot be seen. As far as possible in the act of elimination, out of respect they avoid turning their faces toward the south, not wanting to face in the direction to which they pray. The men urinate crouching down like women, so whoever might urinate standing up would be considered crazy and heretical. They are prohibited by their law from drinking wine, saying that it is the root of all sin and uncleanliness; but they eat grapes and drink their juice. They do not eat meat cooked in its own blood, or pork, or animals they have not killed themselves.

A DECEASED TURK

When a Turk dies, they wash his body and dress it in clean clothes. Then they usually carry him outside the city walls, thinking it improper to bury him in a mosque. Monks carrying lighted candles precede the body, followed by priests singing all the way to the burial site. If the dead man is poor, they collect money in the square, and with these offerings, they pay the priests for their work. The friends of the deceased often return to his grave, laying bread, fish, meat, cheese, eggs, and milk on it for the soul of whoever is buried underneath it; this meal, following ancient custom, is eaten by poor people, ants, and birds, for they say that it is pleasing to God to do good as much to the poor as to birds. So there are many people there, who, seeing bird sellers keeping birds in cages, pay them for them and then, setting them free, let them fly away; and others, for the same reason, give bread to fish, in order to please God.

SEICHIR,
or Holy Men

Among the Turks there are so many religions that it would take much too long to discuss them all. They have many monks who, in the name of piety, live in the woods and deserts, fleeing human contact. Among these, some, being very poor, go almost naked, hardly clothing their private parts and living on alms given to them by Turks and Christians. Some rarely go out in public but confine themselves to temples, near which they have small huts; they wear neither shoes nor clothing but cover only their heads with a canvas shirt, praying for days to God to reveal His secrets to them. These men have won such respect that the King of the Turks, when he goes to war, asks for their advice. The result of so many religions is that everyone follows the one he likes. Their priests are hardly different from laymen; they do not need much knowledge of doctrine as long as they know how to read the Qur'an, and those who know how to interpret the text are considered very learned because it is written not in Turkish but in Arabic, by Mohammed; indeed, they believe it is a grave crime that the text should ever be translated into another language. In return for their services, these holy men receive a certain stipend from the King of the Turks; they have wives and dress as secular men do; if by chance their wages are not sufficient to support their many children, they take up a craft or perform some business suitable for free men. They are always exempt and freed from any tax and from whatever other debt or tribute that the common people have to pay. They wear a toga of coarse wool, white or turquoise, slightly less than ankle-length, with rather

wide sleeves, high-necked, fairly narrow, open in the front and unbelted. They wear long stockings without feet, in the Turkish manner, and also shoes in the Turkish style. As a sign of their profession they carry a book under their arms, and they read from it whenever a suitable occasion arises.

Text on page 464

A DERVISH

These are another kind of religious men, who live in cities and go around begging alms. They wear coarse wool cloth down to the knee, without stockings but only with shoes. On top, they wear a short, sleeveless cape made of sheepskin or thick wool, fastened at the throat and leaving their chest bare and their arms naked; altogether they are poorly dressed. They wear a leather belt with a wooden cup hanging from it, from which they eat and drink. They cover their heads with a flat cap made of turquoise or red wool.

Text on page 465

FRANCO, *OR MERCHANT*
in Constantinople

Because man is by nature inclined toward profit and commerce, to be able to support himself and supply his family with what they need, he leaves his paternal dwelling behind, depriving himself of the cherished sight of his wife, and, departing from his children and the comfort in which they live in their native country, he moves to faraway lands; and there, from the free man that he is, he becomes in a certain sense subject to others. Such men, in Constantinople and throughout the entire East, are called Franchi *[freemen], because they are not slaves. They wear long clothing, like the Turks, and a* sottana *buttoned to the waist, on top of which they wear a toga open in front, of the same length as the* sottana. *These garments are of silk or wool, depending on what they can afford. The color of this overgarment or toga is black. On their heads they usually wear a flat or rounded* berretta à tozzo, *made of silk* canevaccia *or some other coarse-grained cloth or of velvet, around which they wear a band of silk, as is done in Italy.*

Text on page 466

THE CLOTHING OF GREECE

A PATRIARCH
of Constantinople

he Roman Church formerly had the custom of creating four Patriarchs, who were to live in different places: the first in Jerusalem, the second in Antioch, the third in Alexandria, and the fourth in Constantinople. For some time, there were also two in Italy, one in Aquileia and the other in Spado; he was then moved to Venice. These Greeks still have four Patriarchs today, who, because they no longer obey the Roman papacy in all things, do more or less as they like. They live in four regions and have great power in the churches of the East. The principal among them is the one who lives in Constantinople, whom, as head, all the Christians of Greece obey as their superior, as do the people of Macedonia, Epirus, and all of Thrace, the islands of the Archipelago, and all the regions subject to the Empire of Constantinople, even as far as the Muscovites. The second Patriarch lives in Cairo and rules Egypt and Arabia. The third is in Jerusalem and commands Judea, Damascus, Beirut, and Tripoli in Syria. The fourth and last has his residence in Antioch and rules over the Greek Church of Syria. These four Patriarchs are elected by the Metropolitans of their provinces, in the same way that popes are elected by cardinals. These Patriarchs live very simply; they have no income to cover their needs except two hundred ducats a year, which are paid to them by the churches under their authority. They all dress in the same style, no different from the habit of other monks (whom they call Caloieri*), except that the patriarchs wear a large felt hat on their heads, onto which is sewn a strip of gold in the shape of a cross.*

These Patriarchs are distinguished, well-mannered, learned, and mature men, and they never wear clothing of any kind of silk but always of wool.

GREEK PRIEST

The Greeks have two kinds of priests, as do we Roman Catholic Christians: that is, priests and cloistered friars or monks. But they also have some who, living in a secular way, have wives and sometimes children and become priests afterward. Their garments are black on top and rust-colored underneath. If by chance their wives should die, they cannot marry again; if it should be discovered that they are keeping concubines or frequenting women other than their wives, they will be cast off and prevented from becoming Metropolitans. I have no other portrait of them. The Greeks also have certain others, like our friars, who preserve their virginity or life-long chastity; in their monasteries they have no feminine creature, not even hens or female dogs or other similar members of the female sex. These men usually wear coarse wool in a rust or reddish-brown color with a hood, as can be seen in the print, and others among them wear a small cap with a mane of long hair, as long as they remain virgins. Before the Metropolitans invest them as priests, they go through a two-year probation.

A GREEK FRIAR FROM BEHIND, as Further Information

Because these friars wear hoods not well known to everyone, it occurred to me to include this portrait of a back view. These men live in obedience to the Patriarch of Constantinople. Among their great number of monasteries they maintain on a mountain of Thrace called Athos (in the vernacular Monte Santo) between twenty-four and twenty-five monasteries, in which five or six thousand Caloieri live, who have fortified these monasteries extremely well against corsairs. This Mount Athos is so high that it can be seen piercing the clouds, so that many claim that when the sun strikes it with its rays, the shadow cast by this Athos reaches as far as the island of Lemnos, now called Stalimene, which is seventy thousand feet away. When King Xerxes advanced against Greece, he had the mountain cut off from the mainland and made the sea flow over this land, so that it was possible to sail all around it. These Caloieri also have other monasteries on Mount Sinai, which is located in Arabia.

GREEK HOLY WOMAN,
Similar to a Catholic Nun

*Virginity has always been highly regarded in every nation. The Romans, accordingly, seeing that the Vestal Virgins had miraculous powers because one of them filled a sieve with water as proof of her innocence and another pulled a ship into the river all by herself, firmly maintained that such virginity was dearer to God than anything else, and they held virgins in the highest esteem, as the Greeks do today, honoring and revering them in the highest degree. The first nun was created by the apostle and Evangelist Matthew when he brought a girl back to life in a city of Ethiopia and baptized the father and mother of this girl, whose name was Iphigenia. He consecrated her to God as a virgin, with others very like her, and in this way the first convent was established. The dress of these Greek holy women consists of an undergown rather than a tunic, made of black or* rovano *wool; on top of this, they wear a black mantle pulled over their head, almost floor-length. They wear a* bavero *and* soggolo*, as our nuns do, and they carry a rosary for their prayers. Some of them also have been the wives of priests or popes; they cannot remarry after the death of their husbands. They cover their heads with a thin mantle, mid-calf in length.*

A GREEK NOBLEMAN

There is no doubt that the Greek Church has split off from our Catholic Church fourteen times and rejoined it each time. Now it is full of various errors spread by Nestorius, Euticus, Maccherius, and others as time has passed.[1] *As a result of this dissent, the Greeks have been reduced to slaves and are held in contempt wherever they are. The dress of this Greek nobleman consists of a black hat in the style of the Albanians; the color of the merchants' hats is turquoise. Both their under- and overgarments are long and of the finest fabric they can afford, but usually black. They wear many buttons, especially from their belt up to their collar. These garments are cut quite narrow at the sides and they are not wide at the hem. The sleeves of their overgarments are quite full down to the elbow. They wear belts of twisted silk net in different colors, though they avoid white and yellow.*

A GREEK MERCHANT

Commerce is practiced throughout the entire world, but more or less in a particular place depending on whether the land is fertile or sterile, because sterile land makes its men industrious. And for this reason we see a great number of merchants in the most mountainous and sterile regions, such as those from Ragusa, Genoa, Bergamo, and Florence. The clothing of Greek merchants resembles that shown here. On their heads they wear a low cap of wool or silk canevaccia *and they wear full-length stockings, with shoes in our Italian style. Their over- and undergarments are long and usually of thin black wool.*

A GREEK BRIDE in Pera

Pera is a city founded by the Genoese, formerly called Galata, and in ancient times the Horn of Byzantium;[2] *it is now called Pera from a Greek word meaning "over there" because it is located on the far side of the canal, an artillery-shot away from Constantinople, and people are ferried back and forth from one city to the other in boats called* parme. *The port of Pera is one of the most beautiful that can be seen, because it has a circumference of more than five miles and the length of the delta is almost one mile and in some places, a half mile; this channel is so deep that any ship, however large, can make its way up to the banks on which the houses are built. This city of Pera is built partly on level ground and partly on the slope of a hill a little less than three miles in circumference. It is divided into three parts: in one live the native inhabitants of Pera, in another the Greeks, and in the third part the Turks, who rule there. On one side is the arsenal, containing almost a hundred arched vaults used for the maintenance of galleys. Nearby, artillery is made; some, captured in our time by the Turks in Belgrade, Rhodes, and Buda in Hungary, is displayed inland. Outside the city walls are the burial sites of the Turks and the Jews. The freemen and natives of Pera follow Roman Catholicism, in contrast to the Greeks, and these groups dislike each other because of differences in their laws. So if a Greek should marry a woman of Pera, or, on the other hand, a man from Pera should marry a Greek woman, few of them will live in harmony with each other. The clothing of a Greek bride resembles that of Venice and Florence, because their blonde hair makes a lovely sight. They wear a small hat of cloth of gold. At their necks they wear a clasped necklace made of enameled rich gold. Their gown is of* brocatello *or* velluto ad opera, *and floor-length. They have an overskirt of very fine linen that they wear belted and open in front; it is four or six fingers shorter than their gown. They wear an apron and a short collarless bodice, trimmed with gold or silk. On their shoulders they wear a veil that falls here and there under their arms and reaches their waist, and they clasp their hands underneath it; at its ends it is decorated with pearls or some other trim, according to their rank. They wear leather shoes without* pianelle, *but in very lovely colors.*

Text on page 474

A GREEK WOMAN
in Pera

Greek women in Pera usually dress in the Turkish style. They wear very splendid clothing and wherever they go they wear jewelry, and as much of it and as massive as they can. Each of them, at least if she is the wife of a merchant, wears velvet or cremesino *satin or* damasco, *and she embellishes her gowns with woven trim and buttons of gold and silver. Other women of lower status wear* taffetano *and patterned silk from Bursa,[3] and all of them wear gold chains and bracelets set with fine stones. The daughters and newly wedded women cover their heads with a round cap of* cremesino *satin or patterned brocade, around which they wrap a circlet of silk and gold two fingers in width, full of fine pearls. Their* camicie *are made of colored taffeta striped with gold, like those of Turkish women. They cover their faces with make-up to look beautiful, a very immodest style. Walking through the city, they wear a large, thin white veil, which hangs down their backs to mid-thigh; widows wear a yellow veil. Their overgown is of silk, short and open in front. Their* sottana *is a gown of brocade or wool,* pavonazzo *in color; under their veil, they wear a small, round colored cap, of silk trimmed with gold; and they encircle their necks with gold.*

Text on page 475

A GREEK WOMAN
in the Venetian Republic

In the same way that the Jews are scattered far and wide because they crucified Christ, so too are the Greeks, because they don't obey His Vicar, the Roman pope; so neither one people nor the other rules in any region. A Greek woman living in Venetian territory dresses in the Venetian style and almost entirely in black, except that they wear a white fazzuolo *on their heads and shoulders. In their ornaments they imitate Venetian women; and they are shrewd and well informed.*

423

Text on page 476

MEN OF SFAKIA,
on the Island of Candia

The island of Candia was called Crete in ancient times, and the story is that it contained a hundred cities; its people long ago were commended for their shrewdness, so that Cretan shrewdness became proverbial. The country is extremely fertile and especially abundant in rich wines, which are admired everywhere. On this island, now owned by the most Serene Republic of Venice, is a region called Sfakia. Because it is so mountainous, it cannot produce wheat or wine, but milk is very plentiful because of its excellent pastures; it is inhabited by a large number of people, who, like the place in which they are born, are very rough and wild—in fact, practically unconquerable. Nonetheless, they boast of being descended from the Romans, who formerly set up a colony on this island. This group of people, in winter as in summer, dress in black leather, of which they make a garment divided into two sections, one in front and one in back, tying it over their shoulders and under their arms with laces made from the same leather. With these laces they also tie on a pair of leggings, or rather boots, of the same leather, which they wear fitted very tightly to their legs. Their camicie are gathered at the neck and allowed to hang down in front and behind, and the only sleeves they wear are those of these camicie, although they also wear a piece of toughened leather on their left arm to protect themselves against the drawstring of their bows. They wear their hair long and on top a black cap of very coarse wool, not very large. And because they are rough and fierce, like the countryside that produces them, most of the time they sleep in their clothes and rarely take them off. They are always armed with a scimitar and a small dagger of an ancient style, with a belt that is attached at their side and crosses over their shoulder to the hip. From this belt, both behind and in front, hangs a quiver which is also made of black leather and contains arrows, of which they always hold one or two, along with their bow. All this is shown in the present image. They all turn out to be very expert archers and they are divided into two factions, one called the Pateri and the other the Sfachiotti, even though the name "Sfachiotti" is attributed to all the people who live in the region of this name. All the other peasants of Candia dress in white wool cloth, in the style of the porters of Venice, with a sailor's hat and boots on their legs, which they wear at every time of year. In discussing the clothing of Greece, I wanted to mention among those of Candia only the attire of this rough group of people, because noblemen and everyone who lives in the cities of this realm dress as the Venetians do, though some follow the styles of other parts of Italy. Because these have already been mentioned, this is not the place to repeat out of context what can be read in its proper place.

WOMEN OF SFAKIA
and Peasant Women of Candia

*his island of Candia is situated in a climate that suffers no severe cold, so its people never have to endure it; for this reason most of the time the common people, men and women, wear very lightweight clothing. Most of the peasant women, even in winter, go barefoot in their villages without thinking twice about it. As to the rest of their bodies, the women of Sfakia and all the other peasant women of this island dress in white linen or cotton. The dress of some of them includes a* casso, *or stiff bodice in the Venetian style, with woolen sleeves, red or some other color. When they want to cover their legs, they wear stockings of the same color, made of lightweight* rascia. *They wear shoes of black or red needle-worked leather, and they cover their heads with a veil of very light-colored linen, trimmed with needlework, wrapping it around their heads in a way that allows some of the fabric to hang down onto their shoulders. Those most blessed with the gifts of fortune wear two or more hoop earrings of gold, very large, and as a belt they tie on an artfully made silver chain, which hangs down in front of them with two or three pear-shaped chimes or silver bells; on their fingers they usually wear no more than one or two rings. But when, at the death of some relative, they need to show that they are in mourning or grief, they wear this head veil in a dark yellow color for some time; and when they are widowed they wear a gown and head-covering entirely of black. They do not stop wearing this attire until they marry again.*

A NOBLE GIRL
of Macedonia

In ancient times Macedonia had two west-facing cities among other celebrated and noble ones; one of these was Durazzo and the other Apollonia, which was ruled by George Scanderbeg,[4] who spent his life fighting against the Turks and was so valiant that he maintained the Christian faith by himself in that province. At first Macedonia was called Emathia and at its beginning it was a small country, but its kings expanded it so much through the bravery of their armies that it eventually increased to one hundred fifty groups of people. This area stretches from the Aegean to the Adriatic Sea; at the south it includes Thessaly and Magnesia, as far as the mountains of Peonia. It had two great kings among others, King Philip and his son Alexander, who conquered Greece and Thrace and went as far as the Indies.

The clothing of unmarried Macedonian girls has something in common with the clothing of many different peoples. But on their heads they wear a headdress in the shape of a box, made of thin, light woods, covered with a small gold cloth with many beautifully set jewels on it, forming the shape of a crown at the top. At the back it includes a veil of striped silk, from which only one end hangs down; the rest is contained in a circlet of heavy gold, jeweled all over, and it falls down behind the shoulders, along with several braids of hair, one of which dangles near the temple, close to the ear. They adorn their necks and breast with very beautiful, varied ornaments. Their faces are beautiful and pleasant, and over them they wear veils of thin, rich silk that they let fall down to their waists. Their undergarment is of satin or a similar fabric, with a high, ornate bodice, over which they wear a second gown of white ormesino *in the style of a* rocchetto*, long and open down to the middle of the leg. They tie on a very beautiful sash of lovely striped silk.*

Text on page 480

A MARRIED WOMAN of Macedonia

The married women of Macedonia wear a headdress like a turban, made of sessa *or other striped fabric; and on top of this, they wear a thin veil that covers their forehead and, falling past their temples, wraps around their throat up to the chin. They wear an overgown without a bodice, shaped like a* camicia, *with full sleeves. They wear clothing in different colors. Their overgown is of fine wool, in turquoise or some other color, and many of them wear it in black. They live in the Turkish manner, and on their feet they wear a kind of* zoccoli, *finely painted or gilded with ground gold. They wear gold jewelry and use make-up to make themselves beautiful.*

Text on page 481

A BRIDE
of Thessalonia

*his is a densely populated city, beautifully sited and endowed with pleasant women who are very friendly to foreigners; it is only slightly smaller than Constantinople, and it is fortified with strong walls, deep banks and high buildings. The Emperor Theodosius, angered at his citizens, who had killed his judges, had almost a thousand of them put to death; as a result, he was excommunicated from the Church by Saint Ambrose; and wanting to be reconciled to God, he undertook the public penance imposed upon him.*[5] *Then through hereditary succession, the city came under the power of Andronicus. He, hating his brother Giovanni, who had already taken possession of the realm, handed it over to the Venetians, from whom this Andronicus then took it back, after conquering all Macedonia as far as the mountains of Peonia. Then the city came under the dominion of the Turks, in which it remains today, inhabited by Christians, Jews, and Turks, but by Jews in the majority, who have eight synagogues there. The Jews wear a yellow veil on their heads, the Christians a light blue one, and the Turks a white one. The women of this city wear a lot of make-up and rich jewelry on their ears. They wear a* sottana *of turquoise velvet, all in one piece without a bodice and quite long and full, with something of a train. This gown is gathered into pleats or folds and forms a bodice; above their hips they wear a sash of silk striped with gold, which they tie very loosely so that it gives an elegant shape to the body. They wear a long mantle of matching or white silk, which has a small, round* bavero *of* velluto ad opera, *richly trimmed with gold and jewels, which they use to cover their shoulders and breast, fastening it in the middle with a gold jewel of great value. Their sleeves are narrow but quite long, almost covering their hands. But brides, as is usual in most parts of the world, wear more ornaments than other women, as can be seen in the figure shown here in the ornaments of the headdress, which is made first of thin copper or lightweight felt and then covered with a veil of gold and silk, very beautifully needle-worked and trimmed with many different ornaments.*

LADY OF MYTILENE

This city gives its name to the whole island, which is sixty miles in circumference. From this island came: Pittacus, one of the seven wise men of Greece; the poet Alcaeus and his brother Antimenides, a very valiant man of arms; Theophrastus and Phanius, Peripatetic philosophers and relatives of Aristotle; Adonis, an excellent harp player; Sappho, a woman very learned in poetry, who was called the Tenth Muse and numbered among lyric poets; and, in our days, two of the most fortunate brothers in maritime affairs, Cairadino and Arriadeno Barbarossa, who both died possessing the title of King of Algeria. This island produces many very good wines. They wear a fantastic collar raised with copper wire, above which they fit beautiful veils of silk and gold. Their cap is of velvet and it comes so low, with its decorations, that it almost covers their foreheads. The point of the headdress allows them, when they do not want to be seen, to pull it down and cover their faces. At their necks they tie a silk scarf woven in the Moorish style, which they throw full-length back over their shoulders; at its hem are long fringes or twisted threads of silk and gold. They wear a floor-length sottana *without a bodice, of silk or colored wool, and on top a calf-length* guarnaccia *of* ormesino *or very white cotton, very thin, with wide sleeves. At its hem is a border of some matching trim. They wear shoes in the Turkish style, in soft red or* pavonazzo *leather. The women of this island are Greek for the most part, and they have lovely features. They cover themselves up completely and are chaste, and they enjoy needlework and weave very thin, fine cloth.*

A CONCUBINE of Rhodes

The city of Rhodes, from which the island of Rhodes took its name, was given to the priests of the Hospital of Saint John in Jerusalem in 1300, along with the island as a whole. Then in the year 1408 Mehmet, the Ottoman Emperor of the Turks, after taking three hundred thousand soldiers and sixteen large pieces of artillery there, set about capturing it, but he was most ignominiously driven back by the Christians. But the Emperor Suleiman, also the leader of the Turks, returned there in 1522 and did capture it. This island contains three other cities, one called Lindos, where there was a very large colossus; the Sultan of Egypt, once he had seized it, loaded nine hundred camels with the metal from which it had been made and took it to Alexandria. The second city is Camirus and the third is Carisso, later called Rhodes. The courtesans of Rhodes are very beautiful and sensual. They are all the more alluring because they wear all kinds of make-up on their faces and their breasts to make themselves beautiful, and they color their hands, their feet, and their nails red. They load their necks and ears with gold and pearls. The way they style their hair is very elegant and fashioned with marvelous skill; their hair is the color of gold and enclosed in a silver net. On top of this, they wear another headdress of velvet, well-proportioned in height, covered with a lovely veil of striped cloth fastened at the forehead, where it forms a beautiful point and then falls down behind in a most elegant way; and they show off their very white necks. On top of their sotttana, *they wear an overgown usually of cloth of silver, calf-length, open at the sides, which they tie with gold ribbons above the thigh, leaving the rest free. Their* sottana *is of* cremesino *satin, long, with a full train, undecorated. They bind their waists tightly with a silk belt striped in various colors, but they also wear a very precious belt of gold. They wear their* camicie *in the form of an open* bavero, *skillfully needle-worked. And their bodices are cut wide and low, with sleeves made of the same fabric.*

THE END OF THE
CLOTHING OF EUROPE

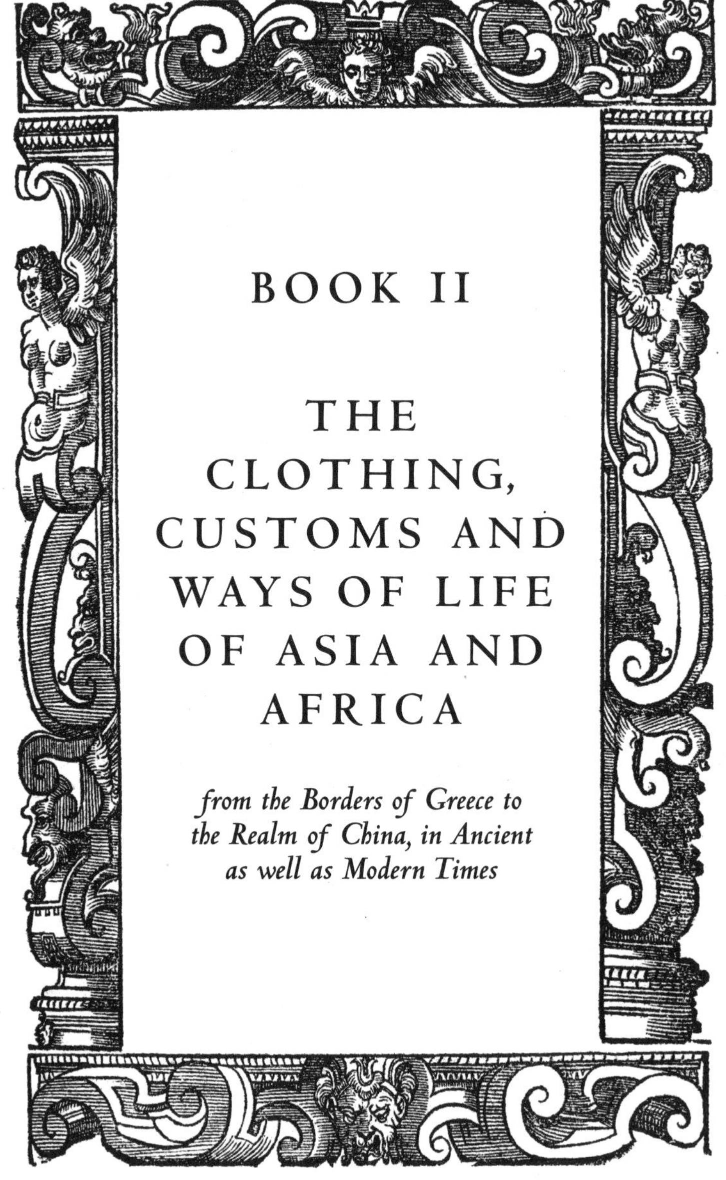

BOOK II

THE CLOTHING, CUSTOMS AND WAYS OF LIFE OF ASIA AND AFRICA

from the Borders of Greece to the Realm of China, in Ancient as well as Modern Times

DISCOURSE
BY CESARE VECELLIO

ON THE CLOTHING, ANCIENT AND MODERN, OF AFRICA AND ASIA

In the first book I showed, with the greatest possible exactness, the styles of dress of all Europe. If I am not mistaken I have succeeded in this, as far as the first third of the world is concerned, because, since it is nobler than the other two and therefore better known, information about it was easier to acquire. Information regarding the other two parts of the world has been less accessible to me because of their great distance from Europe, and it should come as no surprise to anyone if in discussing this part of the world I am briefer than I previously was. Since distance not only makes it more difficult to acquire information but also harder to be sure of the truth of what is said, it was easier for me to discuss the styles of dress of Europe, mostly because I had seen them myself and, if not, people I could trust had told me about them and recounted what they had seen themselves. Accounts of Asia, in contrast, are so uncertain that it is often necessary, because of the geographical distance, to listen to people who speak of things they have not seen themselves but have only heard second-hand. And because those who can describe what they have actually seen are so few in number, the styles of dress I will describe now for this third of the world will also be few in number.

Asia is, in fact, the largest of the three parts of the world, and it contains many kingdoms and many uninhabited and desert regions. It begins at the far side of the North Sea and stretches as far as the greater sea.[1] It shares a border with Greece and extends past the Mediterranean, reaching the Red Sea, though some claim that it is the Nile that divides Asia from Africa. Asia extends to the East Indian Sea and reaches the Indian Ocean, including Japan and the infinite number of islands surrounding it. Now, I have received accurate information about this third part of the world from many people who have been there and also from people who live in its countries, having carried out careful research myself. So in this volume I will speak of some of these styles of dress. But I ask that the reader pardon me if I do not describe them fully, as I did the earlier ones. Let him partly blame the difficulties I have mentioned and partly the fact that I am now tired out by the great effort I have made to gather all these styles of dress together, and eager not to keep them hidden from the world any longer. If my readers show that they value the care I have taken, this will encourage me further to add a second volume, which I plan to set after this second book. In this second volume a great number of new and marvelous styles of dress, never seen before, will be revealed, adding to the clothing of Asia and Africa that of America, that is of the New World; for this I have already prepared many drawings, along with detailed descriptions of the peoples' ways of life and customs. I hope that these will be highly entertaining to see and read about. And I will include some other peoples of the North, entirely unknown to us up to now, which will be equally well received. But to come to our subject, which is the dress of Asia, we will observe the same order as before. And since we have reached the farthest borders of Greece, we will begin with Caramania, which borders on Greece, and we will continue all the way to the great realm of China and then begin describing the dress of the peoples of Africa.

THE CLOTHING OF CARAMANIA

A NOBLEWOMAN of Early Caramania[1]

aramania was originally called Cilicia, and according to Ptolemy it is a province of Asia. At the east it borders Mount Amasos, now called Black Mountain; on the west, it borders a section of Pamphilia; and on the south the tip of the Gulf of Issico, now called Chiasso. This region is surrounded by very steep, high mountains, from which many rivers flow down to the sea. The River Ciane, or Caune, whose source is Mount Taurus, flows across the country. In this river the Emperor Federico Barbarossa[2] *drowned. The great city of Tarsus is located in this province, which was the native land of Saint Paul and produced great philosophers, surpassing those of Athens and Alexandria. This Tarsus and Corice are the principal cities of Caramania. Satalia is located there, too, on the sea coast of Cilicia, but the Gulf of Satalia in ancient times was called Issus and now is called Chiassus. Here Alexander the Great defeated Darius, the mighty King of the Persians, and the city was named Hicopolis, that is, "the City of Victory."*[3] *This Caramania was so powerful that its king could put forty thousand men on horseback into the battlefield. In fact, it was held in such high esteem that Orcan, the son and heir of Osman, who made himself leader of the Turks, before he created nobles among his men and his emperors, deigned to ennoble himself by marrying the daughter of Caramanus, king of the Caramanians, who took their name from him after he had occupied and subjugated their country.*

Such noblewomen of Caramania wear a sottana *of turquoise-colored* velluto ad opera, *which has no bodice but covers the breast and falls to the feet, without many folds; its sleeves cover the arms. They wear no ruffles at their necks but strands of pearls instead. Their headdress resembles a papal miter, covered with* velo *and made of red velvet; in the middle at the front is a strip of cloth of gold, full of jewels. They wear their hair in many small curls and let a lot of it fall loose onto their shoulders, but twisted into rope-like braids. On top they wear a mantle in the style of a* saio *of fine wool, fringed along the edge, and slashed or trimmed with a patterned strip. Under this they wear a gown made in the style of a loose* camicia *like those worn by our priests, and belted with painted* velo. *This style, it seems, is no longer worn today; clothing in the Turkish style is worn instead, in various and beautiful colors, either in wool or silk, with a* sottana *of thin cotton.*

NOBLEWOMAN
of Modern Caramania

This noblewoman of Caramania wears a headdress in the shape of a miter with many ornaments of gold and jewels, in the modern style. She wears earrings of highly valuable jewels, and encircling her chest she wears a necklace of heavy, jeweled gold. She wears a very long colored undergown of patterned silk, without a bodice but cut like a friar's tunic. These women wear beautiful, rich silk sashes woven with stripes of gold and other trim, which they tie to reveal the shape of their breasts and bodies. Over this they wear another beautiful gown, full and ample but short, and white in color; like a zimarra *it has no sleeves, but instead two openings at the side, through which the women put their arms, clothed in the fabric of their full-sleeved* sottana. *This style of dress is no longer being worn, however, as a result of the many payments [to the Turks] that people have to make in this country; as a result, there are many Christians and Greeks who no longer dare to wear luxurious clothing.*

A CARAMANIAN WOMAN
in Constantinople

The women of Caramania who live in Constantinople wear a style of dress similar to that of Turkish women, in various colors; their overgarments are of fine wool in turquoise or pavonazzo *or of scarlet or silk, as well as of satin and* damasco, *according to what they can afford. They are women skilled in business and commerce, and in order to show that they are not Turks, on their heads they wear a small, high, lightweight hat, over which they wear a thin striped veil with many folds covering the cap. Around their necks they wear another veil of silk, in white, and otherwise they dress like Greek or Turkish women, with wide pleated sleeves and a loose* robba, *as shown in the print. There are others among them who wear a round, high hat on their heads, in a cylindrical shape, covered with velvet or another piece of silk. And they wear flat shoes when they leave the house to do business.*

A WEALTHY MAN
of Caramania

he men of Caramania, who live under Turkish control and follow their laws, dress in the Turkish style with little variation. They wear floor-length overgarments of variously colored patterned brocade and other kinds of silk. But those who come to Venice dress for the most part in very fine wool or in scarlet, which makes one think that when they wear them in their own piazzas, these must seem like meadows full of various beautiful and lovely flowers. They cover their heads with sessa, as the Turks do, and they wear shoes or low leather boots in yellow, red, and turquoise. Sitting on carpets on the floor, as do the Turks, they eat a lot of rice, salted meats, and the meat of castrated animals for the most part; and in their banquets they serve only one dish and use only one spoon. When it rains, they wear a woolen or felt cape with a hood, similar to the one shown in this drawing.

A WOMAN OF CARAMANIA
Dressed in More Contemporary Style

The principal and genuinely modern style of dress worn in this country today differs little from that of the Turks except for the headdress, which is formed in the shape of a wooden cylinder, like a box, and covered with a piece of silk in three layers of color, green, red, and white; this piece of silk divides the headdress into three sections. Under it they wear a striped silk veil that covers their hair and falls onto their shoulders, and so dressed, the women of this country leave their houses, but with their faces covered. There are many Christians there, who dress in the Greek style and who now wear fur-lined caps similar to ours on their heads, since Armenians and other Christian peoples who live under the Turks and Persians are prohibited from wearing their own head cloths or turbans, as Muslims and infidels can do.

THE CLOTHING OF ARMENIA

A WEALTHY ARMENIAN MAN

rmenia is very, very large but has a rough terrain because of the high mountains and hills there, which are so high toward Colchis and Hibernia that they are always covered with snow; travelers who want to pass through them, for fear of being snowed under, carry large staffs in their hands so that if they are buried by snow, they can use these sticks to signal for help and be rescued. Many rivers flow through this region, but especially the Tigris, which is so named because of the swiftness of its current: this word in the language of the Medes means "arrow." The region is located in Asia and divided into two parts, that is, into Greater Armenia, today called Turcomania, and lesser Armenia, which still has its own name today. Greater Armenia is inhabited by the Sofi [the Persian ruler], and this is where the principal city of Tauris is located. Lesser Armenia is for the most part in the hands of the Turks, but the people there are Christian, and pay an annual tax of a ducat per person. They are Christians but differ from us Catholics in some ways and from the Greeks in still others. They obey a Catholic leader in spiritual and temporal matters, but their priests are married, following the freedom of the Eastern Church; Ethiopians serve in their churches almost as Latin-speakers do in ours, but in their own language. Their priests have large tonsures on their heads with long hair around them, and long beards. When they stand to listen to the Bible being read, they kiss one another as a sign of reconciliation. Like our priests, they bless the Sacrament in the form of a small wafer, but they use a chalice of glass or wood. They also observe Lent very strictly, eating nothing that has been alive, but in contrast to the Greeks, they eat meat on certain Fridays. The country contains that great Mount Jordan where Noah's Ark landed after the Flood. The Armenians do business as foreigners in Turkey, in Constantinople, in Pera and in the Levant, and they traffic in large quantity ciambellotti, moccajarri, *silks, and Syrian carpets. In Armenia there are very many large, populous cities, such as Leopoli, Theodosia, Sebastia, Comane, and Hicopolis, where the Roman Pompey defeated Mithridates, the King of Pontus, and also Tigranus, King of Greater Armenia.*

The clothing of these Armenian men is usually long, like that of the Greeks and other eastern peoples. On their heads they wear a turban or dolimano *of turquoise, striped with white or red, since only Turks can wear them in white. Their overgarment is long and fastened with ivory buttons. Under this they wear a* guarnaccia, *mid-calf length, also with buttons. They wear boots in the Turkish style, one-piece* bracche *loose on the legs, and shoes in the Turkish style. All of them are naturally brown-skinned but with beautiful features, and they have been Christians since ancient times, from the reign of King Anabagar, who lived in the time of Our Lord. They wear white* camicie *but with full sleeves.*

Text on page 494

ARMENIAN MERCHANT

Armenian merchants, at least those who are Christians, are forced by the Turks to wear caps like ours on their heads, or hats lined with marten or other furs. They usually wear wool, in black or some other color such as blue and pavonazzo, and sometimes satin, ormesino, velvet, and fine wools. They wear long, open zimarre of damasco or another fabric, lined with linen trimmed with borders (and in the winter with fur). On their legs they wear stockings of blue wool with small leather shoes; these stockings are loose and sometimes made of linen. They also wear shoes in the Turkish style.

Text on page 495

A WOMAN OF LOWER ARMENIA

Lower Armenia used to worship Fanais[1] *as its goddess; they not only built altars to her but also consecrated their men and women servants to her, and sometimes also the children of their most illustrious families. It was considered acceptable for their daughters to make their bodies available for carnal pleasures without suffering any infamy, and even if their lovers had had intercourse with them many times, they were not refused as wives by those who wanted to take them in marriage. This was performed between a man and a woman when the man cut off a little of the right ear of his wife and the wife a little of the left ear of her husband. The dress of such an Armenian woman includes a hat made of various colors and then wrapped in a veil similar to those worn by nuns. They wear a beautifully needle-worked* sottana, *and on top a white cotton* rochetto. *Then they wear a piece of cloth similar to a nun's* pacienzia, *needle-worked, longer in back than in front, which they wear in order to see without being seen.*

Text on page 496

A WOMAN OF LOWER ARMENIA,
Devoted to Chastity

The clothing of the woman shown in this drawing in itself signifies modesty and chastity. Certain women in lower Armenia wear a white cotton mantle wrapped around them to cover every visible part of their body, and when they walk on the street, they pull down their headdress like a visor, so that it hangs so low that they prevent anyone from recognizing them. Under this they wear ormesino *bordered and woven with needle-worked strips of silk or* bottana *[sturdy cotton] that reach the ground. On top of this* sottana *they wear a loose smock of silk or white* sessa *arranged in many folds. These Armenians share a border with the Persians and they live almost as the Persians do, in their diet as in their customs. The first son takes only one wife, and they marry their daughters without a dowry. They wear many scents and perfumes, and they are rich in sheep, oxen, and bullocks.*

Text on page 497

A NOBLEMAN
of Lower Armenia

This type of man wears a turban of a certain weight, sky blue, with stripes. He wears a mane of long hair, and also a long beard. As an overgown he wears a monk's cowled tunic or something like it, but in silk or else wool or cotton, and most often in some color. At his neck he wears a cloth of fine silk banded with white and red and other colors, the middle of which rests on his chest while the ends hang down over his shoulders. They wear hobnailed shoes, like the Turks. And they are honored by being assigned certain duties of the nobility. It can also be said that this type of man has something of a priest or Patriarch about him, for not long ago such a man came to Venice wearing almost exactly this style of dress; he remained here several months.

445

Text on page 498

THE CLOTHING OF THE GEORGIANS

Georgia is an infertile country inhabited by Christians, who live poorly because their country is full of mountains and forests. They have wooden houses and are rather coarse in their manners. The men and the women dress in the Persian style but more simply. On their heads the men wear caps lined with marten fur, which can be seen on their turned-back brims; inside they are lined with curly lambskin. From this hat hangs a hood made like a sleeve or a horn, which reaches their shoulders. They have an overgarment or long casacca, *calf-length, which they wrap across their right side in front; it is made of silk or of some other striped cloth with bands woven into it. They arm themselves with bows and quivers and with a Turkish-style scimitar, and in their hands they carry short lances called* zagaglie, *which they throw to wound their enemies from a great distance. They are valiant in battle, and far more loyal to the Persians than to the Turks since most of them are allies of the King of Persia, who protects them faithfully.*

Text on page 499

A PERSIAN WOMAN

The kingdom of Persia was formerly very powerful, and it is surrounded by mountains. The part of it by the sea lacks fruit but is rich in dates, while the middle of the country is made up of pasture and is abundant in all things and an excellent source of food for animals. Various rivers and lakes supply it with water, especially the Araxes river. The main city of this kingdom is Persepolis [Shiraz], where the kings used to reside; they controlled the monarchy after the Medes for 250 years but then were conquered by Alexander the Great.[2] *They never dirtied the water of the Araxes even slightly because they believed that a god lived there. At the time of the birth of Christ, this region was controlled by the Romans; however, its people rebelled and enjoyed freedom until the Saracens took the power to rule from them, which occurred in the year 632. They made Valdacca [Baghdad] the head of the Empire, which replaced Babylon as the ruling city.*[3] *These Persians are bold in warfare and accustomed to the hardships of war from an early age, and they serve their king with great loyalty on horseback and in great numbers: the nobles alone have over fifty thousand horses. They dress in satin, damask, velvet, fine wool, and brocade richly woven with gold and silver, patterned with hunting scenes, animals, and birds. The women, on top of their* camicie, *wear an overgarment partially open in front, as shown in the drawing, and then fastened a quarter of an arm's length below the waist and open from there down to the floor; it is fairly narrow in cut, almost in the style worn by the Turks, and belted with a painted or striped sash of silk, with full, gathered sleeves of the same kind the men wear. These women adorn their necks with long beads in the form of jeweled chains, of gold or silk, whichever suits them; around their foreheads they wrap silk veils, as our nuns do, but they wear their hair long, covered in* velo *down behind their shoulders, with pendant earrings of great value. Underneath they wear* brachesse *of thin* ormesino *and silk, needle-worked from the knees down. Their shoes are of beautifully colored leather, like those of Turkish women.*

A MARRIED WOMAN of Persia

When the married women of Persia leave their houses, they wear a mantle painted with leaves and little animals, all of one piece, which they use to cover themselves from head to foot. They cover their faces, holding this mantle closed with their hands, so that nothing can be seen of them except one eye. They are accompanied by women and men servants in great numbers. And when they marry, they do not follow the custom of bringing their husbands a dowry, except those who, because they are rich, bring beautiful clothes with them to their husbands' houses. Almost all Persian men take only one wife, unless they have no children, in which case they take two. Such women also make themselves very beautiful, and paint their hands and nails in various ways.

A PERSIAN NOBLEMAN

Persian noblemen wear a floor-length overgarment with sleeves as long as the gown. The zimarra *they wear underneath is somewhat shorter, belted with a piece of painted silk voile. They fasten this undergarment on their right side, above the hip, with silk ties or buttons of solid silk. These garments are of patterned brocade and richly needle-worked, as is their custom. They wear rather loose-fitting stockings, resembling* bracche. *The clothing of soldiers is similar to this but somewhat shorter. They wear tall feathers decorated with beautiful pearls and jewels of great value. They perfume themselves, the men as well as the women, with many scents. They admire virtue very much and hold nobility of character in high esteem.*

PERSIAN CAPTAIN
or Soldier

When they go to war, Persian soldiers arm themselves with bows and arrows, short, curved swords, finely worked shields, lances, and muskets, and often a great deal of other artillery. On their bodies they wear jackets of chain mail, corsaletti, corazze, *and* celate. *They armor their horses similarly; they cover them with needle-worked or painted silk, and they do the same with their saddles. They control their horses with bridles appliquéd with gold and jewels, so they look like different kinds of flowers. They eat every sort of food lavishly and drink wine, although it is very expensive.*

PERSIAN GIRL

Shiraz is one of the principal cities of Persia, where the women are so beautiful that they excel all the other women of the East. Mohammed refused to go there, fearing that should he ever taste the delights of such women, he would never go to Paradise afterward. Alexander the Great, after defeating Darius, king of these lands, and holding his daughters prisoners, never wanted to greet them except with lowered eyes, fearing that if he looked at them, he might fall in love with them. The clothing of the young women of the Persian nobility and of young girls is made of many-colored silks and painted cotton. They wear a high hat on their head, made of cloth of gold and decorated with jewels, from which hangs a striped silk veil, with a fringe of silk and gold threads, falling down behind to mid-calf. They wear earrings in the local style. Their overgarment is of turquoise zendado, cut like a zimarra but rather short, with wide, long sleeves; through the openings of these sleeves come their arms, covered in the fabric of their sottana. They wear no ruffles at their neck, nor any other kind of ornament, but show it bare and white. Their sottana is of painted silk fabric, very long. They do not wear pianelle because they are naturally very tall. And they marry according to their own decision, without advice from anyone.

AN UNMARRIED GIRL
of Persia

Persian girls are very modest, as can be seen in the drawing shown here. On their heads they wear a little hat or cap of cloth of gold, almost like the one shown previously; under this they neatly arrange their hair, which falls down onto their shoulders. This little hat is needle-worked in pretty designs and painted, with a very beautiful jewel that rests on their forehead in an unsually lovely way; they arrange their hair in small curls framing their foreheads. Their garments are of silk, exquisitely needle-worked all around in four or five very wide bands. These gowns are usually of silk or cotton or painted linen, fastened at the neck and falling to a palm's length above their feet. They belt them with sashes of plain silk. Their undergowns have sleeves, which are of colored fabric and reach the ground. Their shoes or short boots are in the Turkish style, in yellow or pavonazzo. *They wear make-up on their faces, and when leaving their houses they are well chaperoned and many cover their faces; instead of ruffles or ruffs at their necks, they wear a small veil of very thin silk. They are never without their scents or perfumes, which can be smelled from far away.*

A MARRIED WOMAN of Persia

he married women of Persia walk in public in a way that makes them seem more like nuns than any other kind of woman. They wear a soggolo of sessa or renso or *some other very white fabric, which, tied on top of their heads, creates the effect around their throats and under their chins that can be seen in the drawing shown here. On top of this* soggolo *they set a velvet cap, not very high but well fitted. They wear a* sottana *of silk or some other fabric, floor-length, with a fitted bodice, on top of which they wear a gown of changeable* ormesino *or of cotton fabric. This has open sleeves that reach the ground, and through their openings they bring out their arms. These women, if their husbands, children or relatives die, wear the same clothing but in black; those who want to remarry wear it only for a short while. But if they have children, they rarely take a second husband, because they would be considered wicked if they did.*

PERSIAN FOOT SOLDIER
of the King

he clothing shown here is practical and worn by people who have to fight in situations calling for agility and speed. These Persian soldiers are bold and shrewd and usually quick to conquer; they do not want to endure much discomfort, so they use trickery to help them win. They usually wear a woolen casacca, *half-length, and* brachesse *of coarse wool falling in crosswise folds to their feet because they are so full. They wear shoes in the Turkish style and they cover their heads with a turban with a point at the top, decorated with strips of trim and crimped into twelve bands. They wear a Moorish-style sash at their waists and they always carry a scimitar; they tuck the ends of their* casache *up into their belts, as if they are about to mount a horse.*

THE CLOTHING OF SYRIA AND DAMASCUS

A WOMAN OF DAMASCUS

Damascus in Syria is the principal city in the region called Celisoria, and it is almost the most ancient city in all of Asia, since it was built by the servants of Abraham. It is located on a plain, on infertile land, except for the part of it that is irrigated by water supplied by aqueducts. It is six days' distance from Jerusalem, and it was near Damascus that Saint Paul, falling from his horse, first came to know Christ. This city is also rich in goods; formerly the body of Saint Zachariah, father of Saint John the Baptist, was kept there. The prison where Saint Paul was put is still there, with the window that, every time it was walled up, went back to how it was originally by the following morning.

The women of this city dress very well, with many ornaments of jewels and gold, and they wear beautifully patterned silk. They wear an overgarment of white cotton, sheer, shining, and transparent, like silk. They all wear white laced boots and shoes in red or pavonazzo*, and they wear many jewels around their heads, at their ears, and on their hands. They marry according to their own will, and when they no longer want to remain with their husband, they go to their local* Cadi *[magistrate or judge] and he grants them a separation; they can then marry again and their husbands can take another wife. The men of this country can have two or three wives, and as many as five. They eat on the street, where merchandise is sold. They live on the meat of horses, camels, buffalo, and bullocks, and dairy products of all kinds. The Moors wear long, full robes made of silk or wool, unbelted. The majority of them wear* *cotton trousers with white stockings and white shoes. And the noblewomen in the attire shown here go about with covered faces. In the city of Damascus one can see a Florentine coat of arms, and it is said that the Great Sultan gave this city to a Florentine man to enjoy because he had cured him of a poison. The clothing shown in this print is also worn by women in Aleppo, Beirut, and other cities of this region. These women have five or six husbands, and when they have children, they say that they have this or that father, and people believe them. During the time that this kingdom was ruled by the Mamluks, who were greatly feared, covered women were seized by one man or another and taken to hostelries and other houses, without being uncovered or recognized, so that many men unknowingly had their way with their own relatives.*

Text on page 509

WOMAN
of Tripoli

Tripoli is an ancient commercial city, full of good sailors who are very skillful at sea. Its women are very modest and friendly to foreigners. They wear a headdress shaped like a crown, decorated according to their custom and embellished with many gems and pearls; from this fall onto their shoulders four neatly made braids, two on each side. Underneath they wear a garment of Persian wool, colored and painted, or of silk in various colors. At the back of their crowns, which are made of cloth of gold, they attach beautiful, highly valuable feathers. They wear a thin veil pinned above their forehead and forming a beautiful point; it reaches all the way down to their eyes, while the rest of it falls over their braids behind their shoulders. Their overgown is of white silk in the style of a nun's pacientia, *falling in beautiful full folds from their necks and covering their hands. At the ends of this gown are long silk fringes and gold threads, beautiful to see. They wear colored leather shoes in the Turkish style. When they leave their houses, they cover themselves up, and they wear gold and jewels at their necks.*

457

Text on page 510

WOMAN
of Beirut

Beirut, a very ancient city, is located on the sea; it was once a city rich in commerce, but now little goes on there. The clothing of its women consists of a very beautiful headdress made of a small velvet cap shaped a bit like a horn at the back, while at the front it has two bands of gold or silver, laden with many jewels. On top of this headdress they wear a fazzuolo *of very thin cotton woven in the Moorish style, which covers their temples, shoulders and breast. Their* sottane *are painted with various leafy designs; on top of them they wear a gown of very thin cotton, not very long, with rather full sleeves. They wear low boots in red or* pavonazzo*, or shoes with turned-up toes. They paint their nails, and when they leave their houses, they cover themselves up.*

Text on page 511

NOBLEWOMAN
of Aleppo [Halab]

This city is very beautiful and very large; it is located on the most attractive spot in Syria, eight days' journey from the mainland, and merchandise is brought to it by camel. It has seven hills, like Rome, which formerly subjugated it; it is sixty days away from Constantinople and also from Cairo, and sixty days' distance from Alexandria; it has many merchants from every country. The style of dress shown here is worn by all women. The headdress consists of a gold band around their forehead, attached to a veil; on top of this they wear a fazzuolo, *richly needle-worked in gold and silk, which covers their head and shoulders. At the bottom of this* fazzuolo *hangs a very lovely fringe of silk and gold. They wear a* sottana *made of one piece of cloth without a bodice, floor-length and belted with a striped veil, with sleeves that cover their arms. On top of this, they wear another half-length gown of silk, with full, slit arms, and their arms come through these slits; the gown falls to mid-thigh. Dressed in this way, they leave their houses, wearing no jewelry at their necks, or gold or gems anywhere else.*

Text on page 512

GIRL
of Aleppo

The city of Aleppo, because it is very rich in merchandise, is also very rich because of the great numbers of people from different nations who meet there from all over the world. So among these Mohammedans, whether Moors or Turks, there is a feeling of great pride in this huge gathering, made even larger by the many Persians and Azamini[1] *who come there, too, because this city is a gateway to Turkey and Syria. Many fabrics are brought here, including silks woven in very beautiful patterns, very fine linen and cotton, and the whitest* lisaro *[fine cottons]. All of these things are conveniently and freely available to whoever wants to acquire them and wear them. The noblewomen of this city do this with pleasure, since they can maintain the dignity of their rank with such riches; the married women do so just as much as the brides and unmarried girls.*

They wear a beautiful headdress made of differently colored velvets, in the style of the velvet caps commonly worn throughout Italy in our time; to these they add a band studded with golden brooches and jewels and certain birds' feathers that they prize very highly. Near their ears they wear a braid of their own hair in such a pleasant style that it makes a very pretty sight. Under the cap, they wear narrow bands of various colors, covering their hair and reaching halfway down their backs, on top of their camicie, *which are made of* ormesino *in white or some other color. They wear a full-length overgarment of brocade in the local style or of painted fabric, with a bodice that reaches their throat and makes an ornament of pearls and gold around their necks. They also wear a* rocchetto *of thin, transparent silk, rather short, which covers them from the bodice down; over their bodice they wear a piece of silk in the form of a short mantle, doubled like a burnous or shawl and striped all over with lovely different colors. They go out very rarely, and when they do, they cover their faces, as women still do throughout Syria. It is their custom to paint their skin and fingernails.*

A MARRIED WOMAN
of Syria

Syria is a very large and rich region, and very fertile; it has many famous cities and noble provinces, such as Palestine, Phoenicia, Damascena, Cese, Cornagna, Apamena, Judea, Idumea, and Samaria. This region is located at the center of the world—that is, equidistant from Spain, India, Scythia and Ethiopia[2]*—so it suffers neither great heat nor excessive cold; accordingly, its countryside is fertile and full of animals. Syria was ruled by the Romans for a period of a thousand years and then it was occupied, along with Jerusalem, by the Saracens and owned by them for a hundred years; then it was reconquered by the Christians.*[3]

The women of this country go about very beautifully adorned. Their headdress is similar to that of the women of Caramania and Cairo. It consists of a rather high velvet hat covered in a beautiful design of gold cords, skillfully sewn and enriched with gems set on top; at its base it almost forms a crown of jeweled gold, while at the back is pinned a very thin veil, which falls in a lovely way down onto their shoulders. Their undergown is of gold brocade or of patterned cremesino *velvet, closed in front down to the ground, with sleeves that are narrow but so long that they almost cover their hands. On top they wear another gown of colored* ormesino, *and their arms emerge from its short, open sleeves. On top of this they wear a* corsaletto-*shapaed bodice, expertly needle-worked and embellished with bands of precious gems, which they tie high up with a sash of striped silk. At their necks they wear gold and pearl necklaces, very valuable, with gems falling from them onto their breast. They use a great deal of make-up on their faces, and they paint their nails. They wear the scents of flowers and musk, and they are very seductive, delighting in making themselves beautiful. When they go out, they cover themselves up.*

NEWLY MARRIED WOMAN of Syria

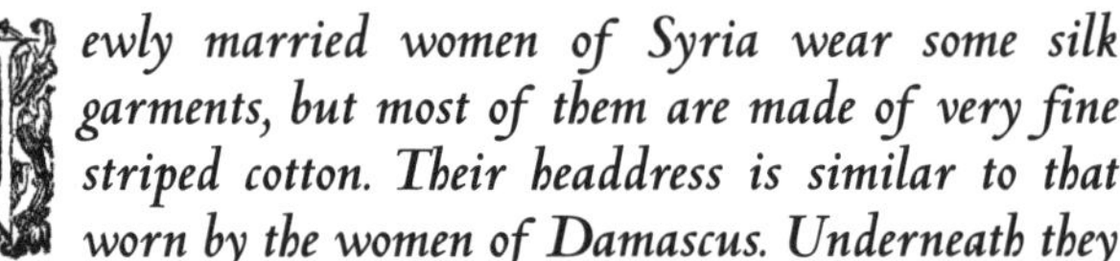

Newly married women of Syria wear some silk garments, but most of them are made of very fine striped cotton. Their headdress is similar to that worn by the women of Damascus. Underneath they wear a gown of silk in the Turkish style, with painted designs and opening in front down to the ground; on top they wear a mantle of cotton, mid-calf in length, with a wide needle-worked border that conceals their hands. Most of the time, they cover themselves, including their faces, with a thin veil and adorn themselves with various jewels in the Moorish style. Under this veil they wear a small velvet cap banded with gold, and under this they wear their hair in braids, which come down in front.

A GREEK WOMAN in Syria

In Syria there are many Greek women who live with their husbands, merchants and businessmen. Some of them even go there to make profits themselves. Their clothing consists of white cotton with many pleats, though some of them wear it of ormesino, *and a few in velvet or satin. Their undergown is floor-length, so their overgarment is shorter, but woven with separate bands of red or* pavonazzo *or some other color. On top of both of these garments they wear a white cotton mantle, which they put over their heads and let fall a palm's length above their overgown. On top of this mantle they wear a low hat divided into sections, which, descending from a silk knob, widens out to cover the head, which they encircle with an ornament embroidered with jewels, pearls and other trim, according to what they can afford.*

JEWISH WOMAN in Syria

There are few places in the world from which the Jews have not been banished. After the final fall of Jerusalem, which was their punishment for the grave sin that they committed, they have always wandered the world as vagabonds, thrown out of one place and then another. So they live in misery, always suspected by everybody and constantly on the move. But even though they are unwillingly tolerated and held in abomination by all nations, wherever they find refuge they always look grand and splendid, both in their clothing and their ornaments. In Syria and in other countries ruled by the Great Turk, there is a great number of Jews, among whom many are very rich. The men dress in Syrian style, in garments similar in every way to those of the Turks, although they wear turbans of velo*, colored yellow, on their heads. These are similar to the kind worn by Levantine Jews in Venice, of whom there is also a very large quantity, who live here permanently with their wives, children and entire families.*

These Jews live in a remote corner of the city called the Ghetto, a place enclosed by canals like a citadel, which can be entered on two sides through two gates, reached by two bridges over the surrounding canal. They dress like Venetians, imitating other merchants and artisans of the city, even though some of them are doctors of medicine and therefore dress differently from people of their own kind. The doctors wear long overgarments with full sleeves, in black, as doctors do; but, to be recognized by others, they are commanded by public law to wear a yellow cap. The women, too, dress differently from Christian women in some ways, especially in their headdress, which includes a yellowish veil; when they go out, they are easily distinguished from other women because, in addition to the difference in headdress, they wear red and white make-up—indeed, they use it so indiscreetly that they seem to be wearing masks, even though some of them are very beautiful. I have made this little digression here because when I was describing Venetian dress earlier, I made no mention of these Jews of Venice.

Now, returning to the Jewish women of Syria, they wear a small hat or high cap, covered with beautifully needle-worked velo*, bordered at the bottom with a circlet of jeweled gold; under this, their hair can be seen, partly uncovered and very finely arranged, under a band of silk, which, starting on the forehead, goes around the back with its ends tied at the nape of the neck. They wear two garments: the* sottana *is of silk or colored wool, with a contrasting border at its hem, and it is so short that it reveals their leather stockings, which they wear in whatever color they like best, as is also the case with their Turkish-style shoes. They wear an overgarment open in front, in the style of a* zimarra*, but short and sleeveless; the bodice is short, but cut so high that it covers their breast. Around the edge of their* camicie*, which also cover their breasts under their overgown, they wear silk needlework in lovely designs, something of which this country can boast of having the best. At their necks, they wear large pearls of great value and, in front, an apron of white silk, decorated with colors and various kinds of silk and gold needlework in Persian style. On top of all these garments, they cover themselves with a cloth of linen or some other fabric, which takes the form of a small mantle. Dressed this way, they go about the city when they have a reason to do so. But if no occasion arises for them to go out, they rarely let themselves be seen.*

465

Text on page 518

WEALTHY EAST INDIAN MAN

There are two Indias, one in the west and one in the east, and it is from the east that this style of dress comes. East India is so large that it takes up the fourth quarter of the world. It is very abundant in wheat, which is harvested twice a year in those countries. They also harvest pepper, spikenard, cinnamon, orris root, and ebony. The region also has many parrots and unicorns,[4] *and many precious stones, such as carbuncles and others like them. The climate there is very good and the inhabitants live to be a hundred and thirty years or more. They wear cotton* camicie *and some go completely nude except for their private parts, which they cover with a bit of cloth hanging down from their heads. There was an African India, ruled by a sultan who ate poison every day, mixed with lime, and whenever he wanted to kill someone, he would spit in his face and the person died immediately.*[5] *He kept four thousand women, and every time he slept with one of them at night, she was found dead in the morning; this sultan ate poison because he had become used to eating it as a little boy. The high-ranking inhabitants of these countries wear a piece of cloth in front, of either silk or wool, with painted trim. On their heads they wear a colored hat bound around with* velo, *and long hair, twisted like braids. From the waist up they are nude, and on their body and legs they wear many bindings of colored cloth and also palm leaves, elegantly made. They wear a mantle of fine cloth brought from Europe, knotted at their necks and reaching down behind to their knees, bordered around the bottom with certain kinds of trim. As weapons they carry bows and arrows. They have sexual relations with one another in the way animals do.*

466

Text on page 519

EASTERN GYPSY,
or Female Vagabond

This is a type of people who live in one place for three days and then in another for another three; they never have a permanent home. They are Christians but vary in some ways from our Catholic faith. Their ruler and others among the nobility powder their faces with flour and the rest of their bodies with ground sandalwood and other very precious scents. They have a ruler whom they call the King of Calicut, who, being a gentile, worships the devil in the form of a painted sculpture, saying that the devil was sent by God to deal out justice, if indeed they still believe in God. This king has certain Brahmins, or priests, whom he respects very much, and when he wants to marry, he has one of the most honored of these priests sleep with his bride before he does and take her virginity; then he pays him four or five hundred ducats and gives him the life-long right to continue sleeping with this queen, under whose rule this type of people live. The clothing of the gypsy woman shown here includes a fitted diadem on her head, made of lightweight wood covered with strips of cloth many arms' lengths long. She wears camicie *of different colors, needle-worked in silk and gold with many lovely designs, and almost floor-length, with wide sleeves, trimmed with beautiful embroidery and needlework. She ties a woolen mantle over one shoulder and drapes it under her other arm, and it is so long that it almost reaches her feet. Her hair falls down to her shoulders. She carries her little child in a sling tied to her neck, and in this way they go wandering.*

Text on page 520

WEALTHY WOMAN
of East India

In the country where the women in the preceding print live, the men, when they take a wife, have a foreigner sleep with her and take her virginity before the marriage, as happened to Lodovico Barthema, who, having been asked to stay by a gentile who was to be married in a few days, remained there with his friends for that reason and, as a result, had good company and many caresses, but then they never slept together again; if a man was found with such a woman after the first time they had been together and he had taken her virginity with her husband's permission, he would have his head cut off on the spot. The dress of these women includes a cotton camicia *with a large piece of cloth that they use as a mantle, knotting it in front. On their heads they wear a headdress of small plates of metal encircled by stiff leaves. They wear leather shoes of various colors; they adorn their arms with different sorts of jewels; they wear their hair loose on their shoulders with a small cap or hat made of palm leaves; and they take their children wherever they go.*

I must not fail to mention something about the customs of Chaldea,[6] in a land called Job, that seems very strange and ridiculous to us. I learned of it in a book written by the Excellent Signor Andrea Butta,[7] a doctor and a nobleman no less wise than well informed, as he showed in both his public and his private activities; I have been encouraged by him, as well as by the Reverend Monsignor Francesco of the noble and ancient Crocecalle family,[8] more courteous than any other, to mention this man, as well as others. He was a saintly and religious person, belonging to the order of the Minor Friars, who traveled through a great part of the world—that is, through Tartary and the upper and lower Indias—in order to disseminate the Gospel. Then, returning after many years to his native land, he was commissioned by his provincial superior, and so wrote an account of his long voyage, including the things that had happened to him and the customs of many peoples; I have taken this information from him because it seems relevant to our subject here. They say that the men of that country are as beautiful as the women of Europe and behave in more or less the same way. They decorate their heads with veils embellished with gold and pearls, and their necks and ears in the same way; they wear beautiful floor-length gowns of silk or other fabric; they walk with small steps and act like women in every way, feeling shame if they are looked at. But in contrast, their women are very ugly and dress in a coarse style, in a knee-length linen camicia *with wide, floor-length sleeves; they go barefoot, in full, floor-length trousers with their hair loose on their shoulders, and they follow the men everywhere, as men follow prostitutes in our country. These regions are abundant in many things, such as sweet resin, the best in the world, and among other things one can buy a pair of partridges for very little money. When these men reach old age, they spin, as our women do.*

AN EAST INDIAN WOMAN of Middle Rank

The women in the clothing shown here love their husbands very deeply, and if they should die before them, fifteen days after they have burned their bodies, they have themselves burnt as well with many accompanying ceremonies, saying that they are going to a better place to eat and sleep with their husbands. Some of the unmarried women court young men, who, to show how sincerely they love these women, soak a rag in oil, set it alight and then burn their naked arms with it in order to show that they love them with all their hearts; these young men are so devoted that they show no sign of pain. In some places, such as the island of Java, children sell their old fathers in the piazza to whoever wants to buy them to eat; they do the same with the sick who have no chance of living. They wear a certain garment most often of cotton and sometimes of silk or ciambellotto, *floor-length with full sleeves, and another piece of cloth that they tie at their waist with striped veils. Their coiffure resembles the one shown here, with circlets of palm leaves or strips of other wood, with their braids divided into four parts, two parts hanging on each side. Their diet consists of rice or some other grain resembling maize, as is shown in this print. They worship the sun, the moon, oxen, or other kinds of crazy thing, or animals such as monkeys and baboons.*

470

ETHIOPIAN NOBLEMAN

There are two Ethiopas, one in Asia and the other in Africa. The one in Africa is today called India and it is bathed on the east by the Red Sea and borders on the north with Libya and Egypt. Toward the west it has the inland area of Libya and the part of it that joins the other Ethiopa, which is larger than this one and further east, and named after Ethiope, the son of Vulcan, who subjugated it. This country is mountainous toward the west, sandy near the Mediterranean, and desert toward the east. It has people of many forms and complexions, who used to be so greatly attached to their kings that if one, by chance, should limp, all of his subjects would limp as well, and if these kings had only one eye, then each man would gouge out one of his. Many of these peoples go naked because of the great heat, covering their pudenda with sheep's tails. They eat dates and elephants for food; these are killed by dragons and other serpents that drink their blood. In these lands there are great numbers of lions, dragons, and basilisks. Jacinths [a red-gold gem], chrysoprase and cinnamon are found there. The two Ethiopias are ruled by Prester John;[9] and the nobles of these lands, like the rest of the people, are Christians, who eat from plates of black earth and keep their wine in jars made of it and make drinking cups of the same material. They sleep on leather and ox skins; some eat ox meat roasted over a fire made of dried and ox dung, and some eat their meat raw. They build their homes without a floor so they sleep on the bare ground, in round houses covered with the shells of ostrich eggs. They sit on the ground on painted mats or carpets. When they are not feeling well, they take no medical treatment except suction cups or tubes to let blood. At the time

of the death of any of their relatives, they shave off their beards and the hair on their heads. They dress in black, and for three days they torment themselves physically, drawing blood once a day and beating their shoulders. Secular men wear a cross at their necks, but the clerics wear a long habit of coarse yellow cotton and carry crosses in their hands. Their weapons are spears and swords, but few daggers. They wear jackets of chain mail, but have only a few of them. They shoot featherless arrows from their bows, carry shields and wear celate. *They still have some artillery today. In their homes they have painted images of many saints, but not of the crucified Christ, Our Lord, because it seems to them that they are not worthy of having him before their eyes. They have been Christians since ancient times and they often take communion, with a piece of thin, round bread. The clothing of the Ethiopian nobility includes a very large* sessa *turban with a short* corno *in the middle. Their garments are made of thin white cotton and of* sessa. *They wear cotton shirts, mid-calf in length, belted with striped cloths to which they attach curved daggers. They wear a mantle of thin white cloth, in the style of a shawl, knotted at the center of their breast, which is so full that it falls to the same length as the* camicie *that they wear as overgowns. They wrap their legs with various bindings and wear shoes of untreated leather, tied on underneath with different kinds of laces.*

Text on page 524

UNMARRIED ETHIOPIAN WOMAN

The girls and brides of Ethiopia wear a long sottana *of silk or cotton, cut into scallops at the hem. On top of this they wear a mantle, sometimes of silk, sometimes of white or yellow cotton. On their heads they wear a beautiful coiffure bound with red or turquoise* velo*; they have gone back to the style of wearing pearls and jewels hanging from their ears. These girls, when they marry, are put into a litter along with their groom; the priests walk ahead singing halleluiahs to them. They do this many times, going round and round this litter, then they cut off a lock of the groom's hair and another lock from the bride, and they give the young girl's hair to him and his to her; sprinkling them on the back with holy water, they then commend them to God. Then they have a great party with music and singing, and with such gaiety the couple is accompanied to the husband's bedchamber, where for a month they maintain their chastity, hardly looking at one another. When the bride leaves the house, she covers her face with a black veil, not taking it off until she is six months pregnant. One man alone can marry two or three women, but a man who does so cannot receive communion. The priests have only one wife each; if they marry more of them, they become laymen; and should they be caught in adultery, they can no longer go to church.*

472

Text on page 525

AN ETHIOPIAN SOLDIER

he clothing shown in this print is worn by one of those who attend the court of the great Prester John. He is a very powerful lord and never stays in the same place but goes about constantly viewing and visiting the lands of his kingdom, accompanied by men-at-arms, soldiers, and other members of his family; all together these number as many as forty thousand, so that in every countryside he stays in, a great city seems to appear because of the pavilions, tents, and small houses they set down to live in. The majority of these people ride mules; only a few ride horses. They dress in many ornaments of gold and jewels, and in white silk and brocade. The apparel shown here consists of a shirt of white silk or some other colored fabric, mid-calf in length, with a fringe made of silk and gold threads. On top the man wears a casacca *of lion skin dyed* rovana, *like a chamois or deer, much longer in the back than in the front and buttoned down to the waist, which they belt with broad, painted ties of silk. They wear long* brachesse, *white and rather full. On their heads they wear turbans of white* sessa, *very large, with a* corno *of the same fabric at its center.*

Text on page 526

MARRIED NOBLEWOMAN of China

The kingdom of China is one of the principal kingdoms of the world; it includes in its territories and regions fifteen provinces containing ninety or a hundred cities, and each one is rich and well supplied with everything necessary and provided by nature. They dress in various styles, and the people of this kingdom have different complexions, as I have seen in paintings from that land. The woman in this drawing or print had very black hair, arranged with many ties decorated with pearls and other valuable jewels. She wore an overgarment with full sleeves, bordered with very beautiful trim of gold and silk; the gown itself was made of velluto riccio, *worn under another, shorter, knee-length garment made of golden brocade. From her belt hung a floor-length silk* fazzuolo *knotted with gold and silk ties, and on top of these garments she wore as a stole a wide band of fabric decorated with beautiful needlework and embroidered with pearls and jewels, which also adorned her breast and the wide sleeves of her garment; two roses made of the same embroidery were set on each side of her breast. They consider small feet a great beauty in women, and when they are young, they bind them very tightly with strips of cloth so that, as a result, they do not allow their feet to grow.*

Text on page 527

NOBLEWOMAN
of China

he women shown in this print are of middling height and olive complexion, and are very modest and chaste, so they are never seen at their windows or at the doors of their houses. They never eat at banquets unless the guests are relatives or very close friends. When they go out to visit their parents, they are carried by four men in a litter enclosed on all sides with very thick blinds made of gold or silver or silk thread, through which they can see other people but cannot be seen themselves. Such women take delight in knowing how to draw and work in bas-relief and carving, and they paint with excellent skill. The clothing of such women resembles the one shown previously. Their headdress is made of pearls in the shape of flowers with jewels in the binding, and they wear ornaments of precious stones at their necks. Their overgarment is of colored silk, floor-length, and belted very high; the sleeves are very wide and bordered with beautiful needlework at their wrists, where they show the sleeves of their very thin camicie. *In their hands they carry beautifully scented flowers such as carnations. They wear many perfumes; they enjoy music and playing different instruments, many of which resemble guitars. They have very beautiful gardens with scented baths and many trees and various delicate fruits, many unknown to us. They wear a great deal of make-up and cosmetics, almost to excess.*

Text on page 528

NOBLEMAN
of China

Noblemen of this country dress very luxuriously and with great decorum, and when they ride, they ride mules richly caparisoned with gold. Their clothing consists of a robe in the style of a toga in silk or in gold or colored brocade, floor-length but slit at the legs, with very long, full sleeves, so that their hands can never be seen; indeed, so long, that they are a half-arm's length longer than their arms. They wear a soggolo *of* ormesino *tied on their head and then covered with a piece of satin or some other cloth of colored silk, which, falling from their head, covers their shoulders. On top of this they set a small cap of red velvet, which keeps their headcloths in place. On their feet they wear boots, not very tight-fitting but of good soft leather in red or yellow or some other color. Their beards are sparse, but they are long and well cared for, as are their moustaches. They live with every sort of elegance and with many perfumes. They never ride horseback except when accompanied by servants holding umbrellas, which they carry to protect them from the sun. Nobles and rich men, when they marry, observe many ceremonies: they give their wives dowries, and the wives give them to their fathers, so that a father with many daughters can say he is rich if they are beautiful and he marries them off. They have many decorations in their houses, such as paintings, sculptures, and carvings, as can be seen in the paintings and bedsteads brought from China to Lisbon in Portugal by Captain Ribora Alguazil, which stunned everybody by their beauty. In whatever they do, they cast many spells and believe in oracles sent through their idols.*

Text on page 529

A MAN OF AVERAGE WEALTH in China

When men marry off their daughters in China, they do the opposite of fathers in other countries, because instead of giving them dowries, they receive these from the husbands in exchange for the trouble they have taken in raising them. This is the case since dowries, in that kingdom, are held in common as long as the fathers of these daughters are alive, and they can spend them as they like; but after the fathers' deaths, they are obliged to return the dowries to their daughters, to whom their husbands have given them, and the daughters then dispose of them as they will. Every man in that kingdom is allowed to marry as many wives as he can support and provide with a dowry, but the first wife is considered the legitimate wife and the others are considered concubines. The men live with their first wives and keep the others in different places. As soon as sons are born to them and begin to talk, they set them to various kinds of study so that they become excellent at various professions and trades. In this kingdom of China there is a province with a large city to which young men looking for wives come for a month each year, as do young girls who want to marry; here, twelve men assigned to this task separate the beautiful girls from the ugly ones and the rich young men from the poor ones, and then they marry the rich men to the beautiful girls and the poor men to the ugly ones. But they follow a law that rich men should contribute as much as they can afford to provide dowries for the ugly girls married to poor men, so that the rich men, happy with the beauty of their wives and the poor men with the dowries, all go away happy.

The clothing in the portrait here, of a man of average wealth, includes a paneled cap of velvet in different colors with a hole on top, through which they tie up their hair. They wrap this cap with velo*, and it is said that they bind their hair on top in this way so that the angels can pick them up by it and take them up to heaven. They wear a* saio *of colored wool, open at the sides and reaching the knee, with long sleeves, more than a half arm's length longer than their arms. They wear long, thin beards, and their moustaches are the same. They wear very full, comfortable trousers, and they enjoy flowers and perfumes very much. The noblemen have their servants carry umbrellas to protect them from the sun and wind. They are all highly active men and strongly opposed to idleness.*

THE CLOTHING OF AFRICA

THE CLOTHING OF CAMPSON GAURI,[1] *the Great Sultan of Cairo*

he ancients divded our world into three parts: that is, Europe, Asia, and Africa. The last of these is separated from Asia by the Nile river, reaching down to Ethiopia in the south and flowing through Egypt, making the land very fertile by watering it, and then entering the sea by seven mouths. This border of Africa, according to some writers, goes as far as the Red Sea in the north.

A very large section of this region of Africa is uncultivated because it is covered with sterile deserts and vexed by various sorts of poisonous animals. It is bordered at the north by the Libyan Sea, at the south by the Ethiopian Sea, and at the west by the Atlantic. It is inhabited by Peru [?] and by Ethiopians, who live in the west and the east of the country. From the beginning they were very crude, like beasts, eating meat and grasses, and having no laws or government, but then they were made more human and reasonable by Hercules. He brought settlers to these lands, who started to sail around these river banks and sea coasts and made them more accessible. In this country there is tremendous heat, and as a result the earth turns into very sterile sand because it receives no rain from the skies. And there are many poisonous animals there, such as dragons and serpents. The men and women have very black skin, more than in any other region, and those of inland Africa live in caves and grottos underground. The land shifts so much that where you see level ground today, tomorrow, because of the wind, it has become a cave or a mountain of sand.

I will describe the clothing worn by the Great Sultan of Cairo, because it is shown here. In 1512 this Great Sultan lived very grandly in the huge city of Cairo, in his castle or palace, according to the report of Messer Zaccaria Pagan, a nobleman of Belluno, who went there with the famous ambassador Domenico Trevisan,[2] *in turn sent by the most Serene Venetian Republic to this Great Sultan. In his palace, then, are many guards stationed at all the doors and in various immense rooms. These rooms are beautifully decorated in gold and other colors, such as turquoise and ultramarine, and make a very beautiful sight; the doors are beautifully inlaid with ivory and ebony, and intricately made, and the windows are of bronze worked in beautiful patterns, and one walks on very fine mosaic floors. In this palace there are two hundred steps. In one of the final rooms sat an Admiral of the Castle, on a seat two feet high called a* Mustabè *in their language, which was surrounded by two hundred slaves playing various instruments including cymbals, flutes, and drums in the Turkish fashion; they had certain shields with which they made a loud noise by clashing them together. Then, passing further through many other doors, they arrived in another room, where two hundred people were working on weapons and armor; from here, going through other rooms full of Mamluks, they entered a large room, two hundred feet long and a hundred feet wide, at the end of which, raised a foot from the ground, on a* Mustabè *covered with green velvet, sat the Great Sultan, who wore on his head a turban of* sessa *with two* corni*, as in the print shown here. He was dressed in a belted* casacca *of white* lisaro *and an overgarment of dark green moiré* ciambellotto *or* zendale. *He sat with his feet crossed and had a shield and scimitar at his side, which it was his habit to take everywhere he went. This Great Sultan had a pleasant appearance and a genial expression, with a brown complexion and a long black beard with a few white hairs. He was large, with a big belly. The palace he lived in was almost three miles in circumference, located on a rock, and in it were very many fountains filled with the water of the Nile, artfully built, and many beautiful gardens, lovely and delightful.*

ADMIRALS AND COUNSELORS
of the Great Sultan

he Great Sultan had almost two hundred Admirals, who all had the title of Colonel or Captain, each of them with about a thousand lancers. They dressed entirely in white with turbans, some tall, some wide and pointed at the sides, and some similar to those worn by the Great Sultan, as can be seen in the drawing shown here. Their garments were of very white lisaro *or* ciambellotto *or moiré* zendado, *beautifully needle-worked and floor-length, fastened in front with gold buttons and belted with pieces of silk. They all stood around the Great Sultan's hall, in addition to the multitude of other kinds of people there. These men made a splendid sight, each one having a handsome appearance, and they responded very reverently to the arrival of the Venetian Ambassador. I will not spend time describing the ceremonies they observe, carried out with a bow, as is their style, in which they place a hand on the ground and then put it to their mouth and onto their head, along with many other rituals; the Ambassador approached and delivered his message. But at the present time many of their customs have changed, for they have changed from the Sultan to the Grand Turk. So they follow the Turkish style more than any other.*

NOBLE MOOR
of Cairo

*ealthy Moors in Cairo wear a sessa turban like that of the Turks on their heads, and a floor-length, white, skillfully needle-worked overgarment with a striped* fazzuolo *at their necks. Their undergown is made of patterned silk and very fine cotton fabrics, which they possess in great quantities, though they also wear some garments in the Persian style, in different colors and hand-painted designs, which they import from Persia. This is the kind worn by the most famous Venetian Ambassador Signor Domenico Trevisan, given to him by the Great Sultan along with some other gowns; but this one was richly woven with gold and silk lined with ermine furs, which are worn only by important people such as the Diodar, who is the Viceroy, and other counselors, but only rarely. It is not surprising that this city of Cairo is considered to be one of the foremost cities of the world, because it is the gathering place of every nation, full of every kind of merchandise from Europe and other parts of the world. In conclusion, there is no rich or beautiful thing that cannot be found there, which I will omit describing to avoid being tedious, since such things have been described in detail by many other writers.*

A WOMAN OF CAIRO

Women in Cairo wear striped gowns belted with silk sashes; these gowns are of silk woven in patterns and of lisaro*. They cover their faces with a kind of cap of cloth of gold, so that nothing but their eyes can be seen, and they cover these caps with a mantle similar to a* lenzuolo *of white* lisaro*. They paint their hands, and they all usually paint their fingernails red. They ride on asses, beautifully caparisoned, with a seat like the ones on pack mules in Spain; they sit on these as men do, with one foot in each stirrup. These women do not spend much time cooking, especially those of the lower classes. Almost all of them eat at inns or taverns, of which there are an infinite number. They cook bread over dried dung from oxen or camels, and food over the leaves and bark of date trees and straw. There are many shops selling cooked food, in addition to the taverns and inns; there are other shops selling waters flavored with every kind of fruit. These waters are very delicate, so all the nobles are in the habit of drinking them; the vendors keep them in glass or tin vessels, worked with great elegance. Others sell sweets made in two ways, with honey or with sugar, very well prepared and different from those of Europe.*

MAMLUKS

These Mamluks were the guards of the Great Sultan, who had great confidence in their valor in battle, on foot as well as on horseback. They covered their heads with a red hat and wore a calf-length belted overgown of white lisaro *with gold and silk buttons. They wore scimitars at their belts and carried iron maces in their right hands, with a gown underneath of patterned silk longer than the one they wore on top. Their stockings were of leather in some beautiful color, and so were their shoes; they were stationed in the palace of the Great Sultan of Cairo, where there was an abundance of fabrics of linen, cotton, cambric,* lisari, *muslins,* sinabusti *[fine cotton or silk from the East], needle-worked silk* fazzuoli, *cloth of wool, satin,* damasco, *and velvet, which had been brought there from Europe. In Cairo there are always fifteen thousand camels that bring water to the city; they make two trips a day. In summer men and women alike sleep uncovered on terraces in the open, without being harmed by the air; they usually dress in white* lisaro *or* ciambellotto, *as their law commands. They have a rich supply of chickens, because the chicks hatch in ovens into which they put thousands of eggs; then, at the right time, they light the fire and so the chicks are born. They are poorly supplied with wood, so they burn camel and ox dung and straw, as I have already said.*

A CHRISTIAN MAN FROM INDIA in Cairo

In this very large city of Cairo one sees baptized Indians, who deal in merchandise; they are baptized with fire, or rather with irons heated in fire, which they put on their faces to signal their identity to others of their kind. These Indians wear a gown of striped cotton and on their heads a felt hat bound with a striped fazzuolo*, which they pull over the top and tuck behind into the band that encircles the hat. This gown has wide sleeves and is cinched with a leather belt; it is floor-length and open in front. They have olive complexions, but are pleasant and diminutive in appearance. At the time that the Venetian Ambassador was in Cairo, two ambassadors arrived, one from the King of Persia and the other from the Georgians, both richly dressed and bringing many gifts. But the Georgian ambassador, who was Christian, begged the Great Sultan to order the route to the Holy Sepulcher to be opened to him, for it was two years since any Christian had been able to go into it. This man was dressed in cloth of gold, with a high pointed hat lined with sable; otherwise he resembled the Persians and also dressed as they did.*

NOBLEMAN
of Barbary

In the part of Africa called Barbary, they live today in Mohammedan fashion, although in earlier times they followed the religion of Christ, which, through the persuasion of the infidels, they then lost. They use the Latin language in many places, but not of a very elegant kind. They take great pleasure in learning, so they devote themselves to the study of the humanities. It is their custom to pay great attention to their paternal lineage; in their signatures they include their own name and their family name. They are very skillful in their arts and they are free of guile; they are truthful and courageous and they keep their promises; they are very jealous over their wives. They dress very elegantly and richly, wearing gowns of lisaro *and other kinds of white cloth, such as* ciambellotto *and other sorts of wool or striped cotton. They wear a turban of* sessa*, striped under its opening. They tie a* fazzuolo *under their beards, as can be seen in the print. They wear stockings and shoes in the Turkish style, and their women dress similarly to the women of Cairo. They also eat the same foods as in Cairo.*

A MOORISH GIRL

Morocco, the metropolitan city of the kingdom of Fez, is full of very beautiful buildings, decorated with gorgeous paintings of fine azure and gold and made very skillfully of stones. They have public baths, as in Germany, which, for lack of wood, they heat with dried ox dung; women bathe separately from men. There are two hundred inns in this city, some of them with more than a hundred rooms, but without beds, instead of which there are only mats and coarse blankets. Their food consists of salted and fresh meat. The inhabitants of that country have three meals a day. When they take a wife, they receive no other dowry than their bride's clothing. These women are led to their husband's house concealed under a baldachin, to the accompaniment of music and the singing of relatives and friends. Once they have arrived there, they are locked in a room where they consummate the marriage, and if the brides are found to be virgins, they open the room right away and the husband displays a bloodied white cloth to everyone there, pronouncing certain words on the subject for the honor of the clan. But if the bride should not be a virgin and they cannot show this bloodied white cloth, she is immediately sent home with little honor. These girls wear gowns of cotton or lisaro or other colored cloth. Their overgarment is a tucked-up white robe, and their headdress resembles the one shown in the print. From their ears hang triangular earrings of beautifully worked gold, decorated with very valuable jewels. They wear other jewelry, circlets of gold and silver of great value on their arms and at their elbows and their knees.

A WEALTHY MOOR

Wealthy Moors in large cities and especially in Tunisia live for the most part on a certain dish of barley, and they eat a certain mixture called Latis *[hashish], weighed by the ounce, which causes them to laugh excessively. They dance a great deal and they are very given to lust; they carry weapons. They wear a long* camicia *with full sleeves, belted with striped, needle-worked veils or* fazzuoli. *They wear white turbans and their clothing is made of cotton. They wear low boots of red leather and shoes of various colors. At their ears they wear gold earrings; across their chests they wear a band of gold with jewels of great value. They arm themselves with scimitars and bows and arrows. They have olive complexions; they eat sitting on the ground, on mats or carpets woven with beautiful designs, and they use neither forks nor knives. They hold literary and religious men in great honor. They are not too rich because they are often robbed by the Arabs, but they live in large rooms beautifully decorated with stucco and gold, in houses only one storey high but with beautiful entrances. Their women dress very elegantly; they are given to all sorts of pleasures and lust.*

BLACK MOORS
of Africa

Because, owing to its great size, there are so many kingdoms and regions in Africa, it is inhabited by people with diverse customs. In Arabia Felix, there is a custom (many claim) that when a daughter is born to her father, he has those body parts made for the procreation of children sewn up completely, except for one small hole, through which she can urinate; the girl, sewn up this way, heals so well that when she has grown up and is ready for marriage, the husband who chooses her cuts the sewing open in order to consummate their marriage. In these regions, those of low rank and income ordinarily wear a garment of cotton cloth from the waist down, and from the waist up they go naked. Both men and women are ugly and black-skinned, and they believe that those with white skins must be bastards. Their noses are blunt, flat and wide, their teeth white, and the whites of their eyes are clear. The clothing of the Moor shown here is an undergarment belted with a scimitar, with mid-length sleeves through which he shows his naked arms; his legs are equally bare. They wear shoes of colored leather. On top of his undergarment, he wears a cloak of coarse wool or cotton, with a large hood that he pulls over his head to protect himself against the sun and rain.

AFRICAN WOMAN

he clothing in the print shown here is very similar to that worn by the married women of ancient Rome, who (some claim) took the style from this one. These African women do not wear much velvet or brocade, except for women in the province of Abyssinia in Egypt and in Prester John's Ethiopia. The clothing shown here is worn by the leading women of the country when they leave their houses. It is a colored camicia *with wide sleeves, with a mantle in black or turquoise, knotted or fastened with a gold or silver pin. They adorn their necks with gold and valuable jewels; on their arms they also wear gold and jeweled bracelets. They cover their hair with a thin colored* velo, *similar to that worn by nuns. Their legs are bare, with anklets of gold. Almost all of them paint their skin and color their nails. They eat sitting on the ground, on carpets, and they sleep on shaggy blankets. The men take many wives, who, because of their olive skin, are not very beautiful; when they are pregnant, their husbands have no carnal relations with them until they give birth.*

CLOTHING OF THE KINGDOM OF TRAMISIN [TLEMCEN][3]

he men of the Kingdom of Tlemcen are very courteous and are great lovers of poetry and enjoy elegant verses. Their region is called Mount Teneis Egozeir. They take pleasure in being very orderly as much in their dress as in their horses and their tents. They live in the countryside, very happily, and practice falcon-hunting a great deal. The men cover their heads with a shaggy hat, rather high, around which they wear a silk band with a beautiful knot in the back. They wear a garment in the form of a camicia *of cotton or other kinds of fabric, mid-calf in length, with a strip of silk, crossing under their left arm and knotted at their right shoulder, hanging down behind the right arm almost to the hem of the shirt. They wear striped sashes at their waist and low-cut leather boots in the style of the Apostles. They arm themselves with curved swords and daggers and they are very strong and courageous.*

AFRICAN WOMAN
of the Kingdom of Tlemcen

The women of this kingdom dress very elegantly. They wear a black camicia *with full sleeves and a mantle of a* lenzuolo, *black or blue, with lace and needlework at its edges; this is fastened on the shoulder with silver and gold clasps worked in a lovely way. On their ears they wear gold earrings, on their fingers rings, and around their ankles thin circlets of gold. Before they marry, they wear creams and paint their faces, breasts, arms, hands, and fingernails in such a way that they are as soft to the touch as velvet.*

AFRICAN WOMAN
of the Middling Sort

he women of this kingdom have an unusual way of wearing a mantle, for those of average wealth wear it in the form of a lenzuolo, *but in black; they wear it in a way that leaves their left arm free. They curl their hair and style it prettily, and they wear many rings at their ears. At their neck they wear necklaces of different stones, in diverse shapes—that is, pointed like diamonds and also square. They are rather brown, not entirely black-skinned. They wear various scents and they, too, wear creams to smooth their faces.*

ARAB NOBLEMAN

*There are three Arabias: Petrea, Deserta, and Felix. The province of Arabia Felix is located in Asia, between Judea and Egypt, from which it looks toward Africa. Arabia Petrea is part of Syria, to the north and west, and Arabia Felix is in the south. In the past the sons of Israel, after passing through the Red Sea, came from there to Arabia Petrea, a place inhabited by serpents, a waterless desert. The inhabitants of this region obey no king; they are nomads and ill-natured; the land, because of its extreme heat and the infertility of its fields, was held in low esteem by the ancients. But we have taken it very seriously because of the divine events that occurred there, since the people of God have held it now for forty years, in addition to the fact that Mount Sinai is located there, on which Moses was miraculously given the Commandments; Ptolemy called it Melane and the Moors Turla. The body of Saint Catherine, virgin and martyr, is also there.*

The second part of the country is called Arabia Deserta. It is inhabited by different people, including the Nabataeans, who live in the eastern part, which is the most deserted and driest. They wander the countryside like thieves, making constant raids on their neighbors and on the caravans or carriers that pass by on their way to Medina and Mecca. In all of Arabia Deserta, there are only two cities and the place called Methath where Mohammed wrote his Qur'an. This country is so infertile that it produces neither trees nor water, or only in very small quantities. No place can compare to it in infertility. They have no ruler, but they live under certain captains, whom they obey; they are Mohammedans.

The third region is called Arabia Felix, so named by an Arab who was the son of Apollo of Babylon and called Eudemon, that is, Happy or Blessed, by the Greeks. On its coast lies the city of

Aden, which, for its great size, power and quantity of people and commerce, is the most famous not only of that province but also of the entire region. On the land around this city, they harvest grains for fodder twice a year; the land is full of rivers, pastures, fruit, animals, and every kind of bird except geese and hens. In this Arabia Felix there are no walled cities because the inhabitants live in peace, and, more important, it is governed by one old man. They are very rich and great merchants; they live near the people of Saba [Sheba]. Among them, anyone who diminishes the wealth of his family is punished, and whoever increases it is honored. They wear soft clothing because their wools are much more delicate than others. The attire of the Arab nobleman consists of a head covering of sessa *in the style of a turban, one part of which hangs down and goes under the chin. These noblemen dress in white, in bordered* lisaro *or other thin cotton fabrics, with full sleeves in* dogalina *style. They devote themselves to literature or to other noble activities. They are sweet and affectionate in their interactions with one another, they admire and are fond of accomplished men, and they are loyal to their faith.*

Text on page 547

AN INDO-AFRICAN
of Ceffala[4]

*ome of the inhabitants of these countries are black-skinned and others have olive complexions; some speak Arabic and some speak the Gentile language of the Indian mainland. From the waist down they wear fabrics of cotton and silk. On their heads they wear hats as part of a bizarre headdress, some wrapped with pieces of silk, and also caps colored red. They also wear wool and* ciambellotto, *beautifully assembled with sections in different styles, very fantastic from the knee down. They use bows and arrows very skillfully, along with spears made of Indian cane, which they carry in their hands to wound enemies from a distance. They eat rice, millet, meat, and fish. Around their hats they wear an ornament of gold, expertly worked and set with beautiful stones. The country produces a great number of lions, bears, deer, boars, and other animals.*

Because there are two Indias, that is, West and East, we will speak here only about the East, from which the styles of dress shown here come. The two Indias are so large that some people claim that they make up the fourth part of the world and that they have so much coastline that a ship could travel along it in full sail for forty days and forty nights. They have five thousand fortified towns, which enjoy a very good climate because of the west wind. They harvest grain twice a year; in the eastern part they raise spikenard, cinnamon, pepper, orris root and ebony. They have parrots and unicorns, and many precious stones, such as beryls and carbuncles. They have two summers, and a gentle wind and a temperate climate; the fertility of the land results from the abundance of water, and for this reason some people live to the age of a hundred and thirty. The trees grow so tall that an arrow shot from a bow cannot fly above them. They produce bamboo trees so large that three men can cross a river in a small trunk of one of them. They produce a great deal of gold and silver, but not much iron.

AN INDO-AFRICAN MAN

The Arabs living in the deserts of Africa go about almost naked, and because they live without laws, they always lie in wait to steal from travelers. They think it is enough to cover their private parts with certain pieces of cloth and, for others, with animal skins. During the day they work at putting their animals out to pasture—lacking any religion, they live according to their impulses. At night they retire into caverns with women, and they sleep with one and then with another. Making their living by robbery, stealing from voyagers, and suspecting that those they prey on have swallowed down some precious piece of gold or jewel, they make them drink camel milk or hot water; then, standing on them with one foot, they force them to vomit up what they suspected them of swallowing, so that nothing is kept from them. They usually carry bows and arrows, and they also make weapons out of camel bones; they feed on camel milk and other coarse foods.

CLOTHING OF GIABEA, a Kingdom of Africa[5]

Giabea is a kingdom of Africa that is very hot and produces a great number of monkeys and baboons. The inhabitants of this land also have a great quantity of civet cats, and they worship idols in various ways and have recourse to incantations and other diabolical things. The children make designs on their breasts, necks, and arms with the point of a needle, as our ivory-workers do; they reinforce these marks with fire so that they will last, thinking this a great form of beauty. For one Barbary horse they pay five or six black slaves. They are valiant warriors; they poison their weapons with such a venom that as soon as they pierce someone, he is certain to die. They are very bold and have no fear of death, as has been seen in their assaults on Portuguese caravans. They eat food similar to that of the black Moors. They dress in a mid-calf-length camicia *of thin cotton with a needle-worked border at the hem, tied at the waist with a striped cotton sash; their shirt has a collar at its neck cut in the shape of a star. On their heads they wear a small white hat with a feather in the middle. They use round leather shields and spears with a poisoned iron tip.*

THE CLOTHING OF CERTAIN BLACK MOORS of Zanzibar, in Africa

The inhabitants of these lands are idolaters and they follow omens and witchcraft to such an extent that when they are planning an important action, if they receive an omen opposed to it, they give up on it. They have frizzy hair, and they go naked from the waist up. From the waist down they cover themselves with colored cloth and with the skins of wild animals; they let the tails of these skins hang down to the ground because they find them beautiful. They carry curved knives with wooden handles, decorated with gold or other metals. They bind their waists with painted cloths; in front, below this belt, they wear a purse attached to it. In their right hands they usually carry spears to wound their enemies from a distance; then they begin to use their bows and with these they fight courageously.

CLOTHING OF THE CANARY ISLANDS

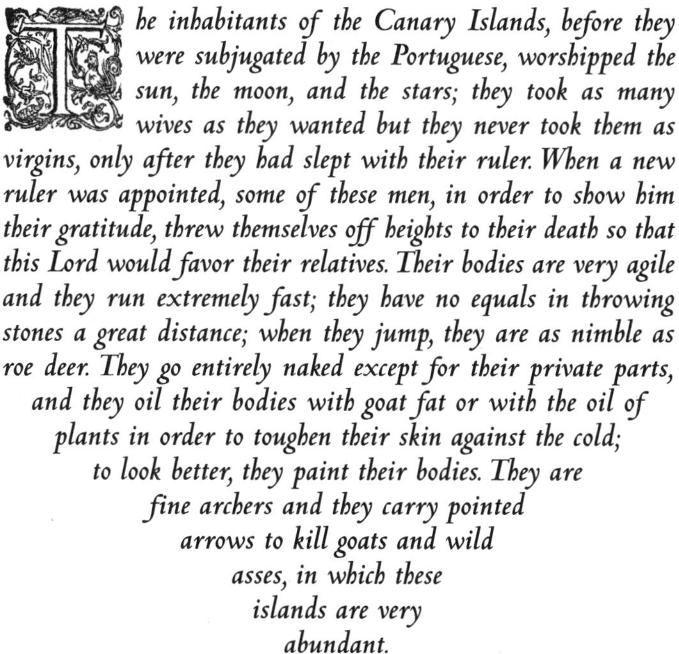

The inhabitants of the Canary Islands, before they were subjugated by the Portuguese, worshipped the sun, the moon, and the stars; they took as many wives as they wanted but they never took them as virgins, only after they had slept with their ruler. When a new ruler was appointed, some of these men, in order to show him their gratitude, threw themselves off heights to their death so that this Lord would favor their relatives. Their bodies are very agile and they run extremely fast; they have no equals in throwing stones a great distance; when they jump, they are as nimble as roe deer. They go entirely naked except for their private parts, and they oil their bodies with goat fat or with the oil of plants in order to toughen their skin against the cold; to look better, they paint their bodies. They are fine archers and they carry pointed arrows to kill goats and wild asses, in which these islands are very abundant.

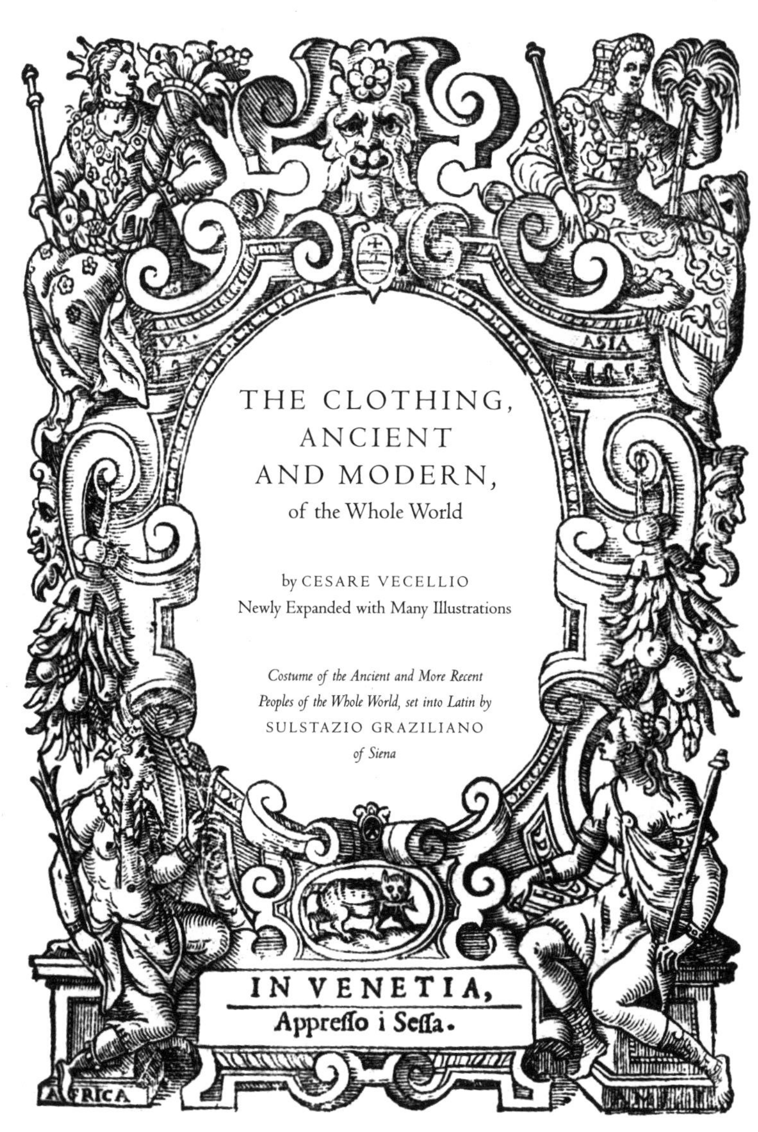
THE CLOTHING,
ANCIENT
AND MODERN,
of the Whole World
by CESARE VECELLIO
Newly Expanded with Many Illustrations
Costume of the Ancient and More Recent
Peoples of the Whole World, set into Latin by
SULSTAZIO GRAZILIANO
of Siena
ASIA
IN VENETIA,
Appresso i Sessa.
AFRICA

THE CLOTHING OF AMERICA

MEN OF PERU

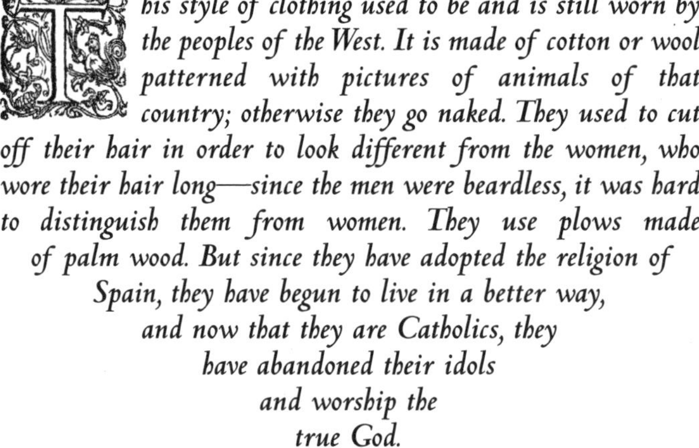

This style of clothing used to be and is still worn by the peoples of the West. It is made of cotton or wool patterned with pictures of animals of that country; otherwise they go naked. They used to cut off their hair in order to look different from the women, who wore their hair long—since the men were beardless, it was hard to distinguish them from women. They use plows made of palm wood. But since they have adopted the religion of Spain, they have begun to live in a better way, and now that they are Catholics, they have abandoned their idols and worship the true God.

NOBLEMAN
of Cuzco

The noblest men of this country that we call America wear various kinds of clothing, but none very costly. On top of an undergarment made of a square of cloth, they used to wear a mantle similar to our lenzuolo, *of black or white cotton or of wool. Today they cover themselves with a mantle that they call a* hacola. *They are delighted by any shirt the Spaniards may give them. They adorn their heads with a band of some lovely color, with two feathers attached above their forehead. They also pierce their ears, into which they put fish bones, but this is permitted only to the noblest men of Cuzco and those living in the areas surrounding it.*

PERUVIAN SOLDIER
Dressed for War

The soldiers of Peru wear this clothing, which consists of a cap padded with cotton, and instead of a corsalette, *a short robe open at the sides—this, too, is padded and covered with cloth. His weapons are slingshots and stones, from a large pouch at his side. They do not use swords, but instead carry a lance with a pointed copper tip. They wear a short garment of cotton, woven of various colors. Otherwise they go naked, in order to be quicker in battle.*

ANOTHER SOLDIER OF PERU, in Battle Dress

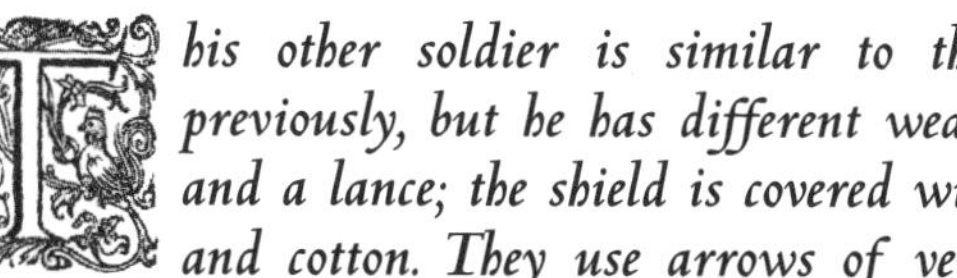

This other soldier is similar to the one shown previously, but he has different weapons, a shield and a lance; the shield is covered with heavy cloth and cotton. They use arrows of very hard palm wood, black in color, which can be shaped only with stone, since they have no iron or steel. If such an arrow falls into the water, it sinks immediately to the bottom. Instead of a sword, they carry a staff similar to a hatchet. They are very skillful in battle and they show the greatest obedience to their king, never turning their back on him. He dresses no differently from them except that on his head he wears a half-circle of gold with a precious stone and a large tassel of red wool with two feathers, similar to those worn by the noblemen of Cuzco.

CLOTHING OF THE WOMEN
of Peru

These women of Peru customarily dress in a way that means they need no tailors. Rather, they take a piece of cloth, wool or cotton, which covers them down to the feet, and they arrange the cloth at their shoulder with pins and cinch it at their waist; they then wrap a band twice around their body below their breasts, and with another band of different colors they wrap their bodies around again. As a result, they always have a healthy posture. They wear their hair loose to their shoulders, with a headband like the one shown. They marry young and go bare-armed. They spin, as can be seen in this print, most often while they are out of the house. Over their shoulders they wear a piece of cloth woven of different colors.

YOUNG MAN
of Mexico

In this province they use many delicate accessories of flowers and scents, and they adorn their heads with flowers and carry many of them in their hands, along with mirrors, which they think of as jewels; these are brought to them from Europe by the Spaniards. They dress as follows: underneath they wear a short garment of very thin cotton, with trousers that end above the knee. Their overgarments are patterned with beautiful designs of flowers, small animals, and bird feathers; otherwise, their arms and legs are naked. Others, from a nearby province called Chichen, go entirely naked because of the heat, covering only their private parts. They sleep in trees; in warfare they use darts.

MEXICAN NOBLEMAN

he more mature men wear a striped mantle arranged over their shoulders. Under it they wear the same clothing as the young man shown here, with the same adornments. They also wear camicie *of very thin fabric, decorated with flowers. They wear their hair long, knotted at their foreheads. They worship the sun and the moon and make sacrifices to them in order to win their help.*

CLOTHING OF THE WOMEN
of Mexico

These women of Mexico, and also those of the province of Nicaqua [now Nicaragua], dress in this way. Their garments for the most part are of wool or cotton, striped in different colors, similar to an uncut piece of cloth, which they gather at their hips and then tie, leaving an opening, and they overlap it at their sides; this comes down to mid-calf and is worn with a short overgarment open at the sides, in various colors. They leave the rest of their bodies bare, with their hair loose on their shoulders. They spin, as shown here. There are others who wear a piece of white cloth or other fabric over their shoulders. Now they follow the Catholic Church.

DESCRIPTION OF THE ISLAND OF VIRGINIA and Its Idol

The island of Virginia in the region of America was discovered in 1587; because of the variety of its dress and customs, I thought I should put it into this book. These people have an infinite number of gods, but one among them is the chief and the governor of all things. They believe that the soul is immortal, and that after death the good are rewarded and the bad are punished. Their idol appears as seen in the print, decorated with chains of copper, and he has a face that seems to be living flesh. It is a custom of the inhabitants that when their princes die, they take out their intestines and put them in the sun and dry them; then they wrap them in certain mats and set them on the highest level of their temples, and the priests care for them constantly.

CLOTHING OF THE KING
of the Island of Florida

he King of Florida wears this clothing, including a deerskin tied over his shoulders. The rest of their bodies are naked. But they take great pleasure in painting themselves and they wear the nails of their fingers and toes long. On their necks they wear a three-strand necklace of copper or silver, and chains of the same metal on their arms and legs, below the knee. They carry tall staffs in their hands, made very elegantly with feathers and tassels at the top. They have servants who hold up their garment so that it does not touch the ground when they go out; two others precede them with fans, to protect them from the sun. They wear their hair tied at the top of their heads, animal tails hang down behind them, and they wear fish bones in their ears.

CLOTHING OF THE QUEEN

his king, when he wants to take a wife, always chooses from among the noblest and most beautiful women who can be found, and he carries out many ceremonies. They set the Queen upon a platform decorated with painted animal skins, and at the back of it they make an arrangement of leaves and flowers for her. Then four men carry the platform; some go ahead of them, sounding trumpets, and two pages hold fans of bird feathers; a great number of unmarried girls carrying baskets full of fruit and flowers follow behind. The queen precedes them with her hair loose on her shoulders, wearing many necklaces on her neck, arms, and legs. They take great pleasure in painting their bodies; they cover their shoulders and private parts with tree leaves; and through their ears they wear fish bones.

CLOTHING OF SOLDIERS
and Captains

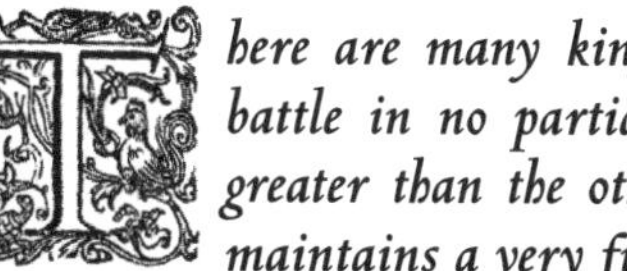*here are many kings on this island, who go into battle in no particular order; Even so, one man greater than the others can always be found, who maintains a very fine order of march and proceeds with his squadrons arranged in place near him; he himself goes at the center, surrounded by the bravest and strongest men in the field. He also has certain men called beaters whose duty it is to spy on the actions of the enemy and report them to the king. They do not use drums or trumpets but raise a terrible yell instead. They set up watches, to protect the king and the entire army. The leaders go into battle nude and terrifyingly painted, with copper circlets on their arms and legs, as can be seen here. They use arrows and decorate their hair with feathers.*

CLOTHING OF PAGES

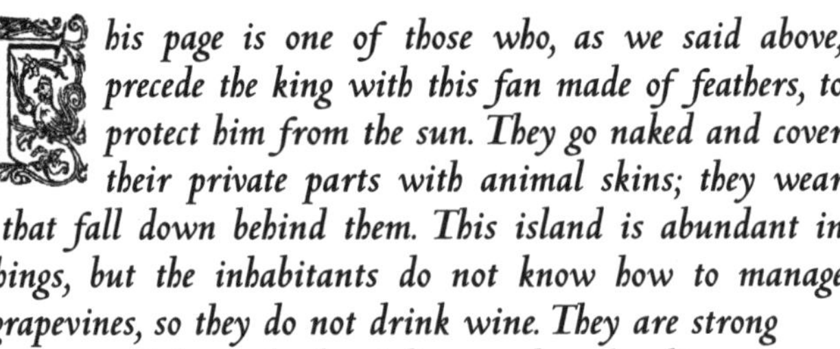

This page is one of those who, as we said above, precede the king with this fan made of feathers, to protect him from the sun. They go naked and cover their private parts with animal skins; they wear tails that fall down behind them. This island is abundant in all things, but the inhabitants do not know how to manage grapevines, so they do not drink wine. They are strong men and do not lead soft lives, and so they live a long time. When they die, their wives weep for them continuously for three days at their graves, without eating or drinking.

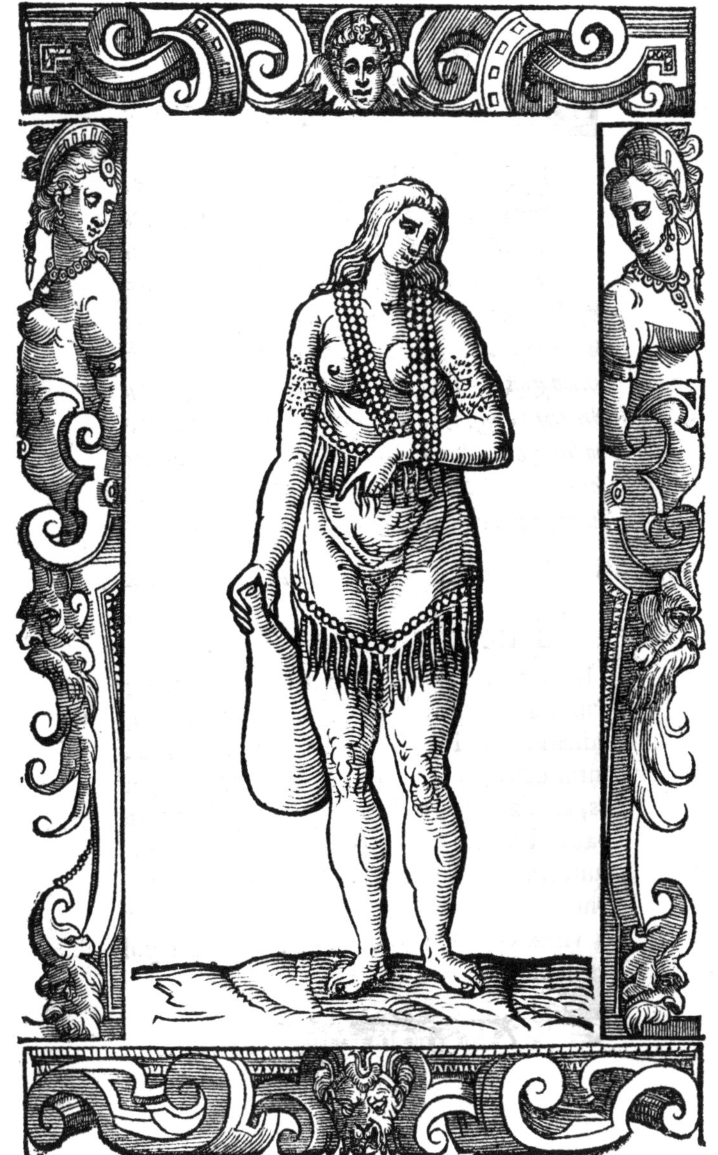

CLOTHING OF THE MARRIED WOMEN and Girls of Virginia

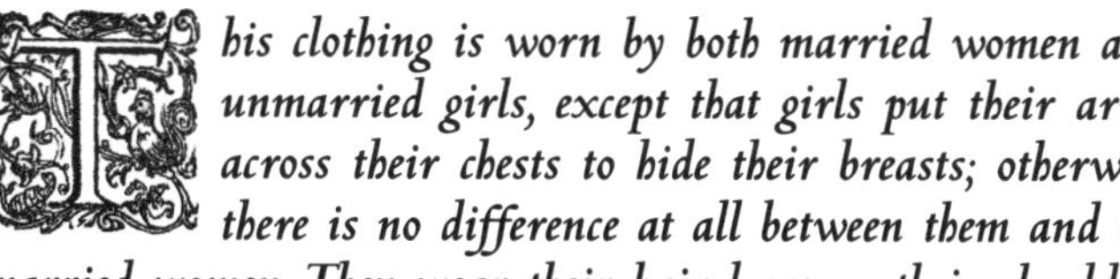

This clothing is worn by both married women and unmarried girls, except that girls put their arms across their chests to hide their breasts; otherwise there is no difference at all between them and the married women. They wear their hair loose on their shoulders and cover their private parts with animal skins. Around their necks they wear copper chains, and they paint themselves in a marvelous way. They have vases that they use to carry water, and they greatly enjoy hunting and fishing.

CLOTHING OF A CENTURION
of Virginia

Centurions wear certain skins of birds on their heads, with their beaks and feet through their ears; they do this in order to look more terrifying. On their chests they wear a particular object of copper or silver. They cover their private parts with skins, from which tails hang down. They have discs of copper at their thighs, and they also wear chains around their legs and arms. In their hands they carry a staff, which, at the top, is like a blade edged with nails, which they use to strike dangerous blows; and in this way they go into battle.

A LEADER
on the Battlefield

This set of clothing is even more beautiful than the previous set. On their heads these leaders wear a lion skin and colored feathers; they cover themselves all over with this kind of skin, and they tie it on with another at their navel. They wear the same things as the preceding man, with the same tails, and they paint themselves in various ways.

504

CLOTHING OF THE WOMEN
of Virginia Island

The women of Virginia Island have an admirable way of carrying their children, resting them on their shoulders, as can be seen in the sketch. They wear their hair long and loose on their shoulders; they wear no clothing except for an animal skin, with which they cover their private parts. They delight in fishing. They have vases of a highly perfected material for cooking, they mix fish with various fruits, and they live in a sober fashion.

CLOTHING OF THE PRIESTS OF SECOTA, on Virginia Island

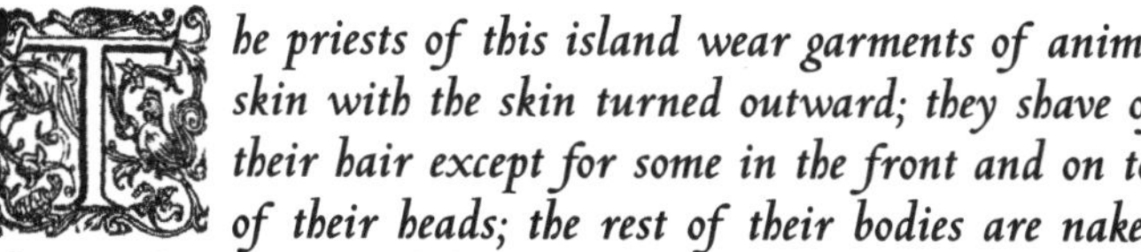

The priests of this island wear garments of animal skin with the skin turned outward; they shave off their hair except for some in the front and on top of their heads; the rest of their bodies are naked, that is, their arms and legs. They practice magic arts, and they enjoy fishing and hunting. The majority of them are old. They inhabit a part of the island called Secota, and for this reason they are called Secotan priests.

506

THE LEADING AND OLDEST MEN
of the Island

The principal and oldest men of the island also shave off their hair, and wear the same crest as the priests. When they speak, they hold their arms in this fashion, saying that it is a sign of prudence. At their necks they wear a medallion of gold or copper, and bracelets on their arms. They cover their private parts with animal skins, but otherwise they go naked, with no covering.

PRINCES
of Virginia Island

These princes, or, rather, minor kings, use arrows, darts, and bows in warfare. They cover themselves with no garment except a small animal skin with which they conceal their private parts. They wear their hair cut short, except for some that they tie over their ears and also some on top of their heads, resembling a crest, along with colored feathers. They attach animal feet to their ears, and they, too, wear copper necklaces. Otherwise, they are not at all different from other men of the island.

THE END

IN VENETIA,
M. D. XCVIII.
Appresso Gio. Bernardo Sessa.

Dedication (pp. 50–51)

1 Pietro Montalbano, Count of Conegliano. See Vecellio's laudatory description of him in his section on Conegliano.

2 For Henri III's stay in Conegliano on his way to Venice, see F. Sansovino, *Venetia città nobilissima*, 1581; facsimile ed. A. Prosperi [Bergamo, (2000), f.162b. Maria of Austria was the wife of the Bohemian king and Holy Roman Emperor Maximilian II (reigned as HRE from 1564–76). A 1550 portrait of her by Anthonis Mor is in the Prado.

Discourse on Ancient and Modern Clothing (pp. 53–64)

1 "Adspirant aurae in noctem, nec candida cursus/ Luna negat" (The breezes blow in the night, nor does/the pale moon prevent his journey), *Aeneid* VII, 8–10, where Virgil describes the moon in the sea as Aeneas sails toward Latium. The same image and motto appear in Vecellio's *Corona delle nobili et virtuose donne*.

2 Senahar (also called Sinhar) was the large region in southeastern Mesopotamia containing the city of Babylon. See the map of "The Kingdoms of the Ancient World," in *The Interpreter's Bible* (New York, 1956), VI: 340.

3 Balsam, or *styrax preparatus*, is a fragrant resin yielded by the Liquidambar orientalis, a tree native to Asia Minor.

4 Flavius Josephus, a Jewish historian (AD c. 37–101), author of *Jewish Antiquities*, a twenty-volume history of the Jews from the Biblical Creation to AD 66.

5 For one version of the story of Europa, see Ovid, *Metamorphoses*, II, 833–75; on her son Minos, King of Crete, see VII, 481 and VIII, 6, 23-35.

6 In the Old Testament (Genesis 13–14), Abraham begins as a wealthy man in Africa and then travels through Egypt to Palestine at God's command.

7 The Meotide Marsh was located north of Moscow; its waters flowed into the Don.

8 Valacchia (Wallachia) was roughly the area now called Romania.

9 Ambrosius Macrobius was a late Roman philosopher and writer of the 5th century AD. His *Saturnalia* (a seven-volume commentary on Virgil) is probably the source of the claim that Hesperus influenced the peninsula of Italy.

10 Terms set in bold type and defined for the first time in brackets can be found, explained more fully, in the Glossary. After their first appearance in our text, they are set in italics.

11 The Latin *candidus* means white.

12 Pliny the Elder (AD 23–79) was a Roman historian and natural philosopher, author of *Historia Naturalis*.

13 Aelianus Claudus (AD 80–140), a Roman philosopher and historian in the reign of Hadrian, was the author of a book on the cities of Italy.

14 Flavio Biondo (1388–1463), an Italian archaeologist and historian, wrote *L'Italia Illustrata* (1474), a description of Italy in fourteen regions.

15 A patriarchal city was one that, in the Byzantine era, had a patriarch, or bishop, appointed to it.

16 Sestertii were the main Roman coins in late republican and early imperial times; a common soldier in Augustus' army earned 900 sestertii a year (www.geocities.com/Athens/Delphi/9601/nummi/coins.html).

17 Sextus Tarquinius, the son of the last Roman king Tarquinius Superbus, raped Lucretia, the wife of Collaltinus; her suicide and call for vengeance led Lucius Junius Brutus, Collaltinus' cousin, to drive the Tarquins out of Rome and to establish a republic. The story is told in Livy's history of Rome, *Ab Urbe Condita*, Book I, LVII–LX.

18 Athaneus, a late Roman historian of the reign of the Emperor Gallienus (AD ?260–68), wrote a book on military machines.

19 Plutarch, a Greek historian who lived in Rome during the time of Hadrian, wrote a series of forty-six parallel lives of Greek and Roman men.

20 Marcellinus Ammianus, a Greek born in Antioch, was a late Roman historian, author of *Rerum Gestarum Libri XXXI* (325–30), a history of the Empire from AD 96 to 378.

21 Marcus Valerius Martialis (AD c. 40–102), a Roman poet, wrote satirical epigrams.

22 Gaius Suetonius (AD 69–140), a Roman historian, wrote *The Lives of the Caesars*, on the first Roman emperors and their families.

23 Aulus Gellius was a Roman grammarian and historian who died about AD 175.

24 Quintus Ennius, a Roman poet (*Annales, Tragoediae*), died in 169 BC.

25 Marcus Terentius Varro (*De Lingua Latina, De Re Rustica*), known mainly for his book on husbandry, died in 27 BC.

26 Lucius Fenestella, a Roman historian, died in about AD 36.

27 Caius Ennius Lucilius, a satiric poet, died in 103 BC.

28 Attilius: probably a Roman consul active during the first Punic War (264–41 BC).

29 Sejanus was a Roman consul condemned in AD 31.

BOOK I

The Clothing of Ancient and Modern Rome (pp. 66–89)

1 Giovanni Maria Bodovino (also Bodino, Boduino) was a manuscript illuminator, born in Friuli in 1503, who spent his working life in Venice, where he died in 1600.

2 Pius V was Pope 1566–72.

The Clothing of Early Venice and the Veneto (pp. 90–154)

1 The Venetian term Vecellio uses here, *fondaço*, meant a warehouse for merchandise or a place where foreign traders were obliged to reside, store their merchandise and conduct their trades. The word had an Eastern origin. Juergen Schulz points out, "The term derives from the Arabic *funduq*, a word for the same sort of institution" (*The New Palaces of Medieval Venice* [University Park, Pa, 2004]), p. 156, n. 123.

2 This was the large ruling body of Venice, with legislative power over the city and its territories; it also elected the doge. The Senate was a smaller body, to which only men able to prove that they came from old Venetian families could belong.

3 Vecellio will continue to call the doge the "Prince," in spite of the fact that the doge ruled by election rather than hereditary right.

4 The word Vecellio uses here is *paludamento*, derived from the Latin *paludamentum*, a general's cloak.

5 The Procurators were appointed for a life term, originally as overseers of churches, almshouses and hospitals in Venice, but their duties grew to include executing wills, collecting and dispensing state monies, participating in the Senate and, up until 1582, the Council of Ten (the senators responsible for public order).

6 The *Savi Grandi*, or Chief Ministers, were the members of a six-man commission that supported the Senate's lawmaking though they themselves lacked the right to vote.

7 The *Arsenale* was the Venetian state shipyard, a large complex at the northwestern edge of the city.

8 *Pietra viva*, a hard, valuable limestone from the peninsula of Istria, in the northwest corner of Croatia.

9 Jacopo Sansovino, a Roman architect who came to Venice in 1537, was hired by the Procurators to work on the complex of San Marco, for which he built not only the library but also the mint and the loggia.

10 The *Compagnie delle Calze* ("tights clubs") were societies of young patrician men; they flourished up to the middle of the sixteenth century. Their members organized and performed in public entertainments of various kinds. For further comments on these groups by Vecellio, see pp. 144–6.

11 Francesco Sansovino, the son of Jacopo, was a printer and the author of two books on the city of Venice, *Tutte le cose notabili che sono in Venetia* (1556) and *Venetia città nobilissima* (1581).

12 Ordelafo Faliero was doge from 1102 to 1117. Vecellio may be confusing him with Vitale Faliero, doge from 1084 to 1096.

13 The Censors oversaw elections, and punished anyone attempting to use improper influence; the Councillors were members of the Great Council; the Savi of the Terra Firma were members of the agency that directed war, finance and military affairs in Venetian territories on the mainland; the Heads of the Council of Ten, occupying short, rotating terms, advised the doge and his six councillors on treason and state policy; the Avogadori del Comun were public attorneys, eligible to attend the meetings of every council and responsible for prosecuting state officials.

14 Titian painted a portrait of a man sometimes identified as this Gregorio Titian (Vecellio's grandfather); the painting is now in the Pinacoteca Ambrosiana in Milan.

15 Herodias was Herod's daughter, identified by Josephus as Salomé, who convinced Herod, by dancing, to execute John the Baptist (Matthew, 14).

16 Francesco Sansovino describes this costume and its prohibition in Book 10 of *Venetia città nobilissima* (facsimile of the edition of 1581, ed. Adriano Prosperi [Bergamo, 2002]), p. 152.

17 Piero [Pietro] Gradenigo was doge from 1289 to 1311.

18 Lucretia was famous for her good housewifery. Livy tells of the exemplary behavior her husband found her engaged in when he arrived home unexpectedly, accompanied by other Roman officers: "Lucretia, though it was late at night, was busily engaged upon her wool, while her maidens toiled about her in the lamplight" (*Ab Urbe Condita*, I, LVII, 8–9).

19 Giambellino: a nickname for Giovanni Bellini (c. 1430–1516), a principal painter of fifteenth-century Venice.

20 This portrait would have been part of the cycle of the Miracles of the True Cross, painted by Gentile Bellini, Carpaccio, and others.

21 Philip II of Spain wore a narrow moustache and a goatee (visible in various portraits of him by Titian); Henri IV of France, after receiving a head wound, wore his hair short and curly.

22 Pietro Loredan was doge from 1567 to 1570.

23 Luigi (Alvise) Vivarini was a member of a family of fifteenth-century Venetian painters.

24 Vecellio refers here to Sebastiano Venier, doge from 1577 to 1578.

25 This is Lorenzo Celsi, doge from 1361 to 1365.

26 Vecellio refers to Francesco Sansovino's second book, *Venetia città nobilissima* (1581).

27 Doge Ziani was Sebastiano Ziani (doge from 1172 to 1178). The Venetians were very proud of the successful defense they mounted for the pope, which they saw as the reason that Barbarossa agreed to a peace treaty in 1176.

28 Lorenzo Priuli was doge from 1556 to 1559.

29 Ezzelino da Romano (1194–1259), an Italian Ghibelline leader, supported the Emperor Frederick II against the pope from 1232 onward; he ruled with famous cruelty in Padua until 1256 but died in prison after an attempt to conquer Milan. Dante sets him (under the name Azzolino) in Canto 12 of *The Inferno* (ll. 109–10), among the tyrants.

30 Campson Gauri (Qansuh al-Ghuri) was the Mamluk sultan in Egypt from 1500 to 1516. Jeannine Guérin Dalle Mese suggests that Vecellio used as a model the figure of the sultan in a painting formerly attributed to Giovanni Bellini, *The Reception of the Venetian Ambassadors*, now in the Louvre (*L'Occhio di Cesare Vecellio: Abiti e costumi esotici nel '500* [Alessandria, Italy, 1998]), pp. 137–8.

31 Vecellio refers here to Vittore Carpaccio (c. 1465–1522), who painted Turkish settings in his cycle on St George for the Scuola di San Giorgio degli Schiavoni in Venice though he probably never went to Turkey himself. For commentary on his use of earlier images of Turkish dress and architecture, see P. Fortini Brown, *Venetian Narrative Painting in the Age of Carpaccio* (New Haven, 1988), pp. 209–16, and J. Raby, *Venice, Dürer and the Oriental Mode* (Florence and London, 1983), pp. 66–81.

32 The Venetian *Bailo* in Constantinople acted as an ambassador to the Sultan and oversaw the welfare of Venetian businessmen working in the city.

33 Pietro Candiano I, the fifteenth doge of Venice, reigned only one year, in 887.

34 Charles V (King Charles I of Spain) ruled as Holy Roman Emperor from 1519 to 1558 and was a patron of Titian and other painters in the Vecellio family.

35 Vecellio refers to Philip II, king of Spain 1556–98.

36 The Collegio was the steering committee of the Senate; the Signoria was the government as a whole.

The Clothing of Modern Venice and the Veneto (pp. 155–234)

1 Venier confronted Selim's Ottomans at Lepanto in October 1571.

2 Governors were officials appointed to oversee Venetian territories on the mainland and islands; these Provedditori were in charge of castles and fortresses in the territories.

3 Consiglieri were the members of the Great Council; the Cancellier Grande, or Head Chancellor, was the head of the state bureaucracy.

4 Theriac was a complex tonic, made from diverse recipes by apothecaries and advertised as a stimulant to masculine potency.

5 For a different translation of these terms and a study of early gondoliers, see Dennis Romano, *Housecraft and Statecraft*, (Balitmore, 1996) chap. 1, p. 28 ff.

6 Vecellio refers jokingly here to Diana, the Roman goddess associated with chastity and represented with a crescent moon on her head.

7 The Sensa was a two-week holiday and fair, held in Venice from Ash Wednesday to Easter, celebrating Christ's ascent into heaven.

8 The fan shown in this print is called a *ventuolo*, or "weathercock fan."

9 The category of *dismessa*, as Virginia Cox explains, meant a lay spinster, planning neither to marry nor to enter a convent, possibly living on a life annuity from her parents and housed with her brothers or other relatives ("The Single Self: Feminist Thought and the Marriage Market in Early Modern Venice," *Renaissance Quarterly* 48 [1995], 513–81). See also Federica Ambrosini, "Toward a Social History of Women in Venice from the Renaissance to the Enlightenment," in *Venice Reconsidered: The History and Civilization of an Italian City-State*, 129–1797, ed. J. Martin and D. Romano (Baltimore, 2000), pp. 420–53.

10 Bartholomeo Bontempele became an extremely wealthy Venetian, owning two shops on the Merceria. Generous to his family (in his will of 1613, he left 100 ducats a year to an unmarried niece), he also left 100,000 ducats to the hospital of San Giovanni and Paolo. The playwright Fabio Glissenti wrote *Il Diligente* in his honor. It is possible that Vecellio hoped for patronage from Bontempele.

11 Hospitals (*Spedali*) were not only shelters for the sick but also charitable institutions founded to house people not otherwise integrated into Venetian society. On their management, see B. Pullan, *Rich and Poor in Renaissance Venice* (Cambridge, 1971), Part II, chaps. 1–2.

12 An intricate legend arose regarding Doge Ziani's mediation between the Holy Roman Emperor, Frederick Barbarossa, and Pope Alexander III, including a successful naval battle against Barbarossa's son Otto led by Ziani and, as marks of gratitude, the donation by the Pope of a set of symbolic objects to Ziani and future doges: a white candle, silver trumpets, leaden seals, an umbrella, a ring, and eight banners. On the legend and the reality, see Edward Muir, *Civic Ritual in Renaissance Venice* (Princeton, 1988), pp. 103–18. Guido Ruggiero identifies the fourteenth-century doge and chronicler Andrea Dandolo as one of the principal elaborators of this myth; see "Politica e Giustizia," in *Storia di Venezia dalle origini alla caduta della Serenissima*, vol. III, *Formazione dello stato patrizio*, ed. A. Tenenti (Rome, 1977).

13 Gioseffo Zarlino (1517–1590) was Chapel Master at San Marco and a prolific composer.

14 Horace, *Odes*, ed. P. Shorey and G. Laing (Chicago, 1919; facsimile, 1962), Book II, 10. Our translation.

15 Basilio Bessarion (1403–1472), a Greek scholar and churchman, studied in Constantinople, lived for a time in Bologna, visited Venice with Pope Giovanni VIII in 1438 and 1460, and left over seven hundred Greek and Latin texts to the Venetian library.

16 This is the first time Vecellio mentions the printmaker Christopher Chrieger, using an Italian version of his name; this was the German printmaker who collaborated with him throughout both his books on costume.

17 In 1569, the Venetians began a war against the Ottoman Emperor Selim over the ownership of Cyprus. They had a first victory that year, though they lost the island to the Turks in 1573.

18 This was the much celebrated sea battle of Lepanto, at which Italian and Spanish galley soldiers defeated the Ottoman navy.

19 Wallonia was a kingdom in present-day south-central Belgium.

20 In 1552 the Ottomans tried but failed to take over the city of Szeged, defended by the Hungarians, its inhabitants, and their allies.

21 Pio Enea degli Obizzi was a captain of Venetian troops, who took part in the siege of Lepanto and later built a great castle in the Eugean hills outside Padua.

22 The *cittadini* were Venetian citizens, either members of longstanding families who regularly filled official positions in the state bureaucracy, or foreigners awarded the title as an honorific.

23 *Bastagi* appears to be derived from the Venetian dialect terms *basta* or *bastin*, the circlet of cloth such porters wore on their heads to protect themselves against injury from the heavy objects they carried.

The Clothing of Lombardy (pp. 235–57)

1 This is the second and last time Vecellio mentions his German collaborator. At this point, Chrieger/Guerra was obviously alive and well, so it must have been at a later date that Vecellio drew and described the "Terza Perspettiva della Piazza San Marco" (appearing toward the end of his section on Venice), in which he mentions Guerra's death.

2 Nasarete Eunuco, or Narses, Roman general (c. 468–c. 573), later identified by Vecellio as the leader of the armies of the Byzantine emperor Justinian (ruled from 527–65).

3 Cristoforo de Maganza lived from 1556 to about 1630.

The Clothing of Liguria or Genoa (pp. 258–77)

1 In his 1598 volume, Vecellio calls this needle-case an *agusello.*

2 This may be the Antonio Cappello (1494–1565) whose paintings appear in the church of Santa Maria del Carmine in Brescia and who, as Provedditore, oversaw the rebuilding of the loggia in the Piazza San Marco.

3 Ezzelino ruled with famous cruelty in Padua until 1256.

4 Giangaleazzo Visconti (1351–1402) became Duke of Milan in 1395 as a reward for his service to the Holy Roman Emperor.

5 Attila, king of the Huns from 434–53, invaded Italy in 452.

6 Vecellio refers here to Henri III's visit to Venice in 1574.

7 A patriarchal city was one large enough to have a patriarch, the equivalent of a chief bishop in the later church.

8 Otto IV, a German king and Holy Roman Emperor (from 1209 to 1215), ceded many Italian territories to the papacy.

9 Odorico and then Giorgio Piloni were Vecellio's patrons in Pieve di Cadore. He continued to work for them and to paint Piloni family portraits up until the 1570s.

10 Bartoli di Sassoferrata (born about 1313) taught law in Pisa and produced a two-part set of lectures on Roman law, *Super Digesto Veteri*. Baldo d'Aguglione, a late thirteenth- and early fourteenth-century Florentine, was one of the compilers of the *Ordinamenti di giustizia*, a summum of Florentine law.

The Clothing of Tuscany (pp. 278–97)

1 This duchess was Eleanora of Toledo, who introduced Spanish styles of dress to Florence.

The Clothing of the Kingdom of Naples (pp. 298–316)

1 Francesco Curia was a Neapolitan painter, who exchanged letters with Vecellio.

2 Charles of Anjou was made king of Naples by Pope Clement IV in 1266.

The Clothing of the Kingdom of France (pp. 317–32)

1 This is Jeanne I of Naples, of the French ducal family of Anjou.

The Clothing of the Kingdom of Spain (pp. 333–44)

1 The Roman Stoic Seneca the Younger committed suicide in AD 65.

2 Averröes, a Greek-Arabic philosopher (Arabic name Ibn Rushd, 1126–98), wrote influential commentaries on Aristotle and Plato. The Church declared him a heretic for arguing that matters of faith and science required different forms of thought.

The Clothing of Germany [including Livonia, Silesia, Danzig, Denmark, Sweden and Bohemia] (pp. 345–86)

1 Otto II was Holy Roman Emperor from 973 to 983.

2 Vecellio seems to be mistaken in his date here. Otto II, who started this process, ruled from 973–983 and probably died in around 1000.

3 Nero Claudius Drusus Germanicus (98–38 BC), the stepson of Augustus Caesar, attacked many parts of Germany and eventually died there.

4 Mary of Hungary (1505–58) was the sister of Charles V, the third Habsburg king of Spain, and the wife of Louis of Hungary.

5 Strabo, a late Greek geographer and philosopher (c. 63 BC–after AD 21), wrote six books on the geography of Europe.

6 This Sigismund, a distinguished humanist, was king of Poland from 1506 to 1548.

The Clothing of Helvetia [including Prussia, the Low Countries, Hungary, Dalmatia, Poland, and Russia] (pp. 387–410)

1 The Uskoks were Christians driven out of Bosnia and Dalmatia by the Ottoman Turks. After the peace between Venice and the Ottomans following the battle of Lepanto (1571), the Uskoks were enlisted by the Hapsburgs under Maximilian II (the grandson of the Holy Roman Emperor Charles V, the Holy Roman Emperor, and the archduke of Austria), to defend their borders against the Turks. The Uskoks (whose name derives from the Croatian word for "refugees") settled in Segna (now Senj, in northwest Croatia) and lived as pirates in the Adriatic. Their name is preserved in their place of origin, a mountainous region of present-day southeast Slovenia bordering on Austria, called Uskokengebirge ("the Uskoks' Mountains") in German.

2 Claudius Ptolemaeus (85–165), an Egyptian mathematician, astronomer, and geographer. His influential *Geography*, based on a Tyrian source, underestimated the size of the earth and had to be radically revised after Europeans circumnavigated the globe.

3 This is the apostle Jude Thaddeus, who preached in Syria, Mesopotamia, and Persia, where he was martyred in the first century AD.

4 Saint Bartholomew, also an apostle, is thought to have preached in Asia Minor and India as well as Armenia, where he was killed by being flayed alive.

5 *Cervosa* (beer) referred at this time to any fermented drink other than wine. *Cervosa* (*cervogia* or *cervisia* in later Italian) could be made from hops and grains, but also from fruit juices and herbs.

6 Gregory XIII was pope from 1572 to 1575. The name of the Jesuit missionary to Moscow who accompanied the Moscovite ambassador on his visit to Venice was Antonio Possevino.

The Clothing of Flanders (pp. 411–16)

1 Marie of Burgundy (a region that included the Low Countries) married Maximilian (who would be Holy Roman Emperor from 1493 to his death in 1519) in 1477; she died in 1482.

2 Mediomatrica was the Roman name for Metz, as the central city and region of Roman holdings in France and Germany.

The Clothing of England [including Gotland and Livellandia] (pp. 416–26)

1 Albion, it was thought, was derived from the Latin *albus*, meaning "white."

2 Vecellio refers here to Henry II, at whose suggestion Thomas Becket, Archbishop of Canterbury, was murdered in 1170.

3 Oland and Gotland are off the southeast coast of Sweden; Sjelland, to the southwest of Sweden, is now part of Denmark.

The Clothing of Turkey (pp. 426–65)

1 This is Osman (or Othman) I (1259–1336), founder of the Ottoman Empire, who took power in 1290 after the collapse of his overlords, the Seljuk Turks. Supported by Muslim forces, he expanded his rule throughout northwest Asia Minor by defeating Christian leaders, but he maintained a policy of religious tolerance in his territories.

2 Constantinople fell to the Ottoman sultan Mohammed II in 1453. The Sultan in power at the time Vecellio wrote was Murad III, the grandson of Suleiman the Magnificent; Murad III ruled from 1574 to 1595. For a useful discussion of Venetian writers on Murad and the Turks in general, see J. G. Dalle Mese, *L'Occhio de Cesare Vecellio* (Alessandria, Italy, 1998), Chapter 2, "Vestire alla turchesca."

3 Romania was the area ruled by the Byzantine church; it is not the present-day Romania.

4 Constantine ordered the building of this new capital city in AD 330.

5 The last Byzantine emperor of Constantinople, when it was captured by Mohammed II in 1453, was Constantine XI.

6 Anatolia, now central Turkey, was the eastern part of the Ottoman Empire.

7 In this sentence Vecellio is emphatically countering the claim, made by a French voyager to Turkey, Nicolas de Nicolay, and other writers, that Turkish women, especially in the baths, had sexual relations with one another. See Nicolay's *Navigations et pérégrinations orientales* (Lyon, 1567), pp. 72–3.

8 *L'ostro*, the word Vecellio uses here, is a synonym for *porpora*. See Glossary.

9 A *canna* was a measuring stick between 2 and 2.6 meters in length.

10 Caramania was a region in south central Turkey, near the present city of Konya, about eighty miles north of the Mediterranean.

11 *Groppi* is Vecellio's version of *gripi*, small sailing vessels used by the Ottomans against Venetian galleys. See Colin Thubron, *The Venetians*, in *The Seafarers* (Alexandria, Va., 1980), p. 107.

12 Cneius Pompeius Magnus (106–48 BC) began his career as a general when he was commissioned in 67 BC to rid the Mediterranean of pirates. He later became part of the triumvirate that also included Octavian and Lepidus.

The Clothing of Greece (pp. 466–84)

1 Nestorius, a fifth-century patriarch of Constantinople, argued that Christ had two separate natures; he established a sect that spread throughout Iran and Iraq. Eutyches (378–452) argued against Nestorius but was deposed by a Catholic council and exiled from Constantinople in 449.

2 Pera/Galata, situated at the meeting-point of the canal called the Golden Horn and the Bosporus directly north and west of Istanbul, was reserved for non-Muslims, including Greeks and Jews, from the mid-fifteenth century. Culturally, it was always oriented toward the West. It is now part of the city of Istanbul.

3 Bursa, a town in northwest Turkey near the Sea of Marmara and the capital of the Ottoman Empire from 1325–65, was located on the Silk Route and famous for the silks it produced.

4 George Castriota, an Albanian national hero (1404–68), the son of a prince of Northern Albania, was named "Iskander Bey" by the Turks, hence "Scanderbeg." Taken hostage and educated in the court of Sultan Murad II, he escaped in 1443, unified warring Albanian chiefs, and defended Albania against repeated Turkish attacks up to 1461.

5 This is Theodosius I, 346–95, emperor first of the Roman and then the Byzantine empire. After defeating the Franks in Gaul, he converted to Christianity in 380 and humbled himself at the cathedral of Milan, at the command of Ambrose, its archbishop.

BOOK II

Discourse on the Clothing, Ancient and Modern, of Africa and Asia (pp. 485–6)

1 By "the greater sea," Vecellio means the Pacific Ocean, first discovered and named by the Spanish explorer Ferdinand Magellan in 1521, though Vecellio thinks of it as the Indian Ocean.

The Clothing of Caramania (pp. 487–91)

1 The Venetian cartographer Paolo Forlani, commenting in 1564 on his map of Caramania, describes it as bounded by the Euphrates on the east and by the Strait of Constantinople on the west. It is now part of south-central part of Turkey, south of the city of Konya, with a coastline along the Mediterranean, north and east of Cyprus.

2 Frederick Barbarossa (1155–90), a German king and Holy Roman Emperor, challenged by Pope Adrian IV, invaded Italy in 1158. During the Third Crusade, he drowned in Cilicia.

3 Alexander the Great (356–23 BC) first defeated Darius, King of Persia (336–30) at Issus in 333.

The Clothing of Armenia [including Georgia and Persia] (pp. 492–506)

1 Probably this is Anahit, a fertility goddess worshipped in pre-Christian Armenia and then associated with Artemis in the Greek pantheon.

2 Alexander made war against the Persians from 327 to 323 when he died in Babylon.

3 Valdacca was the Tuscan word for Baghdad. Arab Muslims led by Abu Bakr captured Ctesiphon, Persias's capital city, in 637, and ruled the region from Baghdad for the next two centuries.

The Clothing of Syria and Damascus [including the East Indies, Ethiopia, China, and Japan] (pp. 507–529)

1 These are travelers from A'zaz, in the northwest corner of Syria.

2 Vecellio here is clearly using the Ptolemaic system of describing the globe, taking Spain as the country farthest west and India as the farthest east.

3 The Romans, under Pompey, conquered Syria in 53 BC. In the fourth century AD the country came under the rule of the Byzantine Empire. After Syria was conquered by Arab Muslims in 640, European Crusaders during the eleventh to fourteenth centuries sometimes succeeded in taking it back.

4 It becomes obvious here that Vecellio, as he admits, is using dubious reports from undependable travelers. On more and less credulous Italians who traveled to India, see J.-P. Rubiés, *Travel and Ethnonology in the Renaissance: South India through European Eyes, 1250–1625* (Cambridge, 2000).

5 This story of the king of Cambay, who poisoned his enemies by spitting at them, comes from Ludovico de Varthema, a Bolognese who traveled in the East from 1501–1508 and personally recounted his voyage to the Venetian senate; this tale he heard told by the Gujarati Muslims of northwest India (Rubiés, *Travel and Ethnonology*, p. 154).

6 This passage is a digression on Vecellio's part because Chaldea was a region not in India but in southern Mesapotamia, sometimes considered to include Babylon.

7 Andrea Butta, member of a famous noble family of Belluno, was the earliest European pilgrim to reach Mecca, in 1503.

8 The Crocevalle family was another famous noble clan of Belluno.

9 Prester John was a legendary Christian priest and king, said from the twelfth century onward to travel around his Asian territories with his entire court; in later versions of the legend, he was said to rule in Africa. See R. Silverberg, *The Realm of Prester John* (Athens, 1972, rpt. 1996) and F. Relaño, *The Shaping of Africa: Cosmographic Discourse and Cartographic Science in Late Medieval and Early Modern Europe* (Burlington, VT., 2002), Part I. Vecellio presents a print of Prester John, one of his courtiers and a page, as the first of three rulers in his 1598 book, *Libro Decimo*, on Africa.

The Clothing of Africa (pp. 530–51)

1 Qansuh al-Ghuri, the last Mamluk sultan of Egypt, was defeated by Selim I in 1517.

2 Domenico Trevisan published an account of his embassy to Cairo, a copy of which Vecellio very likely read in the Piloni library in Belluno (Dalle Mese, *L'Occhio di Cesare Vecellio*, p. 50, n 38).

3 Tlemcen is now a town near the coast of northern Algeria, about halfway between Rabat to the west and Algiers to the east.

4 Ceffala is the modern Sofala in Mozambique, a region halfway down the Indian Ocean coast of the country (Dalle Mese, *L'Occhio di Cesare Vecellio*, p. 179).

5 Giabea, as European explorers used the word in this period, meant present-day Gambia.

GLOSSARY OF COSTUME AND FABRIC

In this glossary, headwords start with the correct form of the term; sometimes two interchangeable forms are given in succession, separated by a comma. Variant forms used by Vecellio are given in parentheses, as are alternative terms; alternatives are introduced by the word 'or'.

OPPOSITE, LEFT AND RIGHT

***balzo* worn by a man** Lorenzo Lotto, *Messer Marsilio and His Wife* (detail), 1523

bavero with gold and pearls Agnolo Bronzino, *Eleonora of Toledo as a Young Woman*, c. 1541

RIGHT AND FAR RIGHT

braghetta Bernardino Licinio, *Ottaviano Grimani, Procurator of San Marco* (detail), 1541

bracciali British school, *A Young Lady aged 21, possibly Helena Snakenborg, later Marchioness of Northampton* (detail), 1569

ARGENTINO: a silver-gray color.

BALZO: a tubular headdress, worn by women and men, made of a willow or metal frame covered with fabric and decorated with various trims, including gold netting, jewels and ribbons.

BAVELLA: floss silk, that is, thread or fabric made of raw (untreated) silk.

BAVERO (*bavaro*): a shoulder covering. As women's attire, a piece of thin silk or linen worn above a bodice to cover the shoulders or breast, sometimes joined to a collar. The word can also mean a broad collar, lapel or short shoulder cape.

BAVERO DI TRINA (or *collaro di trina*); a high, standing collar, often pleated, made of lace or trimmed with lace.

BERETTINO: an ash gray color.

BERRETTA À TAGLIERE: a flat-topped cap of gathered fabric, worn by merchants and older men (from *tagliere,* Venetian dialect for *taglia,* meaning platter).

BERRETTA À TOZZO (from *tozzo,* Venetian dialect for a small, round-bottomed boat): a high, full, rounded cap, usually of velvet, worn by patricians and young men.

BIAVO: sky-blue or bluish color.

BIGIO: a gray color, as in undyed wool.

BISSO: very thin, fine linen.

BOLZACCHINO (*borsachino*): a buskin, or soft, tight boot ending below the knee.

BOTTANA: a sturdy cotton used for veils.

ABOVE, LEFT TO RIGHT

balzo Parmigianino, *The Turkish Slave*, c. 1525

bavero Agnolo Bronzino, *Lucrezia Panciatichi*, c. 1541

bavero di trina Franz Pourbus the Younger, *Maria de' Medici, Queen of France* (detail), 1611

berretta à tozzo Sofonisba Anguissola, *Phillip II of Spain*, c. 1575

ABOVE, LEFT TO RIGHT

bracciali Paolo Veronese, *Portrait of a Woman with a Dog* (detail), 1560–70

bracconi Alonzo Sanchez-Coello, *The Infante Don Carlos*, c. 1564

bracconi Giovanni Battista Moroni, *Gian Girolamo Grumelli*, 1560

braghetta Agnolo Bronzino, *Guidobaldo II della Rovere*, 1531–2

broccatello Paolo Veronese, *The Mystic Marriage of St Catherine* (detail), 1570s

BRACCHETTA (*braghetta*): codpiece, a covering for male genitals, increasingly padded and stiffened from the beginning of the sixteenth century until the 1570s.

BRACCIALI (*braccialetti*; or *spallini*): arm or shoulder rolls, made of fabric in various shapes, sometimes padded or trimmed with puffs of pulled-through *camicia* linen or with veils, used to cover and decorate the points at which the sleeves were attached to a bodice or doublet. Can also mean a short oversleeve covering another sleeve.

BRACCONI: wide, padded breeches.

BRAGHESSE: the Venetian term for breeches (in Italian, *bracche, bracchesse*), usually knee-length in noblemen's clothing, though commoners wore them long.

BROCCATELLO: mixed fabrics whose bottom chain had a silk warp and a weft of waste silk, flax, or cotton. The pattern, which is created on the warp, appears raised. Sometimes mistaken for brocade.

BROCCATO: brocade, usually silk, decorated with woven designs in which the weft (horizontal) threads extend no further than the pattern in which they are used. Often made with gold or silver weft thread.

BURATTO: mixed fabric, with a silk warp and a wool weft. One version was lightweight and transparent, used for veils; a heavier version was used for the awnings of gondolas. Also, in lace, netting used as the basis for drawn threadwork.

BURICHETTO (*buricco, burrichetto*): a short jacket or jerkin.

CALZE: stockings made of wool (or, rarely, silk) cut on the bias to add stretch, and tied to the doublet with strings or metal-tipped laces.

CALZE À BRASOLA: waist-high stockings sewed together in the rear, to form snug, footed trousers.

CALZETTE (*calcetti*): light, short socks of linen, worn over the *calze* and under shoes or boots.

CALZONI INTERE: in the fifteenth century, one-piece, full-length, close-fitting trousers, attached to a doublet with points (metal-tipped laces). In the sixteenth century, *calzoni* became mid-thigh- or knee-length trousers, often with a separately made codpiece attached with ties.

CAMBRAI: cambric, a very fine white linen used for men and women's underclothes, originally made at Cambray, in Flanders.

CAMICIA: a shirt or shift worn as an undergarment by both men and women. In Europe it was made of silk or linen and sometimes trimmed at the neck and wrists with ruffles, which might be needle-worked.

CANEVACCIA: a mixed fabric with a silk warp and a weft of waste silk and flax. In Venice, it could also include gold or silver thread.

CAPPA VENETIANA: a long, wide veil of heavy black silk, often horizontally crimped.

ABOVE, LEFT TO RIGHT

burichetto Jacopo Pontormo (Jacopo Carucci), *Portrait of a Halberdier* (Francesco Guardi?), 1528–30

calze with points Carlo Crivelli, *San Rocco*, 1480 or later

camicia worn by a man Albrecht Dürer, *Self-Portrait*, 1498

camicia worn by a man Agnolo Bronzino, *Portrait of a Young Man*, c. 1535

camicia worn by a woman François Clouet (attributed to), *Jeanne d'Albret* (detail), 1570

ABOVE, LEFT TO RIGHT

colletto Giovanni Battista Moroni, *Portrait of a Knight*, c. 1540

cordellino François Clouet, *Portrait of Henri of Valois (later Henri III of France)*, c. 1562

corazza Titian, *Francesco Maria della Rovere, Duke of Urbino* (detail), 1536–8

corno Giovanni Bellini, *Doge Leonardo Loredan*, after 1505

corno of a turban Gentile Bellini, *Sultan Mehmet II*, 1480

CARPETTA: originally (14th c.) a long undergarment worn by men and women. In 16th-c. Venice, either an undergown worn by noblewomen, or, among lower-ranking women, a floor-length skirt of varying fabrics and colors. In Venice, *carpetta* could also mean a hoopskirt.

CASACCA (*casacchetta*): a man's cloak, or, in the sixteenth century, a wide-bottomed jacket; among poor men, an overshirt.

CELATA: a sallet, or light, round helmet, with a flaring brim at the back.

CENDALE (*sendal*): see ZENDADO

CIAMBELLOTTO: camlet, originally (before the 13th c.) camelhair. In Venice, a hard-wearing cloth with fine hairs, in beige or other colors, which could be of goat, silk, or wool.

COLLETTO: a short, snug, doublet of military origin; a jerkin.

À COMEO (*à cometo*): a long sleeve, very full below the elbow and narrowing at the wrist (from *cometo*, the Venetian dialect term for elbow).

CORAZZA: a cuirass, that is, body armor for the chest and back, usually of steel lined with leather.

CORDELLINO: a narrow cord or ribbon of silk, gold or silver, used for trim or hair decoration.

CORNO: the doge's cap, by the sixteenth century rising in the back into the shape of a rounded horn, usually made of stiffened brocade or cloth of gold. Also the vertical roll of fabric or other substance around which a turban was wound, seen as a finial on top.

CORSALETTO: corselet, light or jousting armor to protect the trunk.

CORTINA: a fabric, often linen, used for curtains and clothing; sometimes used as a veil over the forehead.

COZZETTO: in Neapolitan vocabulary, a woman's *bavero* of *cambrai* or thin *renso.*

CREMESINO: a bright red dye derived from the dried, crushed bodies of the female shield louse, a scale insect (*Kermes ilicis*) living on Mediterranean oaks, the kermes or holm oak; later, a dye made from cochineal, derived from a New World relative of the same insect. Also, fabric dyed this color.

CUFFIA (*scuffia*): a snood, that is, an ornamental hairnet or cap worn at the back of the head.

DAMASCO: damask, a self-patterned, reversible fabric made of fine silk or linen. The pattern is formed using both warp and weft, usually with satin weave, which produces a surface design of shining thread against a matte ground. Of ancient Eastern origin, the fabric was originally made in or traded through the city of Damascus (Syria).

DOGALINA: an overgown worn by noblemen and noblewomen, with long, wide, open sleeves.

DRAPPO: a fabric originally of wool, and a generic term for cloth in general; later, a silk fabric used for church and luxury garments.

DULIMANO (*dolimano*): a dolmen, a Turkish robe, often cut to include sleeves; also worn by sixteenth-century Venetians.

ABOVE, LEFT TO RIGHT

corsaletto French school, *Philippe II of Montmorency (1518–68), Count of Hoorne)*, 16th century

damasco Jacopo Bassano, *Portrait of a Venetian Senator* (Bernardo Morosini?), c. 1542.

damasco Agnolo Bronzino, *Portrait of a Lady*, c. 1550–55

dogalina sleeve Jacopo Tintoretto, *Saint Justine with Three Treasurers and Three Secretaries* (detail), 1580

ABOVE, LEFT TO RIGHT

ferraiuolo Sofonisba Anguissola, *The Duke of Parma*, 1561

ferraiuolo Giovanni Battista Moroni, *Portrait of a Gentleman*, 1554

funghetto Vittore Carpaccio, *Portrait of a Lady*, c. 1510

FALDA: fold or pleat; also, a full skirt.

FALDIGLIA: a farthingale or hoopskirt, with hoops often made of wood; originally a Spanish fashion. Vecellio says that Venetian women of his day call this hoopskirt a *carpetta.*

FAZZUOLO, FAZZOLETTO: a piece of fabric used to cover the head or neck; a kerchief or small shawl; also, a handkerchief.

FERRAIUOLO: a short, wide cape for men, often worn open with sleeves hanging free.

FERRANDINA (*ferandina*): a mixed fabric with a silk warp and a wool weft; originally from Flanders (*Fiandra*).

FRATESCO: light or ash gray, as in the robes of monks.

FUNGO, FUNGHETTO: a hair style of coiled braids including a fringe (bangs) and loose hair at the sides.

FUSTAGNO: fustian, a sturdy fabric of linen and cotton or wool, sometimes napped, suitable for work clothes.

GABBANO: a short or mid-length cape, often worn on horseback; could also be called a TABARRO.

GABBIA: literally, a cage; a high, stiff openwork headdress, of silk or precious metal.

GAVARDINA: a lightweight, short overgarment worn by men.

GIACINTO: a purplish blue color, resembling that of hyacinth flowers; the word is derived from the Latin word *hyacinthus,* defined by Pliny as the blue delphinium or iris.

GIORNEA: an early sixteenth-century overgament, long and open at the sides, sometimes sleeveless; also, a cape, ften lined with fur, or, in summer, silk.

GIUPPONE (*giubbone, zuppone*): a doublet, or close-fitting, vest-like garment, waist-length or longer, often stiffened or slashed, worn over the *camicia* by men and sometimes women.

GONELLA: in Neapolitan vocabulary, a woman's full-length, belted gown.

GORGIERA: in armor, a neckpiece; also, late in the sixteenth century, a detachable ruff.

GRISO: a coarse wool, usually undyed, used in the clothing of servants, workmen and friars.

GROGRANO: a fabric in plain or satin weave with heavier weft threads, giving a ribbed or corded effect. Made from silk, goat's hair or sometimes mixed fabrics.

GUARDACUORE: in Naples, a bodice.

GUARNACCIA: a full-cut, sleeved, mid-length cloak for men.

INCARNATO: a flesh-pink color, derived from *cremesino* dye.

LATTUGA (literally, "lettuce"): a ruffle attached to a man's or woman's *camicia*, at the collar or wrists. After the 1560s, the word could refer to a detachable ruff or detachable sleeve ruffles. Vecellio uses *lattuga* interchangeably with *lattughina*.

LATTUGHINA (*latughetta*): a ruffle sewn to a *camicia*. Often needle-worked with black or red silk.

LENSA: a fine, thin linen; cf. RENSO.

LENZUOLO: a large piece of cloth, worn as a shawl or mantle.

LIONATO: a reddish brown or tawny color, like a lion's mane.

LISARO: a fine cotton used for turbans, from the Arabic *al-hasr*.

ABOVE, LEFT TO RIGHT

giuppone worn by a man Giovanni Battista Moroni, *Portrait of a Man (The Tailor)*, c. 1570

giuppone worn by a woman Lavinia Fontana, *Portrait of a Noblewoman*, c. 1580

gorgiera Titian (attributed to), *Rudolf II*, c. 1575

lattughe worn by a woman Lavinia Fontana, *Ginevra Aldrovandi Hercolani*, c. 1595

Pair of chopines (***pianelle***). Italian (Venice), 1590–1610

MARGARITINE: glass beads, a specialty of Venetian glassmakers, imitating pearls or shaped like flowers and decorated with enamel.

MARIZO AD ONDA: the Venetian term for *marezzo*, moiré, a fabric pressed or stamped to produce wavy lines and a shimmering effect.

MERLETTO AL FUSO: bobbin lace, made by plaiting or twisting together a number of threads, usually linen and sometimes silk, wound on small bobbins of metal, wood or ivory.

MERLETTO DI OPERA D'ACO: needle lace, open work constructed stitch by stitch, using needle and thread. Includes cut-work, made by removing threads from fine linen and adding others to create intricate patterns; also called *punto in aria.*

MOCCAJARRO: a thin fabric of silk mixed with hemp, usually black.

MORRIONE: a crested helmet with an up-pointed brim at the front and the back, often fitted with a jawpiece that could be raised and lowered.

NINFE: ruffles worn at the neck and/or wrist. Often longer or deeper than *lattughe.*

ORMESINO (*ermesino*): a plain, light, and inexpensive silk cloth of Levantine origin, originally made on the island of Hormuz in the Persian Gulf, widely produced in Italy in the sixteenth century, and in Venice in Cannaregio at the Fondamenta degli Ormesini; toward the end of the century also woven with patterns.

PACIENZIA (*pazienzia*): a sleeveless overgarment open at the sides, originally worn by nuns.

PALUDAMENTO (from Latin *paludamentum*): the long mantle of a ancient Roman general, used by Vecellio for the long cloaks worn by Venetian senators.

PANCIERE: sectioned body armor that protects the stomach.

PANNO: fabric in general, but most often, a woolen fabric.

PAVONAZZO: a range of colors, as in a peacock's tail, ranging from purplish-blue to blue-black to peacock blue. In Venice, most often a bright purple, made from a shade of red obtained from a first bath in a red dye and a second in a *vagello,* a blue-dye bath based on indigo with the addition of madder, alum of lees, and bran.

PETTORALE: a plackard or pectoral, a piece of cloth covering the chest, worn by both men and women.

PIANELLE: slip-on shoes leaving the back of the heel bare, worn indoors by both men and women. *Pianelle* had soles of varying heights (some, worn by women, were a foot high or more; the English term for these is "chopines"). They could be made with double soles for outdoor wear, or were worn inside heavier clogs or pattens.

PICCATURA: decorative border or edging of chain mail.

PONTIGGIATO (*punteggiato*): pinked, that is, decorated with short slashes.

PORPORA: a dye extracted from the *Purpura* or *Murex* mollusk, ranging in color from bright red to purple. Known since ancient times, the dye was widely traded by the Phoenicians through the city of Tyre (in Mesopotamia, now Syria).

POSTA: Venetian term for a piece of fine silk related to *cendal,* often net-like, worn as a sash or hatband.

PRETINA: a man's long, narrow overgown fastened down the front with buttons, but worn open indoors.

RASCIA: rash, a twill fabric similar to serge, made in both silk and wool, named after its city of origin, Raska, in Serbia. Used for every-day women's dress, and, in a heavier version, for gondola awnings.

RASCIA FIORENTINA: rash made in Florence beginning in the sixteenth century, a fine-grade woolen cloth without a nap, used especially for men's wear.

RASETTO: satinette, a mixed fabric with a silk warp and a weft of waste silk and flax, woven to look like satin.

RASO: satin, that is, a type of silk cloth with a satin weave that produces a smooth, lustrous surface.

RENSO: a delicate white linen made in Reims beginning in the fourteenth century, used to make luxurious undergarments and collars.

ROBBA: a long, loose overgown worn by both women and men.

ROCCO, ROCCHETTO (*rochetto*): a long sleeveless tunic or overgarment, worn loose (unbelted).

ROMANA: a long, ample overgarment, often lined with fur, named after a gown worn at the papal court in Rome. The secular version was tied at the neck when worn outdoors by Venetian officials but worn open by men and women indoors.

SAIA: a thin woolen fabric with a diagonal weave.

SAIO (or *saione*): a man's coat or jacket for outdoor wear (cf. CASACCA), shin-length up to about 1550, then shorter; made of lightweight fabric for the summer but of heavy fabrics, including velvet, for the winter.

SAMITE: silk or mixed fabric of Greek origin.

SBERNIA: a short, luxurious mantle fastened in front, possibly derived from the Arab *burnous*.

ABOVE, LEFT TO RIGHT

Romana Titian, *Pietro Aretino*, c. 1545

Romana Giovanni Battista Moroni, *Bartolommeo Bonghi*, shortly after 1553

saione Dosso Dossi, *Portrait of a Man in a Black Beret*, c. 1510

saione Titian, *Ippolito de' Medici*, 1533

ABOVE, LEFT TO RIGHT

schinieri Vittore Carpaccio, *A Young Knight in a Landscape*, 1510

sottana Scipione Pulzone, *Portrait of Virginia*, 1590

sottana Alonzo Sanchez-Coello, *Elizabeth de Valois*, c. 1565

SCARLATTO: a bright red dye; also, a cloth of very fine wool or some other high-quality fabric, sometimes dyed this color.

SCHIAVINA: a coarse, heavy woolen cloth, used for blankets and the hooded cloaks of pilgrims and sailors, originally from Schiavonia, in Dalmatia.

SCHIAVONETTO: an unbelted light smock, of silk or light linen, like those worn by Slavic women.

SCHINIERI: in armor, greaves or shin guards

SESSA: gauze, usually light cotton or silk, worn as a veil or wrapped into a turban.

SINABUSTO (*sinabasso*): a valuable fabric of fine cotton or silk imported to Europe from the East.

SOGGOLO: a wimple.

SOTTANA, SOTTANELLA: a long undergown, worn by both men and women, often in colors or patterns contrasting to the overgown.

SPALLACCETTI, SPALLETTI: shoulder rolls, made of variously shaped, trimmed and decorated fabric used to cover the joining of sleeves to a bodice or doublet; cf. BRACCIALI.

SPALLACCI: short oversleeves of a woman's upper gown.

STAME: fine hand-knitted wool from Flanders, used for stockings.

STOCCATO: of a fabric, crimped or pleated.

TABARRO: a short jacket for men, often worn with the sleeves hanging empty; or a hooded, unbelted overgarment; cf. GABBANO.

TABINO (or *tabì*): a fabric of pure silk or mixed with a weft of waste silk and flax; in clothing, a heavy moiré silk, originally made in Attabiya, a section of Baghdad. A luxurious and expensive fabric also used for furnishings.

TAFFETANO: taffeta, a plain and light fabric with the most simple satin weave and a glossy appearance.

TAGLIATO: of a fabric, slashed with long cuts, often to show the fabric or *camicia* underneath.

TANÉ: a chestnut brown color.

TELA: fabric, in general, but most often linen.

TELA D'ORO: cloth of gold.

TESSUTO D'ORO: cloth woven with diagonal gold threads.

TOGA: a long, flowing overgarment worn by Roman citizens. Vecellio also uses the word to mean a loose overgown worn by later Europeans, although, unlike the Roman toga, such a garment was cut and stitched.

TOVAGLIA: kerchief or stole worn over the head.

TRAVERSA: an apron worn by middle-ranking and peasant women, sometimes hitched up with a belt.

TREMOLI: spangles; tiny hanging pieces of silver or gold, sometimes with jewels, sewn onto a garment.

TURCHINO: turquoise blue color.

VAIO: vair, a fur made from the skins of squirrels with gray backs and white bellies.

VASINO: a tall metal sheath, decorating a Turkish court hat.

ABOVE, LEFT TO RIGHT

tagliato sleeve Titian, *Il Bravo*, 1520

tagliato sleeve Titian, *La Bella*, 1536

tagliato overgown Giovanni Battista Moroni, *Portrait of a Lady*, late 1550s

tremoli School of Agnolo Bronzino, *Portrait of a Lady*, 1560

ABOVE, LEFT TO RIGHT

velluto soprariccio Venice, late 16th century

zimarra Giovanni Battista Moroni, *Portait of a Couple*, c. 1560

zimarra Anthonis Mor, *Catherine of Austria*, c. 1552

VELLUTO AD OPERA: velvet with a pattern, often of gold or silver thread, worked across its surface.

VELLUTO ALLUCCIOLATO: velvet woven with the addition of tiny gold or silver loops for a subtle sparkling effect.

VELLUTO RICCIO: single-pile cut velvet made of silk loops woven over rods of the same shape, either round or oval, producing an even, non-reflective surface.

VELLUTO SOPRARICCIO: pile-on-pile velvet, woven with oval and round rods that produced a surface of rings of different heights, creating a two-level pattern with a rich chiaroscuro effect.

VELLUTO TAGLIATO: cut velvet, given a raised surface by the insertion of half-oval shaped rods during the weaving process; the loops were then cut evenly across the top, creating a single-height, light-catching surface.

VELO: a thin voile or gauze fabric, of silk or, less often, cotton.

VERDUCATO (*verdugado*): a farthingale or hoopskirt, with hoops often made of wood; also called a *faldiglia* or *faldea.*

ZENDADO (*zendale, cendale*): cendal, a widely used, light and lustrous silk fabric of Eastern origin.

ZIMARRA: simar, a long gown worn over other clothing by men and women, resembling the *Romana* but usually narrower in cut.

ZOCCOLI: high, open wooden clogs.

ILLUSTRATION CREDITS

Numbers refer to pages.
l = left; *r* = right; *c* = centre; *a* = above; *b* = below

Introduction

2–3 Jost Amman, "Procession of the Doge in Venice", 1560. Hand-colored woodcut in fourteen sections. Print Collection, Stuttgart, Staatsgalerie.

4 Giovanni Battista Moroni, *Portrait of a Man (The Tailor)* (detail), c. 1570. Oil on canvas. National Gallery, London, UK. The Bridgeman Art Library.

8 Venetian possessions in the Adriatic and Aegean, c. 1580. Map 4 from A. Bellavitis, *Identité, mariage, mobilité sociale: citoyennes et citoyens à Venise au XmVIe siècle* (Rome, 2001). By permission of the Ecole Française of Rome.

9 *Venetia,* map engraved by Bernardo Salvioni, printed by Donato Rasciotti, 1597. Museo Civico Correr, Venice.

10*l* Giacomo Franco, "Gentildonna con mercante," *Habiti delle donne Venetiane intagliate in rame* (Venice, 1610), facsimile, ed. Ferdinando Ongania (Venice, 1878). Engraving. Photo: Dick Fish.

10*c* Giacomo Franco, "Noblewoman with a small fan", *Habiti delle donne Venetiane* (Venice, 1610, facsimile 1878). Engraving. Photo: Dick Fish.

10*r* Tiziano Vecellio (Titian), *Young Woman with a Fan,* c. 1555. Oil on canvas. Staatliche Kunstsammlungen Dresden.

11*l* Venetian bookbinding: front binding in leather for the commission certificate of Girolamo da Mula as Procurator, Venice, 1572. Newberry Library, Chicago.

11*r* Drinking glass, Venice, c. 1590. Corning Museum of Glass.

12*a* Cesare Vecellio, *Madonna and Child in Glory, San Fabiano, San Sebastiano e il podestà,* 1585. Oil. Duomo, Belluno. Archivio fotografico della Provincia di Belluno.

12*bl* Cesare Vecellio, *Odorico Piloni,* ?1570, Oil on canvas. Palazzo Piloni, Sala della Rappresentanza, Archivio fotografico della Provincia di Belluno.

12*br* Cesare Vecellio, *Laura contessa di Terlago e Lodrone,* ?1570. Oil on canvas. Palazzo Piloni, Sala della Rappresentanza, Archivio fotografico della Provincia di Belluno.

13*l* Cesare Vecellio, *Degnamerita contessa di Porcia,* 1575. Oil. Palazzo Piloni, Sala della Rappresentanza, Archivio fotografico della Provincia di Belluno.

13*c* Cesare Vecellio, *Giorgio Piloni,* 1575. Oil. Palazzo Piloni, Sala della Rappresentanza. Archivio fotografico della Provincia di Belluno.

13*r* Cesare Vecellio, *Odorico Piloni,* after 1594. Oil on canvas. Palazzo Piloni, Sala della Rappresentanza, Archivio fotografico della Provincia di Belluno.

14*al* Cesare Vecellio, title page of *La Corona delle nobili et virtuose donne* (Venice, 1592/ 1608). Woodcut. By permission of the Folger Shakespeare Library.

14*ar* Cesare Vecellio, diagram of a design for handkerchief corners from *La Corona delle nobili et virtuose donne,* Book 2. Woodcut. By permission of the Folger Shakespeare Library.

14*b* Cesare Vecellio, 4 fore-edge paintings, Courtesy of the Biblioteca Civica, Belluno.

15*l* François Deserps [Desprez], title page of *Recueil de la diversité des habits* (Paris: Richard Breton, 1562). Woodcut. By permission of the Folger Shakespeare Library.

15*cl* Jost Amman, title page of *Gynecaeum, sive Theatrum Mulierum* (Frankfurt: Sigismund Feyerabend), Holbein Society facsimile (London, 1872). Photo: Dick Fish.

15*cr* Hans Weigel and Jost Amman, title page of *Habitus praecipuorum populorum tam virorum...* (Ulm: Kuhnen, 1639). Harry Elkins Widener Collection, Harvard University, HEW 15.8.8.

15*r* Giacomo Franco, title page of *Habiti delle donne Venetiane* (Venice, 1609). Engraving. By permission of the Folger Shakespeare Library.

17 Jean-Jacques Boissard, *Habitus variarum orbis gentium* (Cologne: Kasparrutz, 1581), plate 39, Pyp 520.81. 225. F, Department of Printing and Graphic Arts, Houghton Library, Harvard College Library.

18*l* *Il Rettore in Padova,* 1575–7, from an *album amicorum,* Egerton ms. 1191, fol. 72. Watercolor and gouache. By permission of the British Library.

18*r* *Una Gentildonna Veneziana,* 1575, ms. 457 *Mores Italiae,* fol. 49. Watercolor and gouache. Beinecke Rare Book and Manuscript Library, Yale University.

19 *Sposa Venetiana in Gondola,* 1575–7, from an *album amicorum,* Egerton ms. 1191, fol. 63. Watercolor and gouache. By permission of the British Library.

22 Damask kaftan, Turkey, c. 1530. Topkapi Saray Museum, Istanbul.

23 Vincenzo Catena, *Portrait of Doge Andrea Gritti* (detail), after 1523. Oil. Art Resource/National Gallery, London.

24 Guillaume Le Testu, map of Africa (Tunisia and Algeria) (detail), *Cosmographie universelle selon les navigateurs, tant anciens que modernes,* Paris, 1556. Reproduced in Giovanni Battista Ramusio, *Navigazioni e viaggi,* ed. M. Milanesi. (Turin, 1978–88), vol. 1, facing p. 95. Library of the Ministry of War, Paris.

25*l* Cesare Vecellio, woodcut, title page of *Habiti antichi et moderni* (Venice, 1590), detail, Damian Zenaro's emblem.

25*c* Cesare Vecellio, woodcut, title page of *Habiti antichi et moderni di tutto il mondo* (Venice, 1598), detail, the Sessa brothers' emblem.

25*r* Cesare Vecellio, woodcut, detail of the last page of *Habiti antichi et moderni di tutto il mondo,* showing the Sessa brothers' cat with a kitten.

26 Cesare Vecellio and Cristoforo Guerra [Chrieger], hand-colored woodcut, *Battaglia di Lepanto e delle Curzolari,* 1572, Genoa, Courtesy of Galata Museo del Mare.

27 Ambroise Firmin Didot, *Costumes anciens et modernes/Habiti antichi et moderni...di Cesare Vecellio* (Paris, 1859–60), title page. Wood engraving. Photo: Dick Fish.

28 Juan Pantoja de la Cruz, *Portrait of Margaret of Austria,* 1605. Oil. The Royal Collection © 2007 Her Majesty Queen Elizabeth II.

29*l* Detail of 29*r*.

29*r* Werner Jacobszn, *Members of the Company of Captain Albert Coenraetsz and Lieutenant Pieter Evertsz,* 1625. Oil on canvas. Amsterdams Historisch Museum.

30*c, r* Filippo Calendario, sculpted marble capitals showing a young man and a young woman courting, c. 1340. Ducal Palace, Venice. Photos: Prof. Paola Modesti.

31*l, r* Cesare Vecellio, "Donzella Antica" and "Giovane Antico."

32*a* Cesare Vecellio, "Donzelle, et Fanciulle di Venetia," 1590.

32*b* Ambroise Firmin Didot, *Costumes anciens et modernes* (Paris, 1859–60), plate 101. Wood engraving. Photo: Dick Fish.

35*l* Theodor de Bry, *Les Grands voyages* (Frankfurt, 1590), vol. I, engraving of a Virginian woman carrying her child, based on a watercolor by John White in Thomas Harriot's *A briefe and true report of the new found land of Virginia* (London 1588), plate 10. Annenberg Rare Book and Manuscript Library, University of Pennsylvania.

35*r* Cesare Vecellio, "Donne dell'Isola," from *Habiti antichi,* 1598. Woodcut.

36*l* Theodor De Bry, *Indorum Floridam provinciam inhabitantium eicones* (Frankfurt, 1591), engraving of a king and queen of Florida, based on a 1565 drawing by Jacques le Moyne de Morgues. Annenberg Rare Book and Manuscript Library, University of Pennsylvania.

36*r* Cesare Vecellio, "Habito della Regina," 1598. Woodcut.

39*l* Theodor de Bry, *Les Grands voyages,* I, "A cheiff Ladye of Pomeioc," engraving. Annenberg Rare Book and Manuscript Library, University of Pennsylvania.

39*c* Theodor De Bry, "A cheiff Ladye of Pomeioc," detail, girl's doll.

39*r* Cesare Vecellio, woodcut, "Habito delle matrone e donzelle," 1598.

40 Feather headdress, Peru, 15th–16th century. Cleveland Museum of Art.

Glossary

580*l* Lorenzo Lotto, *Messer Marsilio and His Wife* (detail), 1523. Oil on canvas. Museo del Prado, Madrid.

580*r* Agnolo Bronzino, *Eleonora of Toledo as a Young Woman,* c. 1541. Oil on panel. The National Gallery in Prague.

581*l* Bernardino Licinio, *Ottaviano Grimani, Procurator of San Marco* (detail), 1541. Oil on canvas. Kunsthistorische Museum, Vienna. Erich Lessing/Art Resource, New York.

581*r* British school, *A Young Lady aged 21, possibly Helena Snakenborg, later Marchioness of Northampton* (detail), 1569. Oil on panel. Tate Gallery, London.

582*l* Parmigianino, *The Turkish Slave,* c. 1525. Oil on panel. Galleria Nazionale, Parma. Alinari/Art Resource, New York.

582*cl* Agnolo Bronzino, *Lucretia Panciatichi,* c. 1541. Oil on panel. Uffizi, Florence. Scala/Art Resource, New York.

582*cr* Franz Pourbus the Younger, *Maria de' Medici, Queen of France* (detail), 1611. Oil on canvas. Uffizi, Florence. Erich Lessing/ Art Resource, New York.

582*r* Sofonisba Anguissola, *Phillip II of Spain,* c. 1575. Oil on canvas. Museo del Prado, Madrid.

583*l* Paolo Veronese, *Portrait of a Woman with a Dog* (detail), 1560–70. Oil on canvas. Museo Thyssen-Bornemisza, Madrid.

583*cl* Alonzo Sanchez-Coello, *The Infante Don Carlos,* c. 1564. Kunsthistorische Museum, Vienna. Erich Lessing/Art Resource, New York.

583*c* Giovanni Battista Moroni, *Gian Girolamo Grumelli,* 1560. Oil on canvas. Collection of Count Antonio Moroni, Bergamo, Italy. The Bridgeman Art Library, London.

583*cr* Agnolo Bronzino, *Guidobaldo II della Rovere*, 1531–2. Oil on canvas. Galleria Palatina, Palazzo Pitti. Scala/Art Resource, New York.

583*r* Paolo Veronese, *The Mystic Marriage of Saint Catherine* (detail), 1570s, Gallerie dell'Accademia, Venice. Scala/Art Resource, New York.

584*l* Jacopo Pontormo (Jacopo Carucci), *Portrait of a Halberdier* (Francesco Guardi?), 1528–30. Oil (or oil and tempera) on panel transferred to canvas. 92 x 72 cm (36 ½ x 28 ⅜ in). The J. Paul Getty Museum, Los Angeles.

584*cl* Carlo Crivelli, *San Rocco*. 1480 or later. Oil on panel. By kind permission of the Trustees of the Wallace Collection, London.

584*c* Albrecht Dürer, *Self-Portrait*, 1498. Oil on panel. Museo del Prado, Madrid.

584*cr* Agnolo Bronzino, *Portrait of a Young Man*, c. 1535. Oil on canvas. Hamburger Kunsthalle, Hamburg. Bildarchiv Preussicher Kultur Besitz/Art Resource, New York.

584*r* François Clouet (attributed to), *Jeanne d'Albret* (detail), 1570. Oil on panel. Musée de Condé, Chantilly, France. Giraudon/Art Resource, New York.

585*l* Giovanni Battista Moroni, *Portrait of a Knight*, c. 1540. Oil on canvas. Museo del Prado, Madrid.

585*cl* François Clouet, *Portrait of Henri of Valois (later Henri III of France)*, c. 1562. Pinacoteca Civica, Brescia. Scala/Art Resource, New York.

585*c* Titian (Tiziano Vecellio), *Francesco Maria della Rovere, Duke of Urbino* (detail), 1536–8. Oil on canvas. Uffizi, Florence. Erich Lessing/Art Resource, New York.

585*cr* Giovanni Bellini, *Doge Leonardo Loredan*, after 1505. Oil on panel. National Gallery, London/The Bridgeman Art Library.

585*r* Gentile Bellini, *Sultan Mehmet II*, 1480. Oil on canvas. National Gallery, London/Art Resource, New York.

586*l* French school, *Philippe II of Montmorency (1518–68), Count of Hoorne*, 16th century. Bodycolor on paper. Musée Condé, Chantilly, France. Lauros/Giraudon/The Bridgeman Art Library.

586*cl* Jacopo Bassano, *Portrait of a Venetian Senator (Bernardo Morosini?)*, c. 1542. Oil on canvas. Staatliche Museen, Gemäldegalerie Alte Meister, Kassel, Germany.

586*cr* Agnolo Bronzino, *Portrait of a Lady*, c. 1550–55. Oil on panel. Galleria Sabauda, Turin. Alinari/Art Resource, New York.

586*r* Jacopo Tintoretto, *Saint Justine with Three Treasurers and Three Secretaries* (detail), 1580. Oil on canvas. Gallerie dell'Accademia, Venice.

587*l* Sofonisba Anguissola, *The Duke of Parma*, 1561. Oil on canvas. National Gallery of Ireland, Dublin. Erich Lessing/Art Resource, New York.

587*c* Giovanni Battista Moroni, *Portrait of a Gentleman*, 1554. Pinacoteca Ambrosiana, Milan. Copyrights Biblioteca Ambrosiana Auth. No. F 123/07.

587*r* Vittore Carpaccio, *Portrait of a Lady*, c. 1510. Oil on canvas. Galleria Borghese, Rome. Alinari/Art Resource, New York.

588*l* Giovanni Battista Moroni, *Portrait of a Man (The Tailor)*, c. 1570. Oil on canvas. National Gallery, London, UK. The Bridgeman Art Library.

588*cl* Lavinia Fontana, *Portrait of a Noblewoman*, c. 1580. Oil on canvas, 115 x 89.5 cm (45 ¼ x 35 ¼ in.). National Museum of Women in the Arts, Washington, D.C. Gift of Wallace and Wilhelmina Holladay.

588*cr* Titian (Tiziano Vecellio) (attributed to), *Rudolf II*, c. 1575. Oil on canvas. Portraitgalerie, Schloss Ambras, Innsbruck, Vienna. Erich Lessing/Art Resource, New York.

588*r* Lavinia Fontana, *Ginevra Aldrovandi Hercolani*, c. 1595. Oil on canvas. The Walters Art Museum, Baltimore.

589 Pair of *chopines*. Italian (Venice), 1590–1610. Tooled leather over wood, with metallic braid and silk tassels. 30.2 x 16.2 x 24 cm (11 ⅞ x 6 ⅜ x 9 7/16 in.). Museum of Fine Arts, Boston. The Elizabeth Day McCormick Collection 44.556a-b. Photograph © Fall 2008, Museum of Fine Arts, Boston.

590*l* Titian (Tiziano Vecellio), *Pietro Aretino*, c. 1545. Oil on canvas. Galleria Palatina, Palazzo Pitti, Florence. Erich Lessing/Art Resource, New York.

590*cl* Giovanni Battista Moroni, *Bartolommeo Bonghi* (died 1584), shortly after 1553. Oil on canvas. 40 x 32 ¼ in (101.6 x 81.9 cm). Purchase, Joseph Pulitzer Bequest, 1913 (13.177). The Metropolitan Museum of Art, New York. Image copyright © The Metropolitan Museum of Art, New York. Art Resource, New York.

590*cr* Dosso Dossi, *Portrait of a Man in a Black Beret*, c. 1510, National Museum, Stockholm.

590*r* Titian (Tiziano Vecellio), *Ippolito de' Medici*, 1533. Oil on canvas. Galleria Palatina, Palazzo Pitti, Florence. Scala/Art Resource, New York.

591*l* Vittore Carpaccio, *A Young Knight in a Landscape*, 1510. Museo Thyssen-Bornemisza, Madrid.

591*c* Scipione Pulzone, *Portrait of Virginia*, 1590, Galleria Doria Pamphili, Rome. © ADP, Management, Fratelli Alinari. Alinari/Art Resource, New York.

591*r* Alonzo Sanchez-Coello, *Elizabeth de Valois*, c. 1565. Oil on canvas. Kunsthistorische Museum, Vienna. Erich Lessing/Art Resource, New York.

592*l* Titian (Tiziano Vecellio), *Il Bravo*, 1520. Oil on canvas. Kunsthistorische Museum, Vienna. Erich Lessing/Art Resource, New York.

592*cl* Titian (Tiziano Vecellio), *La Bella*, 1536. Oil on canvas. Galleria Palatina, Palazzo Pitti, Florence. Erich Lessing/Art Resource, New York.

592*cr* Giovanni Battista Moroni, *Portrait of a Lady*, late 1550s. Oil on canvas. Palazzo Pitti, Florence. The Bridgeman Art Library, London.

592*r* School of Agnolo Bronzino, *Portrait of a Lady*, 1560. Oil on canvas. Galleria Palatina, Palazzo Pitti, Florence. Alinari/Art Resource, New York.

593*l* *Velluto soprariccio*, Venice, late 16th century. Courtesy of Doretta Davanzo Poli, Venice.

593*c* Giovanni Battista Moroni, *Portait of a Couple*, c. 1560. Oil on canvas. Galleria Sabauda, Turin. Alinari/Art Resource, New York.

593*r* Anthonis Mor, *Catherine of Austria*, c. 1552. Oil on wood. Museo del Prado, Madrid. Erich Lessing/Art Resource, New York.

ACKNOWLEDGMENTS

Many people and institutions have provided us with invaluable assistance and advice over the years. The early groundwork for our book was made possible with the help of a Renaissance Society of America Grant, a USC College Award for Research Fellowship, faculty research funds from Smith College, and a Los Angeles County Museum of Art Maggie Pexton Murray Grant (Doris Stein Center). We completed the project with the assistance of a two-year National Endowment for the Humanities Collaborative Research Grant, which allowed us to conduct research in Venice, work together translating Vecellio's book in Los Angeles and Northampton, and consult with costume specialists in Italy. The NEH grant provided indispensable leave-time from teaching, which allowed us to devote ourselves full time to most of the writing and translating. To all these institutions we are deeply appreciative. Our special gratitude to Courtney Quaintance, Dartmouth College, for help in last-minute acquisitions of photos and permissions from Italian sources.

Our work was facilitated by the staffs of many libraries and archives: the Getty Research Institute, Houghton Library, Folger Shakespeare Library, the British Library, the National Art Library in London, Special Collections at the University of California, Los Angeles, the University of Pennsylvania's Special Collections, and Venice's Archivio di Stato.

We benefited from the incisive and stimulating comments we received from two publisher's readers of the manuscript, particularly Patricia Brown, who clarified Venetian architectural terms and vocabulary and was generous and supportive all the way through the translation process. For costume terminology, we owe a huge debt to Sandra Rosenbaum and Doretta Davanzo Poli, who have been enormously helpful in teaching us about the intricacies of Renaissance dress. Many other costume historians, too, among them Jane Bridgeman,

Daniela Ferrari, Santina Levey, and Carole Frick, provided us with generous and helpful advice. Errors are ours alone.

Many Venetianists have lent their support and help along the way, either through their own books on Venice or in conversation. For Vecellio's political vocabulary, we have followed Brian Pullan's study, *Rich and Poor in Renaissance Venice*, because it focuses on a time frame closer to Vecellio's than do many other studies of Venice. In particular, Guido Ruggiero and Laura Giannetti generously contributed time and effort by reading our translation carefully and offering many suggestions for improvement. Bronwen Wilson and Diane Owen Hughes helped us to think about the larger implications of Vecellio's books.

Rebecca Wright, a former student at Smith College, helped collect information about printed costume books and compared Vecellio's costume plates to them, and Luisa Rivi, an Italian graduate student at USC, helped revise portions of our translation and researched specific terminologies, geographic locations, and place names in Vecellio's text. Thanks also to Dick Fish of the Imaging Center at Smith College for his amiable promptness and beautiful photographs, Professor Paola Modesti, of the Istituto Universitario di Architettura di Venezia, for her photographs of the Palazzo Ducale, and Mindy Menjou, Administrative Assistant in Comparative Literature at USC, for her untiring assistance in collecting digital images for our introduction and glossary and acquiring permissions.

To our families, thanks for supporting us on Venice's Giudecca while we slaved away translating Vecellio on Signora Franca Sacerdoti's rose-filled balcony with its view of the Redentore church! We will always remember the many good meals and bottles of Prosecco we consumed together after a long day's work.

INDEX

Countries and places are generally indexed by modern names, with cross references from names used by Vecellio when appropriate. On some occasions the original places do not correspond with contemporary regions or states, and thus have been kept. Numbers in *italics* indicate an illustration.